Uniting the Kingdom?

Uniting the Kingdom?

The making of British History

Edited by
Alexander Grant and Keith J. Stringer

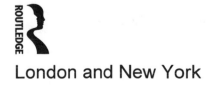

London and New York

First published 1995
by Routledge
11 New Fetter Lane, London EC4P 4EE

Simultaneously published in the USA and Canada
by Routledge
29 West 35th Street, New York, NY 10001

Typeset in 10/12 Garamond by
Aligra Lancaster
Printed and bound in Great Britain by
Biddles Ltd, Guildford and King's Lynn

British Library Cataloguing in Publication Data
A catalogue record for this book is available from the British Library

Library of Congress Cataloguing in Publication Data
A catalogue record for this book has been requested

ISBN 0–415–13041–7

Contents

Contributors

James Campbell is a Reader in Medieval History at the University of Oxford, and Lightbody Fellow of Worcester College

David Cannadine is Moore Collegiate Professor of History at Columbia University, New York

Nicholas Canny is Professor of Modern History at the University College, Galway, within the National University of Ireland

S. J. Connolly is a Reader in History at the University of Ulster

Eric Evans is Professor of Social History at the University of Lancaster

Robin Frame is Professor of Medieval History at the University of Durham

John Gillingham is Professor of History at the London School of Economics

Alexander Grant is a Senior Lecturer in History at the University of Lancaster

David Marquand is Director of the Political Economy Research Centre, and Professor of Politics at the University of Sheffield

P. J. Marshall is Professor Emeritus of Imperial History at King's College, London

Marcus Merriman is a Senior Lecturer in History at the University of Lancaster

John Morrill is a Reader in Early Modern History at the University of Cambridge, and Vice-Master of Selwyn College

P. K. O'Brien is Director of the Institute of Historical Research, and Professor of Economic History at the University of London

J. G. A. Pocock is Professor of History at The Johns Hopkins University, Baltimore

Keith Robbins is Principal of St David's University College, Lampeter

Conrad Russell is Professor of History at King's College, London

Keith Stringer is a Senior Lecturer in History at the University of Lancaster

John Turner is Professor of Modern History and Politics at Royal Holloway and Bedford New College, London

Jenny Wormald is V. H. Galbraith Fellow and Tutor in Modern History at St Hilda's College, Oxford

Foreword

P. K. O'Brien
Institute of Historical Research

The Institute of Historical Research, founded in 1921, has long been acknowledged as the national, and a leading international, centre for promoting the advanced study of history. Of its many programmes, one of the most important is the Anglo-American Conference of Historians, which has met no fewer than sixty-four times since 1921. The present invaluable volume has its origins in the 63rd Conference, convened in the Senate House of London University in the summer of 1994 with the support of a grant from the British Academy.

A Steering Committee of historians, including Dr Sean Connolly, Professor Rees Davies, Professor Harry Dickinson, Dr John Morrill, Professor Keith Robbins and myself, constructed a programme to address critically the theme 'The Formation of the United Kingdom' – a programme which ranged across the centuries, gave due attention to the converging and separate histories of England, Wales, Ireland and Scotland, and provided the opportunity for broad scholarly debate. It was our view, given the uncertain nature of present-day 'Britain' and 'Britishness', that such a conference had a pronounced topical relevance. Moreover, there was an impressive range of scholarly expertise that we could hope to recruit to discuss the making of British History. In the event, thirteen distinguished lecturers looked anew, within their particular fields of specialist knowledge, at national identities, religious diversity, cultural assimilation and resistance, the political tensions arising from conquests and constitutional incorporations, and much more besides. Each lecturer was paired with respondents, and many members of the large audience – there were 400 participants in all – contributed vigorously from the floor.

This book contains contributions from fifteen of the lecturers and respondents, and from a further three historians to whom special thanks are due for agreeing to expand the debate in fresh directions. Similarly, Dr Alexander Grant and Dr Keith Stringer are to be congratulated for the labour and care they have put into the construction of a fitting memorial to a major intellectual event, and for conveying these top-class essays to a wider public.

Historians are too wise to claim that there are easy lessons to be learned from their discipline, but they know that history matters, and the scholarship and insights embodied in these essays can undoubtedly play a vital role in informing current debates about the future of the United Kingdom.

Part I

Prologue

Prologue

Chapter 1

Introduction
The enigma of British History

Alexander Grant and *Keith Stringer*

'Continental Europeans will have become aware through football matches, if through nothing else, that Great Britain is a multinational state.'[1] That was how, some years ago, a German historian began a study of the Scottish Wars of Independence. We, too, find that the world of sport offers a good way of introducing the complexities and anomalies of the relationship between the United Kingdom as a unitary state on the one hand, and England, Scotland, Wales and Ireland on the other. For instance, with association football, every sovereign state has its own 'national team', except for the United Kingdom, which has four: a source of much irritation elsewhere. Until recently, most Scottish, Welsh and Northern Irish footballers of international status belonged to English clubs; but, nowadays, new European rulings mean that such players count as foreigners in England. With rugby union, too, the four 'Home Nations' are separate, each on a par with France in the Five Nations' Championship — but, in rugby, Ireland comprises both Northern Ireland *and* the separately sovereign Republic of Ireland. Rugby league, in contrast, has a Great Britain side – which invariably plays its home internationals in England. With cricket, on the other hand, the UK equals England; if Scotland, Wales and Ireland produce high-quality players, they go on to represent England (as an Australian-born cricketer did recently, by virtue of his Northern Irish grandmother). With other sports, such as athletics or swimming, there are English, Scottish, Irish and Welsh teams for internal UK competitions, but one United Kingdom team for international competitions. In sport, the concept of the UK is a veritable enigma.

This has a wide significance; after all, international sport is a way of sublimating international rivalries. It is no coincidence that, in the years since the abolition of British football's 'Home Internationals' – which happened because the English and Scottish Football Associations became more interested in European and World Championships – the annual Scotland–England rugby union international has attracted nationalistic passions, especially in Scotland. Scottish rugby's adoption of the evocative song 'Flower of Scotland', and the jingle '1314 Bannockburn, 13–7 Murrayfield' coined after

[1] A. Kalckhoff, *Schottischer Regionalismus im Spätmittlealter* (Frankfurt am Main, 1983), p. 1.

the Scottish 'Grand Slam' victory of 1990, show how antipathy towards 'the auld inemie' can be expressed on the sports field. But it is not simply the Scots who link sport and politics. Harold Wilson blamed England's 1970 World Cup defeat by West Germany for his subsequent defeat in that year's general election; while there is a connection between extreme right-wing political parties and the darker side of English international football support. Then there is the 'Tebbit test': Norman Tebbit has argued that supporting England at cricket should be a test of the loyalty of people of West Indian, Indian or Pakistani origin to the United Kingdom in which they live (but should not the same reasoning apply to all those Scottish, Welsh and Irish football and rugby supporters who live in England?). This highlights the seriousness that can lie behind questions of sport, and in particular raises the question of how much the United Kingdom state – or UK politicians – can recognise members of the ethnic minorities as being 'truly British'. That question has almost a thousand years of history behind it (Gillingham, ch. 4).

The same point is raised by an issue that hit the headlines just as this book was going to press. As a *Guardian* report put it:

> The Government's chief adviser on school curriculums last night defended his call for the development of a British cultural identity in all schoolchildren regardless of their ethnic background ... Dr Nick Tate, chief executive of the School Curriculum and Assessment Authority ... advocated the teaching of the majority culture, with the emphasis on the English language, English history and literary heritage, and the study of Christianity and the classical world.[2]

English language, *English* history and literary heritage are here being taken as the constituents of a *British* cultural identity. The idea that all inhabitants of the British Isles should be taught to an English norm is, not surprisingly, raising heated objections among the ethnic minorities who have become UK citizens in recent years – but it is equally objectionable to members of the much 'older' ethnic minorities, namely the Scots, Welsh and Irish. In reality, a *British* cultural identity depends no more than partly on Englishness. There is vastly more to the language and literary heritage of the UK than that which is written in standard English: contributions, for example, in regional forms of English and in varieties of Scots (from Robert Henryson to Robert Burns to Hugh MacDiarmid); contributions from the Celtic world, not only in Welsh and Gaelic, but also in the way 'Celtic' writers (such as James Joyce and Dylan Thomas) use English; and, nowadays, contributions from the 'new' ethnic minorities (of which Salman Rushdie's are the best known).

This applies equally, of course, to history. Although the equation of British history with the history of England held sway for most of the nineteenth and twentieth centuries (Cannadine, p. 16), today few professional historians would seriously contend that the only significant historical dimension of

---

2 *The Guardian*, 19 July 1995. Our thanks to Bruce Webster for drawing this to our attention.

British cultural identity was the English one. Instead, J. G. A. Pocock's 1974 argument for a 'new' British history,[3] covering not only England but Scotland, Wales and Ireland, together with the 'British' colonies, Empire and Commonwealth, has been widely accepted and even practised – as the following essays (which conclude with Pocock's own reflections on the current state of the 'new subject'), and the bibliographical references contained within them, make abundantly clear.

As a result, it is now possible to contemplate teaching what we would call genuine 'British history' courses, which grapple with the past of all four countries of the British Isles together,[4] rather than concentrating almost exclusively on England. Among the main themes of these courses would be the social and political interrelationships of all the various peoples, or ethnic groupings, living within the British Isles, and the extent to which they were integrated together into one 'British' people. That, of course, would be the proper way to approach 'the development of a British cultural identity'. As the essays in this book demonstrate, however, such interrelationships were by no means invariably successful. 'British history' is not simply the history of the coming together of the British: for much of the time, the theme of integration is matched by those of rejection and conflict. Thus British – let alone English – triumphalism is out of place. But we must remember that one of the vital functions of historical study is to display the lessons, and warnings, of the past. In today's multiracial and multicultural United Kingdom, there can be few historical subjects more worth understanding than the past successes and failures in the interrelationships of the peoples of the British Isles.

If that is one reason for studying 'British history', a second takes us more directly into the political sphere. At the present time, the United Kingdom as a whole is very much on the political agenda. The civil war in Northern Ireland has now been given a top priority;[5] partly as a consequence, the 'Troubles' have halted, and (at the time of writing) the prospects for long-term peace seem better than at any period in the last twenty-five years. On the other hand, the future of the Union with Wales and, especially, with

---

[3] J. G. A. Pocock, 'British History: a plea for a new subject', *New Zealand Historical Journal*, viii (1974), reprinted in *Journal of Modern History*, xlvii (1975).

[4] The principle that British history covers Scotland and Wales as well as England is straightforward enough, but the assertion that it covers Ireland too is more contentious. 'Britain' encompasses only England, Wales and Scotland, and the habit of using it to include Ireland is very irritating to the Irish, just as the habit of using 'England' to include Scotland and Wales irritates the Scots and Welsh; we therefore appreciate how Irish historians can be 'Brito-sceptics' (Canny, p. 147). Historians have coined, as an alternative, terms such as 'the (East) Atlantic archipelago' and 'these islands' to refer collectively to England, Scotland, Wales and Ireland. Yet, as we have found in editing this book, such terminology is generally too clumsy for convenient use, especially adjectivally; so, like others before us, we have fallen back on the terms 'British Isles' and 'British history'. That does not imply that Ireland is actually subsumed within Britain; but it does reflect the fact that the history of the island of Ireland has been intimately connected with, and in some ways determined by, the history of the island of Britain for well over eight hundred years.

[5] Unlike in 1974, when the remarkable power-sharing initiative was fatally undermined by the general election of that year, held for essentially *English* political reasons.

Scotland appears increasingly problematic. One of the factors which is believed to have won the 1992 general election for the 'Conservative and Unionist Party' is Mr Major's last-minute call to maintain the integrity of the United Kingdom, and it is highly likely that the same strategy will be given an even higher profile in the election which will (presumably) be held in 1997: a vote for Labour will be a vote for the break-up of the United Kingdom, it will doubtless be claimed, in England as well as in Scotland and Wales. Thus it is not too difficult to predict that 'British' political and constitutional questions, concerning the UK as a whole, will bulk larger in our politics at the end of the twentieth century than at any time since its opening decades. And, beside them, there will of course be that other problem, of the UK's place in and relationship with the European Union. This, too, is a genuinely 'British' issue, particularly since the Scots and Welsh seem mostly more positive about the EU than are many of the English. As several contributors stress, however, further prediction is impossible: our future British history is certainly an enigma at the present time. But there is one point to be made. Whereas 'to most Victorian historians and constitutional commentators ... the manifest destiny of a United Kingdom had been achieved' (Robbins, p. 245), nowadays no serious historian would believe that the UK is *bound* to last for ever. Its creation was by no means automatic or inevitable; and it has already broken up in 1922 – with the acquiescence of the Conservative and Unionist Party (Turner, ch. 15). So, whatever might happen in the future, one thing is certain: the cohesion of what is left of the United Kingdom cannot simply be taken for granted.

Awareness of the uncertainties about the UK's future is what led to the holding of the 1994 Anglo-American Conference of Historians, on which this book is based. The contributors – to the conference and to the book – were asked to reflect on the evolution of the United Kingdom in the light of their own expertise in particular periods, which when taken together span the whole spectrum of post-Roman 'British history'. They did not set out to write a connected narrative account of the history of the British Isles. But, from the various essays that follow, most of the main strands, and problems, of such a narrative certainly emerge – making it abundantly clear that the evolution of the UK was not a straightforward linear progression. Running through the entire book are the twin themes of convergence and divergence: in political, as in social, history, some factors can always be found which pull the parts of the British Isles together, while others push them apart. The balance between pull and push, between convergence and divergence, varied from period to period, but both can always be found operating simultaneously. And from that, above all else, derives the enigma of 'British history'.

Of the main factors producing this convergence/divergence interplay, we would highlight first the effects of contingency. Many of the essays discuss complicated chains of events, in which unexpected accidents played a vital role in determining the course of 'British history'. For example, had it not been for the whirligig of chance, England and Scotland might well have experienced a union of the Crowns in the early fourteenth century (Frame, pp. 66, 83; Stringer, p. 89); and other contingencies diverted the English Crown's interests into France (Frame, p. 83). The Union of Crowns that did take place in 1603 was as much the consequence of 'Tudor/Stewart dynastic roulette' (Morrill, p. 172) as of any conscious British state-building (Merriman, pp. 117ff.). Or, to take a different kind of contingency, consider how the sudden collapse of the European international order in 1914 helped to bring about the release of Southern Ireland from Westminster's political embrace (Robbins, p. 246; Turner, p. 262). Contingency is a permanent feature of our history, and constantly reminds us of two fundamental points. First, outcomes of historical processes are never predetermined, and therefore historians should beware of Whiggishly reading history backwards. Second, to be successful, all polities must be able to adapt rapidly to unexpected challenges, constraints and accidents; 'events' are what cause the worst problems, Mrs Thatcher once remarked.

That leads us to ask how well the UK polity, in its various forms, has survived the pressures of events. The answer, probably, is surprisingly well, despite much tension and conflict – and especially so by comparison with the failures of multiple states elsewhere (Russell, p. 135). Thus, while the regnal Union of 1603 was most imperfect (Wormald, pp. 123ff.; Morrill, p. 173), it did lead eventually (along a very rocky path) to the incorporating Union of 1707. Even during the mid-seventeenth-century 'War(s) of the Three Kingdoms', which were sparked off by Scottish rebellion, the Scots wanted to maintain the regnal Union, albeit on redefined terms; and when the English Parliament broke it by executing Charles I, they fought to reconstruct it for Charles II (Morrill, pp. 172, 178). Similarly, for all the violence of the Jacobite rebellions, eighteenth-century Jacobitism was 'a British political ideology' (Connolly, p. 197). In the nineteenth century, many Irish Catholic landowners – even, for a time, Daniel O'Connell – accepted the Anglo-Irish Union (Connolly, p. 207). And despite the break-away of Southern Ireland (which even nowadays is not quite absolute: Frame, p. 65), the majority of what made up the United Kingdom of Great Britain and Ireland in 1801 still survives intact.

Thus, although rule from Westminster has been and is often resented elsewhere in the British Isles, paradoxically the magnetic pull of the Westminster power mass is one of the factors keeping the United Kingdom together. The location of the political centre of gravity in southern England is a fact of British geopolitics dating back over a thousand years to the Anglo-Saxons – who had created a consolidated nation-state by 1066 (Campbell, pp. 31, 44). To the Anglo-Saxons, we also owe the English shires, where there developed 'loyalties to local units which had been created for the purposes of the central authority, loyalties which generally did not so much contradict as reinforce that authority' – 'arguably one of the principal keys to the long success of the English state' (Campbell, p. 35). And from them, too, derive the origins of what had already by the thirteenth century become the aggressively centralised system of English government, which enabled Edward I to assert his power so effectively across almost the whole of the British Isles (Frame, pp. 65ff.).

Yet, as Edward and his successors found out, aggressively centralised government, operating on the basis that it is better for the ruler to be feared than to be loved, is not the only, or necessarily the most effective, means of power-building and successful integration. The history of thirteenth-century Scotland, where an equally successful monarchy developed in tandem with that of England but in a much more relaxed and 'loose-jointed' fashion, bears that point out (Stringer, pp. 90ff.). In the later Middle Ages, the defence of Scottish independence against English governance proved critical for the shape of 'British history' (Grant, pp. 97ff.). After 1603, the contrast in the styles of Scottish and English government helps to explain why James VI was a more successful king than James I (Wormald, pp. 123ff.).

Nevertheless, the centralising path taken by the medieval English Crown is of fundamental relevance to the dynamics of state-formation and political interaction within the British Isles – in both convergent and divergent directions. During the Middle Ages, it determined the modes and scale of medieval English domination over outlying power structures (Gillingham, ch. 4; Frame, ch. 5). In the early modern era, it obstructed effective compromises between the interests of the Crown and the wider communities, resulting in severe political tensions: for instance, the way English administrators overrode the Irish Parliament helped to provoke Irish rebellion in the 1640s (Canny, p. 165; Morrill, p. 176), and antagonised even the Protestant elite of eighteenth-century Ireland (Connolly, p. 197). Eighteenth-century American colonists feared that their 'liberty' was jeopardised by intrusive executive government directed from Westminster (Marshall, p. 219). Similarly, radical reformers in eighteenth- and early nineteenth-century Britain agitated for the rescue of 'English liberties' from the 'Norman Yoke' of state intrusiveness, and, north of the Border, depicted Scotland as 'groaning under the chains of England' (Evans, pp. 235, 242). The legacy of Scotland's old non-centralising style of government, however, helped to keep the chains much lighter than in Ireland (Connolly, pp. 199ff.) – until, perhaps, the modern era, when, despite the 'anti-government' rhetoric of Thatcherism, there has been a fresh shift of power into the hands of the central state (Marquand, p. 281).

The centralising drive of English/British government is closely linked with the sovereignty of 'King-in-Parliament', a doctrine which grew to maturity between the reigns of Edward I and Henry VIII. This has had far-reaching and lasting repercussions. Although in many ways it underpinned the development of British liberal democracy, it also seriously compromised the ability of English/British governments to forge strong loyalties throughout the British Isles and Empire by means of compromise and accommodation. For example, English parliamentarians could never take account of the parallel development of Scotland as an independent nation-state in its own right (Stringer, pp. 90ff.) – even though the principles of *Scottish* sovereignty were a major factor in the Wars of Independence (Grant, pp. 97ff.), and produced several head-on collisions between 1603 and 1707 (Morrill, ch. 10).

In fact, while the absolute sovereignty of 'King-in-[English]-Parliament' had great advantages for a single highly unified kingdom, it caused (and causes) acute problems in dealing with any kind of multiple state, as the histories of Ireland, Scotland, the Empire, and the European Community and Union all bear witness in their various ways. Thus, after 1603, 'the English were ... locked into the nightmare of either believing that England had lost its sovereignty, or ... that no union had taken place' (Russell, p. 144). In the 1640s, the English Parliament preferred to ignore Scotland (Morrill, pp. 172, 185), but full incorporation within a United Kingdom was the only logical solution, as eventually happened in 1707 and 1801 – though the fact that 'the only union [the English] could understand was annexation' (Russell, p. 145) significantly unbalanced the result. Similar considerations help to explain why the American colonies could not be kept (Marshall, p. 219; Pocock, p. 294), and why in 1922 Ireland had to be partitioned (Marquand, p. 284). The British state and Parliament are incompatible with federal or confederal associations – which brings us to current problems: power is still seen as a 'hard, impervious cricket ball, which ... cannot, by its very nature, be shared' (Marquand, p. 284). It is extremely difficult to see how effective power-sharing institutions can be constructed within the UK – though there are now, *perhaps*, promising developments with respect to Northern Ireland. And then there is the conundrum of the European Union! To medieval historians, the supranational institutions of the EU look very much like those of the medieval Catholic Church – but it was in revolt against Rome that the sovereignty of 'King-in-Parliament' was fully adumbrated. In years to come, will there be an anti-Brussels 'Reformation'?

Behind all these problems of power, government and sovereignty lies the all-important question of the relationship between ruled and their rulers, which is encapsulated in the issue of legitimacy: 'Why *should* we obey the state?' Theorists argue that authority is legitimate only if it is recognised as justified and acceptable by the people over whom it is exercised. But when social-science models of the ruler-ruled relationship are applied to present-day Britain, the conclusion is that 'the British state today is much less legitimate, the identity or identities it claims to embody are more contentious and more problematic, and the political economy is less prone to generate social cohesion', than was the case earlier this century (Marquand, p. 277).

What of past centuries? Throughout this book, we are reminded time and again that state authority was effective only when it enjoyed the consent of the governed – which was achieved by giving them an adequate 'voice' (Marquand, p. 278) or 'say' in the process of government. Early examples of success in this respect include pre-Conquest and post-Conquest England, which, while created through 'brute force' (Campbell, p. 37), exhibited an all-embracing sense of Englishness and relatively extensive participation by freemen in their governance (Campbell, pp. 35ff.; Gillingham, ch. 4); and medieval Scotland, where, remarkably, different peoples were brought together into a hybrid kingdom, whose rulers specifically allowed for, and safeguarded, plural traditions and customs, thereby producing a strong sense of loyalty among the people of Scotland (Stringer, pp. 94ff.). On the other hand, early examples of failure in this respect would include thirteenth- and fourteenth-century England, where authoritarian principles were taken to excess, especially in dealings with the rest of the British Isles (Frame, ch. 5; Grant, pp. 97ff.); and the British Isles in the seventeenth-century era of the 'War(s) of the Three Kingdoms' (Canny, ch. 9; Morrill, ch. 10).

Difficulties over legitimising 'British' regimes are attributable to the polarisation of society into insiders and outsiders – the latter being those who were more or less excluded from political society and participation – which happened elsewhere than in medieval Scotland. The Westminster-based state has always been essentially English (did the Anglo-Saxons do their job *too* well?), and easily slides into a 'Little Englandism' which significantly limits the normal means for expression and redress of grievances open to non-English; while the cultural pluralities of Britain/Ireland were rarely recognised fully in practice. This has often produced perceptions that there was not equality of rights and citizenship within a just political order, and hence created a sense of alienation and abandonment.

In medieval England, indeed, a concept of what we would now call 'apartheid' came into existence, based on a striking growth of English military and economic might that produced the imperialistic image of 'civilised' superiority in England and 'barbaric' inferiority elsewhere. This meant that 'from the twelfth century onwards there was to be a crucial fragility at the heart of the English empire' (Gillingham, p. 64); and that 'traditions of dissent ... were ... built into the fabric of the United Kingdom' (Frame, p. 74). The effect, however, varied. It was worst in Ireland, where the Gaelic Irish were almost always completely alienated. Perceptions of Welsh barbarity gradually faded, however – no doubt because the Welsh managed to achieve a 'voice' in their affairs, and eventually accepted their 'perfect' union with England (Grant, p. 104; Russell, p. 135; Connolly, p. 199). Similarly, perceptions of Lowland Scotland changed after it was 'civilised' in the twelfth century – but from the fifteenth century Scotland's Gaelic world was increasingly viewed in the same way as Ireland's (by both English and Lowland Scots), and in the first half of the eighteenth century it was regarded as an even greater threat (Connolly, pp. 194ff.). In the post-Reformation era, too, alienation was compounded by religious differences. Catholics were often regarded as enemies of the state, especially in Ireland, where the Pale 'became the first coherent Counter-Reformation community under the ... English Crown' (Canny, p. 152). Hence not only the Gaelic Irish, but also the 'Old English' were excluded from the governance of Ireland (Canny, p. 153; Connolly, p. 194).

Moreover, as the modern British Empire extended across the world, new 'barbarian' races were encountered, and the dichotomy came to be between 'British' and others, not English and others. Imperialism, indeed, was an exceptionally powerful force in the creation of Britishness (Robbins, p. 253), particularly significant for integrating Scots, Welsh and Protestant Irish into the British state, and giving them a strong 'voice' in running the Empire. But the assimilating effects of Empire only really applied to the people of Britain. Just as the ties between the medieval English colonies in Ireland and France dissolved (Frame, p. 81), so the eighteenth-century American colonists came to be excluded – or, eventually, excluded themselves – from the status of 'British' (Marshall, pp. 220ff). And the same, to a large extent, has happened with the post-1783 British Empire – with the last straw, perhaps, being the rejection of the Britishness of, say, New Zealand when the UK joined the European Community (Pocock, p. 297).

As with the rest of the factors discussed in this introduction – and with many others analysed in the following essays, which space has prevented us from treating here – the effect of the British Empire can thus be seen in terms of both convergence and divergence. And if, here, we have concentrated more on the divergences, then that is perhaps because historians tend to gravitate towards problems and difficulties. Certainly, there was much convergence – especially at times of political and economic expansion: the thirteenth, sixteenth, eighteenth and nineteenth centuries are probably the most 'British' in our history. Conversely, times of economic contraction tended also to be times of divergence, as in the post-Black Death era (Grant, pp. 101ff.) – yet what does that imply about the current state of the UK?

There is one final point to be made. In all the periods of expansion, more people were brought within the orbit or under the power of the British state(s); many of these stayed in their own lands, but many others migrated towards the centre. Such immigration was and is, of course, a particularly significant consequence of the British Empire. Now, if this book has any lesson, it is that the Westminster-based state has at times found it difficult to give equal treatment to all the peoples who constitute it – and that the result has often been one of acute tensions. It is, therefore, worth reminding readers of the remark of King Stephen of Hungary (d. 1038), that 'a kingdom of one language and one way of life would be weak and fragile ... Foreigners should be welcomed: their different languages and customs, their example and their arms, would ... enrich the kingdom and deter its enemies.'[6] When we read, in another account of the current 'British culture' controversy, that the headmaster of John Major's old school in south London has pupils with roots in twenty different countries,[7] we can only hope that he and they take heed of King Stephen's wise words – and learn from the enigmas of 'British history'.

[6] S. Reynolds, *Kingdoms and Communities in Western Europe, 900–1300* (Oxford, 1984), p. 257.
[7] *Sunday Telegraph*, 23 July 1995.

Chapter 2

British History as a 'new subject'
Politics, perspectives and prospects[1]

David Cannadine

During the election campaign for the European Parliament which was fought out in May 1994, the Prime Minister, John Major, offered this version of the history of the country whose government he led:

> This British nation has a monarchy founded by the Kings of Wessex over eleven hundred years ago, a Parliament and universities formed over seven hundred years ago, a language with its roots in the mists of time, and the richest vocabulary in the world. This is no recent historical invention: it is the cherished creation of generations, and as we work to build a new and better Europe, we must never forget the traditions and inheritance of our past. I never leave Britain without the spirit sinking just a little, and it always lifts the heart to set foot here once again.[2]

Albeit in less strident form, these rather idiosyncratic comments of Mr Major echo those made by Lady Thatcher in Paris at the bicentennial of the French Revolution, when she spoke with more force than accuracy about Magna Carta and 1688.[3] Taken together, their remarks suggest that when it comes to producing a contemporary account of Britain's past, the most unreconstructed and uncompromising form of Whig history which survives today is that preached from 10 Downing Street by Tory Prime Ministers. In more ways than one, it is a suggestive and significant irony.

For their account is not only Whig history implausibly masquerading as

---

[1] British history has been described both as an 'unknown' and as a 'new' subject: J. G. A. Pocock, 'British History: a plea for a new subject', *Journal of Modern History*, xlvii (1975); J. G. A. Pocock, 'The limits and divisions of British History: in search of the unknown subject', *American Historical Review*, lxxxvii (1982).

[2] *The Times*, 24 May 1994. It is worth quoting the riposte by Lord Jenkins of Hillhead, who rightly took exception to 'some rather curious history': 'I'm not sure many parts of the United Kingdom regard their monarchy as being descended from Wessex, nor that it is very natural to cite our two seven-hundred-year-old universities, together with our languages, as being worthy signs of our ancient separateness and ancient insularity ... For a substantial number of centuries, the universities operated almost exclusively, not in the indigenous language, but in one which attempted a European universality' (*The Independent*, 26 May 1994). For Britain as an 'invented nation', see P. Scott, *Knowledge and Nation* (Edinburgh, 1990), p. 168.

[3] M. Thatcher, *The Downing Street Years* (London, 1993), p. 753.

Conservative propaganda. Notwithstanding their ritual invocation of the word 'Britain', it is also emphatically 'Little England' history. Both Thatcher and Major assert the essential Englishness of the United Kingdom, its separateness from the rest of Europe, the long and unbroken continuity of its traditions and precedents, and its unique characteristics and institutions. But the reason that they feel obliged to reaffirm these beliefs is that recent developments abroad and at home have thrown virtually every one of them into question. And those developments have not merely changed the contemporary political landscape; they have also inspired many scholars to look again and anew at the nation's history. During the last two decades, an emerging school of self-consciously 'British' historians has been evolving a very different interpretation of Britain's past from that espoused by the Prime Minister and his immediate predecessor. Indeed, it is an interpretation so different that it is doubtful whether either of them would readily understand what 'British history', as it is now defined, practised and understood by professional historians, actually is.

Inasmuch as they are both reacting to the same external stimuli, provided by recent and current events, it must always be remembered that there is a real and important connection between the past and present premiers on the one side, and the 'new' British historians on the other. But they are clearly reacting in significantly different ways. The two top Tories have responded by reviving and restating the traditional view of the national past; the new British historians have responded by redefining and rethinking it. And so, while Thatcher and Major will reappear occasionally in the course of this essay, where it is appropriate and necessary for them to do so, its chief concern is to explain, explore and evaluate the results of this scholarly labour of redefining and rethinking. The first section discusses the Whig interpretation of English history, against which the new British historians have been reacting. The second examines changes in the international, domestic and academic environments, which have rendered English history less compelling and have helped to bring this new form of British history into being and into prominence. The last considers the strengths and weaknesses which have thus far characterised this latest approach to the national past, and suggests some directions in which British history might (and might not) proceed in the future.

One problem with discussing the traditional Whig interpretation of English history is in knowing where to begin. After all, the Venerable Bede completed his *History of the English Church and Nation* in 731, and there is a more or less continuous tradition of national history writing thereafter. For present purposes, it is best to confine the discussion to books which appeared between the middle of the nineteenth century and the outbreak of the Second World War, the years which are generally regarded as having marked the zenith of the modern nation-state. This was the period which saw the reconstruction of the United States in the aftermath of the Civil War, the creation of new nations in Europe in 1870 and again in 1919, the partition of Africa by the Great Powers during the last decades of the nineteenth century, and the Confederation of Canada, Federation of Australia and Union of South Africa. It witnessed mass electorates, mass political parties, mass education, mass transport, mass mobilisation – and mass war. And one result of these developments, which further helped to define and consolidate the identities of these new countries, was the rise of nationalist history in Germany, in France, in the United States – and also in Britain itself.[4]

It is easy to understand why this was so. The years from 1800 to 1922 saw the creation, survival and modification of the United Kingdom of Great Britain and Ireland. They witnessed the inexorable expansion of that greater Britain beyond the seas, as the Empire reached its territorial zenith in the years immediately after the First World War. Forster's Education Act of 1870 created a mass literate public; the Reform Acts of 1885 and 1919 created a mass voting public. Both internationally, in terms of dominion, and domestically, in terms of citizens, the boundaries of the nation were (as A. C. Benson observed in 'Land of Hope and Glory') being set wider than ever before. One of the ways in which this new nation was defined, its unity asserted, and its mission proclaimed was by giving unprecedented attention to its past. At elementary schools, grammar schools and public schools, the history of the nation became an essential subject. At Cambridge, a History Tripos was inaugurated, and at Oxford a History School, which meant that Clio soon superseded the Classics as the most appropriate training for statesmen. And in London, Oxbridge and the new provincial universities, scholarly, rigorous, academic history was established for the first time.[5]

From the standpoint of the British reading public, the national past came presented and packaged in three different versions. Initially, pride of place went to those multi-volume single-authored works, written by gentlemen amateurs, which were so fashionable during the reign of Queen Victoria. The most famous and most successful was Macaulay's *History of England*, published in four volumes between 1855 and 1861. But he was far from being alone: during the same period, H. T. Buckle began (but, like Macaulay, did not live to finish) his *History of Civilisation in England*. Then, between 1873 and 1878, Stubbs produced his *Constitutional History of England* in three volumes; and in 1902 Gardiner published his *Student's History of England* at

    [4] P. M. Kennedy, 'The decline of nationalistic history in the West, 1900–1970', in W. Laqueur and G. L. Mosse (eds.), *Historians on Politics* (London, 1974).
    [5] V. Chancellor, *History For Their Masters: Opinion in the English History Text Book, 1800–1914* (Bath, 1970); G. Kitson Clark, 'A hundred years of history teaching at Cambridge, 1873–1973', *Historical Journal*, xvi (1973); D. S. Goldstein, 'The organisational development of the British historical profession, 1884–1921', *Bulletin of the Institute of Historical Research*, lv (1982); R. Soffer, 'Nation, duty, character and confidence: History at Oxford, 1850–1914', *Historical Journal*, xxx (1987).

the same length. That work spanned the whole of British history, from Caesar's invasion to the death of Queen Victoria. But Gardiner also wrote in much greater detail on the seventeenth century, and other writers also concentrated on similar shorter periods: among them Froude (*History of England from the Fall of Wolsey to the Defeat of the Spanish Armada*, twelve volumes, 1856–70); Freeman (*History of the Norman Conquest*, six volumes, 1867–79); and Lecky (*History of England in the Eighteenth Century*, eight volumes, 1878–90).

Towards the end of Victoria's reign, these lengthy, leisurely surveys were going out of fashion, and they were replaced by new single-volume histories, which were better suited to the mass audience that had recently come into being. They were less expensive, they told the whole of the story from beginning to end, they were ideal text books for schools and universities, and they genuinely seem to have reached that long since defunct category, the general reader. The most important was J. R. Green's *Short History of the English People*, first published in 1874, so soon after Forster's Act that it surely cannot be coincidence. For two generations, Green's book held the field: it was endlessly reprinted and updated, and a multi-volume illustrated edition was later brought out by his wife Alice.[6] Only in 1926 was it superseded, when G. M. Trevelyan published his *History of England*, which served its day and generation as effectively as Green had done, selling 200,000 copies during the next twenty years. Such was its appeal and its renown that it may even have inspired the publication of that most memorable and affectionate parody of the one-volume text-book history, Sellar and Yeatman's *1066 and All That*, which appeared in 1930.[7]

By this time, the third version of the nation's history was also well established: the multi-volume, multi-authored series, written by a team of academic professionals, most of whom confined themselves to their realm of scholarly expertise. Here was emphatic indication not only of the increased quantity and complexity of historical knowledge, but also of the expanding market for detailed histories which had come into being. These collaborative ventures first appeared during the early years of the twentieth century, just as the single-author multi-volume histories were beginning to fade from the scene. Methuen produced *A History of England* in seven volumes, edited by Sir Charles Oman, with contributions from H. W. C. Davis (who wrote *England Under the Normans and Angevins*) and G. M. Trevelyan (who produced *England Under the Stuarts*). Longman replied with a twelve-volume *Political History of England*, co-edited by William Hunt and Reginald Lane Poole, with books by T. F. Tout, Sir Charles Oman, H. A. L. Fisher, A. F. Pollard, and Sir Richard Lodge. Finally, the early 1930s witnessed the launch of the most comprehensive and authoritative multi-authored work, *The Oxford History of*

---

[6] A. S. Green, 'Preface to the illustrated edition', and 'Introduction' to J. R. Green, *A Short History of the English People: Illustrated Edition* (2nd edn, London, 1902–3), i, pp. v–xxiii.
[7] D. Cannadine, *G. M. Trevelyan: A Life in History* (London, 1992), pp. 109–14.

England, under the general editorship of G. N. Clark, which was eventually completed, in fifteen volumes, thirty years later.

Inevitably, these three different versions of the national past varied greatly in their content, their quality, and their argumentation.[8] But they also had much in common. To begin with, it cannot be too much stressed that they were all conceived, written and marketed as histories of *England*. The word Britain did not appear in the title of any of the series that have been mentioned. These years may have witnessed the zenith of the British nation-state, of the United Kingdom, and of the British Empire, but the nation whose history they recounted and whose identity they helped to proclaim was England.[9] Moreover, these books were almost without exception in praise of England. They celebrated parliamentary government, the Common Law, the Church of England, ordered progress towards democracy, and the avoidance of revolution. They took English exceptionalism for granted: it existed, it was good, and it was the historian's task to explain it and to applaud it. And they generally supposed that this history was a success story: as the authors of *1066 and All That* argued, when England ceased to be top nation, history came to a full stop.[10]

These characteristics are the commonplaces of the Whig interpretation of English history which is now so much derided in professional circles, even if it retains its allure for Tory Prime Ministers. In retrospect, it is also easy to dismiss these books as having been wholly devoid of any awareness of the separate identities and the separate histories of England, Ireland, Scotland and Wales, let alone those of Great Britain, of the United Kingdom, and of the British Empire. Almost without exception, they indiscriminately interchanged the words England and Britain, as if they were no more than different names for the same country, to be used in the interests of stylistic variation. And to the extent that they did deal with the British Isles, these authors wrote from a very anglocentric perspective: insofar as they possessed any geographical range and territorial teleology, they were concerned to describe the gradual expansion of England, slowly but inexorably overwhelming, absorbing and dominating its near neighbours. The history of Britain was merely the history of England as and when it took place elsewhere.

It is these attitudes, assumptions and arguments which now seem so unacceptable and so outmoded. But before we dismiss this earlier historiography completely out of hand, it should be said in its defence that some of these

---

[8] J. W. Burrow, *A Liberal Descent: Victorian Historians and the English Past* (Cambridge, 1981).

[9] Cf. A. J. P. Taylor, *English History, 1914–1945* (Oxford, 1965), p. v: 'When the *Oxford History of England* was launched a generation ago, "England" was still an all-embracing word. It meant indiscriminately England and Wales; Great Britain; the United Kingdom; and even the British Empire.' For much of the 18th and early 19th centuries, histories of Britain and of its constituent parts were readily available. When and why they came to an end are subjects still awaiting their historian; for some suggestive ideas, see P. Morgan, *A New History of Wales: The Eighteenth-Century Renaissance* (Llandybie, Glamorgan, 1981); and M. Ash, *The Strange Death of Scottish History* (Edinburgh, 1980).

[10] W. C. Sellar and R. J. Yeatman, *1066 and All That* (London, 1930), p. 123.

books were not so unthinkingly anglocentric as it is now fashionable to deride them for having been. Even among the single-author multi-volume writers, Macaulay was exceptionally sensitive to the histories of the three kingdoms, and Lecky devoted considerable attention to relations between Great Britain and Ireland during the eighteenth century. The same can be said of the single-author single-volume surveys, and of the multi-author multi-volume series. They always treated Roman Britain as Roman *Britain*. The books or chapters on the twelfth and thirteenth centuries dealt in detail with the changing relations between England, Ireland, Scotland and Wales. And the same was true when it came to the 'long' seventeenth century, from the advent of James VI and I, via the Civil War, to the Act of Union with Scotland.[11] Only thereafter did interest in greater Britain somewhat diminish – the very time, it bears repeating, when greater Britain itself was undeniably at its greatest.

Despite these qualifications, the fact remains that during the heyday of the *British* state, nation and Empire, it was the *English* version of Whig history which was the prevailing mode. And it proved remarkably tenacious, long outliving the era in which it had blossomed, and the circumstances which had given it such resonance. The last single-author multi-volume history appeared during the late 1950s: Sir Winston Churchill's aptly named *History of the English-Speaking Peoples*, a time-warp work, owing much to such best-selling authors of his youth as Lecky and Green. Sir Keith Feiling and Sir George Clark produced single-volume histories of England, in 1949 and 1971 respectively, which were very much in the Trevelyan mould. The last volume of the *Oxford History of England* contained A. J. P. Taylor's celebrated (or notorious) denial that such a thing as Britain had ever existed.[12] And in the post-war, welfare-state era, there was a veritable glut of multi-authored, multi-volume series: from Penguin, Nelson, Longman, Paladin and Edward Arnold. All of them were conventionally styled *Histories of England*, and they continued to appear as late as the 1970s and 1980s. But by then, this traditional English history no longer seemed as confident or as convincing as it had in earlier decades.

What have been the changes in context and circumstance which have lead to the recent rethinking of national history, not only in Britain, but elsewhere? The most significant international development has been the unexpected and

[11] For the Longman series, see T. F. Tout, *From the Accession of Henry III to the Death of Edward III (1216–1377)* (London, 1920 edn), chs. 8–11; and R. Lodge, *From the Restoration to the Death of William III (1660–1702)* (London, 1923 edn), chs. 2, 3, 9, 13, 14. For the *Oxford History of England*, see R. G. Collingwood and J. N. L. Myers, *Roman Britain and the English Settlements* (Oxford, 1936), books 1–4; A. L. Poole, *From Domesday Book to Magna Carta, 1087–1216* (Oxford, 1951), ch. 9; F. M. Powicke, *The Thirteenth Century, 1216–1307* (Oxford, 1953), chs. 9, 12; and G. N. Clark, *The Later Stuarts, 1660–1714* (Oxford, 1934), chs. 12, 13.
[12] K. Feiling, *A History of England* (London, 1949), G. N. Clark, *English History: A Survey* (Oxford, 1971); Taylor, *English History, 1914–1945*, pp. v–vi.

unprecedented break-up of nation-states, many of them created less than a century ago. The demise of Communism since 1989 has brought an end to the Union of Soviet Socialist Republics, and has seen the establishment or re-establishment of many new countries in Eastern Europe and Central Asia. The collapse of the Warsaw Pact has brought freedom to many nations; but in certain cases, it has been a freedom which they have been unable to sustain. In Czechoslovakia, the break-up has been amicable: in Yugoslavia, it has been horrendous. And there is no guarantee that this is the end of the story. There are separatist movements in Spain; Italy has been on the brink of dissolution; the Canadian Confederation is in serious crisis; there are even predictions that, in the long run, the United States is bound to collapse into different ethnic and linguistic constituencies. Nationalism is once again alive, aggressive and on the march; but much of the most fervent national feeling is no longer consistent with the units of nationhood as they were created and consolidated between 1870 and 1919.[13]

This melt-down of some countries into smaller and less stable units is not the only way in which recent developments have undermined national identity. The enlargement of the European Union, the creation of the single market, and the seemingly inexorable shift of power to the Strasbourg Parliament and the Brussels bureaucrats, mean that state sovereignty is being rapidly and substantially eroded. No-one can know whether the single currency and the single bank are going to come into being, or what will be the result of the re-appraisal of the EU institutions due in the not too distant future. But whatever the outcome, the undermining of national sovereignty seems likely to go on. For it is not simply a political erosion. The globalisation of the economy means that decisions affecting particular nations or regions of Europe are as likely to be taken in New York or Tokyo or Hong Kong as they are in Berlin or Birmingham or Barcelona. And the still incomplete revolution in communications technology has only served to break down national identities still further. As the multinational, multi-media empire of Rupert Murdoch so vividly reminds us, the information super-highway knows no national boundaries or barriers.

Not surprisingly, then, the nation-state is widely regarded as being one of the most significant casualties of our post-modern world. Fernand Braudel devoted the last years of his life to trying to find *The Identity of France*. It eluded him – albeit in several volumes. The reunification of Germany, instead of stemming the tide of national dissolution, seems to have renewed, rather than lessened, German anxieties about their identity.[14] More generally,

[13] J. Breuilly, *Nationalism and the State* (2nd edn, Manchester, 1982); E. Gellner, *Nations and Nationalism* (Oxford, 1983); E. J. Hobsbawm, *Nations and Nationalism since 1870: Programme, Myth, Reality* (2nd edn, Cambridge, 1992); L. Greenfield, *Nationalism: Five Roads to Modernity* (Cambridge, Mass., 1992).

[14] F. Braudel, *The Identity of France* (London, 1988–90); P. Burke, 'French historians and their cultural identities', in E. Tonkin *et al.* (eds.), *History and Ethnicity* (London, 1989); R. Gildea, *The Past in French History* (New Haven, 1994); R. J. Evans, 'The new Nationalism and the old

Benedict Anderson has argued that nations should properly be understood as 'imagined communities': invented associations, encompassing a multitude of shifting boundaries and subjective identities. Thus regarded, there is nothing absolute, unchanging or immutable about the late nineteenth- and early twentieth-century nation-state. On the contrary, it was merely one provisional, temporary and contingent way of organising, governing and identifying large numbers of people, which invariably rested on manufactured myths and invented traditions.[15] By deconstructing these myths and traditions, historians are no longer reinforcing national identity as they did in the heyday of the nation-state: instead, they are intensifying the identity crisis through which many countries now seem to be passing.[16]

Once again, Britain has fully shared in these recent developments: both internationally and domestically, its identity seems increasingly problematic and uncertain. On the global stage, it no longer has the comforting reassurance of being a great power: since 1945, Britain's standing in the world has declined with astonishing and unrivalled rapidity, and for all Mrs Thatcher's bluster and bravura, this is a decline which she conspicuously failed to reverse. It no longer has the secure satisfaction of being the metropolis of a greater Britain flung far beyond the seas. The Empire has gone, the Commonwealth is multi-racial, and apart from the present Queen Elizabeth, there are few people today who believe in it, or even know what it is. And many Britons no longer feel separate from and superior to 'Europe'. As the opening of the Channel Tunnel makes plain, the ties to the rest of the Continent get closer all the time. For a nation that has, throughout so much of its history, defined itself over and against 'Europe' as something different, something exceptional, something better, this is proving to be very traumatic indeed.[17]

These globally conditioned anxieties about Britain's late twentieth-century identity have been reinforced by three domestic developments. First, the

History: perspectives on the West German *Historikerstreit*', *Journal of Modern History*, lix (1987); C. S. Maier, *The Unmasterable Past: History, Holocaust and German National Identity* (Cambridge, Mass., 1988); G. Eley, 'Nazism, politics and the image of the past: thoughts on the West German *Historikerstreit*', *Past and Present*, cxxi (1988); H. James, *A German Identity, 1770–1990* (revised edn, London, 1990).

[15] B. Anderson, *Imagined Communities: Reflections on the Origin and Spread of Nationalism* (London, 1983); P. Sahlins, *Boundaries: The Making of France and Spain in the Pyrenees* (Berkeley, 1989).

[16] For examples of such work, concerned with England, Wales, Scotland and Britain, see E. J. Hobsbawm and T. Ranger (eds.), *The Invention of Tradition* (Cambridge, 1983); T. Curtis (ed.), *Wales: The Imagined Nation: Essays on Culture and National Identity* (Bridgend, 1986); D. Cannadine, *The Pleasures of the Past* (London, 1989); R. Samuel (ed.), *Patriotism: The Making and Unmaking of British National Identity* (London, 1989); M. G. H. Pittock, *The Invention of Scotland: The Stuart Myth and the Scottish Identity, 1638 to the Present* (London, 1991); R. Porter (ed.), *Myths of the English* (Cambridge, 1992); and K. Robbins, *History, Religion and Identity in Modern Britain* (London, 1993).

[17] L. Colley, 'Britishness and Otherness: an argument'; J. G. A. Pocock, 'History and sovereignty: the historiographical response to Europeanization in two cultures'; G. Eley, 'Culture, Britain and Europe': all in *Journal of British Studies*, xxxi (1992); also J. Black, *Convergence or Divergence? Britain and the Continent* (London, 1994).

obverse of post-war decolonisation has been a massive influx of immigrants, especially from South Asia and the Caribbean; to an unprecedented degree, Britain is now a multi-racial, multi-ethnic, multi-cultural society, where there are more Moslems than Methodists. Second, the 'troubles' in Northern Ireland, which have lasted for a quarter of a century, combined with the resurgence of Welsh and Scottish nationalism since the 1970s, have led many commentators to predict (and some to hope for) the break-up of Britain as a nation-state into its separate, historic, constituent parts of England, Scotland, Wales and (presumably) a re-united Ireland.[18] Third, many institutions which seemed for so long the very embodiment of national identity and national success seem to have lost their sense of purpose and the confidence of the public – the monarchy, Parliament, the Church of England, the police.

At the same time, there have also been significant changes and developments in British historical scholarship since 1945, away from the earlier concern with, and celebration of, the English nation-state. In England itself, university-based history greatly expanded during the immediate post-war years, and again in the 1960s and 1970s. But although traditional English political and constitutional history was still taught, with the aid of the new multi-authored series that were then being produced, it was no longer as unchallenged as it had been.[19] For the new, burgeoning, fashionable sub-disciplines which came to prominence and maturity during those years were little concerned with questions and units of national identity. Economic historians preferred to deal with smaller areas (especially Lancashire) or larger (usually Europe). Local historians and urban historians concentrated on particular regions and individual cities. Social historians were more interested in classes than in nations. And historians of ideas, of culture, of capitalism, of technology, of population, of race, of sex, of gender and of religion were rarely concerned with specific national boundaries at all.

Elsewhere in the British Isles, English history was faced with a different, but no less powerful challenge: the emergence of Irish, Welsh and Scottish history as separate self-conscious academic subjects.[20] The post-war expansion of universities, combined with the Irish 'troubles' and the upsurge of Scottish and Welsh nationalism, undoubtedly gave a great impetus to non-English

---

[18] T. Nairn, *The Break-Up of Britain: Crisis and Neo-Nationalism* (London, 1977); V. Bogdanor, *Devolution* (Oxford, 1979); H. M. Drucker, *The Politics of Nationalism and Devolution* (London, 1980); J. Osmond, *The Divided Kingdom* (London, 1988); N. Evans (ed.), *National Identity in the British Isles* (Harlech, 1989); B. Crick (ed.), *National Identities: The Constitution of the United Kingdom* (Oxford, 1991).

[19] For a vigorous protest against these developments, see G. R. Elton's (first) inaugural lecture, as Professor of English Constitutional History at Cambridge, 'The future of the past': reprinted in G. R. Elton, *Return to Essentials* (Cambridge, 1991).

[20] B. Lenman, 'The teaching of Scottish history in the Scottish universities', *Scottish Historical Review*, lii (1973); G. Williams, 'Local and national history in Wales', *Welsh History Review*, v (1970–1); T. W. Moody, 'The first forty years', *Irish Historical Studies*, xx (1977); R. F. Foster, 'History and the Irish Question', *Transactions of the Royal Historical Society*, 5th ser., xxxiii (1983); P. Jenkins, *A History of Modern Wales, 1536–1990* (London, 1992), pp. 407–29.

(and sometimes anglophobic) historical studies in these three nations. One sign of this was the advent of a cohort of outstanding scholars, including T. W. Moody and F. S. L. Lyons in Ireland, Rosalind Mitchison, Gordon Donaldson and Geoffrey Barrow in Scotland, and Glanmor Williams and Gwyn A. Williams in Wales. Another was the proliferation of separate scholarly journals: the *Scottish Historical Review* was revived and rejuvenated after 1945; *Irish Historical Studies* became the major forum for rethinking Irish history; and they were joined by the *Welsh History Review* in 1961. Yet a third was the appearance of new single-volume histories of the three nations, consolidating the detailed research now being done, and establishing new, non-anglocentric interpretations.[21]

Together, these international, domestic and scholarly developments have substantially undermined the presumptions and presuppositions which characterised English history-writing in the heyday of the nation-state, and of Britain as top nation. Globally, it is no longer convincing to depict the history of England as the successful and still unfinished epic of the rise of a great power and the winning and consolidation of a great empire. Continentally, it is no longer convincing to depict the history of England as one of providential exceptionalism, intermittent involvement, and ordered and inexorable progress. Domestically, it is no longer convincing to depict the history of England as the process whereby it inexorably assimilated the rest of the British Isles. And academically, it is no longer convincing to write the history of England without some awareness of the separate but interlocking histories of Ireland, Scotland and Wales, and without giving thought to the different identities (and histories) implied by the words England, Great Britain, the United Kingdom, the British Isles, and the British Empire.

Accordingly, the 1970s and 1980s witnessed the gradual abandonment of the Whiggish history of England, and the first tentative moves towards a new and more sophisticated form of genuinely British history. Michael Hechter's study of England and the Celtic fringe seems retrospectively too anglocentric, but at the time it appeared, it was the British dimension of the work which rightly impressed. Oxford University Press published a one-volume history which had Britain in the text as well as the title, and Cambridge responded with an encyclopaedia which embraced both Britain and Ireland.[22] Most importantly, J. G. A. Pocock produced two seminal articles, which urged the creation and recognition of British history 'as a new subject'. It should be concerned for the early period with the archipelago as a whole (a period for which the designation 'British Isles' is not at all appropriate). It should be concerned for the seventeenth and eighteenth centuries with the greater

---

[21] E.g., D. Williams, *A History of Modern Wales* (London, 1950); J. C. Beckett, *The Making of Modern Ireland* (London, 1966); R. Mitchison, *A History of Scotland* (London, 1970).

[22] M. Hechter, *Internal Colonialism: The Celtic Fringe in British National Development* (Berkeley, 1975); K. O. Morgan (ed.), *The Oxford Illustrated History of Britain* (Oxford, 1984); C. Haigh (ed.), *The Cambridge Historical Encyclopaedia of Great Britain and Ireland* (Cambridge, 1985).

British transatlantic world, which was shattered by the civil war that began in 1776. And it should be concerned for the nineteenth and twentieth centuries with imperial Britain, encompassing North America, parts of Africa, much of India, and all of the Antipodes.[23]

This was a powerful programmatic polemic, much influenced by contemporary developments, and it naturally took some time to influence the course of historical thinking, research and writing. As late as 1986, Rees Davies lamented that:

> British history has been much in the air of late; but it still seems strangely reluctant to come down to earth ... British history has not in truth arrived. The programmatic rhetoric, as is usual in these matters, has been more impressive than the practical achievement.[24]

So, indeed, at the time it was. But what a change the intervening years have wrought. Today, there can scarcely be a historian left in these islands who would still unthinkingly interchange the words England and Britain, who is ignorant of the work done in Irish, Scottish and Welsh history, who pays no heed to connections and contrasts across the Channel, or who fails to recognise that 'British history' is something substantively different from 'English history' writ larger. Articles, monographs and general surveys regularly appear, proclaiming their commitment to the 'new British history'. But what exactly is it? How new is it? What are its prospects and its problems?

It is helpful, in addressing these questions, to recall an observation of Conrad Russell, namely that it is not clear that 'British history' can be undertaken for every century of Britain's past with the same degree of plausibility, conviction or success.[25] Before we reach the early modern period, the 'new British history' seems to flourish most vigorously and self-consciously in the twelfth, thirteenth and seventeenth centuries.[26] Nor should this come as any great surprise. For if we look back on the many English histories of the past, be they the single-author multi-volume works, the single-author single-volume surveys, or the multi-author multi-volume series, it was in precisely these same centuries that most attention was lavished on the affairs, not just of England, but also of Wales, Scotland and Ireland. And how could it have been

---

[23] Pocock, 'British History: a plea for a new subject', and 'Limits and divisions of British History'.

[24] R. R. Davies, 'In praise of British History', in R. R. Davies (ed.), *The British Isles 1100–1500: Comparisons, Contrasts and Connections* (Edinburgh, 1988), p. 9.

[25] C. Russell, 'John Bull's other nations', *Times Literary Supplement*, 12 March 1993, pp. 3–4.

[26] In addition to the works cited below, see R. Frame, *The Political Development of the British Isles 1100–1400* (Oxford, 1990); J. Wormald, 'The creation of Britain: multiple kingdoms or core and colonies?', *Transactions of the Royal Historical Society*, 6th ser., ii (1992); J. Morrill (ed.), *The Scottish National Covenant in its British Context* (Edinburgh, 1990); and B. P. Levack, *The Formation of the British State: England, Scotland and the Union, 1603–1707* (Oxford, 1987).

otherwise, given that the histories of the four (or the three) kingdoms interacted more intensely and intensively during these centuries than those either side? From this perspective, the 'new British history' now being undertaken, for the period of the first Pocockian paradigm, is not always quite as new or as original as some might be inclined to think.

When we turn to the broader, transatlantic British world that was founded, flourished and fell apart during the seventeenth and eighteenth centuries, the picture changes dramatically. The great English historians of the past did not view things from a Pocockian perspective: they wrote about the establishment of colonies on the Eastern Seaboard, and about the American War of Independence, but they did not see these activities as defining a discrete phase (or area) of British history. In recent years, however, this period and this community have become much studied: a great array of 'Atlanticist' scholars have been exploring the demographic, economic, social, political and ideological links which bound together, and eventually drove apart, this greater British realm located on both the eastern and the western perimeters of the Atlantic Ocean.[27] And for a later period, Peter Marshall and C. A. Bayly have been exploring the beginnings of a new British Empire that was being founded in India.[28] Amidst such a wealth of meritorious endeavour, only Ireland seems to have received rather less attention than perhaps it should have.

When we reach the nineteenth and twentieth centuries, the period of the third and most expanded British community, the picture changes again, but this time not for the better. It is worth repeating that the histories written in the heyday of the United Kingdom and the British Empire were generally indifferent to that Kingdom and Empire, in the sense that they simply took it for granted. The ending, since the Second World War, of this most extended and most recent phase of British history-making might have been expected to

[27] J. G. A. Pocock (ed.), *Three British Revolutions: 1641, 1688, 1776* (Princeton, 1980); J. G. A. Pocock (ed.), *The Varieties of British Political Thought, 1500–1800* (Cambridge, 1993); K. R. Andrews, N. P. Canny and P. E. H. Hair (eds.), *The Westwards Enterprise: English Activities in Ireland, the Atlantic and America, 1480–1650* (Liverpool, 1978); N. Canny, *Kingdom and Colony: Ireland in the Atlantic World, 1560–1800* (Baltimore, 1988); N. Canny and A. Pagden (eds.), *Colonial Identity in the Atlantic World, 1500–1800* (Princeton, 1987); J. P. Greene, *Peripheries and Center: Constitutional Development in the Extended Polities of the British Empire and United States, 1607–1788* (Athens, Georgia, 1986); J. P. Greene, *Pursuits of Happiness: The Social Development of Early Modern British Colonies and the Formation of American Culture* (New York, 1988); B. Bailyn, *The Peopling of British North America* (New York, 1986); B. Bailyn, *Voyagers to the West* (New York, 1986); D. H. Fischer, *Albion's Seed: Four British Folkways in America* (New York, 1989); B. Bailyn and P. D. Morgan (eds.), *Strangers Within the Realm: Cultural Margins of the First British Empire* (Chapel Hill, North Carolina, 1991); D. Armitage, 'The Cromwellian Protectorate and the language of Empire', *Historical Journal*, xxxv (1992); J. C. D. Clark, *The Language of Liberty, 1660–1832: Political Discourse and Social Dynamics in the Anglo-American World* (Cambridge, 1994).

[28] C. A. Bayly, *Indian Society and the Making of the British Empire* (Cambridge, 1988); C. A. Bayly, *Imperial Meridian: The British Empire and the World, 1780–1830* (London, 1989); P. J. Marshall, *Problems of Empire: Britain and India, 1757–1813* (London, 1968); P. J. Marshall, *Bengal, the British Bridgehead* (Cambridge, 1987).

lead to an upsurge in British history-writing about it. But this has rarely yet been the case. With the exception of the work of Keith Robbins, there is very little authentic, self-conscious 'British history' – and as he would be the first to admit, his work does not extend much to Ireland or the Empire. Peter Cain and A. G. Hopkins have audaciously reconnected metropolitan Britain and its Empire; but they never address, let alone resolve, the central contradiction of their book, namely that they see the *British* Empire as the result of exporting the *English* gentlemanly ideal overseas. Beyond that, there is next to nothing.[29] How odd it is that 'British history' as a subject should be at its weakest for the very period when British history itself in many ways reached its zenith.

'British history', it should be clear, means different things in different centuries. But this is not just in terms of when and where it can be deemed to have taken place, nor in terms of how much of it there can be – or should be. It is also that this new, fashionable, generic heading conceals – or encompasses – a variety of very different problems and issues, approaches and methodologies. Rees Davies has shown how the kings and aristocracy of England sought to extend their dominion, by military conquest, over Wales, Scotland and Ireland during the twelfth and thirteenth centuries. Conrad Russell has sought to explain what used to be called the English Civil War as a British War of the Three Kingdoms.[30] Linda Colley has looked at the many ways in which a new sense of British national identity was created and forged at all social levels during the eighteenth century. And Keith Robbins has investigated the integration of nineteenth-century Britain via the arts, religion, politics, business, education and recreation.[31] These are excessively oversimplified summaries of works of great subtlety, insight and complexity. But it is surely correct to note that these historians are looking at very different forms of Britishness, and so are writing very different forms of 'British history'.

There is, in short, no one single, dominant methodology for the 'new British history'. Nor should there be. Put another way, this means that the 'four nations' approach, so brilliantly pioneered by Hugh Kearney, should not be allowed to dominate the subject.[32] Clearly, there are some aspects and some centuries of British history which it illuminates with unique force and power. But, as Kearney himself admitted, this is not the whole story. The

[29] K. Robbins, *Nineteenth-Century Britain: Integration and Diversity* (Oxford, 1988); P. J. Cain and A. G. Hopkins, *British Imperialism*, vol. I: *Innovation and Expansion, 1688-1914*; vol. II: *Crisis and Deconstruction, 1914-1990* (London, 1993). For another attempt to write British history in the modern era, see D. Cannadine, *The Decline and Fall of the British Aristocracy* (New Haven, 1990).

[30] R. R. Davies, *Domination and Conquest: The Experience of Ireland, Scotland and Wales 1100-1300* (Cambridge, 1990); C. Russell, 'The British problem and the English Civil War', *History*, lxxii (1987); C. Russell, 'The British background to the Irish rebellion of 1641', *Historical Research*, lxi (1988); C. Russell, *The Fall of the British Monarchies, 1637-1642* (Oxford, 1991).

[31] L. Colley, *Britons: Forging the Nation, 1707-1837* (New Haven, 1992); Robbins, *Nineteenth-Century Britain*.

[32] H. Kearney, *The British Isles: A History of Four Nations* (Cambridge, 1989).

four nations evolved in different ways and at different speeds. At certain stages in their histories, they had different state structures, different monarchies, different religions, different national identities. There were important internal divisions, between the north and the south of England, between the Lowlands and Highlands of Scotland, between Protestant and Catholic Ireland. The borders and boundaries between the four nations were often contested and shifting. And England's eventual incorporation of Wales was different from its incorporation of Scotland, which was different again from its incorporation of Ireland. The danger with the 'four nations' methodology is that it sometimes pays insufficient attention to the important variations between and within them.[33]

Indeed, in the opening pages of his book, Kearney comes close to subverting the very conceptual framework which, thereafter, he utilises with such brio and élan. For, as he points out, there are other ways of dividing up the British Isles, and thus of conceptualising its history, than that embodied in the 'four nations' approach. Suppose, for instance, a history of the British Isles was organised, not around the interconnections between England, Ireland, Scotland and Wales, but around the differences between lowland and upland regions.[34] This might lead to an alternative form of 'British history', briefly suggested by Pocock, but which has never been taken up. Almost as an aside, he notes that the 'new British history' does not have to be political and constitutional. It could, he seems to be implying, be social history, economic history, demographic history, environmental history, maritime history. It could – and this is his own shorthand term – be Braudellian history: a much more broadly conceived history of the British Isles than that provided by political historians, whether they use the 'four nations' approach or not.[35]

That is surely the most important challenge which this new brand of British history has not yet begun to face: namely that political history has run far ahead of other, no less essential, ways of looking at the British past. In this sense, we need more 'British history', not less. Yet at the same time, we should not expect more from this new subject than it can realistically be expected to deliver. One danger is that too much British history will merely replace the political teleology of ordered constitutional development, and the

[33] Colley, 'Britishness and Otherness', pp. 313–16. For some valuable works of comparative history, dealing with some, but not all, of the 'four nations', see L. M. Cullen and T. C. Smout (eds.), *Comparative Aspects of Scottish and Irish Economic and Social History, 1600–1900* (Edinburgh, 1977); T. M. Devine and D. Dickson (eds.), *Ireland and Scotland, 1600–1850: Parallels and Contrasts in Economic and Social Development* (Edinburgh, 1983); R. A. Mason (ed.), *Scotland and England, 1286–1815* (Edinburgh, 1987); and K. Wrightson, 'Kindred adjoining kingdoms: an English perspective on the social and economic history of early modern Scotland', in R. A. Houston and I. D. Whyte (eds.), *Scottish Society, 1500–1800* (Cambridge, 1989).

[34] Kearney, *British Isles*, pp. 1–9. For some suggestive hints, see H. M. Jewell, *The North–South Divide: The Origins of Northern Consciousness in England* (Manchester, 1994). No historian has yet explored the implications for Britain of Professor Bailyn's findings about the different emigration patterns to 18th-century America from the North and the South: Bailyn, *Voyagers to the West*, especially pp. 13/–41.

[35] Pocock, 'Limits and divisions of British History', pp. 317–18.

sociological teleology of an ever-rising middle class, with an indentificational teleology which merely and mindlessly claims that, at any given time, the British were actively engaged in the process of becoming more British than they ever had been before. Another is that an excessive concentration on 'Britishness' may lead historians to ignore those many alternative individual identities, sometimes complementary, sometimes contradictory, which are more locally – but no less powerfully – articulated. Even in the post-modern era of decentred discourse, it bears repeating that the creation of a British identity did not entail or require the abandonment of English or Scottish or Welsh or Irish identities, or of more regional loyalties to county, city or village.

It is, then, neither surprising nor wrong that separate histories of England, Ireland, Scotland and Wales are continuing to flourish alongside newly conceptualised and newly commissioned histories of Britain.[36] After all, it was the Irish 'troubles' and the growth of Welsh and Scottish nationalism that helped to make us more aware of the 'British' problem, and this has stimulated Irish, Welsh and Scottish history at the same time that it has stimulated the 'new British history'. The last fifteen years have witnessed the appearance of Edward Arnold's *New History of Scotland* in eight volumes;[37] of Oxford University Press's *New History of Ireland*, to be in a projected ten volumes; and of the Oxford University Press/University of Wales Press *History of Wales*, of which four volumes have so far appeared. Nor is the history of England going into terminal decline. Sir Geoffrey Elton's single-volume survey, *The English*, while impressively up to date with revisionist scholarship, celebrates English exceptionalism and institutions with an enthusiastic ardour that G. M. Trevelyan barely equalled.[38] And it looks as though the *New Oxford History of England* is going to be no more British-minded and British-ranging than was the old series it has been designed to replace.[39]

To be sure, there may still be too much anglocentric history produced in some English quarters, and too much anglophobic history undertaken in some of the more distant reaches of the British Isles. Be that as it may, the 'new British history', whether it is the history of Britain, or of Britishness, or of the United Kingdom, or of the British Empire, should not be – and must not be – a denial of those separate histories and separate

---

[36] J. Davies, *A History of Wales* (London, 1993); M. Lynch, *Scotland: A New History* (London, 1991); R. F. Foster, *Modern Ireland, 1600–1972* (London, 1988).

[37] Though, slightly earlier, the decade 1965–75 saw the publication of the four-volume *Edinburgh History of Scotland*.

[38] G. R. Elton, *The English* (Oxford, 1992). See also his (second) inaugural lecture, as Regius Professor of Modern History at Cambridge, 'The History of England': reprinted in Elton, *Return to Essentials*, especially pp. 110–15. For other studies of England, see R. Colls and P. Dodds (eds.), *Englishness: Politics and Culture, 1880–1920* (Beckenham, Kent, 1986); and G. Newman, *The Rise of English Nationalism: A Cultural History, 1740–1830* (London, 1987).

[39] J. Roberts, 'General editor's preface', in P. Langford, *A Polite and Commercial People: England, 1727–1783* (Oxford, 1989), pp. vii–viii.

identities of England, Ireland, Scotland and Wales. All too often in the past, histories of England, Ireland, Scotland and Wales ignored (or resented) the British dimensions. It would be an unhappy irony if the newly emergent histories of Britain ignored (or resented) the English, Welsh, Scottish and Irish dimension.[40] Beyond any doubt, there are some aspects of our past where the 'new British history' has been successful and illuminating, and there are others where it urgently needs to be undertaken. But it is also necessary to insist that we should not claim more for 'British history as a new subject' than it is right, sensible and appropriate to do.

To say this is not to provide inadvertent scholarly endorsement for the 'Little England' Whiggism of Thatcher and Major, with which this essay briefly but appropriately began. They may refer to Britain in their speeches, but their notion of Britishness is excessively and anachronistically anglocentric, and as such it tells us much about the evolution of Conservative attitudes and electoral fortunes in the years since the Second World War. The party that once championed the British Empire is now more inclined to dismiss the whole imperial adventure and its Commonwealth aftermath as a distorting aberration from English history.[41] The party which changed its name to defend the Union with Ireland is today widely distrusted by the Protestant loyalists of Belfast. And in Wales and Scotland, popular Toryism has seemed for some time almost a contradiction in terms. As so often in the past, the Conservative Party has once again become pre-eminently the party of English nationalism.[42] When Tories pledge themselves to maintain the United Kingdom intact, they do so to perpetuate traditional English dominance within it, rather than out of any sympathy with its broader British identity.

For reasons that are precisely the opposite, but are no less cogent, the Labour Party also needs to preserve the United Kingdom intact. Unlike the Conservatives, it is electorally essential for it to do so. The party may have been – and may still be – committed to some degree of devolution for Scotland and Wales. But this is because it is also crucially dependent for its national success on Welsh and Scottish votes. For a future Labour government to devolve so much power to Scottish and Welsh assemblies that the

[40] For recent discussions of these separate histories and historiographies, see R. Mitchison (ed.), *Why Scottish History Matters* (Edinburgh, 1993); G. Donaldson, *Scottish History: Approaches and Reflections* (Edinburgh, 1994); B. Bradshaw, 'Nationalism and historical scholarship in modern Ireland', *Irish Historical Studies*, xxvi (1989); S. G. Ellis, 'Historiographical debate: representations of the past in Ireland: whose past and whose present?', *Irish Historical Studies*, xxvii (1991); N. Evans, 'Debate: British History: past, present – and future?', *Past and Present*, cxix (1988); and R. Merfyn Jones, 'Beyond identity: the reconstruction of the Welsh', *Journal of British Studies*, xxxi (1992).

[41] This was an especially pronounced theme in many of the speeches of Enoch Powell: see Nairn, *Break-Up of Britain*, pp. 256–91.

[42] Elton, *The English*, pp. 233–5; R. Blake, *The Conservative Party from Peel to Churchill* (London, 1970), p. 273; R. Blake (ed.), *The English World: History, Character and People* (New York, 1982).

number of MPs at Westminster had to be substantially reduced would be to commit electoral suicide. Labour cannot win British elections without the Welsh and Scottish electorate, and it is hardly coincidental that so many of its leaders have come from Scotland and Wales. Thus described, the Labour Party, like the Liberals before them, is British in a way that the Conservative Party has rarely been in the past, and is not now. The Tories use England as the means to dominate Britain; Labour needs Britain as the means to dominate England.

Notwithstanding the 'Little England' rhetoric of the Conservatives, and the devolutionist obligations of Labour, the two main political parties thus have very good (albeit very different) reasons for wanting to keep the United Kingdom intact. And so, while the predicted or hoped-for or despaired-of break-up of Britain could still occur, it seems equally likely that it will not. Even in the 1990s, nations that have survived far outnumber nations that have dissolved, and the forces holding the United Kingdom together may yet turn out to be much stronger than those pulling it apart. British historians, of whatever political persuasion or local loyalty, would do well to ponder this. For while the 'new British history' has been significantly stimulated by what seemed to be the impending dissolution of Britain, the continued validity and vitality of the subject do not depend upon such an apocalyptic outcome. All that can be said with certainty at present is that Britain still exists, that British history is still being made, and that it will continue to be made for the foreseeable future. This is not the only reason why scholars should continue to study and to rethink 'British history'. But it is certainly a most compelling one.[43]

43 In revising this essay for publication, I have benefited greatly from the comments and advice of David Armitage, Linda Colley, Willy Malley and Kenneth Morgan. For some earlier thoughts on related issues, but which use the term 'British history' in rather a different way, see D. Cannadine, 'British History: past, present – and future?', *Past and Present*, cxvi (1987).

Part II

Medieval foundations

Chapter 3

The United Kingdom of England
The Anglo-Saxon achievement[1]

James Campbell

England was, and is, the preponderant element in the United Kingdom. Historical understanding of the United Kingdom must involve consideration of when, how, and why England itself became united. Inquiry into this can begin by addressing sharp contrasts: between England and the Continent, between the seventh century and the eleventh. In the seventh century, England (or, to be precise, what was to become England) was occupied by many small 'kingdoms'. The old historiographical topos that this was the period of seven kingdoms, the 'heptarchy', is misleading. Reality was more complicated. But there is useful crude sense in the antique term as a formula for extreme division of authority. There were other parts of north-western Europe where authority was comparably divided: Ireland, the areas in British hands in western parts of our island, and probably the future Norway. But Ireland and Norway had not been part of the Roman Empire; most of Britain had been. Its post-imperial state contrasts with that of the remainder of the former Western Empire. There was no 'heptarchic element' in Spain, Italy and Gaul; rather did the Visigothic, Lombard and Frankish kings rule over substantial realms.

Contrast the position in 1066. England was by then a nation-state. It is highly improbable that any European rulers enjoyed closely organised authority over so wide an area as did its kings. The dominions of the German King Henry IV were far more extensive, but the extent of his authority varied from area to area; his government was by no means uniformly integrated; and he did not rule a state in the sense that Edward the Confessor did. There is no question of there having been anything comparable to the English state in France, Spain or Italy. In four centuries a position had been completely reversed. The area of the former Western Empire where authority had disintegrated furthest had become the largest area of integrated power.

It may seem extravagant to describe early England as a 'nation-state'. Nevertheless it is unavoidable. South of the Tees and the Ribble (the area surveyed by the Domesday commissioners) England had a system of government which was substantially uniform. The shires, many of them

[1] This sketch does not profess to do more than identify some of the salient issues. References have been kept to a minimum.

created in some fairly recent generation, were the basic units of royal authority, and, broadly, what applied in one of them applied in all. Hundreds or wapentakes, the subdivisions of the shires, varied more from area to area, but resemblances were more important than differences. Shires, hundreds and wapentakes had courts which were part of a system of royal justice and in a significant sense were 'popular'. A major indication of the power of the English state was the scale and scope of the system of assessment for taxation. The Domesday survey proves that virtually every village and every estate was assessed in terms of hides or carucates. The system was such as to have made it possible for rulers of England to raise taxes on a scale unparalleled elsewhere.[2]

A special, but a very solid, demonstration of the power of the English state is the coinage. Its kings issued an abundant silver coinage, whose nature was such as to permit numismatists to estimate the number of coins struck in successive issues.[3] By Michael Metcalf's estimates the most abundant of these, the 'Quatrefoil' issue of Cnut, contained something of the order of forty million coins; the issues of the Confessor's reign were much less abundant, averaging about seven million, but were current for shorter periods. The evidence of hoards is that the only coin allowed to circulate in England was that of the English kings. This is itself a demonstration of effective royal power. No less so is the fact that the coinage was run on a system of *renovatio* by which at intervals of a few years the current type of penny was demonetised and replaced by a new one. The coins themselves were powerful messengers of royal authority. They always bore on one side the name and portrait of the king. The other bore a symbol, sometimes one such as to give the coin a moral force. Thus early issues in Æthelred II's reign bore on one side the king's head, and on the other the Hand of God. Numismatic evidence illuminates the unity of England in another way. It shows not only that England was an integrated state but that it had a considerably integrated economy. Of coins of the period 1018–86 found singly, more than a third were discovered over a hundred kilometres from their places of minting.[4]

It might, however, be contended that, notwithstanding these indications of extensive royal authority and of detailed control in the provinces, there are also contrary indications of historically rooted provincialism. Particular stress would here be laid on the position of the great earls and on provincial variations in law.

Late Anglo-Saxon England was divided into units of authority called in the tenth century ealdordoms, in the eleventh earldoms.[5] In the tenth century,

---

[2] J. Campbell, *Essays in Anglo-Saxon History* (London, 1986), pp. 155–70; P. Wormald, '*Engla Land*: the making of an allegiance', *Journal of Historical Sociology*, vii (1994).

[3] See D. M. Metcalf, 'Continuity and change in English monetary history, c.973–1086', which appears in two parts in *British Numismatic Journal*, l (1980), and li (1982).

[4] Metcalf, 'Continuity and change', Part I, p. 29, note.

[5] H. M. Chadwick, *Studies on Anglo-Saxon Institutions* (Cambridge, 1905), pp. 161–97; L. N. Banton, 'Ealdormen and Earls in England from the Reign of Alfred to the Reign of Æthelred II' (Oxford University D.Phil. thesis, 1981).

two of these, East Anglia and Essex, corresponded approximately to earlier kingdoms. As a result of a reorganisation under Cnut, the number of earldoms increased. There were now earls of East Anglia, Wessex, Mercia and Northumbria. The *Anglo-Saxon Chronicle*'s annal for 1017 could create the impression of a reversion to the circumstances of the early ninth century: 'In this year King Cnut succeeded to all the kingdom of England and divided it into four, Wessex for himself, East Anglia for Thorkel, Mercia for Eadric and Northumbria for Eric.'[6] Such an impression is misleading. The degree of semi-independence enjoyed by Eadric can be judged from the fact that he was killed, presumably by Cnut, before the year was out;[7] Thorkel was exiled in 1021;[8] Eric seems to have died not long after but may possibly have been exiled.[9] Nevertheless the four major earldoms did persist, though sometimes we also find earls with authority over individual shires. From Cnut's time until the Conquest all the major earldoms were held by three men appointed by Cnut – Godwin, Leofric and Siward – or by their descendants.

Did the powers and position of such men embody or encourage historically rooted provincial particularism? What were the powers of an earl in the last years of the Old English state? To the extent that they may have varied from earldom to earldom, the principal variations are likely to have been between Northumbria, particularly the lands beyond the Tees and the Ribble, and the other earldoms. Everywhere the earl was supposed to preside in the shire court and to lead the shire levies. That he was absolute in either function is unlikely. The king regularly dispatched *legati*, probably with judicial functions, even to Northumbria.[10] The annals suggest that the king had overriding powers over the fyrd. By the Confessor's reign much local administrative responsibility fell to the sheriff. If, as is very possible but not demonstrable, sheriffs were generally appointed not by the relevant earl but by the king, then a large part of the apparatus of government could have been independent of the earl. The sheriffs were probably largely responsible for the management of the important royal lands which lay in most shires. Although Domesday shows that earls had a third share of certain royal revenues, particularly urban revenues, this demonstrates that the king received two-thirds of these.[11] There is no evidence for earls having a share in the geld. A certain limitation on the power of the earls is indicated by the fact that they did not issue charters. The witness lists of royal charters show how frequently earls, even those of

[6] *Two of the Anglo-Saxon Chronicles Parallel*, ed. C. Plummer (Oxford, 1896), i, pp. 154–5. The translation is that of D. Whitelock *et al.*, *The Anglo-Saxon Chronicle: A Revised Translation*, (2nd [corrected] edn, London, 1965), p. 97.

[7] *Two of the Anglo-Saxon Chronicles*, i, p. 154.

[8] Ibid., i, p. 155.

[9] L. M. Larson, *Cnut the Great* (London and New York, 1912), p. 148.

[10] *Domesday Book, Lincolnshire*, ed. P. Morgan and C. Thorn (Chichester, 1986), i, p. T (i, f. 337ª). I am assuming the circumstances described antedate the Conquest.

[11] J. Tait, *The Medieval English Borough* (Manchester, 1936), pp. 64–5, 141–9.

Northumbria, attended the royal court.[12] A clear demonstration that the ealdormen of the tenth century and the earls of the eleventh did not enjoy vice-regal status is that for most of the period England was completely divided up into ealdordoms/earldoms; after all, if Cnut's earls had been virtual viceroys, that king would have left himself with virtually no power in England after 1019 – a most unlikely hypothesis. Earls were evidently important: but they were not pre-eminently the beneficiaries or representatives of provincialism. Indeed, the reverse could be the case. When the West Saxon Tostig was appointed earl of Northumbria in 1055, his role was seen by a contemporary as that of repressing the violence of Northumbrian society.[13] When the Northumbrians rebelled against him in 1065, they came south to ask the king for a new earl, and the new earl they were given was another non-Northumbrian, Morcar.

The great English families were not 'provincial' even in the sense in which, say, the counts of Anjou were provincial. They acted on an all-English stage. The extent to which their estates were scattered in relatively small units, not held in big blocs, is itself indicative of how far the earls, like their lands, were integrated into a wider whole.[14] The estates of many of the nobility below the earls were similarly dispersed. Although the estates of some important nobles of the Confessor's day were concentrated within a relatively small area, others were widely scattered. Extreme cases are those of Wulfweard White with lands in twelve shires, and Wulfwynn of Creslow with nine manors spread from Dorset to Hertfordshire.[15]

Another factor in fostering national unity must have been the intermarriage within the nobility. In the tenth century the high nobility were extensively interrelated, and the royal family was very much part of an extended noble cousinhood.[16] No member of the royal family is known to have married outside England between the marriages of daughters of Æthelstan to continental potentates in the 910s and 920s and Æthelred II's marriage to Emma of Normandy in 1002.

Even if it is admitted that earldoms were only in limited senses expressive of provincial particularism, the question may fairly be asked, were there not major provincial distinctions in law? It is true that some tenth-century laws imply separate provision for all or part of the lands which had been conquered by the Danes – the Danelaw. It is also true that post-Conquest compilations refer to England as divided into three legal zones: those of West Saxon law, Mercian law, and the Danelaw. There were significant differences between these in certain elements of law, especially in regard to the sum fixed

[12] T. J. Oleson, *The Witenagemot in the Reign of Edward the Confessor* (Oxford, 1955), pp. 53–4 and Appendix H.

[13] *Vita Edwardi Regis*, ed. F. Barlow (London, 1962), pp. 50–1.

[14] D. Hill, *An Atlas of Anglo-Saxon England* (Oxford, 1981), maps nos. 181 and 182.

[15] P. A. Clarke, *The English Nobility under Edward the Confessor* (Oxford, 1994), especially p. 37.

[16] W. G. Searle, *Anglo-Saxon Bishops, Kings and Nobles* (Cambridge, 1899), is still the best prosopographical conspectus in print.

for fines and compensations. But the weight of evidence is that there was far more uniformity than diversity, and the law 'codes' of the reigns of Æthelred II and Cnut make no special provincial provisions.

Domesday gives important information of local variations in law, insofar as for some shires it reveals shire *consuetudines*. Not all relate to law in a strict sense, and that a custom is recorded for one shire need not mean that it did not prevail in others. All the same, these *consuetudines* do indicate a degree of local variation in law. What were probably the most important local variations (not revealed in Domesday) relate to Kent. They were certainly the longest lasting: gavelkind, an almost specifically Kentish form of land-tenure, was not abolished until 1926. There clearly was a distinct early spirit of Kentishness, to be found, for example, in an apocryphal early thirteenth-century account of Kentish resistance to William the Conqueror.[17] Yet such a legend does not appear to draw on memories of the long-distant independent Kent. That the Kentish sense of identity was one in relation rather than in opposition to the English state can be seen in an earlier story about Kent, given by John of Salisbury in his *Policraticus* (written in the later 1150s): he says that in the order of battle of the English army the men of Kent formed the first line.[18] Such an indication of shire-consciousness, again in a military context, appears in the *Chronicle* account of a battle against the Danes in 1010: it says 'then stood Cambridgeshire firm'.[19] Here we see arguably one of the principal keys to the long success of the English state: the development of loyalties to local units which had been created for the purposes of the central authority, loyalties which generally did not so much contradict as reinforce that authority.

This raises big questions about the nature and foundations of the late Anglo-Saxon kingdom. How far was there a sense of emotional and ideological commitment to the English state: a 'nationalist' commitment? If there was such a commitment, how far down society did it go? To put both questions in crude blunt form: was there a 'political nation', and, if so, who was in it? In the absence of sources which provide direct access to the thoughts of individuals, the attitudes of the high nobility have to be reached largely by a process of induction from the course of events. The remarkable extent to which the English nobility avoided civil war is arguably a tribute to their 'national' outlook. In the tenth century, there was recurrent dynastic stress, in particular in 899–902, 957–9 and 975–8, and perhaps not only during those years. The troubled early career of a high-born courtier cleric such as Dunstan is itself an indication of factional stresses. Yet no civil strife came about of the kind which was common on the Continent: considerable tension with some violence, yes; war, no. The same can be said of the reign of Edward the Confessor. There

---

[17] J. C. Holt, *Magna Carta and Medieval Government* (London, 1985), pp. 10–13.
[18] *Ioannis Saresberiensis Episcopi Carnotensis Policratici*, ed. C. C. J. Webb (Oxford, 1909), ii, pp. 4/–8.
[19] *Two of the Anglo-Saxon Chronicles*, i, p. 140.

was very serious political trouble in 1051–2; but the expulsion of Godwin and his family, and their return, were accomplished without warfare, though not without the use of some force, particularly in 1052, and the threat of more. An observation of the *Chronicle* (version D) in the context of the stand-off between Edward and Godwin in Gloucestershire in 1051 is revealing.

> Then some of them thought it would be a great piece of folly if they joined battle, for in the two hosts there was most of what was noblest in England, and they considered that they would be opening a way for our enemies to enter the country and to cause much ruin among ourselves.[20]

Thus the memory of Viking invasion and the imminent threat of more to come had a unifying force.

One may get some idea of the attitudes of the ruling few at about the end of the tenth century by considering the famous poem on the battle of Maldon (991). National consciousness is to be found in Byrhtnoth's shout to the Vikings: 'This is Æthelred's land!' It probably matters that the poem brings out elements of Mercian and Northumbrian involvement.[21] And an interesting case has been put for its including passages intended to emphasise social cohesion: a series of brave speeches made in support of Byrhtnoth by a range of individuals such as to represent different ranks of free society, from important nobility down to ceorl.[22]

In different ways Susan Reynolds and Patrick Wormald have drawn attention to the power and scope of national consciousness in eleventh-century England; one by emphasising the extent to which people identified themselves as Anglo-Saxons, the other especially (but not only) by emphasising how the power of the consciousness of Englishness and of the English *patria* is demonstrated by the strength with which such feelings survived the Conquest. They determined some of the attitudes of the great Anglo-Norman historians, soon affected members of the Anglo-Norman ruling class, and in the long run became dominant.[23]

There is no doubt that considerable elements of the free classes participated in government to the extent that they shared in the proceedings of the courts of shire and hundred. It is impossible to be precise about the scale and nature of attendance at such courts: by the thirteenth century attendance at a big and well-attended shire court could reach two hundred or more. Comparable assemblies, albeit doubtless in considerable measure dominated by the great, probably took place in late Anglo-Saxon England.

---

[20] Ibid., i, p. 179; trans. Whitelock *et al.*, p. 118.

[21] J. Campbell, 'England in *c.*991', in J. Cooper (ed.), *The Battle of Maldon in Fact and Fiction* (London, 1993).

[22] A. Williams, 'The battle of Maldon and "The Battle of Maldon": history, poetry and propaganda', *Medieval History*, ii (1992).

[23] What is suggested in this and the following four paragraphs is discussed in more detail with references in my Raleigh Lecture, 'The late Anglo-Saxon state: a maximum view', to be published in the *Proceedings of the British Academy*.

What was the nature of the communication of such courts and the kind of men who attended them with the royal authority and 'national' affairs? This question raises others about the frequency and, so to speak, density of communication between court and countryside in late Anglo-Saxon England. Written communication in the decades immediately before the Conquest could have been by writ. Not many more than a hundred writs survive, but there are several reasons for supposing that they may have been far more numerous. For example, their very nature suggests that the writ form was intended to facilitate multiple production. Equally suggestive is the contrast between the numerous references to writs in Domesday Book and the tiny number actually surviving from the reign of the Conqueror. Also, almost all the surviving writs are evidence of title to land; it could well be that many, maybe many more, conveyed ephemeral executive orders.

The most important intimation of a connection between royal power, a fairly wide political nation, and written communication, comes from two letters from Cnut, one from 1019 or 1020, the other from 1027, which were addressed generally: one made promises of good government, the other related, in particular, to his journey to Rome. There is reason to suppose that there were other such widely distributed and programmatic letters from Cnut, and also from Æthelred II. It is very hard not to see these letters as 'political', as means of raising support, conciliating opinion, and so forth. In this they resemble such a later effort as the coronation charter of Henry I, a widely distributed bundle of promises which extended to concessions to *milites*. A more distant, but in a way more striking, resemblance is that to the first certainly known governmental document in English issued after the reign of William I: this is the proclamation to the shire courts sent out by Henry III in 1263, proclaiming his adhesion to the Provisions of Oxford.

The 'political' implications of the public letters of Cnut and comparable documents are reinforced by arresting evidence which indicates that England in 1066 was a political entity of a much more 'modern' kind than the casual observer might suppose. The annalistic accounts of such crises as those of 1051–2 and 1066 suggest the importance of formal procedures and extensive noble participation. Consideration of the way in which the tax assessments of whole areas in the eleventh century were altered suggests a political culture in which areas mattered as much as individuals. Consideration of the possible composition of shire courts largely in the light of what is known of them later suggests that they could have been the vehicle for fairly extensive participation by what would later have been called the gentry and yeomanry. Domesday's evidence on commendation in some shires suggests that it may have had a by no means exclusively local but rather a more general significance.

How had this united polity come to be? A short answer is: by brute force. A telegraphic account is as follows. When the first Viking assaults on England began, towards the end of the eighth century, the 'heptarchic' kingdoms had been reduced to four: Northumbria, Mercia, Wessex and East Anglia. The Vikings took over East Anglia, reduced English power in Northumbria to a non-regal rump, in Mercia first established a puppet regime and then divided the kingdom with Alfred. Quite soon the pendulum swung the other way. Between 909 and 920 Alfred's son Edward conquered much of the area ruled by the Danes, and thereafter the southern Danelaw was part of the dominions of the house of Wessex. Further north there was an ebb and flow of power between the English kings and various Viking rulers. From 954 onwards the English were in control. But how and by what stages the lands acquired by these kings were integrated into the organisation of the English state as we know it to have been in 1000 is still unclear. It is an indication of how imperfect is our knowledge of what simply must have been major acts of administration that the nearest we can get to full certainty on the date of the creation of many of the midland shires is to say that it cannot have been earlier than the reign of Edward the Elder, or later than that of Æthelred II. Equally baffling, but in a different way, is the wide range of titular descriptions used by those who drew up charters to honour the tenth-century kings in whose names they were issued. They vary very much and deserve much closer analysis than is possible in this cursory essay.[24] From Æthelstan's reign on they sometimes include the imperial term *basileus* – for example, in a charter of Æthelstan, 'Basileus Anglorum et equæ totius Bryttaniæ orbis curagulus'.[25] This may have indicated something hopefully meaningful about the relations between this ruler's power and his aspirations. But when Eadwig (955–9) was described as 'gentis Anglorum cæterarumque per gyrum nationum basileus' there must have been more wind than substance in the claim.[26] Edgar (959–75) has a wide range of descriptions from plain 'Rex Anglorum' to 'totius Britanniae basileus gubernator et rector'.[27] One deduction from this material is that in the 'imperial' claims implied by these grand 'titles' a distinction is almost always drawn between the *Anglii* and the inhabitants of the rest of Britain or Albion. There is a mismatch here between such charter evidence and that which indicates that in the context of coronation rituals the kings could be regarded as kings of the Saxons, Mercians and Northumbrians, though also of the whole of Albion.[28] A flickering, but probably meaningful, consciousness of Mercia as a political entity remains

---

[24] The best analysis is that of H. Kleinschmidt, *Untersuchungen über des englische Königtum in 10. Jahrhundert* (Göttingen, 1979), ch. 2.

[25] P. H. Sawyer, *Anglo-Saxon Charters: An Annotated List and Bibliography*, revised edn by S. E. Kelly (n.p., 1994), no. 430.

[26] Ibid., nos. 600–1.

[27] Ibid., nos. 707, 727. For indications of 'hegemonial imperialism' by Edgar, see J. L. Nelson, *Politics and Ritual in Early Medieval Europe* (London, 1986), pp. 299–303.

[28] Ibid., p. 363; C. Hohler, 'Some service books of the late Saxon Church', in D. Parsons (ed.), *Tenth-Century Studies* (Chichester, 1975), especially pp. 67–8. The most likely explanation for the mismatch is that the language of the relevant elements in coronation *ordines* goes back to the later 9th and early 10th centuries.

until the time of Edgar.[29] There is little sign of it in the language of the charters.

One thing we can be certain of is that the Church played an important part in the administrative and psychological unification of England. It was important that southern and midland England had for centuries been one ecclesiastical province (though, conversely, the existence of a separate metropolitan at York could be an impediment to unification). At a more immediately emotive level the cults and movements of saints are revealing, not least for the buttressing of royal claims and the creation of national consciousness. Thus northern saints were moved to new southern or midland homes: Wilfrid from Ripon to Canterbury, Oswald from Bardney to Gloucester. Elements in the cult of St Edmund are interesting in relation to the spirit of unity. One might have supposed that Edmund, a king of East Anglia martyred by the Danes, would have been an ideal focus of East Anglian particularism, should there have been such a thing. Nothing of the kind happened. Some of his relics were taken to Ramsey, outside East Anglia, and it was there that his first *Vita* was written. Late traditions (but by no means necessarily late inventions) provide him with a sainted brother, for whom there was a cult at Cerne, in the depths of Wessex. West Saxon kings claimed to be related to Edmund. Another tradition claimed that he was related to Offa, king of the Mercians.[30] When the centre of his cult became a great royal abbey at Bury, who should patronise it but the great Danish king, Cnut. The cults of saints are nodes and links in a network which connected royal power to local piety over most of England.

An important role in unification was played by the English monastic movement of the tenth century, commonly called 'the Tenth-Century Reformation'. Perhaps it was not too dissimilar to the real Reformation. In tenth-century England, as in seventh-century Gaul, as more generally in sixteenth-century Europe, very remarkable things happened when some determined and determinative part of the ruling few got religion. The case for the unifying force of the tenth-century Reformation has been most vigorously put by the late Nicholas Banton.[31] His contentions are these. The monastic movement was an important element in the integration of Mercia and Wessex. It was not for nothing that so many of the monasteries founded or refounded by King Edgar (959-75) were in Mercia. A strong emphasis on 'England' as a single entity was associated with the monastic movement; some of the most eminent participants in the monastic movement did put a special emphasis on unity. A tract on Edgar's foundation of monasteries complained of his brother and predecessor, Eadwig, that 'he divided this kingdom and parted its

[29] F. M. Stenton, *Anglo-Saxon England* (2nd edn, Oxford, 1947), pp. 325–6, 361.

[30] For the cult of Edmund, see D. Rollason, *Saints and Relics in Anglo-Saxon England* (Oxford, 1989), pp. 155–7; and S. J. Ridyard, *The Royal Saints of Anglo-Saxon England* (Cambridge, 1988), pp. 61–9, 217 note.

[31] N. Banton, 'Monastic reform and the unification of tenth-century England', in S. Mews (ed.), *Religion and National Identity* (Studies in Church History, 1982).

unity'.[32] The very idea that there should be a uniform rule for all the reformed monasteries, that is the *Regularis Concordia*, promulgated in about 970, is itself indicative of the connection between monastic reform and English unity; these monasteries with their standard rule were all linked to the monarchy and, according to the *Concordia*, were to pray for the royal family seven times daily. A strong impression of the integration of Church and State and so of the integration of the English state is given by the proceedings of some of the later councils of Æthelred II, which were homilectic and penitential, requiring for example national fasts and the observance of the cult of King Edward the Martyr.[33] The Church served to create a background of commitment to king and country.

How far was there a degree of English unity, some kind of paving the way for ultimate unification, before the tenth century? A common answer has long been on these lines: that there is indeed a significant 'prehistory' of English unity, extending back to the seventh century or even before. Although the early Anglo-Saxons were divided into so many kingdoms, there was at least at times an element of political unity. The key text here is a passage in Bede's *Ecclesiastical History*, where he says that there were seven kings who had *imperium* over all or nearly all the others.[34] Such unity as there may have been was reinforced by the introduction of Christianity and the creation of ecclesiastical institutions which transcended the bounds of kingdoms. From about 635 until 735 Canterbury was the only archdiocese. From 671 there were regular councils for all the bishops; and there is evidence to suggest that such councils, and the archbishops, enjoyed considerable authority. The Church introduced a special element of unification, insofar as men could be appointed as bishops in kingdoms other than their own. According to the conventional arguments, the next stage in the development of English unity came with the regime of the Mercian kings Æthelbald (716–57) and Offa (757–96). Bede says that all the kingdoms south of the Humber were subject to Æthelbald. It would appear that Offa enjoyed comparable authority at least for part of his reign. The Mercian regime is seen as greatly reducing the number of independent or quasi-independent kingdoms: thus by the end of the eighth century Kent no longer had kings of its own. The survival of part of the archive of the church of Worcester most interestingly enables us to see the formerly independent dynasty of the Hwicce reduced to *comes* status. Through such instances it can be argued that the Mercian regime prepared the way for the rise of the house of Wessex in the ninth century. It has, of course, to be admitted that the Vikings played a crucial role by destroying the

---

[32] *Leechdoms, Wortcunning and Starcraft of Early England*, ed. O. Cockayne (Rolls Series, 1864–6), iii, pp. 434–7.
[33] *The Laws of the Kings of England from Edmund to Henry I*, ed. and trans. A. J. Robertson (Cambridge, 1925), p. 84.
[34] *Baedae Opera Historica*, ed. C. Plummer (Oxford, 1896), i, pp. 89–90.

kingdoms other than Wessex. But the partial unity established by the Mercian kings helps to explain Alfred's capacity to be projected as ruler of all the Christian English, not just as king of the West Saxons but rather of the 'Anglo-Saxons'.

There is something superficially bovine about these arguments. A herd of historians chew over the same old sources with a near unanimity which is tedious. A refreshing note of innovatory iconoclasm has been introduced by Patrick Wormald.[35] For him most of the forgoing argument is misleading. He sees it as coloured and distorted by nineteenth-century views which saw the 'creation of national unity' as manifest destiny, and argues that had it not been for the Viking assault England might perfectly well have remained a land of four independent states: Wessex, Mercia, East Anglia and Northumbria. He will allow little or no institutional force to the *imperium* referred to by Bede in relation to the seven kings or to the regime of Æthelbald. To the extent that English unity, and the consciousness of English unity, were not created by force in the ninth and tenth centuries, he sees its origins not in the polities of the eighth century and earlier, but in Rome, the Church and the Christian faith. His case in that respect is as follows. 'English', *Anglii*, was the term adopted by Gregory I to describe the Germanic inhabitants of Britain. In a religious context the Angles, Saxons and Jutes all came to see themselves as 'English'. That is why Bede could call them all *gens Anglorum*; and why he emphasised elements of unity, for example seeing the saints of the various *provinciae* as common property. The 'English' could see themselves as a people of God, a new Israel. In addition, a powerful brand of providential history was mediated through Bede, in particular to the important extent that he drew on Gildas. This emphasises the intimacy of a people's relationship with God, both as the agent of His will, and as the subject, when it errs, of His punishment.

Wormald's argument is a most interesting one, forcefully expressed. It is at its most powerful in its positive aspects. That Biblical attitudes, especially as they can be found in Bede's *Ecclesiastical History*, influenced some, perhaps many, important people's sense of nationality, and helped to create the urge towards unity which can be traced in action and in writing in the late tenth century. In the light of Wormald's important insight we can see how some of the vernacular Biblical poetry which was valued in the tenth century may have had more political importance than at first appears: for example, how appropriate the long poem based on *Exodus* could have been for an elite whose predecessors had passed through the desert of the Viking invasions.

We cannot, however, but have serious doubts about his negative contentions. First, on *imperium*: few, if any, scholars would think it at all likely that we have here anything like a clearly and continuously established institution;

[35] P. Wormald, 'Bede, the *Bretwaldas* and the *Gens Anglorum*', in P. Wormald *et al.* (eds.), *Ideal and Reality in Frankish and Anglo-Saxon Society: Studies Presented to J. M. Wallace-Hadrill* (Oxford, 1983).

the term *bretwalda* is almost certainly honorific rather than specific. So much must be common ground. It is, however, a different matter to exclude the strong possibility that there were conventions on the relationships between powerful kings and those who were subordinated to them. Thus Bede says that St Augustine went from Kent to the borders of the Hwicce (somewhere in modern Oxfordshire, perhaps).[36] The observation is frequently made that this suggests that an overlord such as Æthelbert could grant an extensive safe-conduct through kingdoms other than his own. Wormald will not have it. He suggests that what Bede tells us would be consonant with no more than Æthelbert's having provided Augustine with a heavy escort.

Well, yes, this could, fairly arguably, be the case: but it by no means has to be the case. Similarly with Bede's account of the power of Æthelbald. In the penultimate chapter of his *Ecclesiastical History*, he states that all the kingdoms south of the Humber 'subiectae sunt' to Æthelbald.[37] Vague though this is, it does create an impression of accepted, conceivably even ordered, authority. Wormald is uneasy about such impressions. He suggests that Bede has to an extent been misled by Mercian informants, in particular Nothelm. Again, this is possible; when sources are thin, all sorts of things are arguably possible. But Bede was a well-connected man with many informants; it would not seem *prima facie* likely that he would have been misled in making his generalisation about Æthelbald's power. Similarly negative arguments might be directed against making anything of Bede's reference to a (probable) overlord participating in a land grant by a lesser ruler in the 630s.[38] Maybe, writing a century after the event, Bede was mistaken; but even if he were, and he is making an anachronistic assumption, it would still tell us something about how Bede saw overlordship in his own day.

One does not have to believe in 'bretwaldaship' as an institution to accept that the kings and kingdoms of England were so interconnected that, notwithstanding their frequent and cruel wars, they formed a community with elements relevant to the later accomplishment of unity. Marriage was one such element. All but one of the royal marriages which Bede mentions were between members of two English royal or near-royal families. When a princess married into another kingdom she took a household of her own with her and retained contact with her homeland. Another bond was service. Young noblemen took service with kings other than their own. This was often, but not always, due to the exigencies of exile. Exile in another kingdom was a common element in aristocratic life. Successful kings were served in war by lesser ones. Kings visited the courts of overlords, and perhaps visited one another in other circumstances.[39]

There were many other interconnections; some we can be sure of, others

---

[36] *Baedae Opera Historica*, i, p. 81.
[37] Ibid., i, p. 350.
[38] Ibid., i, p. 139.
[39] Campbell, *Essays in Anglo-Saxon History*, pp. 93–5.

are more obscure. The Church was a source of unity in more ways than those already mentioned. Thus Wilfrid's seventh-century ecclesiastical empire included monasteries in at least three kingdoms. Such a midland monastery as Medeshamstede could have a dependent house at Hoo in Kent.[40]

A most important unifying element in early England was language. Bede is categorical about language as a distinguishing factor. There were, he said, five languages in Britain: English, Irish, Pictish, British and Latin.[41] It is important here that he saw English as a distinct language; this agrees with the findings of modern scholars who, although they detect important dialectal differences in early English, do not suggest that there was a significant lack of mutual intelligibility among the Anglo-Saxons.[42]

However one judges the extent and ways in which England was or was not unified in the seventh and eighth centuries, there is no doubt that it was a unified country by 1066 (albeit imperfectly so in the far North). The stages and nature of the process of unification were reflected in the nature of England as it appears not only in the eleventh century but also later. It can be divided into three zones which may loosely be characterised as follows: first, a zone of palaces and councils; second, a zone lacking palaces and royal meeting-places, but having uniform institutions; third, a frontier zone.

To consider a map of the places at which royal councils or national meetings were held in late Anglo-Saxon England, or to consider the itineraries of its kings is to be reminded very forcibly that the heartland of the English dynasty was the former kingdom of Wessex.[43] The residences of the kings and the normal meeting-places of their councils were all within that kingdom or within the areas added to it before the death of Alfred. Of course, kings did move beyond Watling Street, but when they did so it was for special purposes and special occasions, for war, for great diplomatic meetings, or perhaps sometimes for a grand provincial tour. Occasions such as those on which Edward the Elder or Æthelstan or Cnut sallied to the North to fight, to negotiate or to demonstrate their power, were important indeed. But these were not normal events. The kings not only had no residences (though they did own lands) outside Wessex, the Thames valley and west Mercia, but also had no regular visiting-places outside these areas. Many observations might be made about this phenomenon, but I will offer only these. First, this is a demonstration of how strongly the nature of the English state was determined by its origins in West Saxon power. The old centres of Mercian authority and dynastic grandeur, Repton, Tamworth and Winchcombe, fall into insignificance, or relative insignificance. It is true that London, not by long history a

---

[40] F. M. Stenton, *Preparatory to Anglo-Saxon England* (Oxford, 1970), pp. 189–90.
[41] *Baedae Opera Historica*, i, p. 11.
[42] T. E. Toon, 'Old English dialects', in R. M. Hogg (ed.), *The Cambridge History of the English Language*, i (Cambridge, 1992), is a recent summary.
[43] Hill, *Atlas of Anglo-Saxon England*, maps nos. 154–63.

West Saxon centre, became a major centre of authority, but it is interesting to note that by the time of the Conquest the king was establishing his major base not in the City where, so it is reasonably guessed, the Mercian kings had had their base in the Roman fort in the north-west corner, but rather in a new palace and monastery complex at Westminster. Second, the zonal difference remained significant for long after 1066. For a time it was indicated by the three places which the Norman kings used for their great crown-wearing days: Winchester, Gloucester and Westminster. The councils and meetings of the twelfth- and thirteenth-century kings seldom extended far beyond the corresponding limits for their Anglo-Saxon predecessors.[44] Henry II seems never to have held a council further to the north-east than Northampton. Henry III hardly ventured so far for such a purpose. A considerable change comes, of course, once Edward I moved his government north to fight the Scots. All the same, if we exclude the meetings held at York in association with such transfers of the seat of government and consider the limited number of occasions on which the medieval English Parliament met outside Westminster, we find that only on very rare occasions did it meet in a place which had not been under the authority of King Alfred. More striking still is the way in which the ordinary residences of all the rulers of England until Queen Victoria were within the same southern and western zone. Until Victoria acquired Balmoral and the future Edward VII acquired Sandringham, the monarchs of England had no significant residence north or east of Watling Street. Westminster, Windsor, Winchester, Woodstock, Clarendon – places such as these were the normal homes of our rulers. Third, if we compare the itineraries of the kings of late Anglo-Saxon England with those of their German contemporaries, we can see significant resemblances; thus the concentration of the West Saxon kings in greater Wessex roughly corresponds to the way in which the Ottonians were to be found above all in their Saxon homeland and in their Rhineland palaces. There seems, however, to be a contrast to an extent, in that the Ottonians and Salians seem to have itinerated over their much larger area of authority on a rather more regular and wider basis than did their Anglo-Saxon counterparts.[45]

If the first zone is that of palaces and councils, I have called my second that of uniform administration. By that I mean the areas which, though they did not have the pleasures, or the reverse, of seeing their king on quite frequent occasions, were nevertheless organised in ways which gave them substantial uniformity and strong resemblances to those which were on the regular royal beat. The lands concerned, to a large extent those conquered from Danish rulers by the kings of the house of Wessex in the tenth century, had elements in their organisation which marked them off from greater Wessex. They were

---

[44] E. B. Fryde et al. (eds.), *Handbook of British Chronology* (revised edn, London, 1986), pp. 533–72, lists conciliar meetings.
[45] *Westermanns Atlas zur Weltgeschichte*, ed. H.-E. Stier et al. (Berlin, 1956), p. 62, provides appropriate maps.

to a large extent assessed in carucates not hides; the major sub-units of local government below the shire were in wide areas called wapentakes not hundreds; there were legal differences sufficient to be remarked upon in the early twelfth century. For all that, the shired lands of the North and East were recognised by eleventh- and twelfth-century contemporaries as integral parts of a unified England which could be regarded for administrative purposes as an aggregation of units of the same kind. To the organisers of the Domesday survey, England south of the Tees and the Ribble was, in the most important ways, one.[46]

Beyond those rivers there was a third zone which might be called that of the frontier lordships. The greatest of these was that of the community of St Cuthbert, which enjoyed wide powers over a vast region, powers probably of great antiquity.[47] There were other comparable, if lesser, lordships elsewhere in the far north of England. These lordships presented marked contrasts to those to be found further south. In 1066 they did not form part of the shired structure and they consisted of continuous blocks of territory resembling the feudal lordships of contemporary France or the little kingdoms of Wales and Ireland, rather than the generally scattered, if collectively extremely extensive, landholdings of the English noblemen south of the Tees and the Ribble. The northern frontier zone did become integrated into the uniform English kingdom, but it took a long time, and the integration was for long incomplete. Westmorland and Cumberland do not appear as shires until the reign of Henry II and then they present features which marked them off from other shires. It is an interesting, even possibly meaningful, fact that three historic shires which disappeared completely as a result of the changes introduced in 1974, Cumberland, Westmorland and Rutland, had all been created after the Conquest. Great lordships of the North presented a contrast to what was to be found in the South for many centuries. The great quasi-independent franchises of Northumberland, such as Tynedale, remained until the sixteenth century. The extreme case, of course, is that of the bishopric of Durham, which survived as a separate lordship until the Act of 1836 abolished the palatine jurisdiction.

Such a sketch as this of the so-to-speak historical geology of England cannot take full account of a paradox. The historic kingdom of England is defined not only by the successes of Anglo-Saxon rulers and elites, but also by their failures. That we still think of this island as divided into England, Scotland and Wales demonstrates the determinative force, in Britain, of Dark Age events. Bede tells us that three of the Northumbrian kings who held *imperium* in the seventh century had authority over nearly the whole island. His brief

---

[46] Though the shiring only extended to the Mersey; in Domesday the North-West beyond the Mersey was surveyed as 'Inter Ripam et Mersham': 'Between the Ribble and the Mersey'.

[47] D. J. Hall, 'The Community of St Cuthbert: The Properties, Rights and Claims from the Ninth Century to the Twelfth' (Oxford University D.Phil. thesis, 1983), ch. 9.

account is richer in provoking questions than in providing answers. Historians are apt to take refuge in expressions such as 'vague overlordship'. But they do not know how vague or otherwise, though obviously shortlived, the supremacy of these rulers was. What they are actually telling us is that they are, necessarily, vague about it. It is, however, worth noting Bede's categorical statement that these rulers had authority over Anglesey and Man, and that he gives what sounds like an assessment figure for Iona, where the last really powerful Northumbrian king, Ecgfrith, was buried.[48] Northumbria was the central kingdom of the island of Britain, and if our island has a natural capital, it is York. We have to admit the possibility that, for a time in the seventh century, there was a Northumbrian empire covering almost the whole of Britain – though, if so, it was a fleeting empire indeed. But in the tenth century, although such great kings as Edward the Elder and, more particularly, Æthelstan and Edgar tried hard to extend their authority beyond England, in anything more than the very short run they failed.

Why did the formidable Anglo-Saxon state fail to absorb Wales and Scotland? Within the limits of the few words available it is impossible to offer more than passing over-generalisations. Wales, more precisely the Welsh, look like a long-lasting frontier problem – so that if we are seeking modern parallels we should think of India's north-west frontier or even of Afghanistan. We should ask ourselves, for example, why it is that quite close to one another in the south-east corner of Wales are to be found three of the most formidable fortifications of Western Europe. First, there is Caerleon, a fortified barracks into which in the second century were neatly packed in standardised accommodation the 6,000 men of a Roman legion, about the same sized force with which William conquered England. Not so far off is part of Offa's Dyke, the most impressive earthwork in Europe. It has been suggested that it was built as a kind of demonstration, but surely it is more probable that, whatever its argued tactical inadequacies, it was more like Hadrian's Wall than the Pyramids of Egypt. In the same area we find the most extensive of the English castles built against the Welsh, Caerphilly. What were Caerleon, Offa's Dyke and Caerphilly for, if not to contain a fiercely dangerous, aggressive and parasitic people in Wales? When in Edward the Confessor's reign the Welsh danger reached one of its recurrent peaks, it was contained, but only by mustering the military force of much of England. Nevertheless one can imagine how, had the dice fallen just a little differently, parts of Wales, especially of south Wales, might have been absorbed into England. What Asser has to tell us about the subordination of southern Welsh princes to Alfred is suggestive here.[49] So too, perhaps even more so, is his own career, passing from St Davids to the richly rewarding service of Alfred, apparently on an arrangement whereby he spent half his time in England and

[48] *Baedae Opera Historica*, i, pp. 89, 97, 133.
[49] *Asser's Life of Alfred*, ed. W. H. Stevenson (Oxford, 1904), ch. 80.

half in Wales.[50] The interest displayed by 'Nennius' in English events and genealogies suggests a degree of Anglo-Welsh osmosis by the ninth century.[51] British Wales had, of course, quite easy sea-communication with partly British Wessex. Geography can hardly suffice to explain the long escape of south Wales from the English yoke.

Geography plainly does more to explain Scotland's independent survival. Scotland is the most problematic, because the worst documented, of early European kingdoms. The sources are not such as to enable us fully to understand an extraordinary story of political success, the creation of a medieval kingdom from five different groups with different languages – the Picts, Irish, Britons, English, Norse – and ultimately with Norman-French participation also. That a Scottish state based north of the Forth gained effective control of all or much of Lothian in the later tenth and earlier eleventh centuries must have been a recognition of the effective limits of the power of the late Anglo-Saxon state, whose centre of gravity (in striking contrast to that of seventh-century Northumbria) lay very much in the southern part of the island. The kings of the house of Wessex could project their power a long way: Æthelred the Unready could use his naval power to reach as far as Cumbria, Man or the Cotentin.[52] But Scotland – especially *Scotia* north of the Forth – lay even beyond the frontier zone of English royal power. The inclusion of Lothian into the mysteriously emergent kingdom of Scotland had long-lasting effects.[53] It looks as if key elements in the organisation of that kingdom were, as its language became, English; it is almost as if there are two Englands and one of them is called Scotland.

This is, it may well be, a controversial statement. What is more certain is that the history of the United Kingdom cannot be understood without consideration of how some thousand years ago England became a united kingdom, but failed to incorporate the far West and the long North of our island.

---

[50] Ibid., ch. 79.

[51] *Nennius: British History and the Welsh Annals*, ed. and trans. J. Morris (Chichester, 1980); e.g. chs. 31–8 and, more particularly, chs. 57–65.

[52] *Two of the Anglo-Saxon Chronicles*, i, p. 133; Campbell, *Essays in Anglo-Saxon History*, pp. 199–200.

[53] A. A. M. Duncan, *Scotland: The Making of the Kingdom* (Edinburgh, 1975), pp. 97–8; B. T. Hudson, *Kings of Celtic Scotland* (Westport, Connecticut, 1994), pp. 99–101.

Chapter 4

Foundations of a disunited kingdom

John Gillingham

I begin with the view from London. The late twelfth-century historian, Ralph, dean of St Paul's, regarded the kingdom of England as a model state – literally the model on which he believed that a new king of France, Philip Augustus, intended to pattern his own kingdom. This model state was, in Ralph's words, 'wide in extent, peacefully governed, and contained within it some very barbarous inhabitants, the Scots and the Welsh'.[1] Dean Ralph's view encapsulates two perceptions of fundamental importance for the history of the United Kingdom: the first, that the king of England is the ruler of Britain; the second, that some of his subjects are barbarians. Since in this passage Ralph was limiting his remarks to Britain, he made no mention of the latest of Henry II's acquisitions, Ireland. Had he done so, he would certainly have added the Irish to the list of Henry's barbarous subjects. By the 1180s, when Dean Ralph was writing, the foundations of an English empire had been well and truly laid – 'an empire based on the wealth, population and resources of southern England over the rest of the British Isles'.[2] That there was an English empire of Britain had been claimed two hundred years earlier still, in the 980s – not surprisingly, given the military and political achievements of the tenth-century West Saxons. But what was new about the twelfth-century 'empire' was the assumption that some of the ruler's subjects were barbarians. Given that, for all its power then and in subsequent centuries, the English state never managed to introduce measures for the effective integration of the 'Celtic' parts of the British Isles which it controlled into its own, distinctively English, political community, this new assumption was to be of critical significance. It meant that those whose lands were taken often remained undervalued and alienated.[3] If English power tended to unite Britain and

---

[1] '... a tam barbaris nationibus Scotis videlicet et Walensibus inhabitatum': *The Historical Works of Master Ralph de Diceto*, ed. W. Stubbs (Rolls Series, 1876), ii, p. 8. Ralph, it should be noted, was thinking of a time when Henry II's garrisons were installed in Scotland's largest town, Berwick, and also in Edinburgh and Roxburgh.

[2] H. Kearney, *The British Isles: A History of Four Nations* (Cambridge, 1989), p. 106, where the phrase is applied to 16th-century developments.

[3] R. R. Davies, 'The English state and the "Celtic" peoples 1100–1400', *Journal of Historical Sociology*, vi (1993), pp. 12–13. For some of the many reasons why 'Celtic' is a very misleading, if convenient, word, see M. Chapman, *The Celts: The Construction of a Myth* (London, 1992).

Ireland, English attitudes tended to divide; hence the long history of a disunited kingdom.

By the 1180s the movement that Rees Davies has characterised as 'the second tidal wave of Anglo-Saxon or English colonisation' was in full flood: that migration of primarily English settlers into lowland Wales, Scotland and Ireland which began in the late eleventh century and which flowed more or less strongly for roughly two hundred years.[4] These settlers lived dangerously. In Wales and Ireland they had muscled their way in by force of arms and, as stealers of other men's lands, they sometimes had to pay a high price. In 1171 the natives, wrote Gerald of Wales, 'cruelly put to death any English they found on the streets of Waterford or in the houses, without respect for sex or age'.[5] Even in Scotland, where they were not following in the wake of military conquest, the incomers were often resented, and in 1174, after the defeat of King William of Scotland's invasion of the north of England, the Scots took their revenge. 'The towns and boroughs of the kingdom of Scotland are inhabited by English, and the Scots hate them, so they killed as many of the English as they could.'[6] Many centuries earlier, at the time of the first great tidal wave of Anglo-Saxon colonisation, the lives of the settlers had been just as precarious, but at that time there had also been a strong tide flowing in the opposite direction. Irish colonisation of northern and western Britain had – arguably – been just as important as Anglo-Saxon colonisation of the South and East. Irish settlements lay at the foundations of the kingdom of Scotland, much as the Anglo-Saxon settlements led ultimately to the kingdom of England. By contrast, in the twelfth century, and with the important exception of Stephen's reign – significant for this and for other reasons (to which I shall return) – the tide appeared to be flowing in one direction only. It was not just those whose lands were being invaded who were alarmed. In 1171 the king of the Isle of Man and other lords of the Isles came to the aid of the Irish who were fighting to retain control of Dublin. According to Gerald, one of the reasons they did so was because 'English successes meant that they too now feared English dominion'.[7]

What lay behind those English successes? First and most obvious was the creation of the kingdom of England itself, those economic, political and military developments which changed for ever the political configuration of the British Isles and which in this volume are dealt with by James Campbell. Compared with contemporary 'Celtic' societies, tenth-century England was

---

[4] R. R. Davies, *Domination and Conquest: The Experience of Ireland, Scotland and Wales 1100–1300* (Cambridge, 1990), p. 12.

[5] Giraldus Cambrensis [Gerald of Wales], *Expugnatio Hibernica*, ed. and trans. A. B. Scott and F. X. Martin (Dublin, 1978), p. 140. On contemporary use of the word 'English' to refer to the invaders, see J. Gillingham, 'The English invasion of Ireland', in B. Bradshaw *et al.* (eds.), *Representing Ireland: Literature and the Origins of Conflict* (Cambridge, 1993).

[6] William of Newburgh, *Historia Rerum Anglicarum*, in *Chronicles of the Reigns of Stephen, Henry II and Richard I*, ed. R. Howlett (Rolls Series, 1884–90), i, p. 186

[7] Gerald of Wales, *Expugnatio*, p. 78.

both relatively peaceful and economically advanced. Beyond England there were hardly any coins and hardly any towns – just a few coastal emporia. Economically and politically England had been transformed; 'Celtic' societies had not.[8] Not surprisingly, tenth-century English kings, notably Edgar, were described by contemporaries – English ones of course – in terms which accorded them some sort of imperial overlordship over the whole of Britain. There may have been earlier Anglo-Saxon overlordships from the seventh century onwards – Bede certainly claims as much – but it was tenth-century overlordship which had staying power. In place of a British Isles composed of a large number of political communities with fluid frontiers and more-or-less ephemeral overlordships, from now on there existed a single state in the richer lands of lowland Britain and a large number of smaller and poorer kingships to the north and west. By the time Dean Ralph wrote, England had been, with rare and transitory exceptions, a united kingdom for more than two hundred years. Wales and Ireland had continued to be politically fragmented, Ireland especially so. As William of Newburgh, writing in the 1190s, put it when explaining the background to the conquest of the Irish by the English (his words), Ireland in 1170 was like the England of long ago, a land of many kingdoms and a seemingly endless round of war and slaughter.[9] So long as England remained united, it was bound to be the dominant power. Its only rival lay in the north, but in 1100 'as a kingdom Scotland was still very much in the making. The authority of the kings of Scots was barely nominal in Galloway or Moray; in Argyll or Caithness, as of course in the Isles, it faded out in the face of a world of virtually autonomous chiefs under the loose overlordship of Norway.'[10] True, the kingdom of Scotland had not suffered the eleventh-century English fate of being twice conquered. On these grounds it can be argued that it was the Scots, not the English, who 'established the most stable and successful kingdom in Britain prior to the Norman Invasion'.[11] But it was more limited in extent and much poorer than

[8] Though the process was beginning in Scotland; see, e.g. B. T. Hudson, 'Kings and Church in early Scotland', *Scottish Historical Review*, lxxiii (1994); and A. Grant, 'Thanes and thanages from the eleventh to the fourteenth centuries', in A. Grant and K. J. Stringer (eds.), *Medieval Scotland: Crown, Lordship and Community. Essays presented to G. W. S. Barrow* (Edinburgh, 1993), pp. 40–7.

[9] William of Newburgh, *Historia*, p. 167.

[10] R. Frame, *The Political Development of the British Isles 1100–1400* (Oxford, 1990), pp. 10–11; but see Grant, 'Thanes and thanages', pp. 46–7; and E. J. Cowan, 'The historical MacBeth', in W. D. H. Sellar (ed.), *Moray: Province and People* (Edinburgh, 1993).

[11] A. Smyth, *Warlords and Holy Men: Scotland AD 80–1000* (London, 1984), p. 238. However, as Smyth acknowledges, the king of Scots 'did not command resources comparable with those of his English counterpart'. Moreover the 12th-century kingdom of Scotland seems to have been ethnically more divided even than Anglo-Norman England. See above, note 6, and below, note 59; and see also Richard of Hexham's account of ferocious splits within King David I's army in 1138: 'After the battle his men scattered, and in flight they dealt with each other not as friends but as foes. For the English and the Scots and the Galwegians and the rest of the barbarians, whenever they chanced upon each other ... took the opportunity to kill, wound or rob the other. Thus by a just judgement of God they were oppressed as much by their own kind as by outsiders' (Richard of Hexham, *De Gestis Regis Stephani*, in *Chronicles of Stephen, Henry II and Richard I*, ed. Howlett, iii, pp. 165–6).

England; and from the late eleventh century onwards its culture was increasingly influenced by incomers from the south.

Thus it was the English empire established in the tenth century – a thousand-year *Reich* in the making – which really impressed itself upon subsequent historical consciousness. By the twelfth century it was commonplace for English authors to see their history in imperial terms. In this version of their past, King Edgar was the ideal ruler. According to John of Worcester, Simeon of Durham, Ailred of Rievaulx and Roger of Howden, Edgar was to the English what Charlemagne was to the French and Alexander to the Greeks.[12] This is how another twelfth-century author, Geoffrey Gaimar, described Edgar's reign.

> He held the land as emperor
> In his time he improved the land.
> Everywhere there was peace, nowhere war.
> He alone ruled over all the kings
> And over the Scots and the Welsh.
> Never since Arthur departed
> Has any king held such power.[13]

Gaimar's words were taken over by the late medieval chronicle known as the prose *Brut*, the chronicle which survives in more manuscripts than any other English historical work, which was the earliest English history to be printed (by Caxton in 1480), and which had been reprinted no less than eleven times by 1528. Thus this most popular view of English history came to include the notion of an empire founded in the tenth century.[14]

After 1066, and riding on the back of Anglo-Saxon achievement, the new Norman rulers were soon to assert greater dominance both in Scotland and in Wales than their predecessors had done. From this time onwards the native Welsh histories began to acknowledge the pre-eminent position of the king of England. The *Chronicle of the Princes* referred to 'William the Bastard, prince of the Normans and king of the Saxons and Britons and Scots'. In the *Red Book of Hergest* version, Henry I was called 'king of England and Wales and all the island besides'.[15] According to the author of the *Gesta Stephani*, after the Normans had conquered England, they added Wales to their dominion, civilised it, and 'made the land so productive as to be in no way inferior to the

[12] When, at the end of the 12th century, Roger of Howden borrowed from his predecessors this estimate of Edgar's place in English history, he added a comparison of his own, 'as Arthur to the Britons': *Chronica Rogeri de Houedene*, ed. W. Stubbs (Rolls Series, 1868–71), i, p. 64.

[13] *L'Estoire des Engleis by Geffrei Gaimar*, ed. A. Bell (Anglo-Norman Text Society, 1960), ll. 3562–8.

[14] J. Gillingham, 'Gaimar, the prose *Brut* and the making of English history', in J.-P. Genet (ed.), *Historiographie médiévale* (forthcoming).

[15] *Brut y Tywysogyon or The Chronicle of the Princes: Peniarth MS 20 version*, ed. and trans. T. Jones (Cardiff, 1952), p. 18; *Brut y Tywysogyon: Red Book of Hergest version*, ed. and trans. T. Jones (Cardiff, 1955), p. 113.

most fertile part of Britain'.[16] In Scotland, English influence was strong at the court of Malcolm Canmore and Margaret; their anglicised son Edgar may have accepted that he owed his throne in part 'to the gift of King William his lord'. In 1124 the earl of Huntingdon (as the English saw it) became King David I of Scotland, accelerating the process of Anglo-Norman penetration into Scotland.[17] When, writing at the end of the tenth century, Aelfric of Eynsham had referred to Roman Britain as England, it may have been just – just! – an early example of what Patrick Wormald has called 'the Englishman's tendency to confuse the identities of England and Britain'.[18] By the 1120s Henry of Huntingdon was turning it into an explicit point. 'This, the most noble of islands, 800 miles long and 200 broad, was first called Albion, then Britain and is now known as England.' And, Henry continued, its abundant wealth, including flourishing vineyards, meant that an extensive foreign trade brought in so much silver that there appeared to be more silver here than in Germany itself. Thus the inhabitants of this England were, in Henry's opinion, superior in life-style and in dress to all other peoples.[19] By the 1120s a combination of politics, war, economics and fashion was creating an apparently inexorable drive towards a culturally homogeneous island in which the overlordship of the king of England was becoming an ever greater reality.[20]

As it happened, however, this process was to be halted – in some senses reversed, and in others profoundly transformed – during the crisis of Stephen's reign.

Since English dominion depended on the unity of the English state, the prolonged civil war of Stephen's reign was the period when the empire of the kings of England was most at risk, most in danger of being overthrown by the military successes of the Scottish and Welsh kings. For Stephen, the decisive moment came when he was captured at the battle of Lincoln (1141). In addition to its other consequences, this allowed King David of Scotland, who had already led invasions in 1136 and 1138, to extend and consolidate his takeover of all of England north of the River Tees, including north Lancashire and parts of Yorkshire as well as all Cumberland and Northumberland. From

[16] *Gesta Stephani*, ed. and trans. K. R. Potter and R. H. C. Davis (Oxford, 1976), p. 15.

[17] A. A. M. Duncan, *Scotland: The Making of the Kingdom* (Edinburgh, 1975), pp. 122–7, 134–5. An English army put Edgar on the throne, and William Rufus doubtless regarded him as a vassal. It is harder to be sure about what Edgar thought. The quotation comes from a charter (or diploma) which (if genuine) was issued at Durham in 1095, two years before he became king; the text is quite possibly a 13th-century forgery; and in all his later charters Edgar is simply styled 'king of Scots'. See J. Donnelly, 'The earliest Scottish charters?', *Scottish Historical Review*, lxviii (1989).

[18] P. Wormald, 'The Venerable Bede and the "Church of the English"', in G. Rowell (ed.), *The English Religious Tradition and the Genius of Anglicanism* (Wantage, 1992), note 27.

[19] Henry of Huntingdon, *Historia Anglorum*, ed. T. Arnold (Rolls Series, 1879), pp. 6, 10.

[20] The European dimensions of these trends are best set out in R. Bartlett, *The Making of Europe: Conquest, Colonization and Cultural Change 950–1350* (London, 1993).

then until his death in 1153, King David regularly held court at Carlisle and Newcastle, and issued coin from mints at Carlisle, Corbridge and Bamburgh. After Lincoln, as Keith Stringer has pointed out, the North was bound more tightly to Scotland than ever it had been to England.[21] Arguably it was the Welsh contingents fighting for the Angevin cause at Lincoln who gave the Scots this golden opportunity. According to Orderic Vitalis, the first of Stephen's men to take to flight were those who had found themselves facing 'the fierce mob of Welshmen'.[22] The Welsh mob at Lincoln was led by three remarkable kings: Cadwaladr ap Gruffydd of Gwynedd, Madog ap Maredudd of Powys, and Morgan ap Owain from south-east Wales. All three had played – and would continue to play – leading roles in what Sir John Lloyd labelled the 'National Revival', the great Welsh revolt which had broken out following the death of Henry I. In 1136 Cadwaladr and his brother Owain led the biggest and most dramatically successful Welsh armies. In the words of the *Brut Y Tywysogyon*, they were 'two exalted kings and two generous ones, two brave lions, two wise ones, defenders of the poor, slayers of their enemies, predominant in soul and body, together they upheld the whole kingdom of the Britons'.[23] Madog ap Maredudd of Powys (1132–60) was to capture Oswestry and see Welsh settlement pushed eastwards towards Cheshire and Shropshire. A great patron of poets, Madog also was praised in extravagant language as 'a firm anchor in a deep sea'.[24] The third king, Morgan ap Owain, is less well known – indeed until recently the evidence for his presence at Lincoln has been overlooked[25] – but it was he who gave the signal for the great revolt by killing Richard FitzGilbert before going on to capture the castle of Caerleon. The revolt and Morgan's capture of Caerleon were, I have suggested, events of major significance in the literary history of Britain, helping to inspire Geoffrey of Monmouth's figure of King Arthur, the all-conquering British king whose reign, in Geoffrey's version, came to a grand climax with a crown-wearing at Caerleon. It is, I think, to the period of the Welsh revolt that we can date the Anglo-Norman vernacular *Description of England*, with the lines:

[21] K. J. Stringer, *The Reign of Stephen: Kingship, Warfare and Government in Twelfth-Century England* (London, 1993), pp. 28–37.
[22] *The Ecclesiastical History of Orderic Vitalis*, ed. and trans. M. Chibnall (Oxford, 1968–80), vi, p. 542.
[23] *Brut Peniarth*, p. 51; *Brut Hergest*, pp. 113–15.
[24] R. R. Davies, *Conquest, Coexistence and Change: Wales 1063–1415* (Oxford, 1987), pp. 46, 49–50, 57, 233.
[25] As noted by D. Crouch, 'The March and the Welsh kings', in E. King (ed.), *The Anarchy of King Stephen's Reign* (Oxford, 1994), p. 273, note 41. Madog's presence at Lincoln is vouched for by the author of the *Liber Eliensis*, ed. E. O. Blake (Camden Society, 1962), p. 321. Although, on the authority of J. E. Lloyd, *A History of Wales* (3rd edn, London, 1939), ii, pp. 478, 489, 507, this has long been thought to be a mistake, the fact that between 1140 and 1142 Bishop Nigel of Ely took refuge at Gloucester suggests that at the critical period he was well placed to learn about Robert of Gloucester's Welsh allies and hence to pass that information on to the author of the Book of Ely.

> Well have the Welsh revenged themselves ...
> Some of our castles they have taken,
> Fiercely they threaten us,
> Openly they go about saying,
> That in the end they will have all,
> By means of Arthur they will have it back ...
> They will call it Britain again.[26]

In this crisis of empire, when the Crown of England was in dispute and when ground was being lost to both Scots and Welsh, two perceptions took root.[27] The first was the emergence of a new sense of national identity after the traumas of the Norman Conquest. In answer to the question of the date at which the descendants of those newcomers who settled in England in the wake of the Norman Conquest began to think of themselves as English, historians have often said 'by the end of the twelfth century'. However, I am convinced that it was by 1140, at the latest.[28] If we frame the question of national identity in terms of self-identification, it is apparent that William of Malmesbury and Henry of Huntingdon, authors who left behind a sufficient body of relevant evidence for their own sense of national identity to be ascertained with reasonable confidence, both thought of themselves as English. In what they wrote in the 1120s it is possible to discern a lingering reminiscence of a perception of themselves as English in the sense of being members of a subject population – the down-trodden English oppressed by French (or Norman) lords. But by the time of their later writings this sense of oppression is absent. Now the clear sense in which they felt themselves to be English was in terms of 'we are English and we are members of a ruling elite'.

Equally striking is the work of Geoffrey Gaimar. His *Estoire des Engleis*, written in the late 1130s for the wife of a Lincolnshire landowner, is the earliest extant history written in French, yet it is not a history of the French, but of the English.[29] What Geoffrey's *Estoire* suggests is, as Sir Richard Southern pointed out, that by the 1130s the Francophone secular elite, the gentry of the time, could see the Anglo-Saxon past as their past, and could, for example, regard a Hereward the Wake as one of their own heroes.[30] Doubtless the king and a tiny handful of the greatest magnates, holding vast estates in

---

[26] J. Gillingham, 'The context and the purposes of the *History of the Kings of Britain*', *Anglo-Norman Studies*, xiii (1990).

[27] 'The ambitions of England's rulers ... were given literary shape during Stephen's reign, when the kingdom was torn by civil war': M. T. Clanchy, *England and its Rulers* (Glasgow, 1983), pp. 29–30.

[28] In what follows, I am summarising the argument in J. Gillingham, 'Henry of Huntingdon and the twelfth-century revival of the English nation', in L. Johnson and A. Murray (eds.), *Concepts of National Identity in the Middle Ages* (Leeds, 1995).

[29] Manuscript evidence supports the use of the familiar title: *Estoire des Engleis*, p. xi. On the circumstances in which Gaimar wrote, see I. Short, 'Gaimar's Epilogue and Geoffrey of Monmouth's *Liber Vetustissimus*', *Speculum*, lxix (1994).

[30] R. W. Southern, *Medieval Humanism* (Oxford, 1970), pp. 154–5.

Normandy as well as in England (though this too was not to be so easy in Stephen's reign after 1141), may have thought of themselves primarily as Norman-French, but the overwhelming majority of the landowners of England knew that they were English, of mixed ancestry and proud of their French forefathers' achievements, bilingual if not trilingual, but English nonetheless, believing that Old English law was their law.[31]

Now the context in which Henry of Huntingdon, that learned and poetic canon of Lincoln, most explicitly gave voice to his *Wirgefühl* was in his account of the great battle fought in 1138 between the northern barons and the Scots, the battle of the Standard. 'We were victorious', he wrote.[32] A contemporary of his, John of Worcester, responded in the same way. The first occasions in his chronicle that he used the word 'we' were when writing of 'our' wars against the Welsh and the Scots in 1138.[33] It looks as though one of the consequences of the wars against the Welsh and the Scots in Stephen's reign was to crystallise a newly re-emerging sense of English solidarity and identity – a solidarity linking men from Lincoln and Worcester with northerners.

I should stress that I am concerned here with nationality in terms of self-identification. This is not necessarily how others would have identified them, almost certainly not the Scots, and certainly not the Welsh. Welsh narrative sources continue to use the term 'the French' when writing of the people whom I am calling the English. This is not surprising. The Welsh had a centuries-old experience of facing invaders from the east. Before 1066 they had called them the Saxons. After 1066, when the most prominent invaders were now speaking another language, they gave them another name. The Welsh had made their identification of the invaders on the basis of language, and just because the Francophone settlers of England began to think of themselves as English, that was no reason for the Welsh to stop using a term which still made perfectly good linguistic sense to them. Not until the end of the twelfth century do Welsh sources get round to using the word 'Saxon' of French-speaking English. Native Scottish narrative sources, had any such existed, might well have seen a similar development.[34]

The second perception to take root during Stephen's reign was the

[31] On English law in the early 12th century, see P. Wormald, 'Quadripartitus', in G. Garnett and J. Hudson (eds.), *Law and Government in Medieval England and Normandy* (Cambridge, 1994).

[32] Henry of Huntingdon, *Historia*, p. 264. This is the one and only time he brings English and Normans together in a single *gens*, the 'gens Normannorum et Anglorum in una acie'. This is the nearest any contemporary writing in England came to using a term approximating to the 18th-century concept 'Anglo-Norman'. A little later in the same passage Henry referred to the northern army as 'populus Anglorum'.

[33] *The Chronicle of John of Worcester*, ed. J. R. H. Weaver (Oxford, 1908), pp. 46, 49, 51.

[34] The French figure prominently in the address clauses of 12th-century charters drawn up in Scotland as well as in England and Ireland, but I would argue that the legalistic formulae of address are, in the context of perceptions of national identity, less significant than the usage of contemporary narratives; see Gillingham, 'English invasion of Ireland', pp. 32–3. There are occasional references to the newcomers in Scotland and Ireland as 'French' rather than 'English' in 13th-century narratives – but these are exceptional, and explicable in terms of the exceptional circumstances in which they were written.

perception of 'Celtic' peoples as barbarians. Thus the emerging sense of Englishness came to be partly based on the perception of 'Celts' as significantly different and inferior. The period of the first tidal wave of Anglo-Saxon colonisation had also seen great antipathies. In the early eighth century Bede was prepared to call a British king – a fellow-Christian – a barbarian, and early West Saxon law codes treated the Welsh as 'second-class citizens'.[35] But in the lull between the two great tidal waves, we seem to have a period – and it is an enormously long period – characterised by the absence of any sharply defined attitude towards the Welsh and Scots. Works written in England during the ninth, tenth and eleventh centuries contain none of the language of alienation and superiority which later bulks so large. Moreover, it seemed to Liebermann, comparing the late Anglo-Saxon law code of the *Dunsaete* with the early – *c*.700 – laws of Wessex, that the former's even-handed treatment of Welsh and English marked 'an advance towards the reconciliation of the races'.[36] It might be argued that the absence of condemnatory language is just an apparent absence, a reflection of the paucity of sources and of the silence of those few that do exist. In this case all that would have happened is that the greater volume of sources in the twelfth century would have enabled historians belatedly to detect views which had been held for centuries. But the writings of early twelfth-century authors such as Orderic Vitalis and John of Worcester suggest that attitudes were changing during their lifetimes. Orderic was at work on his great *History* from about 1115 to 1141. In what he wrote about the Welsh and Scots up to the mid-1130s, he is neutral or even sympathetic. But by the end of that decade his tone was very different. In 1138 the Scots 'invaded England with the utmost brutality and giving full rein to their barbarity treated the peoples of the Borders with bestial cruelty'. Of the Welsh, he now noted that they are called barbarians and are going around slaughtering people like cattle.[37] John of Worcester, too, was originally sympathetic towards the Welsh, but in the late 1130s adopted a more hostile tone.[38] The Welsh rising and the Scottish invasions of the North unleashed an unprecedented deluge of vituperation over the heads of the Welsh and Scots. It is the language of peoples at war, doubtless, but these were peoples who had been at war with each other for many centuries without all this verbal ferocity. So why now?

I have suggested that the new vocabulary should be linked to a socio-economic development of fundamental importance: the demise of

---

[35] Bede, *Ecclesiastical History of the English People*, ed. and trans. B. Colgrave and R. A. B. Mynors (Oxford, 1969), p. 202; *The Laws of the Earliest English Kings*, ed. and trans. F. L. Attenborough (Cambridge, 1922), pp. 36–61. In these early centuries learned Britons from Gildas to 'Nennius' referred to the Saxons as barbarians.

[36] F. Liebermann, *Die Gesetze der Angelsachsen* (Halle, 1903–16), iii, p. 217.

[37] *Ecclesiastical History of Orderic Vitalis*, vi, pp. 518, 536.

[38] Compare the sympathetic treatment of Welsh revolts during the 1090s in Florence of Worcester, *Chronicon e Chronicis*, ed. B. Thorpe (London, 1848–9), ii, pp. 35, 41–2, with the more critical notes heard after 1135 (ibid., ii, p. 97, and *Chronicle of John of Worcester*, p. 43).

slavery.[39] Slavery went out of fashion in England in the early twelfth century. But it survived for longer in Wales, Ireland and Scotland – perhaps for not much longer, but for long enough to have had a dramatic impact upon the Englishman's perception of his neighbours. Obviously those who no longer practised slavery or engaged in the slave-trade found it easy to condemn those who did. Particularly important in the context of forming opinion was the fact that the Scots, Welsh and Irish continued to practise war as slave-hunt – a kind of total war. This is how one contemporary, Richard of Hexham, described the Scots in the North in 1138.

> [They] slaughtered husbands in the sight of their wives, then they carried off the women together with their spoil. The women, both widows and maidens, were stripped, bound and then roped together by cords and thongs, and were driven off at arrow point, goaded by spears ... Those bestial men who think nothing of adultery, incest and other crimes, when they were tired of abusing their victims, either kept them as slaves or sold them to other barbarians in exchange for cattle.[40]

As this passage, like many others written in the mid-twelfth century, makes clear, war as slave-hunt was war targeted against non-combatants, whereas by this date 'civilised' war elsewhere in England or on the Continent meant war against combatants and against property. But slave-raiders found it in practice necessary to kill not only anyone who put up a fight but also anyone whose lamenting or clinging presence got in the way of the business of seizing potential slaves and dragging them off into captivity. Thus the Scots, in Richard of Hexham's words, 'by the sword's edge or the spear's point slaughtered the sick on their beds, women pregnant and in labour, babes in their cradles or at their mothers' breasts or in their arms; they slaughtered worn-out old men, feeble old women, and anyone who was disabled'.[41] As Richard of Hexham's language makes plain, authors like him now regarded as utterly bestial a form of war once taken for granted as the way everyone made war and always had done. Hence the newly hysterical language applied to the conduct of the Scottish and Welsh war-parties in the later 1130s.

Once English authors had in this way been made forcibly aware of the Scots and Welsh, then they noticed other things about them. For example, they began to talk about their 'nakedness'. This did not, of course, mean that they invaded England in the nude, but that their lack of adequate armour made their bodies look very vulnerable – as indeed they were. Even the royal army of David of Scotland at the Standard included only 200 mailed soldiers;

[39] J. Gillingham, 'The beginnings of English imperialism', *Journal of Historical Sociology*, v (1992); also J. Gillingham, 'Conquering the barbarians: war and chivalry in twelfth-century Britain', *Haskins Society Journal*, iv (1993).

[40] Richard of Hexham, *De Gestis Regis Stephani*, p. 152.

[41] Ibid., pp. 156–7. Henry of Huntingdon, Ailred of Rievaulx, John of Hexham and John of Worcester all wrote of the Scots in similar terms.

the rest of his troops lacked body-armour and in consequence, as was observed by all commentators on the battle, they suffered terribly from the fire of the English archers.[42] Similarly, during the invasion of Ireland it was, in Gerald of Wales's judgement, the arrows of the English which spread terror among the Irish. Superior armour and firepower gave the invaders a decisive advantage, enabling them to win the control which gave them time to build the castles which further reinforced and stabilised that control.[43] In terms of armour and ammunition (arrowheads), the English economy was clearly capable of out-producing that of any 'Celtic' power. In a vivid image of Henry II's knights riding out to war, Jordan Fantosme, author of a vernacular account of the Anglo-Scottish war of 1173–4, used the contrast to make a point.

> See now the knights coming down from the castle, seizing their arms, putting on hauberks and coats of mail, lacing on their new helmets ... in battle array they come forth from the town, some 60,000 of them ... and not one of them but thinks himself the equal of a Welsh king.[44]

The 60,000 is, no doubt, an exaggeration, but the point remains that in Jordan's mind there were very large numbers of men who could afford to be 'royally', by Welsh standards, armed and armoured. And, indeed, that the numbers able to obtain high-quality armour had reached new – if still unquantifiable – levels is suggested by that other twelfth-century phenomenon, the tournament. To engage in tournaments was to proclaim your membership of a heavily armoured elite, the exclusive club of international chivalry. In the 1150s and 1160s we can see kings of Scotland, Malcolm IV and William the Lion, working hard to join the club; but, kings apart, there were few living north or west of England who could afford the entrance fee.

War between the English, with their towns, castles, hauberks and helmets, and any of their 'Celtic' neighbours (including, at this stage of their development, the Scots) was an unequal struggle between an industrially advanced power and a comparatively primitive economy. Thus when twelfth-century English writers looked at the Welsh and Scots they saw savage and poorly equipped people. In consequence they looked at them with hostile and condescending eyes. As Jordan Fantosme's language implies, this attitude is unlikely to have been restricted to the Latin-writing clerical elite. Chrétien of Troyes probably became familiar with the 'Matter of Britain' at Henry II's court and, in Chrétien's *Perceval*, one of King Arthur's knights is made to observe that 'all Welshmen are more stupid than beasts of the field'. In Guillaume le Clerc's *Fergus*, this characterisation was transferred to the

---

[42] M. Strickland, 'Securing the North: invasion and the strategy of defence in twelfth-century Anglo-Scottish warfare', *Anglo-Norman Studies*, xii (1989).

[43] Gerald of Wales, *Expugnatio*, pp. 230, 248; 'incastellata' was Gerald's term for a properly subjected land: ibid., p. 232, and cf. p. 104. See also Bartlett, *Making of Europe*, pp. 63–84.

[44] *Jordan Fantosme's Chronicle*, ed. and trans. R. C. Johnston (Oxford, 1981), ll. 153–61.

Galwegians.[45] Routinely, learned men such as Dean Ralph, Richard of Hexham and William of Newburgh began to refer to these crude, stupid and feckless people as 'barbarians'.

But why did those who came to look down on their 'Celtic' neighbours choose to describe them precisely as *barbari*? In earlier centuries the word 'barbarian' had been used by Latin Christian authors as a synonym for 'pagan', so *prima facie* it is odd to see it applied to the Christian Irish, Welsh and Scots.[46] I am inclined to think that at least part of the responsibility for this – one of the most devastating ideological shifts in the course of British history – should be borne by a historian: William of Malmesbury, one of the most creative of all English historians, and, in his influential *Deeds of the Kings of England* (completed by 1125), an early exponent of the splendid English habit of regarding the course of English history as the triumph of civilisation over barbarism. William's crucial intellectual step was to take the religious component out of the concept of barbarian and redefine it in terms of secular and material culture. His comments on King David of Scotland show that he regarded polished manners and a sophisticated life-style as among the hallmarks of civilised society. According to William, David 'promised tax exemptions to any of his subjects who would live in a more civilised style, dress with more elegance and learn to eat with more refinement'. And where had David acquired his notions of civilised behaviour? William was in no doubt. 'From the time he had spent with us ['familiaritas nostrorum'] he had been made more courtly and the rust of his native barbarism had been polished away.'[47] Later in the century we can see Henry II holding court at Dublin and trying to impress the Irish by a demonstration of a kind of *nouvelle cuisine*. According to Gerald of Wales, Henry made the Irish kings and chiefs eat crane – a bird they had never before thought of as a delicacy. Moreover, Exchequer records show that Henry's logistical preparations for his 1171–2 expedition to Ireland included 569 pounds of almonds.[48]

More fundamentally, William explicitly associated high culture with economic development. Of the Irish – whom he refers to as barbarians – he says that 'ignorant of agriculture, they live in rustic squalor, unlike the English and French who live in towns, who are familiar with commerce and

---

[45] Chrétien de Troyes, *Arthurian Romances*, trans. W. W. Kibler (Harmondsworth, 1991), p. 384; Guillaume le Clerc, *Fergus of Galloway*, trans. D. D. R. Owen (London, 1991), p. 4. The Galwegians seem to have been regarded as peculiarly savage by many of their neighbours.

[46] W. R. Jones, 'The image of the barbarian in medieval Europe', *Comparative Studies in Society and History*, xiii (1971); W. R. Jones, 'England against the Celtic fringe: a study in cultural stereotypes', *Journal of World History*, xiii (1971).

[47] William of Malmesbury, *Gesta Regum Anglorum*, ed. W. Stubbs (Rolls Series, 1887–9), ii, pp. 476–7.

[48] Gerald of Wales, *Expugnatio*, p. 96. In addition to carrying almonds and massive quantities of ironware, Henry II's fleet to Ireland also brought 1,000 lb. of wax, presumably to seal documents and to shed light in the dark corners of the land. See J. F. Lydon, *The Lordship of Ireland* (Dublin, 1972), pp. 40–1.

enjoy a more cultivated style of life'.[49] He clearly accepted the ancient notion that pastoral economies were unable to sustain civilised life. Here we have one of the consequences of the unequal rate of economic development in different parts of the British Isles. Whereas for centuries the Anglo-Saxon and 'Celtic' worlds had been, as Patrick Wormald has argued, very similar, by the early twelfth century they were different enough for the differences to be visible to contemporaries. The author who first gave expression to this perception of significant otherness was William of Malmesbury. After centuries in which the term 'barbarian' was understood in religious terms, William's remarkable familiarity with classical literature and his admiration for the values of the ancient world enabled him to rediscover the classical concept of the barbarian and to discover that it applied to 'Celtic' peoples in his own day. In British history, at any rate, this is the truly significant Renaissance. William's revival of Greco-Roman modes of perception resulted in the Christian view of the world, one which divided men and women into two basic groups – Christian and non-Christian – being decisively supplemented by a non-religious system of classification, one which divided men and women into the 'civilised' and the 'barbarous'. In the course of British history this was to be the great divide, the creation of an imperialist English culture.

It may be that William's way of seeing the societies of the British Isles would have caught on anyway. But, as it happened, ten years or so after he completed his *History of the Kings of England,* the events of Stephen's reign brought two of William's barbarian races, the Welsh and the Scots, to people's attention, and did so with shocking violence. Thus the author of the *Deeds of Stephen* began his narrative of Stephen's reign with an account of the Welsh revolt, which led him to offer an analysis of Welsh society. This he did in Malmesbury's terms. The Welsh, it appears, are a barbarous people, of untamed savagery, and they live in a 'country of woodland and pasture ... abounding in deer and fish, milk and herds ... a country breeding men of a bestial type'.[50] By the later twelfth century it had become commonplace to note the relative lack of towns, commerce and agriculture in Ireland and Wales – though in Scotland these were now to be found.[51] The author who, above all others, took up and elaborated this point of view was Gerald of Wales. According to him, the Welsh lived almost entirely on oats and milk, cheese and butter – the produce of their herds; they ate plenty of meat but

---

[49] William of Malmesbury, *Gesta Regum,* ii, p. 485.

[50] *Gesta Stephani,* p. 14.

[51] It is important for the way anglicised Lowland Scotland was developing to note that in the 1150s one well-informed observer, Ailred of Rievaulx, praised King David for having made an uncultivated and barren land bring forth fruit, for building castles and towns, and for filling its markets with goods from abroad: *Eulogium Davidis Regis Scottorum,* in *Pinkerton's Lives of the Scottish Saints,* ed. W. M. Metcalfe (Paisley, 1889), ii, p. 279. Perhaps the tax exemptions attributed to David by William of Malmesbury had had the desired pump-priming effect.

very little bread, and paid no attention to commerce, shipping or industry.[52] He painted a picture of Ireland as a country rich in natural resources but undeveloped owing to lack of industry on the part of the natives, a land of gold and rain-forests where the savages whiled away their lives in brutality, sexual licence and laziness, an Eldorado waiting for the arrival of the enterprising and clean-living Englishman.[53]

Of course twelfth-century writers exaggerated the extent to which 'Celtic' societies were pastoral; here the point is that this is how those societies were perceived and presented to English audiences. So far as Ireland and Wales were concerned, one consequence was that they were perceived as economically dependent on England, and hence as vulnerable to the power of the rulers of England. According to William of Malmesbury, Irish kings were careful to remain in Henry I's good books. One who stepped out of line for a moment was quickly brought to heel by a trade embargo: 'For what would Ireland be worth if goods were not brought to it from England?'[54] According to William of Newburgh, Wales 'is incapable of supplying its inhabitants with food except by imports from neighbouring English counties – and thus it is inevitably subject to the power of the king of England'. When Gerald advised the English on how to conquer the Welsh, he advocated an embargo. 'Every effort must be made to stop them from buying the cloth, salt and corn which they usually import from England. Ships manned with picked troops must patrol the coast to ensure that these goods are not brought by water across the Irish or the Severn Sea.'[55]

A second consequence of seeing Ireland and Wales as economically undeveloped was the conviction that under proper (that is, English) management and with strong government to curb native lawlessness, they could be brought to peace and prosperity. According to the author of the *Gesta Stephani*, conquerors and settlers in Wales 'had made the country so abound in peace and productivity that it might easily have been thought a second England'. In the same vein, Gerald argued that if the Irish could be compelled to obey the king of England, then they would enjoy the benefits of peace and be introduced to 'a better way of life'.[56] 'Let them eat crane', as Henry II might have said. The better way was the English way. In stark contrast to their image of their 'Celtic' neighbours, the English perceived themselves as prosperous, urbanised, enterprising, peaceful, law-abiding and with higher moral standards. At the Synod of Cashel (1172) it was announced that in

---

[52] Gerald of Wales, *The Journey through Wales and The Description of Wales*, trans. L. Thorpe (Harmondsworth, 1978), p. 233.

[53] Gerald of Wales, *Expugnatio*, p. 170; Gerald of Wales, *The Topography of Ireland*, trans. J. J. O'Meara (Harmondsworth, 1982), *passim*.

[54] William of Malmesbury, *Gesta Regum*, ii, pp. 484–5. Gerald made a similar point: 'Ireland cannot survive without the goods and trade which come to it from Britain' (Gerald of Wales, *Expugnatio*, p. 252).

[55] William of Newburgh, *Historia*, p. 107; Gerald of Wales, *Journey through Wales*, p. 267.

[56] *Gesta Stephani*, p. 16; Gerald of Wales, *Expugnatio*, pp. 100, 250.

future the Irish Church was in all matters to be conducted in line with the observance of the English Church – above all, the dean of St Paul's noted, in matters of marriage, one of many indications that church 'reformers', from the time of Pope Gregory VII and Lanfranc onwards, had regarded 'Celtic' family law as immoral. In 1174 a captive King William was forced to agree that the Church of Scotland would be subject to the English Church, albeit in vague terms. England's neighbours were being offered a co-prosperity sphere and a New Order. But is it not misleading to apply, as here, the vocabulary of twentieth-century imperialism to twelfth-century conditions? After all 'everyone knows' that things were different then. Looking back from the twentieth century, we can see that medieval England was an overwhelmingly rural economy, a primitive society. But this was precisely what twelfth-century Englishmen saw when they looked towards their 'Celtic' neighbours. When they called them barbarians they did not merely mean 'we are better than you'. They meant 'we are so much better as to have reached a higher stage of human development than you'.[57]

One measure of the economic and political strength of the structures underpinning the English position within the British Isles is the speed with which, after the crisis of Stephen's reign, Henry II was able to re-impose the old patterns. In Gerald's words, 'He remarkably extended the kingdom's borders and limits until they reached from the sea to the south to the Orkney Islands in the north. Within his powerful grasp he included the whole island of Britain in one monarchy.'[58] In doing this he was materially helped by the fact that divisions within Scotland and Wales were fiercer and more fundamental than those which had recently disturbed the English kingdom. King David had 'modernised' Scotland with the help of émigrés from south of the Border, but this may have exacerbated ethnic tensions and added to the difficulties faced by his successor, Malcolm IV.[59] In 1157 the young king of Scots had to submit to Henry II's bullying and restore the territorial gains which David had made at English expense. In 1158 Morgan of Caerleon was 'slain through treachery' by a fellow Welshman; in 1171, on his way to Ireland, Henry confiscated the castle of Caerleon.[60] Part of the pattern was that those who, in Gerald's words, 'feed constantly on the hope of recovering the lands which the English have taken from them' would naturally take

[57] R. Bartlett, *Gerald of Wales* (Oxford, 1982), p. 176, for the parallels between some of these 12th-century concepts – the ladder of evolution of human societies and the persistence of primitive survivals – and 19th- (and 20th-) century anthropological thought.

[58] Gerald of Wales, *Opera*, ed. J. S. Brewer *et al.* (Rolls Series, 1861–91), viii, p. 156.

[59] For Malcolm's problems with the Gaelic world, notably from 'the barbarous hands' of Somerled of Argyll and his kin, see the passages from the Chronicles of Holyrood, Melrose and Man, and above all from the *Carmen de morte Sumerledi*, all translated in A. O. Anderson, *Early Sources of Scottish History* (reprint, Stamford, 1990), ii, pp. 223–4, 254–8. The point is argued vigorously in R. A. McDonald and S. A. McLean, 'Somerled of Argyll: a new look at old problems', *Scottish Historical Review*, lxxi (1992). But for a different view, see Duncan, *Making of the Kingdom*, pp. 166–7.

[60] *Brut Peniarth*, p. 66; *Brut Hergest*, p. 137.

advantage of any serious dissension within the English establishment. For example, the rebellion of his family against Henry II in 1173-4 triggered Irish, Scottish and – by Morgan's successor, Iorwerth of Caerleon – Welsh recovery attempts.[61] Similarly, the war at the end of John's reign, the Magna Carta revolt as it appears from an English perspective, was also a war of the allies, the French, the Welsh and the Scots against the English – and was so perceived at the time.[62] In this war no-one fought on more obstinately than did the lord of Caerleon.[63]

There is one striking exception to this pattern. This is when Richard I was in prison in Germany and his brother John in revolt against him – a moment of acute weakness for the English Crown, and an ideal opportunity for any of England's 'Celtic' neighbours to exploit. Yet, unlike the king of France, not one of them made any attempt to do so. Not the Irish.[64] Not the Welsh princes – perhaps thanks in part to Gerald of Wales's diplomatic activity, though at the cost of his own ecclesiastical career.[65] Not the Scots. William the Lion not only refused to exploit the situation, but even made a substantial contribution to Richard's ransom. Peace, not war, characterised the relations between Scots and English in Richard's reign. In the words of the first historian of Scotland, John of Fordun, there was 'so hearty a union between the two countries and so great a friendship of real affection knit the two kings ... that the two peoples were reckoned as one and the same'.[66] This, of course, was in the reign of an exceptional king.

Henry II's reign had witnessed the re-imposition of old patterns. This, indeed, is what he had set out to achieve – the recovery of what he called the rights of his grandfather. In this context Walter Map's styling of Henry I as

---

[61] Gerald of Wales, *Expugnatio*, p. 134. For the interdependence of these events, see Gerald of Wales, *Journey through Wales*, pp. 119-20.

[62] T. Wright, *The Political Songs of England from the Reign of John to that of Edward II* (Camden Society, 1839), pp. 19-20. For the continuing concern of the English government with alliances of this kind, see S. Duffy, 'The Bruce brothers and the Irish Sea world, 1306-29', *Cambridge Medieval Celtic Studies*, xxi (1991).

[63] See D. A. Carpenter, *The Minority of Henry III* (London, 1990), pp. 70, 77, 192, 294, 308.

[64] To judge from the Irish annals, in Ireland it was business as usual – perhaps the only corner of Christian Europe to display no interest in the crusades. Modern books on medieval Irish history have tended to ignore Richard I's reign – a mistake, as is shown in M. T. Flanagan, *Irish Society, Anglo-Norman Settlers, Angevin Kingship: Interactions in Ireland in the Late Twelfth Century* (Oxford, 1989), especially pp. 266-7, on the appointment and activities of John de Courcy as Justiciar of Ireland in 1194-5.

[65] Gerald of Wales, *Opera* , i, pp. 295-300.

[66] Fordun called Richard 'that noble king of England so friendly to the Scots': John of Fordun, *Cronica Gentis Scotorum*, ed. and trans. W. F. and F. H. Skene (Edinburgh, 1871-2), ii, pp. 269-71. This is not surprising, since Richard's 1189 Quitclaim of Canterbury (ibid., pp. 267-8) released Scotland, in the words of the Melrose Chronicle (Anderson, *Early Sources of Scottish History*, ii, p. 322), 'from the heavy yoke of domination and servitude'. As the aftermath indicated, this was a well calculated act of political generosity, of enormous advantage to Richard as well as to the independence of Scotland. But many modern English historians have preferred to echo the view expressed by Gerald of Wales (*Opera*, viii, p. 156) that the Quitclaim represented a shameful loss to the English Crown.

'king of England, duke of Normandy, count of Brittany and Maine, lord of Scotland, Galloway and of the whole English island' gives a good indication of the way men thought at Henry II's court, as does also Map's reference to 'our island England'.[67] But in some vital respects Henry II's reign marked the New Order. First and most fateful was the fact that the English invaded Ireland. In the words of William of Newburgh, this meant that a people who had been free since time immemorial, unconquered even by the Romans, a people for whom liberty seemed, as he put it, an inborn right, had now fallen into the power of the king of England.[68] The second was that as a consequence of government in late twelfth-century England becoming significantly more bureaucratic, so English domination was increasingly to be expressed in institutional and administrative forms. The third was that a regime which claimed to be bringing the delights of modern government and prosperity to its neighbours was doing so at a time when the perception of the king's 'Celtic' subjects as barbarians was no longer just the clever idea of a clever historian, but had become deeply entrenched in English thought. Thanks to Richard I, Scotland regained its independence in 1189 – as was always likely given its own internal development – but in Ireland and Wales this way of seeing and describing differences between peoples set up ideological barriers between invader and invaded, between coloniser and colonised.[69] From the twelfth century onwards there was to be a crucial fragility at the heart of the English empire.[70]

[67] Walter Map, *De Nugis Curialium*, ed. and trans. M. R. James *et al.* (Oxford, 1983), pp. 166, 472.

[68] William of Newburgh, *Historia*, pp. 165–8.

[69] As is shown by Keith Stringer, 'Scottish foundations: thirteenth-century perspectives', below, ch. 6, these perceptions were softened so far as the Scots were concerned, especially in the 13th century.

[70] Davies, 'English state and the "Celtic" peoples', pp. 10–13.

Chapter 5

Overlordship and reaction, c.1200–c.1450

Robin Frame

This essay has two parts, dividing in the early fourteenth century. The first chimes with the agreeably Whiggish title of this section of the volume, which commands the medievalists to consider the 'foundations' of the United Kingdom – the Westminster-centred state which was at its height between 1801 and 1922, and most of which still exists. (Indeed, whether through arrogance, absence of mind, muddle or guilt, that state, so strict in its treatment of Commonwealth citizens, has never brought itself to regard the inhabitants of the bit that has seceded – the citizens of the Irish Republic – as aliens.) Until the early fourteenth century, the historian surveying the British Isles with later events in mind can discover an organising theme ready made: English expansion and responses to it.[1] In the later Middle Ages, however, English power ceased to spread; in Ireland it receded. The proto-United Kingdom often attributed to Edward I proved to be built on sand. Its crumbling, at a time when the eyes of the more effective English kings were firmly fixed on France, may prompt another, prior, question. How appropriate is it to take the British Isles as our mental arena, in an age when the kings of England were also continental rulers, and when into the bargain they shared the island of Britain with kings of Scots whose royal status was recognised by Popes, by other European rulers, and indeed by the kings of England themselves? These are issues to which I shall return.

Let us begin by glancing at the scene as it might have appeared to Edward I in the year 1290, when his authority was little challenged. English rule in medieval Ireland, which had begun in a small way with the visit of Henry II in 1171–2, was well rooted, with perhaps half of the island governed directly from Dublin and most of the rest dominated by a settler aristocracy.[2] In

---

[1] This is a major theme of two recent studies: R. R. Davies, *Domination and Conquest: The Experience of Ireland, Scotland and Wales 1100–1300* (Cambridge, 1990); and R. Frame, *The Political Development of the British Isles 1100–1400* (Oxford, 1990).

[2] See, e.g., A. J. Otway-Ruthven, *A History of Medieval Ireland* (London, 1968), chs. 1–6; R. Frame, *Colonial Ireland 1169–1369* (Dublin, 1981), chs. 1–5; A. Cosgrove (ed.), *A New History of Ireland*, vol. II: *Medieval Ireland 1169–1534* (Oxford, 1987), chs. 1–6, 8, 15, by F. X. Martin, J. F. Lydon, R. E. Glasscock and K. Down.

Wales the native principality had recently been conquered and equipped with an English legal and institutional superstructure.[3] Scotland, which after nearly seventy years of peace had unexpectedly become problematical through the deaths between 1281 and 1286 of Alexander III and his sons, seemed as though it might be drawn more fully within the English sphere by the planned marriage of the future Edward II to Alexander's sole living descendant, his granddaughter, Margaret 'the Maid of Norway'.[4] To Edward, we must assume, the prospect was pleasing. The whole of Britain and Ireland would be within the control of the Plantagenet house, and closed to French marital meddling. England, Wales and Ireland were already held in the grip of a governmental system able to raise revenues and do justice in Cumberland, Merioneth or Limerick. The proposed dynastic link with Scotland was subject, as agreed in the Treaty of Birgham,[5] to respect for Scots law and institutions; but those, unlike their native Welsh and Irish counterparts, were broadly compatible with English systems, and furthermore the two kingdoms were bridged by a cross-Border aristocracy.[6] It is possible to imagine England and Scotland being managed much as Edward's brother-in-law, Sancho of Castile, handled his kingdoms of Castile and Leon, or as the count-kings of Barcelona, Aragon and Valencia ruled their tripartite realm.[7]

1290 may indeed look more promising than 1305, when direct English control was probably at its zenith. In that year, after almost a decade of war, Edward laid out a scheme for the government of Scotland. Although his arrangements rested on harnessing rather than excluding such of the Scottish elites as would co-operate, English garrisons dotted the Lowlands; English nobles had been granted tracts of land north of the Tweed and the Solway; Berwick, like Dublin and Caernarfon, was the seat of an English

[3] Among the more important modern works on this subject are: R. R. Davies, *Conquest, Coexistence and Change: Wales 1063–1415* (Oxford, 1987), Part IV; J. Given, *State and Society in Medieval Europe: Gwynedd and Languedoc under Outside Rule* (Ithaca and London, 1990); A. J. Taylor, *The Welsh Castles of Edward I* (London, 1986); and L. B. Smith, 'The Statute of Wales, 1284', *Welsh History Review*, x (1981).

[4] The classic account is G. W. S. Barrow, *Robert Bruce and the Community of the Realm of Scotland* (3rd edn, Edinburgh, 1988), chs. 1, 2; see also R. Nicholson, *Scotland: The Later Middle Ages* (Edinburgh, 1974), ch. 2. The story is told from the English perspective in M. Prestwich, *Edward I* (London, 1988), pp. 356–62.

[5] For a translation of and commentary on this treaty, see G. W. S. Barrow, 'A kingdom in crisis: Scotland and the Maid of Norway', *Scottish Historical Review*, lxix (1990).

[6] For Scots law, see W. D. H. Sellar, 'The Common Law of Scotland and the Common Law of England', in R. R. Davies (ed.), *The British Isles 1100–1500: Comparisons, Contrasts and Connections* (Edinburgh, 1988); and H. L. MacQueen, *Common Law and Feudal Society in Medieval Scotland* (Edinburgh, 1993). Cross-Border landholding is discussed in K. J. Stringer, *Earl David of Huntingdon, 1152–1219: A Study in Anglo-Scottish History* (Edinburgh, 1985), ch. 9, and in A. Young, 'Noble families and political factions in the reign of Alexander III', in N. H. Reid (ed.), *Scotland in the Reign of Alexander III 1249–1286* (Edinburgh, 1990).

[7] See J. N. Hillgarth, *The Spanish Kingdoms 1250–1516*, i (Oxford, 1976), Part II; and T. N. Bisson, *The Medieval Crown of Aragon: A Short History* (Oxford, 1986), especially the comments at pp. 1–4. For a gloomier view of medieval dynastic unions, see M. Prestwich, 'Edward I and the Maid of Norway', *Scottish Historical Review*, lxix (1990), pp. 172–3.

exchequer.[8] These facts testified to a degree of state military and fiscal activity probably unequalled in the British Isles until the seventeenth century.[9] But they also show the limits of the possible. Dynastic unions were one thing; the conquest and administrative absorption of a medium-sized kingdom, with an old regnal tradition and an awkward physical geography, was quite another. So it seems appropriate to linger a little longer in the world as it was before it sprang apart in the wars that began in 1296.

While there is little to suggest that English kings – even Edward I – had the attainment of direct rule over the British Isles as a conscious goal, let alone one to whose steady pursuit they gave priority, the degree of domination achieved during the later twelfth and the thirteenth centuries is striking. One simple testimony to this is the English royal centres that existed in 1290, but had not existed in 1170: Chester, Flint, Conwy, Caernarfon, Harlech, Aberystwyth; Dublin, Drogheda, Waterford, Cork, Limerick, Athlone, Roscommon. The extension of English power westwards can be measured in another way. The Welsh king Gruffudd ap Cynan, who ruled on and off in north Wales from 1075 to 1137, showed great powers of resistance in the face of the Normans. This was largely because he could retreat to Ireland and gather troops there:[10] the Irish Sea was still a Celtic-Scandinavian lake. The 1240s provide a sharp contrast. When Gruffudd's descendant, Dafydd son of Llywelyn the Great, offended Henry III, the result was utterly different. The English regime at Dublin shipped in materials for Henry's new castle at Degannwy, and the justiciar of Ireland raised a large force, including contingents led by the king of Connacht, to attack Anglesey.[11] This was the shape of things to come: in the early fourteenth century the English often mobilised much of Wales and Ireland against the Scots.

The impact of English power and influence is apparent not just in material terms but also in identities and perceptions. I wish to offer three contrasting examples, the first amounting to what might be described as a transplanted identity, the other two involving the reactions of those who were on the receiving end of English aggression.

Colonisation in Ireland, which was probably at its peak between the 1170s

---

[8] See Barrow, *Robert Bruce*, pp. 132–6; and M. Prestwich, 'Colonial Scotland: the English in Scotland under Edward I', in R. A. Mason (ed.), *Scotland and England 1286–1815* (Edinburgh, 1987).

[9] For the size of English armies under Edward I compared to their early modern successors, see M. Prestwich, *War, Politics and Finance under Edward I* (London, 1972), p. 113.

[10] Contacts between Wales and Ireland, and the 'Irish Sea world' in general in the 11th and early 12th centuries, have been the subject of several recent studies, in all of which Gruffudd figures. See, e.g., K. L. Maund, *Ireland, Wales, and England in the Eleventh Century* (Woodbridge, 1991), especially chs. 2–4; M. T. Flanagan, *Irish Society, Anglo-Norman Settlers, Angevin Kingship: Interactions in Ireland in the Late Twelfth Century* (Oxford, 1989), ch. 2; and S. Duffy, 'Irishmen and Islesmen in the kingdoms of Dublin and Man, 1052–1171', *Ériu*, xliii (1992).

[11] On this episode, see G. H. Orpen, *Ireland under the Normans 1169–1333* (Oxford, 1911–20), iii, pp. 227–30. Its significance is brought out in A. D. Carr, *Medieval Anglesey* (Llangefni, 1982), pp. 46–8.

and the 1220s, led to the creation of an 'English Ireland', which at least in its institutional forms closely mirrored England itself. Irish historians (until recently almost the only ones interested) have understandably tended to focus upon its incompleteness and upon its negative sides: the unpleasant face of English triumphalism and exclusiveness; the fact that English control and cultural influence declined from the fourteenth century; the ambiguities and tensions that came to be associated with the settler identity. It is easy to forget – though less so since the appearance of Robert Bartlett's *The Making of Europe*[12] – that this was a major, and in some ways very successful, example of high medieval colonial enterprise.

That those who went to Ireland in the late twelfth century already saw themselves, and were seen by others, as English has been argued by John Gillingham.[13] During the thirteenth century much of Ireland formed a single zone with England, within which English Common Law and English government developed.[14] The emerging English lordship was not a bureaucratic figment, or the product of royal prescription. It was rooted in considerable numbers of men, women and institutions with property and lives on both sides of the sea: landed magnates, widows and heiresses, lesser lords, officials, beneficed clergy, monasteries, merchants. It was also present in the self-interest and self-identification of substantial settler communities.[15] In a recent paper I have tried to trace the sharpening of this expatriate Englishness which became the distinguishing mark of a self-conscious political society, stretching far beyond the territory of the later Pale.[16] One of the influences that shaped it was an experience already touched upon: that of being organised by the Crown against its enemies, not just within Ireland but outside it. The corn lands and ports of the South and East were scoured for supplies and shipping; taxes were asked for, and conceded, in Irish parliaments and councils; between 1296 and 1335 six expeditions sailed against the Scots; lords from Ireland

12 R. Bartlett, *The Making of Europe: Conquest, Colonization and Cultural Change 950–1350* (London, 1993), which considers English settlement in Ireland in the context of Christian expansion in the Slav lands, Spain and Outremer.

13 J. Gillingham, 'The beginnings of English imperialism', *Journal of Historical Sociology*, v (1992); J. Gillingham, 'The English invasion of Ireland', in B. Bradshaw *et al.* (eds.), *Representing Ireland: Literature and the Origins of Conflict* (Cambridge, 1993); see also J. Gillingham, 'Foundations of a disunited kingdom', above, ch. 4.

14 On this point, see the comments in P. Brand, 'Ireland and the literature of the early Common Law', *Irish Jurist*, xvi (1981). The development of English government in Ireland is succinctly traced in Otway-Ruthven, *History of Medieval Ireland*, ch. 5.

15 Ties between Ireland and England are discussed in R. Frame, 'King Henry III and Ireland: the shaping of a peripheral lordship', in P. R. Coss and S. D. Lloyd (eds.), *Thirteenth Century England IV: Proceedings of the Newcastle-upon-Tyne Conference, 1991* (Woodbridge, 1992). On the settlements, see A. J. Otway-Ruthven, 'The character of Norman settlement in Ireland', in J. L. McCracken (ed.), *Historical Studies V* (London, 1965); C. A. Empey, 'Conquest and settlement: patterns of Anglo-Norman settlement in north Munster and south Leinster', *Irish Economic and Social History*, xiii (1986); and Bartlett, *Making of Europe, passim*.

16 R. Frame, '"Les Engleys nées en Irlande": the English political identity in medieval Ireland', *Transactions of the Royal Historical Society*, 6th ser., iii (1993).

served at the siege of Calais in 1347.[17] Even more significant were the events of 1315–18 when the Scots under Edward Bruce, assisted during the early months of 1317 by King Robert himself, invaded Ireland. Despite the emphasis placed by some earlier historians on examples of dubious loyalty on the part of certain settler lords, a more notable feature of the period is the extent to which their allegiance, and that of the towns, held firm: there is no doubt that for most the king's enemies were also the enemies of the lordship of Ireland. Indeed the only significant English victory of Edward II's wretched reign was that won for him by the English of Ireland in October 1318 near Dundalk, where Edward Bruce, the 'king of Ireland', fell. English chroniclers, and Edward II, made much of it; indeed throughout the emergency, the king showered lands, liberties and titles upon his lords and towns in Ireland.[18]

The collaboration of the English of Ireland in wider undertakings is visible in the Latin annals compiled in Dublin and Kilkenny, which are as aware of the martial deeds of Edward I and Edward III as are any English local chronicle.[19] Their outlook is apparent, for instance, in an incident reported by John Clyn of Kilkenny in 1345. The earl of Oxford, returning from Brittany, was blown by tempests to the shores of Connacht where, landing among the Irish, he and his men were attacked and robbed, 'escaping from the shipwreck semi-naked'. Henry Scrope, on the other hand, made landfall in Cork, 'but this was among loyal people who did him no harm'. By 'loyal', of course, Clyn meant 'English'.[20] A petition sent to Edward III from 'the earls, barons and community of Ireland' in 1341, when they were at odds with royal ministers, catches exactly the link between involvement in the king's wars and the sense of being English:

> whereas various people of your allegiance, as of Scotland, Gascony and Wales, often in times past have levied war against their liege lord, at all times your English liege people of Ireland have behaved themselves well and loyally, holding your land for your ancestors and yourself both against the Scots and against the Irish, your enemies.[21]

Needless to say, this Irish Englishness was not a straightforward phenomenon; 1341 saw the first of many political clashes between dependency and metropolis. But it was more than just a reflection of the fact that there was no

---

[17] J. F. Lydon, in ch. 7 of *New History of Ireland*, ii, pp. 195–204; R. Frame, *English Lordship in Ireland 1318–1361* (Oxford, 1982), ch. 4.

[18] R. Frame, 'The Bruces in Ireland, 1315–1318', *Irish Historical Studies*, xix (1974); J. R. S. Phillips, 'The mission of John de Hothum to Ireland, 1315–1316', in J. Lydon (ed.), *England and Ireland in the Later Middle Ages* (Dublin, 1981); S. Duffy, 'The "Continuation" of Nicholas Trevet: a new source for the Bruce invasion', *Proceedings of the Royal Irish Academy*, xci C (1991).

[19] E.g. *Chartularies of St Mary's Abbey, Dublin*, ed. J. T. Gilbert (Rolls Series, 1884–6), ii, pp. 325–9, 334–5, 390; *Annals of Ireland by Friar John Clyn*, ed. R. Butler (Dublin, 1849), pp. 24–6, 28–9, 33–4.

[20] Ibid., p. 32.

[21] *Statutes, Ordinances and Acts of the Parliament of Ireland, King John to Henry V*, ed. H. F. Berry (Dublin, 1907), pp. 342–5. For the background, see Frame, *English Lordship*, ch. 7.

alternative label available, of the sort that enables modern Ulstermen to maintain a 'British' allegiance while articulating a loathing of the English equal to anything to be heard in a Glasgow bar. The English had transferred themselves to Ireland, creating a world that for a century and a half had developed in many respects (though not of course in all) in close parallel with England itself.

My second example concerns not the transplantation of English identity (though this did happen in Wales at local level)[22] but the impact of the English on a native political society. It did not need the English of this period to engineer a Welsh identity. Awareness of a distinct British past was already present, at least among the Welsh intelligentsia; it had been nourished by hostility to Anglo-Saxon intrusions. But the consciousness of difference, enshrined from different perspectives by Geoffrey of Monmouth and Gerald of Wales, was not accompanied by political unity, in the sense of a settled link between a stable territory and a ruling dynasty.[23] This came – up to a point – later, through the rulers who consolidated their position in north Wales, and aspired to be princes of all Wales. No doubt economic change and ecclesiastical reform would have altered authority and perceptions in Wales even without Anglo-Norman intervention and settlement.[24] But what did occur was certainly affected by the English power against which Welsh leaders defined themselves and their country.

This is apparent, for instance, in the nomenclature of authority. In the later twelfth century, major Welsh rulers tended to abandon their traditional royal styles in favour of the title 'prince' (*tywysog*). David Crouch has argued that this was not something required of them by the English: Henry II was happy enough to have Welsh (or Irish) kings under him.[25] Chroniclers might put them in their place by calling them 'kinglets' (*reguli*),[26] just as the verse history of the conquest of Ireland says, condescendingly, 'there are as many kings in Ireland as there are counts elsewhere'.[27] The adoption of the new-fangled title 'prince', which has parallels on the Continent and in Outremer, marked the bigger Welsh rulers out from the general run of native royalty,

---

[22] R. R. Davies, 'In praise of British history', in Davies, *British Isles 1100–1500*, p. 14.

[23] See Davies, *Conquest, Coexistence and Change*, pp. 15–20, 78–80; and W. Davies, *Wales in the Early Middle Ages* (Leicester, 1982), p. 196. Both stress that the existence of a sense of identity should not lead us to conclude that there was a linear trend towards political unity. See also W. Davies, *Patterns of Power in Early Wales* (Oxford, 1990), chs. 3, 6.

[24] R. R. Davies, *Conquest, Coexistence and Change*, chs. 6, 7; H. Pryce, *Native Law and the Church in Medieval Wales* (Oxford, 1993).

[25] D. Crouch, *The Image of Aristocracy in Britain 1000–1300* (London, 1992), pp. 85–95. The Treaty of Windsor of 1175, in which Henry accepted Ruaidrí Ua Conchobair of Connacht as king over the native zones of Ireland, states that Ruaidrí should be 'king under him' ('quod sit rex sub eo'): Flanagan, *Irish Society*, p. 312.

[26] For instance Roger Howden, describing the 1177 Council of Oxford, calls each of the Welsh leaders who attended a *subregulus*: *Chronica Rogeri de Houedene*, ed. W. Stubbs (Rolls Series, 1868–71), ii, pp. 133–4. In the text of 'Benedict of Peterborough', however, they are called *reges*: *Gesta Regis Henrici Secundi Benedicti Abbatis*, ed. W. Stubbs (Rolls Series, 1867), i, p. 162.

[27] *The Song of Dermot and the Earl*, ed. G. H. Orpen (Oxford, 1892), ll. 2190–2.

claiming for them a place above barons or earls. And prince of what? Of 'North Wales' or of 'South Wales', even of 'Wales'. 'Welsh' was an English word, meaning 'foreigner'. If the term 'prince' signified a riposte to English overlordship, the adoption of these territorial titles marked the domestication of an English view of the way the world was arranged.[28]

In the thirteenth century, English might showed itself in legal intrusiveness, which demanded a response. The same legal system that was throwing a cloak of formal Englishness over the settlements in Ireland forced other powers to explain themselves; Welsh rulers, like marcher barons, had to learn to make the right noises.[29] In 1224, for instance, Llywelyn, who had harboured the disgraced Norman lord, Fawkes de Breauté, argued a key question with Henry III. A subject of the king should not receive outlaws; but Llywelyn claimed to be no ordinary subject but a ruler of equal rank with the king of Scots, who could receive whom he wished.[30] Such attempts to acquire status in terms the outside world understood were intertwined with the building of jurisdiction over those within Wales whom the princes chose to regard as their subjects. In the 1260s Llywelyn ap Gruffudd was concerned both to define his relationship with other Welsh lords through written bonds, and to gain English recognition of the fact that they owed homage to him.[31]

In all this, native law, which the princes manipulated to their advantage, was an unreliable weapon.[32] It was customary and regional, and in the care of jurists who might feel menaced by the claims of assertive, 'modernising' rulers. It could also offer arguments to other native lords, who were anxious to preserve traditions of regal equality. But by the time of Edward I, English demands, spearheaded by officials working from Chester or Montgomery, led to a papering over of the cracks. Llywelyn presented himself both to the king and to the Welsh as the defender of a national custom. It was in this context

[28] See M. Richter, 'The political and institutional background to national consciousness in medieval Wales', in T. W. Moody (ed.), *Historical Studies XI: Nationality and the Pursuit of National Independence* (Belfast, 1978). This may have had its beginnings in the 11th century (W. Davies, *Patterns of Power*, p. 88).

[29] See, in particular, R. R. Davies, 'Kings, lords and liberties in the March of Wales, 1066–1272', *Transactions of the Royal Historical Society*, 5th ser., xxix (1979); and Davies, *Conquest, Coexistence and Change*, ch. 11.

[30] *Royal and other Historical Letters illustrative of the Reign of Henry III*, ed. W. W. Shirley (Rolls Series, 1862–6), i, pp. 229–30; *Calendar of Ancient Correspondence concerning Wales*, ed. J. G. Edwards (Cardiff, 1935), pp. 24–5.

[31] E.g., *Littere Wallie*, ed. J. G. Edwards (Cardiff, 1940), nos. 147, 199, 204. For discussion, see ibid., pp. xli–xlvi; D. Stephenson, 'Llywelyn ap Gruffydd and the struggle for the Principality of Wales', *Transactions of the Honourable Society of Cymmrodorion* (1983), pp. 36–40; and Davies, *Conquest, Coexistence and Change*, pp. 316–20. The capacity of the demands of an external overlord to intensify lordship within a dependent polity, a familiar concept among early medievalists, is discussed in W. Davies, *Patterns of Power*, pp. 84–8.

[32] For what follows, see R. R. Davies, 'Law and national identity in medieval Wales', in R. R. Davies et al. (eds.), *Welsh Society and Nationhood: Historical Essays presented to Glanmor Williams* (Cardiff, 1984). The complex relationship between the legal tradition and princely power is discussed in H. Pryce, 'The prologues to the Welsh lawbooks', *Bulletin of the Board of Celtic Studies*, xxxiii (1986).

that his brother, Dafydd, argued famously that, since Edward I was 'lord of divers countries and of divers peoples, and divers laws are administered in them and are not changed', Welsh law should remain inviolate – a protest that began by accepting the political hierarchy as the English saw it.[33]

Such a hierarchy was necessary to the princes. They were thrusting themselves upon a native Wales that was highly fissile; the habit of rule by a single member of a single princely house had yet to be created. Outside acceptance was a trump card. Although Llywelyn the Great had had dealings with Philip Augustus in 1212 and Dafydd ap Llywelyn had obtained fleeting recognition from the Pope in 1244, almost always acceptance had to come from the English king.[34] Recognition depended on playing the game by his rules; the construction of a small state on the outskirts of a large kingdom demanded a finely judged mixture of resistance, circumspection, and emulation. In the event English and Welsh perceptions of what the relationship between prince and Crown should be proved incompatible. The nucleation and definition the house of Gwynedd had achieved could not be maintained, let alone pressed further, in the face of internal splits and English might; and in 1282 the Saxon took over. That moment appears to be an abrupt change of direction in Welsh history – as indeed it was. Yet there were continuities. What the princes had built, partly through interaction with the English, aided the assimilation of north Wales into the Plantagenet realm. The conquerors kept the core of the princely dominion as a unit; they perpetuated the notion of a principality; and they harnessed the Welsh local elites and courts that had been part of the structure of princely rule. Viewed in this way – as it could not be by contemporaries – 1282–4 was one stage in a longer process of incorporation, which itself reflected the weight of English power upon a neighbouring polity.[35]

The third measure of the English impact takes us beyond the experience of a single country. Recent work on the Irish Sea Province, or more accurately the area as far south as Anglesey (for St George's Channel belonged pretty firmly to St George), has assembled evidence of lines of contact and influence that continued to criss-cross the old Celtic–Norse zone. These drew together western Scotland and the Isles, northern Ireland, Galloway and Man; here bards, clergy, mercenaries, traders, and sometimes diplomats, came and went.[36]

---

[33] *Calendar of Ancient Correspondence concerning Wales*, p. 73.

[34] R. F. Treharne, 'The Franco-Welsh treaty of alliance in 1212', *Bulletin of the Board of Celtic Studies*, xviii (1958–60); M. Richter, 'David ap Llywelyn, the first Prince of Wales', *Welsh History Review*, v (1970–1).

[35] See J. G. Edwards, *The Principality of Wales 1267–1967: A Study in Constitutional History* (Caernarfon, 1969), pp. 9–11; and W. H. Waters, *The Edwardian Settlement of North Wales in its Administrative and Legal Aspects (1284–1343)* (Cardiff, 1935). D. Stephenson, *The Governance of Gwynedd* (Cardiff, 1984), ch. 7, brings out the closeness of the links between the princely administrative elite and the English even before 1282.

[36] Such links are explored in, e.g., J. Bannerman, 'The king's poet and the inauguration of Alexander III', *Scottish Historical Review*, lxviii (1989), pp. 141–7; and S. Duffy, 'The Bruce brothers and the Irish Sea world, 1306–29', *Cambridge Medieval Celtic Studies*, xxi (1991).

In 1224 we saw Llywelyn the Great make a comparison between his status and that of the king of Scots. In 1258 his grandson entered a brief alliance with a Scottish baronial faction.[37] When King Hakon of Norway appeared off Scotland in 1263, there were reverberations in Ireland – unsurprisingly, since troops from the western Highlands and the Isles (where Norwegian influence was still strong) were already finding employment with Gaelic rulers in Ulster and Connacht, at a time when the remnants of the native polity were under threat from a late ripple of English expansion into Ireland. It was even rumoured that an offer of lordship was made by the Irish to Hakon at this time.[38] With the outbreak of the Anglo-Scottish wars, such interactions became more significant, and worried the English authorities. There is clear evidence of a sense of shared oppression. Native Irish annalists lamented defeats of the Welsh and the Scots;[39] Merlinic prophecies circulated in Scotland;[40] Robert and Edward Bruce devised propaganda stressing the common language and descent of the Scots and the Irish;[41] they also wrote to the Welsh about the common experience of dispossession by the Saxons.[42] None of this was enough to nurture an organised resistance, let alone to fabricate a working 'Celtic' identity: apart from anything else, the more effectively articulated clumps of English settlement, administration and sentiment in western Britain and Ireland stood in the way. But there can be no doubt that in the early fourteenth century a single English realm was coming close enough to heighten the sense of being 'not English', and of suffering for it.[43] Such feelings lasted. When in the 1360s the Scots contemplated a possible Plantagenet succession to the childless David II, one of the arguments put forward against it was the treatment the Irish and Welsh had already received at the hands of the English.[44]

Around 1300, therefore, those eager to read history backwards will find plenty to encourage them. Essential building blocks of the United Kingdom were certainly in place as a result of this period of English expansion. There was an ingrained assumption of English supremacy in relation to Wales and

[37] *Littere Wallie*, no. 317. See G. W. S. Barrow, 'Wales and Scotland in the Middle Ages', *Welsh History Review*, x (1981), pp. 311–12.

[38] See Duffy, 'Bruce brothers', pp. 68–70; and for the 'ripple of expansion', Frame, 'King Henry III and Ireland', pp. 194–202.

[39] E.g. *Annals of Connacht*, ed. A. M. Freeman (Dublin, 1944), *s.a.* 1296, 1301, 1303; *Annals of Inisfallen*, ed. S. Mac Airt (Dublin, 1951), *s.a.* 1282, 1296, 1307.

[40] See Barrow, *Robert Bruce*, pp. 172–3.

[41] *Formulary E. Scottish Letters and Brieves 1286–1424*, ed. A. A. M. Duncan (Glasgow, 1976), p. 44; R. Nicholson, 'A sequel to Edward Bruce's invasion of Ireland', *Scottish Historical Review*, xlii (1963), pp. 38–9. The date of this letter is reconsidered in Duffy, 'Bruce brothers', pp. 64–5.

[42] J. B. Smith, 'Gruffydd Llwyd and the Celtic alliance, 1315–18', *Bulletin of the Board of Celtic Studies*, xxvi (1976).

[43] See Davies, *Domination and Conquest*, pp. 126–8.

[44] 'Papers relating to the captivity and release of David II', ed. E. W. M. Balfour-Melville, in *Scottish History Society Miscellany, IX* (Edinburgh, 1958), p. 42. Archdeacon Barbour, writing slightly later, also refers to the 'thraldom' imposed by Edward I on the Welsh and Irish: R. J. Goldstein, *The Matter of Scotland: Historical Narrative in Medieval Scotland* (Lincoln, Nebraska, 1993), pp. 157–8.

Ireland. Wales was already united to England, not just through the admini-stration of the newly incorporated Principality, but through the accumulation of marcher lordships in the hands of aristocratic families with property elsewhere, a process that was to continue during the fourteenth and fifteenth centuries.[45] The Act of Union of 1536 might change the terms of the integration; but the decisive work was that of a Plantagenet state capable of deploying resources on a large scale. In Ireland of course there was more to do – including such minutiae as reconquest and plantation! But reports of the death of the medieval lordship have been exaggerated. Fifteenth-century Ireland, still sadly neglected by historians, was a complex, decentralised polity rather than a wholly decomposed one. The legacy of the period from Henry II to Edward I included an English title to the island, sizeable colonial bridgeheads, a settler aristocracy with continued ties to the English court, municipal government, traces of a county system, a parliamentary history that was to remain continuous to 1800, and a common law tradition that is still largely intact.[46]

There was also a less comfortable inheritance. After 1284 many members of the Welsh elites found employment under the Crown; Welsh men and women also discovered advantages in some English customs. But the sense of distinctness, and of having been expropriated and marginalised, remained strong. In certain circumstances – most notably those surrounding the rebellion of Owain Glyn Dŵr in the early fifteenth century – it could provide a stimulus to, and a rationalisation of, resistance.[47] In Ireland the Gaelic learned classes were the guardians of an ancient cultural inheritance that had long been expressed in national terms, for instance when it came to recording (retrospectively) the story of the Viking attacks; such traditions were already exploited for political purposes by the publicists of Gaelic kings in the pre-Norman period. The responses of Irish leaders to the English presence may have been determined by local practicalities; but commentators continued to interpret events along ethnic lines, and to fit them into the established pat-terns of a national past.[48] These traditions of dissent, with their accumulating layers, were themselves to be built into the fabric of the United Kingdom.

[45] R. R. Davies, *Lordship and Society in the March of Wales 1282–1400* (Oxford, 1978), ch. 2.

[46] D. B. Quinn has perceptively described the Pale as a 'fulcrum for action' (in *New History of Ireland*, ii, p. 637). In several studies Steven Ellis has sought to counter the traditional gloomy view of the Yorkist and early Tudor lordship and to set Ireland in a broader context: see, e.g., S. G. Ellis, *Reform and Revival: English Government in Ireland 1470–1534* (Woodbridge, 1986); and S. G. Ellis, *The Pale and the Far North: Government and Society in Two Early Tudor Borderlands* (O'Donnell Lecture, Galway, 1988). But there is an urgent need for studies of the articulation of power, formal and informal, in later medieval Ireland.

[47] See, e.g., Davies, *Conquest, Coexistence and Change*, Part V; and G. Williams, 'Prophecy, poetry and politics in medieval and Tudor Wales', in G. Williams, *Religion, Language and Nationality in Wales* (Cardiff, 1979).

[48] This theme was the subject of a valuable response at the 1994 Conference by Dr Brendan Smith. See, e.g., F. J. Byrne, 'Senchas: the nature of Gaelic historical tradition', in J. G. Barry (ed.), *Historical Studies IX* (Belfast, 1974); and D. Ó Corráin, 'Nationality and kingship in pre-Norman Ireland', in Moody, *Historical Studies XI*.

Scotland, whose rulers successfully resisted English threats and blandishments, is the subject of a separate chapter of this volume. It is clear that the strength of the northern kingdom, which contrasts sharply with the fragility of the multiple royal regimes of Wales and Ireland, owed much to men and institutional borrowings from south of the Tweed.[49] Indeed Robert Bruce's reconstruction of Scottish government after 1314 shows that the process of borrowing, in the legal sphere at least, was not occluded by the Anglo-Scottish wars.[50] But equally, the capacity of the kings of Scots to manage and exploit new influences in the twelfth and thirteenth centuries suggests that a stable regal tradition and an organised territorial base already existed. That Scottish historians by and large *want* to demonstrate the precocity of the kingdom should not lead outsiders into exaggerated scepticism: recent work has done much to confirm that royal power was well rooted and institutionalised long before 1100 in the area between the Forth and the Moray Firth.[51] It was this that enabled later kings confidently (if not always consciously) to borrow features of the Anglo-Norman world and turn them to their advantage. Such comparative regnal solidity, which native Wales and Ireland lacked, made Scotland amenable to dynastic association (and perhaps gradual assimilation), but not to conquest and incorporation.

How should the story go from here? In the late Middle Ages English expansion ceased within the archipelago. Demographic trends, while not ruling further colonisation out – as the state-sponsored English settlements in early fifteenth-century Normandy and Maine show – were strongly against it. Direct crown control in Ireland shrank. Protracted war loosened, though it did not destroy, conventional English administration in the northern shires.[52] Continued Scottish resistance ensured that the kingdom of the Scots would follow an increasingly divergent path. Rees Davies has suggested that the most 'Britannic' medieval century ended around 1340.[53] That date serves to recall the question I ducked at the outset: whether the British Isles should in any case form the mould in which we cast our thoughts.

In 1340 Edward III publicly assumed in Ghent the title and arms of France. His success on the Continent, and the obligations it imposed on his successors, were to turn Scotland, let alone Ireland, into a side-show for several generations. But was it not the case that – despite the energy Edward I had devoted to Wales and Scotland – this is what for the Norman and Plantagenet

[49] The classic works on this topic are by G. W. S. Barrow: *The Kingdom of the Scots* (London, 1973); and *The Anglo-Norman Era in Scottish History* (Oxford, 1980).

[50] MacQueen, *Common Law and Feudal Society*, pp. 152–3, 264–6.

[51] See, especially, A. Grant, 'Thanes and thanages from the eleventh to the fourteenth centuries', in A. Grant and K. J. Stringer (eds.), *Medieval Scotland: Crown, Lordship and Community. Essays presented to G. W. S. Barrow* (Edinburgh, 1993).

[52] For a recent assessment, see C. J. Neville, 'Keeping the peace on the northern Marches in the late Middle Ages', *English Historical Review*, cix (1994).

[53] Davies, 'In praise of British history', p. 22.

kings they always had been, and that historians' pursuit of an embryonic British realm is a chimera? Conrad Russell has claimed that

> there is no case for a medieval British [political] history, which would be as much an abstraction as European history, and a slightly less logical one. The history of the Angevin Empire which is still needed would be an Anglo-French, not a British, history. From 1066 to the death of Henry III, London looked south and east, not north and west, and integrated political history should reflect that fact.[54]

Up to a point, perhaps. Of course thirteenth-century kings presided over an Anglo-French 'realm'. But this does not alter the fact that, despite the occasional foreign *curialis* who benefited from the westwards expansion (such as Maurice son of Guy de Rochfort, a Poitevin who founded a landed family in Ireland in the mid-thirteenth century),[55] the dominance achieved within the archipelago was an English one, and was perceived as such by those who were agents of it, who endured it, or who resisted it. In England itself, as Michael Clanchy and others have argued, national identity had been clarified by political tensions during the reigns of John and Henry III, when continental members of the royal circle were used as scapegoats.[56] After 1204 even a Norman, such as Fawkes de Breauté, might be stigmatised as an alien.[57] In that sense the Englishness that spilled outwards in Britain and Ireland was amplified, not muted, by the overseas interests of the king. Indeed it has been acutely observed that the very Englishness of the enterprise made accommodations with Welsh and Irish society more difficult than they might otherwise have been.[58]

In 1340, however, when the English were on the defensive within the British Isles, the French involvement was about to grow dramatically. There is no doubt that the attention and resources of the monarchy were thereafter drawn to France on a scale and with a persistence unparalleled since the defeat of John's allies at Bouvines in 1214. But the point is that this too was now unmistakably an *English* undertaking. In the thirteenth century, especially after Henry III's military failure in western France in 1230, activities on the Continent had been of concern only to a cosmopolitan court and a handful of

[54] C. Russell, 'John Bull's other nations', *Times Literary Supplement*, no. 4693 (12 March 1993), p. 3.

[55] Frame, 'King Henry III and Ireland', p. 193.

[56] M. T. Clanchy, *England and its Rulers: Foreign Lordship and National Identity* (London, 1983), ch. 10. Cf. the recent comment by David Carpenter that the mid-13th century 'marked a stage in the "making" of England, when political society was almost completely Anglicized, but monarchy still retained vestiges of the imperial outlook of the Angevin kings': D. Carpenter, 'King Henry III's "Statute" against aliens: July 1263', *English Historical Review*, cvii (1992), pp. 942–3.

[57] J. C. Holt, 'Feudal society and the family in early medieval England: IV. The heiress and the alien', *Transactions of the Royal Historical Society*, 5th ser., xxxv (1985), pp. 27–8.

[58] R. R. Davies, 'The English state and the "Celtic" peoples 1100–1400', *Journal of Historical Sociology*, vi (1993), pp. 12–13.

magnates.[59] In the fourteenth, by contrast, they became, thanks to Edward III's victories of 1346–56 and his gift for domestic propaganda, an enterprise with which the English political class identified itself. Moreover, that class had widened and deepened as a result of the mobilisation of human and fiscal resources required by successive military efforts especially from the 1290s onwards. This so-called 'war state' had, as we have seen, its attendant satellite in English Ireland.[60]

If we seek a way of thinking about the political structures that emerged as a result of these developments, there is an obvious possibility. The late Middle Ages were the era of a particular sort of dynastic state, which had as one typical feature interaction between rulers or their agents and national or provincial communities in parliaments, estates or *cortes*.[61] As commitments in France grew, England may be seen as the core of such a state. Normally we arrange the scene differently, by studying the political society of England itself; equipping England with a 'foreign policy'; and leaving the outlying lands to be picked over separately by specialists. In view of the antiquity, wealth and relative coherence of the kingdom of England, this approach is probably inescapable. But a shift of viewpoint can be fruitful, as Mark Ormrod has shown in his essay on Edward III's family policy, or Ralph Griffiths in his study of the legal and national status of the king's subjects across his entire dominions.[62] A glance at some aspects of the overseas territories, diverse as they were, may help to make the point.

The oldest outlier – associated with the royal house from the marriage of Henry II to Eleanor of Aquitaine in 1152, and so pre-dating Ireland by some twenty years – was Gascony. Despite the title of a well-known book,[63] Gascony was not a 'colony' in the same sense as Ireland and Wales were to become, for it had not been even partially settled by the English. It was a continental duchy, with its own customs, Church and aristocracy. The self-interest of the local mercantile, and a majority of the landed, elite bolstered Plantagenet rule, but the English presence was limited to transient governors, soldiers and traders. Yet this was no medieval Hanover. When in 1254 Henry III had created an apanage for the future Edward I (made up of

[59] R. Stacey, *Politics, Policy and Finance under Henry III 1216–1245* (Oxford, 1987), pp. 168–73.

[60] For a valuable overview of recent work on this theme, see G. L. Harriss, 'Political society and the growth of government in late medieval England', *Past and Present*, cxxxviii (1993).

[61] See, e.g., B. Guenée, *States and Rulers in Later Medieval Europe*, trans. J. Vale (Oxford, 1985), chs. 10, 11.

[62] W. M. Ormrod, 'Edward III and his family', *Journal of British Studies*, xxvi (1987); R. A. Griffiths, 'The English realm and dominions and the king's subjects in the later Middle Ages', in R. A. Griffiths, *King and Country: England and Wales in the Fifteenth Century* (London, 1991).

[63] M. W. Labarge, *Gascony: England's First Colony 1204–1453* (London, 1980). That Ireland rather than Gascony deserves this description is cogently argued by J. A. Watt in *New History of Ireland*, ii, pp. 312–13. See also R. R. Davies, 'Lordship or colony?', in J. Lydon (ed.), *The English in Medieval Ireland* (Dublin, 1984). On the colonial status of Wales, see R. R. Davies, 'Colonial Wales', *Past and Present*, lxv (1974).

Gascony, Ireland, the royal possessions in Wales, and some English lands), the award included the proviso that these should never be separated from the Crown of England. This clause may have been devised partly to allay Gascon fear of the French.[64] But the idea that the duchy was an inalienable *English* land became an article of faith. When in the 1390s Richard II thought of paying liege homage to Charles VI for the duchy in return for peace, he risked offending not just the Gascons but mainstream English opinion, which saw such a surrender of hard-won sovereignty – the issue on which Edward III had held absolutely firm – as dismemberment of the Crown of England.[65]

Except from 1254 to 1272 (when the Lord Edward's regime was strictly limited and supervised) and briefly during the 1380s (when the maverick Richard II allowed writs from the Irish chancery to run in the name of his favourite, Robert de Vere, Earl of Oxford, whom he made marquess of Dublin and duke of Ireland),[66] Ireland remained under the direct rule of the king's representatives from John's accession to the English throne in 1199 to the extinction of the medieval lordship in 1541. In the later Middle Ages the English in Ireland, defined as they were by English law, and sharing the experience of English government and English forms of military service, possessed the stigmata of a mature political community, which mimicked that of England itself. They had a historical perspective, with at its best an almost Kiplingesque sense of duty. (It was rarely at its best.) In 1290 Geoffrey de Joinville, lord of Meath (no Englishman but that is beside the present point), included the following statement in a petition seeking a papal dispensation for his son's marriage:

Henry [II] of happy memory, former king of the English, by the wish of the apostolic see, entered that land with armed force, and reduced it and its inhabitants so far as he could to his obedience and that of the papacy; and both he and his successors in that kingdom tried as time went by to place upright men of a different nation in that land of Ireland to encourage papal obedience there; among them this same Geoffrey, who acquired much land in Ireland by means of a marriage with a noble lady of those parts; and he [Geoffrey] has tried and still tries, by himself and through his people, to carry out as best he can the aim of those kings, to

[64] *Calendar of Documents relating to Ireland, 1252–84*, ed. H. S. Sweetman (London, 1877), no. 326. See Prestwich, *Edward I*, pp. 7–14. While the charter of 1254 may symbolise the emergence of an England-centred state, that state was both more and (without Scotland) less than a monarchy of the British Isles; see J. Le Patourel, 'The Plantagenet dominions', *History*, l (1965), pp. 298–308.

[65] A. Tuck, 'Richard II and the Hundred Years War', in J. Taylor and W. Childs (eds.), *Politics and Crisis in Fourteenth Century England* (Gloucester, 1990); M. Jones, 'Relations with France, 1337–1399', in M. Jones and M. Vale (eds.), *England and her Neighbours, 1066–1453: Essays in Honour of Pierre Chaplais* (London, 1989), pp. 257–8.

[66] J. R. Studd, 'The Lord Edward and Henry III', *Bulletin of the Institute of Historical Research*, l (1977); A. Tuck, 'Anglo-Irish relations, 1382–93', *Proceedings of the Royal Irish Academy*, lxix C (1970), pp. 23–6.

keep the natives within that obedience and earnestly to foster peace amongst them.[67]

This view of the English role in Ireland, planted by Gerald of Wales and by papal documents of the twelfth century, constantly recurs. It might be accompanied by the belief, no doubt encouraged by the royal servants who inhabited the chapter of St Patrick's Cathedral, Dublin, that a providential link could be traced between the Patrician mission of the fifth century and the coming of the reforming English in the twelfth, by-passing the era of native disorder in between.[68] That these attitudes were widely shared is suggested by an episode in 1346, when jurors in south-west Ireland, scraping around for dirt to dish on the unruly first earl of Desmond, accused him of telling Clement VI that Edward III was failing to rule Ireland according to the terms of the original papal grant.[69]

During the fourteenth century instances accumulate of the English of Ireland, like the English of England, voicing grievances against the rulers who were frequently assembling them and placing burdens upon them. An early hint of collective, critical views is present in the Middle English Kildare poems. Among these is 'A Song on the Times', whose vocabulary places its Irish provenance beyond doubt. This poem visualises a community, referred to as 'the land', and articulates its resentments:

> Would Holy Church use its might,
> And law of land use it too,
> Then should covetise and unright
> Out of the land be banished.

> That king's ministers be disgraced
> To right and law that should take heed
> And all the land for to amend.[70]

As in England, parliaments served as occasions for grumbling and redress. Some of the resentments, notably to do with financial demands and the misdeeds of officials, were shared with England. Others reflected the particular features of Ireland. They included appeals for a royal presence and

---

[67] *Vetera monumenta Hibernorum et Scotorum historiam illustrantia*, ed. A. Theiner (Rome, 1864), no. 331.

[68] For this notion, see a petition of the 'middling people of Ireland', *c.*1318, in *Documents on the Affairs of Ireland before the King's Council*, ed. G. O. Sayles (Dublin, 1979), no. 136. A justification of the English position, partly on historical grounds, sent to the Pope around 1331 can be associated with St Patrick's: J. A. Watt, 'Negotiations between Edward II and John XXII concerning Ireland', *Irish Historical Studies*, x (1956), pp. 14, 18–20.

[69] 'Legal proceedings against the first earl of Desmond', ed. G. O. Sayles, *Analecta Hibernica*, xxiii (1966), p. 44.

[70] W. Heuser, *Die Kildare-Gedichte: Die Ältesten Mittelenglischen Denkmäler in Anglo-Irischer Überlieferung* (Bonn, 1904), pp. 133–9. For similar poems of English provenance, see T. Turville-Petre, 'The "nation" in English writings of the early fourteenth century', in N. Rogers (ed.), *England in the Fourteenth Century* (Stamford, 1993), pp. 129–31.

help against the native Irish; the alleged maldistribution of gifts and offices between locals and men who blew in with English governors; neglect by absentee lords; and the tendency of the metropolis to define loyalty in terms of birth in England, or of a narrow uniformity, which might even call in question the Englishness that was the foundation of settler privilege. In return, ministers from England had their own grumbles, not least at the way resident lords frustrated governmental purposes by exploiting their direct links with the Plantagenet court.[71] It is possible, I believe, to glimpse in the Anglo-Irish relations of the fourteenth and fifteenth centuries most of the structural features and almost every source of tension (save religion) that historians of the seventeenth century have identified as characteristic of the early modern 'multiple state' or 'composite monarchy'.

Despite the very different origins of the Anglo-Gascon and Anglo-Irish relationships, the contrasting societies of Gascony and Ireland (the one relatively homogeneous, the other divided between English settler and Irish native), and the much greater significance of Gascony on the international stage, the two countries shared, not just a ruler and a similar model of devolved government, but some similar structural tensions and political debates. This is specially noticeable between the 1340s and the 1370s. For several years in the 1360s Edward III's eldest son, the Black Prince, ruled in Gascony as prince of Aquitaine, while his second surviving son, Lionel of Antwerp, governed Ireland as king's lieutenant and earl of Ulster. The prince's first expedition to Gascony, in 1355, had been preceded by requests from the Gascons for royal attention; lobbying by the English of Ireland had helped to bring about Lionel's dispatch there.[72] English princes and nobles went to Gascony with administrators and troops, who had to be supported. The borders of Gascony, like those of English Ireland, were vulnerable, and its revenues shrunken: in both territories taxation and threatened resumptions of gifts that had been made to the local elites were political flash-points. Under the Black Prince – whose rule in Wales also was exacting and abrasive – financial pressures led to heavy demands for subsidies, which soured relations with the Gascon Estates.[73] In Ireland the 1370s saw a fiscal crisis, turning essentially on the question of whether the English taxpayer or the inhabitants of the lordship of Ireland should pay for defence by English expeditionary forces. By 1375 these difficulties were focused in dramatic form on the Irish Parliament; when adequate subsidies were refused, despite the dispatch of special emissaries to strengthen the arm of the Governor, William of Windsor,

[71] On this political agenda, see further Frame, *Political Development*, pp. 184–7; and Frame, "'Les Engleys nées en Irlande'", pp. 94–103. More detailed illustration is to be found in Frame, *English Lordship*, especially pp. 72–4, 114–23, and chs. 7–9.

[72] H. J. Hewitt, *The Black Prince's Expedition of 1355–7* (Manchester, 1958), p. 3; Frame, *English Lordship*, pp. 320–5.

[73] See, e.g., K. Fowler, *The King's Lieutenant: Henry of Grosmont, First Duke of Lancaster, 1310–1361* (London, 1969), pp. 42–9, 73–4; and R. Barber, *Edward, Prince of Wales and Aquitaine* (Woodbridge, 1978), pp. 181–2, 208–13.

Edward III proposed bringing representatives of the Irish Commons to England; a demand to which local communities responded by denying their representatives plenipotentiary authority.[74] The political histories of Gascony and Ireland have been explored in some detail at this period, and each has been separately related to the financial and political crises that occurred in England as a result of the stresses created by the renewal of the Hundred Years War in 1369.[75] There is, however, room to consider them *together*, in the setting of the Plantagenet lands as a whole.

Between 1420 and 1450 the scope and complexity of those lands was increased by the addition of Normandy and its fringes, where the victories of Henry V and the duke of Bedford led to the establishment of an English presence whose character has been dissected by Christopher Allmand and others, who have drawn attention to parallels between settlement in Normandy and earlier colonisation within the British Isles.[76] On the face of it, the conquest of Normandy produced something different in nature from either Ireland or Gascony. Normandy was like Ireland in the presence of English settlers; but it was like Gascony, in that Bedford and his successors had to work with conventional – by which I suppose I mean non-Celtic – indigenous elites and customs. Furthermore, in Normandy both native and newcomer were acceptable, whereas in Ireland the Gaelic lords remained outside the formal legal and political system, and lacked the collective institutions necessary to function as a political community. Nevertheless, Maurice Keen has pointed to intriguing parallels. Just as the English of Ireland were sufficiently distanced from, and politically ill at ease with, the English of England to appear at times a distinct group,[77] so the English domiciled in Normandy quickly began to have interests that were not necessarily congruent with those of the metropolis. The failure of resources and nerve under Henry VI, when English opinion was into the bargain affected by Henry's status as king of France, exaggerated the stresses between the homeland and the expatriate English who felt increasingly abandoned by it.[78]

There is a need for further comparative studies, and for a greater willingness to set the kingdom of England in the context of the royal dominions as a

[74] See especially J. F. Lydon, 'William of Windsor and the Irish Parliament', *English Historical Review*, lxxx (1965).

[75] See G. Holmes, *The Good Parliament* (Oxford, 1975); and S. Harbison, 'William of Windsor, the court party and the administration of Ireland', in Lydon, *England and Ireland*.

[76] See, e.g., C. T. Allmand, *Lancastrian Normandy 1415–1450: The History of a Medieval Occupation* (Oxford, 1983); C. T. Allmand, 'The Lancastrian land settlement in Normandy, 1417–50', *Economic History Review*, xxi (1968); and R. Massey, 'The land settlement in Lancastrian Normandy', in A. J. Pollard (ed.), *Property and Politics: Essays in Later Medieval English History* (Gloucester, 1984).

[77] M. Keen, 'The end of the Hundred Years War: Lancastrian France and Lancastrian England', in Jones and Vale, *England and her Neighbours*. Cf. C. T. Allmand, 'La Normandie devant l'opinion anglaise à la fin de la Guerre de Cent Ans', *Bibliothèque de l'Ecole des Chartes*, cxxviii (1970).

[78] The same failure contributed to a collapse of pro-English sentiment among the Gascon lords: M. G. A. Vale, *English Gascony 1399–1453* (Oxford, 1970), pp. 206–15, 217–19.

whole. Small parts of the story may emerge through exploration of the careers of magnates such as Richard Duke of York or John Talbot, Earl of Shrewsbury and Waterford, who served and held property in more than one sphere.[79] But major themes remain to be tackled directly. It is, for instance, worth recalling that, with the addition of Normandy, Lancastrian kings, their councils and representatives were for some thirty years involved in dealings with an array of representative institutions, including the English and Irish Parliaments, and the Gascon and Norman Estates.[80] Is there perhaps a subject here? We might also hope that some of the sophistication on display in recent studies of regional societies in fifteenth-century England might be extended to the outskirts of the English territories, now that county communities have somewhat belatedly appeared on the agenda of Irish medievalists.[81]

If there are histories of the English dominions in the late Middle Ages still to be written, Scotland can reasonably stand outside them. Claims to English overlordship, while not wholly abandoned, had little substance in the late fourteenth and early fifteenth centuries, and the two kingdoms diverged more than they converged. But there is one obvious way – besides that of making instructive contrasts, pioneered by Alexander Grant[82] – of drawing Scotland into the discussion. The English lands formed an assemblage of political communities, some with imperfectly absorbed fringes, such as Gaelic Ireland or, for a time, Maine. This dynastic aggregation, volatile at its edges, was in competition with the complex state presided over by the Valois kings of France. Scotland, as a small but independent kingdom within the same geographical orbit, had to find its way in the interstices of the broader competition; indeed its own 'Celtic fringe' interacted with Gaelic Ireland in ways that created difficulties for both Edinburgh and Dublin.[83] The French option, exploited occasionally since the twelfth century and frequently from 1295, helped to confirm Scotland's separate identity by supplying a distinctive

---

[79] See P. A. Johnson, *Duke Richard of York, 1411–1460* (Oxford, 1988); Talbot's important Irish career, understandably, figures little in A. J. Pollard, *John Talbot and the War in France 1427–1453* (London, 1983).

[80] There has been little work on the Irish Parliament in the period c.1300–1460 since the publication of H. G. Richardson and G. O. Sayles, *The Irish Parliament in the Middle Ages* (Philadelphia, 1952; 2nd edn, 1964). For Gascony, see R. Boutruche, *La crise d'une société: seigneurs et paysans du Bordelais pendant la Guerre de Cent Ans* (Paris, 1947), pp. 132, 182, 224–5, 244, 267, 406; J. J. N. Palmer, *England, France and Christendom 1377–1399* (London, 1972), pp. 154–63; and Vale, *English Gascony*, pp. 28, 35, 63, 69, 81, 86, 198. On Normandy, see B. J. H. Rowe, 'The Estates of Normandy under the duke of Bedford, 1422–1435', *English Historical Review*, xlvi (1931); and Allmand, *Lancastrian Normandy*, pp. 171–86.

[81] B. Smith, 'A county community in early fourteenth-century Ireland: the case of Louth', *English Historical Review*, cvii (1993). There are some suggestions for an agenda in R. Frame, 'Commissions of the Peace in Ireland, 1302–1461', *Analecta Hibernica*, xxxv (1992), pp. 3–7.

[82] A. Grant, 'Crown and nobility in late medieval Britain', in Mason, *Scotland and England 1286–1815*; Frame, *Political Development*, pp. 187–97.

[83] See A. Grant, 'Scotland's "Celtic Fringe" in the late Middle Ages: the Macdonald Lords of the Isles and the kingdom of Scotland', in Davies, *British Isles 1100–1500*; and, for comments on the Irish-Scottish Gaelic links, S. G. Ellis, 'Nationalist historiography and the English and Gaelic worlds in the late Middle Ages', *Irish Historical Studies*, xxv (1986), pp. 6–9.

external orientation.[84] Once the Bruce monarchy had shaken off its origins in homicide and usurpation, the direct link between the Scottish Church and the Papacy had a similar effect, especially during the Great Schism, which allowed England and Scotland to give allegiance to different Popes.[85] And the Anglo-Scottish wars themselves ended most cross-Border landholding for many generations. If the eventual dynastic merger of 1603 was between kingdoms that differed more widely from each other than would have been the case in 1290, the explanation lies in the fourteenth and fifteenth centuries as well as in the experience of the Reformation period.

The later Middle Ages may seem to shovel less concrete into the 'foundations' of the United Kingdom than did the twelfth and thirteenth centuries, when English power was extended and institutionalised in Wales and Ireland. Even so, they are of interest to the historian searching for antecedents, or (less Whiggishly) simply for profitable questions to think about. They saw a focusing of the communities of kingdoms and provinces through deeper princely legal and fiscal penetration, and through dialogue in parliaments and councils. This took place in an intensely dynastic, and hence unpredictable, world. In 1281, when Alexander III was only forty, and had two living sons, the royal line of Scotland seemed more likely to last than to die out; had it survived, much would have differed, throughout Britain and Ireland, and indeed Western Europe. Or again, the Maid of Norway's actuarial rating may not have been good, nor were the consequences of the birth of children to her and Edward II fully thought through by contemporaries; even so, England and Scotland *might* have shared a line of kings after the death of Edward I in 1307 – just as they might not have shared one from 1603. Similarly, only the unlikely deaths of four youngish kings of France during the years 1316–28 opened the possibility of a Plantagenet claim to a Crown that had passed unbroken from father to son for the previous three hundred years. Without those deaths, Edward III might have devoted more of his considerable political and military gifts to Ireland. He had made all the preparations for an expedition to the lordship in 1332, before a Scottish opportunity, and then the French threat and temptation, distracted him. Who knows what difference a royal visit would have made at this critical stage: certainly it would have prevented the circumstances that led to the catastrophic assassination in 1333 of William de Burgh, the last resident earl of Ulster and lord of Connacht, who was not merely crucial to the management of the north and west of Ireland, but also (as heir through his mother to one third of the estates of the Clare earls of Gloucester) the single most important link between the nobilities of Ireland and England.[86]

There may be value in such counterfactual whimsy, if only to remind us

---

[84] For a recent discussion, see A. Curry, *The Hundred Years War* (London, 1993), pp. 137–50.

[85] See, e.g., M. Lynch, *Scotland: A New History* (London, 1991), pp. 99–104.

[86] Frame, *English Lordship*, pp. 197–202. Though I remain unconvinced that a sustained commitment to Ireland on the part of the English monarchy was likely (see ibid., pp. 224–5).

that in 1290 a number of futures were possible for the British Isles, among which hugely protracted Anglo-Scottish and Anglo-French wars might have seemed less likely than the emergence of some sort of greater British realm, under the lordship of the Plantagenet house. The materials for such a structure were not lacking: concepts of kingship and law, sinews of administration, fiscal and military capacity, and coherent, though not all-encompassing, political communities and national or sub-national identities, on both sides of the Irish Sea. (Admittedly the development of some of these would have been different had major wars not occurred to force the pace.) If the biological dice had rolled differently, fourteenth-century historians might be debating some of the 'three kingdoms' issues that preoccupy early modernists. Even as things stand, there is room to explore the links and resemblances as well as the discontinuities and contrasts between late medieval political structures and problems and those of later times.

Chapter 6

Scottish foundations

Keith Stringer and *Alexander Grant*

Thirteenth-century perspectives
Keith Stringer

> You have offered much solace for our grief by [saying] ... that although
> death has ... borne away your kindred in these parts, we are united
> together perpetually, God willing, by the tie of indissoluble affection: we
> are bound to thank your dear highness, beyond what is due for other
> courtesies and kindnesses, in that you value our kinship, and ... much
> good may yet come to pass through ... the daughter of your niece, the
> daughter, too, of our beloved [daughter], the late queen of Norway, who
> is now our heir-apparent.[1]

It was thus that in April 1284 Alexander III of Scotland acknowledged
Edward I's condolences on the death of the last of his three children. This
might seem an oddly cosy starting-point. After all, less than twelve years later
Scotland and England embarked on a nationalistic war of endurance that
would embitter Anglo-Scottish relations for the next three centuries. Yet the
outbreak of the Wars of Independence must be seen for what it was: not the
inevitable result of deep-seated incompatibilities, but the product of a rapid
and profound deterioration in relations shaped by the particular conjuncture
of the extinction of the ancient Scottish royal line and Edward I's determined
assault on Scottish liberties as he chose to disregard the established conventions of Anglo-Scottish diplomacy and take full advantage of Scotland's
unexpected and acute misfortunes. The first task, therefore, is to get away
from what happened in 1296 by identifying and exploring those themes of
convergence which, had the Scottish heiress, Margaret 'the Maid of Norway',
lived long enough, might have helped to produce an entirely different
outcome.

The history of Anglo-Scottish relations between December 1217 and March
1296 is a record of unbroken peace, in part because hostilities had become too
risky for cautious rulers to contemplate – if the war of 1215–17 had ended

---

[1] *Anglo-Scottish Relations 1174–1328: Some Selected Documents*, ed. E. L. G. Stones (2nd edn,
Oxford, 1970), no. 13.

badly for the Scots, in 1216 (albeit when England seethed with rebellion) even the Yorkshire barons had paid homage to Alexander II, and a Scottish force had marched as far south as Dover. But this lengthy peace was not so much a precarious equilibrium as a sturdy *modus vivendi*. Tensions were never wholly eradicated; yet unless we seek to read history backwards from the 1290s, relations were probably as intimate and productive as relations between medieval states could ever become. Alexander II's marriage to Henry III's sister in 1221 paved the way for a definitive solution to the problem of northern England, for long the main stumbling-block to Anglo-Scottish harmony, and English claims to the overlordship of Scotland had only an occasional airing. Superficially, the Treaty of York (1237), by which Alexander II renounced all claims to the northern English counties for a promise of lands worth £200 annually, appears primarily to have benefited England. But of central importance was its form as an amicable compromise between equals, one which – in contrast to William the Lion's involuntary submissions to the English Crown – took account of Scottish feelings by its 'implicit acceptance' of Scotland's separate status as an independent kingdom.[2] Accord was cemented in 1251 by Alexander III's marriage to Henry III's daughter, celebrated on a prodigiously extravagant scale,[3] and while the honeyed phrases of diplomatic correspondence can mislead, there is no gainsaying the blossoming affection between the two royal families. Alexander III's minority (1249–60) was a critical period. It brought clear openings for English diplomacy to exploit, and the view (of a Scottish historian) that Henry III's machinations were those of 'an innocent mischief-maker' may be overly indulgent.[4] Nevertheless, though anxious to influence the membership and policies of the young king's council, Henry refrained from hard-nosed interventions, and none of the noble factions involved in the minority power struggles was pushed irrevocably into an anti-English stance. Equally striking is how speedily and effectively peace-keeping mechanisms were employed whenever relations were jeopardised. Even when in 1244 hostilities seemed imminent, the crisis was quickly defused and both armies 'returned home with rejoicing'.[5] It was a sign of the times that nobles in the Borders began to build non-defensive hall-houses; that in 1251 the clerk of works at York castle was a Scot; that Carlisle castle was semi-ruinous by 1256, and still 'greatly dilapidated' in the 1280s.[6] This was a world in which peace

[2] G. W. S. Barrow, *Kingship and Unity: Scotland 1000–1306* (2nd edn, Edinburgh, 1989), pp. 150–1.

[3] K. Staniland, 'The nuptials of Alexander III of Scotland and Margaret Plantagenet', *Nottingham Medieval Studies*, xxx (1986).

[4] A. A. M. Duncan, *Scotland: The Making of the Kingdom* (Edinburgh, 1975), p. 568.

[5] *Chronicon de Lanercost* (Maitland Club, Edinburgh, 1839), p. 51.

[6] P. Dixon, 'From hall to tower: the change in seigneurial houses on the Anglo-Scottish Border after c.1250', in P. R. Coss and S. D. Lloyd (eds.), *Thirteenth Century England IV: Proceedings of the Newcastle-upon-Tyne Conference 1991* (Woodbridge, 1992), pp. 87–96; *Calendar of Documents relating to Scotland*, ed. J. Bain et al. (Edinburgh, 1881–1986), i, no. 1857; M. R. McCarthy, H. R. T. Summerson and R. G. Annis, *Carlisle Castle: A Survey and Documentary History* (Historic Buildings and Monuments Commission for England, 1990), pp. 128–32.

had become the norm and neither government wanted or expected war.

Cordial relations, moreover, were not merely a matter of royal diplomacy. In itself, peaceful coexistence ensured that the imperialist 'anti-Celtic' English culture, highlighted by John Gillingham and Rees Davies,[7] was relatively speaking much less scornful of the Scots, at any rate until the 1290s. More importantly, unlike native Wales and Ireland, Scotland had already begun to participate vigorously in the institutional, economic and socio-cultural developments reshaping Europe into an 'increasingly homogeneous society'.[8] Thus, however wide the perceived gulf between the English community and the Welsh and Irish peoples, Scotland's different trajectory was bringing all but its remotest parts into fuller correspondence with England in language, customs and practices.

In particular, close kinship between the royal houses was underpinned by ties between the two aristocracies, and, through marriage, inheritance and royal patronage, the Anglo-Scottish nexus came to be more elaborately woven than it had ever been in the past.[9] It embraced English newcomers to Scotland like the earl of Pembroke (lord of Haddington) and the de Umfravilles (earls of Angus); the native earls of Atholl (lord of Chilham), Dunbar (lords of Beanley) and others besides; Anglo-Norman families long established north of the Tweed such as the Lovels (lords of Hawick and Castle Cary); and cadets of the Scottish royal house itself (earls of Huntingdon and Chester). Statistically, no fewer than nine Scottish earldoms and about half of Scotland's 'provincial lordships' were held at some stage between 1200 and 1296 by lords who were also English landowners. Put another way, one in three English earldoms and one in five English baronies (or shares of them) then went together with Scottish estates, though not always for long periods. Few 'cross-Border' magnates had dominant positions in both countries, and many families did not expand from one kingdom to the other. But even these bald figures graphically illustrate that Anglo-Scottish landholders formed a very significant body among Scotland's higher nobility. Unsurprisingly, cross-frontier bonds were most pronounced in southern Scotland and the far north of England, yet overall they extended from the Great Glen to the Channel Islands, and were strikingly multi-layered, for they also involved lesser nobles, burgesses, religious corporations, some bishops and numerous lesser churchmen. At least forty religious houses, for example, engaged in property-owning across the thirteenth-century Border, sometimes on a substantial scale. Seventeen were

[7] See most recently the essay by J. Gillingham, 'Foundations of a disunited kingdom', above, ch. 4; and R. R. Davies, 'The English state and the "Celtic" peoples 1100–1400', *Journal of Historical Sociology*, vi (1993).

[8] R. Bartlett, *The Making of Europe: Conquest, Colonization and Cultural Change 950–1350* (London, 1993), p. 3.

[9] This paragraph and the next are based on K. J. Stringer, *Earl David of Huntingdon, 1152–1219: A Study in Anglo-Scottish History* (Edinburgh, 1985), especially ch. 9; and K. J. Stringer, 'Identities in thirteenth-century England: frontier society in the far North', in C. Bjørn, A. Grant and K. J. Stringer (eds.), *Social and Political Identities in Western History* (Copenhagen, 1994).

Scottish, with interests scattered throughout northern England and the Midlands; and twenty-three were English, including Bromholm Priory (Norfolk), Sempringham Priory (Lincolnshire) and, more remarkably, the tiny hospital of Brackley (Northamptonshire), which took a special interest in its valuable Perthshire assets. On another level, in the 1260s native-born Englishmen held the bishoprics of Aberdeen, Dunblane, Glasgow and the Isles. Nor was the traffic all one way. On the unanimous election to Durham of William Stichill in 1226, Henry III had had the election quashed, protesting how 'perilous it would be for a Scotsman to control the bishopric, especially because of its nearness to Scotland'.[10] By 1260, however, attitudes had changed, and there was no royal dissent when Durham passed in that year to Robert Stichill.

All in all, this takes us a long way from the intense and persistent opposition of nationalities characteristic of Anglo-Scottish relations in the later Middle Ages. In the thirteenth century, no less than today, identities are not reducible to hard-and-fast definitions. Alan of Galloway (d. 1234) had no difficulty in seeing himself as a Gaelic chieftain, the constable of Scotland and a great Scottish feudal magnate, a highly favoured ally in 1212–15 of King John (whom he counselled to grant Magna Carta), the son and husband of Anglo-Norman noblewomen, and a knight of the English shires, who held manors in Yorkshire and Rutland, endowed St Andrew's Priory at Northampton (his father's burial-place), and went on pilgrimage to Canterbury.[11] Or, consider the transnational attachments and loyalties of the soldier-diplomat, John de Vescy of Alnwick (d. 1289). A prominent English war captain and negotiator for Edward I with the European courts, he was also William the Lion's great-grandson, lord of the regality of Sprouston (Roxburghshire), and a commander of the army sent by Alexander III to the Isle of Man in 1275. Another leader of this expedition was John Comyn, lord of the Highland fastnesses of Badenoch and Lochaber, justiciar of Galloway, a powerful near-neighbour of de Vescy in Northumberland, and a former member of the English royal household who, with other magnates of Scotland, had brought a vast force of Scottish infantry to fight for Henry III at the battle of Lewes (1264).

While such pluralism deserves more recognition and study, it would be entirely wrong to suggest that it entailed the denial of English or Scots identity. In fact, many cross-Border proprietors had predominantly Scottish careers and associations, and in a crisis they would normally wish to take the Scottish side. But before protracted war inflamed national differences, it was almost taken for granted that individuals could regard themselves as loyal

---

[10] *Rotuli Litterarum Clausarum in Turri Londinensi asservati*, ed. T. D. Hardy (Record Commission, 1833–4), ii, p. 207.

[11] See most recently K. J. Stringer, 'Periphery and core in thirteenth-century Scotland: Alan son of Roland, lord of Galloway and constable of Scotland', in A. Grant and K. J. Stringer (eds.), *Medieval Scotland: Crown, Lordship and Community. Essays presented to G. W. S. Barrow* (Edinburgh, 1993).

subjects of each king, move freely in both societies, and generally benefit from their experiences. Especially among the greater nobles, the pattern of family ties and landholding criss-crossing the national boundary became very finely textured, and it brought the political elites into a degree of common fellowship not to be seen again until the emergence of a 'new British upper class' after 1707. This gradual melding was in part a natural consequence of the great change in direction set in train by David I (1124–53): the introduction of a feudalised society by the Scots kings and their Anglo-Norman followers, whose 'settlement greatly reinforced the Middle English elements in Scots speech and culture, and had a decisive effect upon the texture of Scottish society as a whole'.[12] But it was also the product of sustained good neighbourliness between adjacent kingdoms, and striking testimony in itself to 'an easy rapport and fruitful exchange between the two communities'.[13]

That is part of the essential backdrop to the events immediately following Alexander III's untimely death. There is no reason to doubt a later chronicler's statement that in 1286 the Scots specifically requested Edward I's help in their leaderless condition; and it is easy to see why the planned marriage between Margaret of Norway and Edward of Caernarfon (the future Edward II) was widely welcomed. What might have happened had the marriage taken place and children issued from it is an inescapable question. In 1290 no deep thought was apparently given to the long-term implications, and there are other grounds for concluding that the negotiations were flawed.[14] But if we take our lead from studies of the later successes, and failures, of composite monarchies,[15] the underlying conditions were arguably more favourable to an ultimate union of the realms than has sometimes been supposed. There existed the obvious structural advantages not only of territorial contiguity and institutional similarities, but also of 'conformity' in terms, after all, of extensive social interpenetration. Against this has to be balanced, among other considerations, the fact that Edward I was unwisely attempting to force matters even before Margaret died.[16] But he was not yet pushing *too* hard, and it might be hazarded that, compared to the situation in 1603, the chances of going on to surmount the intrinsic difficulties of regnal unions were rather stronger, if only because of the absence of centuries of bitter strife. Any unifying programme would need to soothe Scottish anxieties about English domination. But given the common ground already established in the Anglo-

---

[12] G. W. S. Barrow, *The Anglo-Norman Era in Scottish History* (Oxford, 1980), p. 117.

[13] R. R. Davies, 'The failure of the first British empire? England's relations with Ireland, Scotland and Wales 1066–1500', in N. Saul (ed.), *England in Europe 1066–1453* (London, 1994), p. 126.

[14] M. Prestwich, 'Edward I and the Maid of Norway', *Scottish Historical Review*, lxix (1990).

[15] For a recent overview, see J. Robertson, 'Empire and union: two concepts of the early modern European political order', in J. Robertson (ed.), *A Union For Empire: Political Thought and the British Union of 1707* (Cambridge, 1995).

[16] G. W. S. Barrow, 'A kingdom in crisis: Scotland and the Maid of Norway', *Scottish Historical Review*, lxix (1990), pp. 132–6.

Scottish relationship, an eventual effective union, even if it fell far short of the kind of 'perfect union' to which King James would aspire, might have held firm. In the meantime, England would have been spared having to pour resources into the exhausting Scottish wars, and could possibly have devoted them instead to a redoubling of its effort in Ireland, with the added advantage of Scottish support.[17] To pursue this line of thought, it seems that, for a fleeting moment, the creation of a 'united kingdom' was potentially realisable much earlier than was actually the case.

But the Maid of Norway's premature death brings us back to the real world. Crucially, the Scottish negotiators had considered very carefully what the 1290 alliance should entail in the short term. Incorporation was not on their agenda, and the guarantees of Scottish independence then written into the Treaty of Birgham left Scotland with its own Church, Parliament, legal system and administrative autonomy. Thus Birgham envisaged unity *and* equality – a dynastic alliance of England and Scotland, each 'ruled separately though in harmony by a king and queen respectively, whose sovereignties would remain distinct'.[18]

So here were two good neighbours prepared to co-operate to a striking degree. But another cardinal aspect of the relationship was that between them there existed a formal parity of status which, in 1290, even Edward I conceded; and this constitutional antithesis supplies a powerful alternative model to that of convergence. Historians have over the past thirty years produced a stream of studies making us more aware of the long continuity of 'Scotland' as a political community, its growing governmental, economic and military power, and the other central features which made the Scottish realm one of the most effective medium-sized states of the high Middle Ages. So extensive is this literature that it is quite impossible to do justice to it here.[19] We have, however, been repeatedly and forcibly reminded that the most apt comparison is provided not by the vulnerable and unstable native power-structures of Wales and Ireland, but rather by the English polity itself.[20] The essential reason for this is that during the twelfth and thirteenth centuries the processes of Normanisation (or anglicisation) followed a very different path

---

[17] Co-ordinated Anglo-Scottish action in Ireland was not unprecedented. See especially Stringer, 'Periphery and core', pp. 85ff.

[18] G. W. S. Barrow, *Robert Bruce and the Community of the Realm of Scotland* (3rd edn, Edinburgh, 1988), p. 28; followed in Prestwich, 'Edward I and the Maid of Norway', p. 172.

[19] The fundamental general studies are Duncan, *Making of the Kingdom*, Barrow, *Anglo-Norman Era*, and Barrow, *Kingship and Unity*. Among the most recent publications are: H. L. MacQueen, *Common Law and Feudal Society in Medieval Scotland* (Edinburgh, 1993); B. T. Hudson, *Kings of Celtic Scotland* (Westport, Connecticut, 1994); and essays in the following collections: N. H. Reid (ed.), *Scotland in the Reign of Alexander III 1249–1286* (Edinburgh, 1990); G. W. S. Barrow, *Scotland and its Neighbours in the Middle Ages* (London, 1992); Grant and Stringer, *Medieval Scotland*; C. Bjørn, A. Grant and K. J. Stringer (eds.), *Nations, Nationalism and Patriotism in the European Past* (Copenhagen, 1994).

[20] A point readily conceded by Welsh and Irish historians: cf. R. R. Davies, *Conquest, Coexistence and Change: Wales 1063–1415* (Oxford, 1987), pp. 269–70; R. Frame, *Colonial Ireland, 1169–1369* (Dublin, 1981), p. 117.

from that taken in the rest of the 'Celtic fringe', for the Scots kings had already established a sufficiently powerful and unitary monarchy to ensure that change operated in their interests, not against them. Scotland still lacked the vast resources possessed by the English Crown; its government remained less complex and deeply dependent on co-operation with the nobility; and it is increasingly clear that there was considerable interaction between Gaelic tradition and 'modernisation'. But the result was a European-style monarchy, and one obvious way forward is to look more closely at thirteenth-century perceptions of Scotland as a kingdom, in the Treaty of Birgham's terminology, 'separated ... and free in itself, without subjection to the English realm'.

Often quoted is the resounding defence of Scotland's political autonomy attributed to Alexander III in 1278 – 'No-one has a right to homage for my kingdom save God alone.' He needed no reminding that, save between 1174 and 1189, the kings of Scots had never explicitly acknowledged the feudal subjection of Scotland to England, and the maturity of Scottish constitutionalism was why Edward I's assertion of superior lordship from 1291 proved to be so explosive. Earlier, sustained English lobbying had blocked papal permission for the Scots king to be anointed and crowned on his inauguration; undaunted, the Scots emphasised the dignity and prestige of their kingship by astute manipulation of the symbols and motifs of royalty.[21] Yet it is not the Scottish monarchy's determination to 'keep up with the Plantagenets'[22] which is really striking so much as how far the English Crown, for all its ingrained assumptions of political pre-eminence, had been prepared to accept that Scotland was *de facto* a sovereign entity. In brief, it accorded the Scots kings a very different status from that of the provincial kings of Wales and Ireland, whose position was drastically undermined by the 'ever more monopolistic authority' of the English state.[23] Whereas English attitudes and ambitions *vis-à-vis* the Welsh and Irish became increasingly uncompromising, Anglo-Scottish politics were perceived on both sides as conforming in essence to the niceties of diplomacy between national kingdoms. On the rare instances when claims to English overlordship were rehearsed (1235, 1251, 1278), they were speedily dropped after predictably vigorous Scottish ripostes, and we are left to conclude that they were not so much ends in themselves as *pièces d'occasion* devised to gain some diplomatic leverage.[24] Nor was Henry III merely dissembling when he repeatedly reassured Alexander III of his respect for the honour and liberties of Scotland, and in 1258 urged the new Scottish council to maintain Alexander's royal dignity and uphold the laws and customs of the realm.[25]

---

[21] A fine instance is Alexander III's small seal of minority, replete with the emblems of sovereignty, including a foliated sceptre and a crown: G. G. Simpson, 'Kingship in miniature: a seal of minority of Alexander III, 1249–1257', in Grant and Stringer, *Medieval Scotland*.

[22] Barrow, *Scotland and its Neighbours*, p. 35.

[23] R. Frame, *The Political Development of the British Isles 1100–1400* (Oxford, 1990), p. 98.

[24] Duncan, *Making of the Kingdom*, pp. 536–7, 591.

[25] *Cal. Docs. Scot.*, i, nos. 1995, 2002, 2004, 2040; *Anglo-Scottish Relations*, ed. Stones, nos. 10, 11.

In all this, the English Crown, however reluctantly, was in effect acknowledging the existence of a viable state able to sustain an alternative lordship to its own – something that did not exist in Wales or Ireland. There was no absolute segregation of jurisdictions; but it was accepted that such fuzziness as occurred was very limited, and by no means exclusively to Scotland's prejudice. When in 1262 a case came before the Bedford assizes concerning an estate in Scotland, the defendants insisted they were not obliged to answer in an English court; and in 1277 it was Edward I's royal dignity that had to be defended when the earl of Buchan initiated litigation over English lands in the Scottish courts.[26] Nowhere was the reality of Scotland's separate sovereign status more evident than at the Border itself – 'for most of the middle ages the only formally constituted, internationally defined land frontier in Britain'.[27] There, each kingdom came up against the limits to its territorial sovereignty in an exceptionally precise manner for a boundary between medieval states. Any 'slippage' normally worked to the Scots' advantage, as at Canonbie and Kirkandrews-on-Esk in the western Borders; and the consternation of Edward I's judges can easily be imagined when English jurors at Newcastle in 1279 solemnly informed them that Alexander III's highly privileged liberty of Tynedale (west Northumberland) lay 'outside the kingdom of England in the kingdom of Scotland'.[28] Certainly, the sheriff of Northumberland was taught a swift lesson when in 1290 he had the impertinence to arrive in Scotland demanding to survey the de Vescy barony of Sprouston: *rex est imperator in regno suo*.[29] It follows that men like John de Vescy were playing an entirely different game from that of English lords who held Welsh or Irish lands and remained a colonial aristocracy subject to the English Crown. Socially the Border was permeable. But time and again we are reminded of Scotland's constitutional separateness from England, of distinct conceptions of sovereignty and law, and of the fact that it would be wholly inappropriate to characterise thirteenth-century Anglo-Scottish relations in terms of the 'core-colony' phraseology with which England's relationship with Wales and Ireland is conventionally addressed.

Nevertheless, from a Scottish standpoint it cannot help but be said that, despite the magisterial achievements of the 'new British history', centre-periphery relations in medieval Britain still tend to be treated in an overly anglocentric way. Further consideration of the capacity and character of Scottish rule might bring matters into clearer focus. The new feudalism of

[26] *Cal. Docs. Scot.*, i, no. 2302; ii, nos. 91–2.

[27] G. W. S. Barrow, 'The Anglo-Scottish Border: growth and structure in the Middle Ages', in W. Haubrichs and R. Schneider (eds.), *Grenzen und Grenzregionen: Frontières et régions frontalières: Borders and Border Regions* (Saarbrücken, 1994), p. 209.

[28] G. W. S. Barrow, *The Kingdom of the Scots* (London, 1973), pp. 145–6; Stringer, 'Identities in thirteenth-century England', p. 47. The bishopric of Galloway (Whithorn) remained formally within the York province until 1355; but, for the Scots king's right of patronage, see R. D. Oram, 'In obedience and reverence: Whithorn and York c.1128–c.1250', *Innes Review*, xlii (1991), pp. 96–8.

[29] He was arrested immediately on crossing the Border and imprisoned in Roxburgh castle: Barrow, 'Kingdom in crisis', pp. 131–2.

twelfth-century Scotland had impacted primarily on the east-coast Lowlands, leaving a vast, strongly Norse-Gaelic outer zone where regional potentates governed their domains with considerable autonomy and even regal authority. Thus, around the year 1200 the problems of the far North and the western Highlands and Islands from Edinburgh's viewpoint were akin to those of Wales and Ireland as perceived from Westminster.[30] Indeed, they were arguably more daunting. The awesome military and naval power of the great Hebridean sea-lords raised the prospect of 'a self-sustaining kingdom … from Man to the Butt of Lewis and encompassing a considerable chunk of the western seaboard';[31] and from about 1220 the Scots had to contend with another major player in North Atlantic affairs, the resurgent Norwegian monarchy. Nonetheless, the two Alexanders presided over one of the most successful programmes of territorial consolidation and expansion to be seen in the British Isles since the Norman Conquest itself. Ross and Caithness had been pacified by the early 1230s; the 'independence' of Galloway, already in fact a shadow of its former self, was suppressed in 1235; and royal dominance over mainland Argyll had been achieved by the 1250s. Strikingly, so skilled had the Scots kings become in co-opting local support that their opponents in the far North and Galloway had depended on Irish and Hebridean allies to make a fight of it; and when the struggle with Norway for supremacy in the Western Isles climaxed in 1263, Hebridean chiefs lined up to do battle on either side – a key reason why King Hakon's offensive, itself an abysmal failure, was followed in 1266 by the outright transfer of sovereignty over Man and the Isles from Norway to Scotland.

Above all, it is this substantial extension of Scottish royal power, a phenomenon as impressive and important as Scotland's later ability to withstand English aggression, which suggests how thirteenth-century Scotland might best be located in British history. It is generally assumed that from the tenth century England was the supreme, if not the only, expansionist power in the British Isles. But while English resources were greatly superior, one of the most fundamental – if inconvenient – points about Britain's 'medieval foundations' is that there were *two* powerful core areas seeking to absorb peripheral regions. In the Scottish case, territorial expansion had been a leading motif since the emergence of the original kingdom of Alba or 'Scotland' (between the Forth and the Spey) by the end of the ninth century. Moreover, the consolidation of 'greater Scotland' under the Alexanders presents a very clear contrast to the fortunes of English expansionism under Henry III, notably in Ireland where 'the periphery … proved decisively resistant to the impact of the core'.[32] Nor should it be forgotten that Man's

---

[30] Cf. D. Broun, 'Defining Scotland and the Scots before the Wars of Independence', in *Nationalism and Identity: The Search for Scotland* (Association of Scottish Historical Studies, 1994).

[31] E. J. Cowan, 'Norwegian sunset – Scottish dawn: Hakon IV and Alexander III', in Reid, *Alexander III*, p. 125.

[32] R. Frame, 'King Henry III and Ireland: the shaping of a peripheral lordship', in Coss and Lloyd, *Thirteenth Century England IV*, p. 201.

annexation to Scotland, symbolised by Alexander III's grant of Holy Trinity church in Ramsey to Whithorn Priory,[33] was a direct check to English ambitions, given Henry III's well-attested designs to bring Man within his orbit.

It was in fact the very 'peripheral' position of Scotland that now helped to make it such a pivotal force north of St George's Channel, and the remote Westminster 'core' seem less dynamic. Further explanation of this contrast reveals some very instructive differences between the nature of Scottish and English kingship. Important as it was, too much can possibly be made of the native Scottish monarchy's greater store of 'legitimacy'. How power was projected and perceived was also a matter of royal personality, policy and judgement, and the Plantagenets gained a reputation as oppressors even of their English subjects. But Scottish kingship, for all its 'modernity', was by no means typically English in intensity and style. Lacking the English Crown's superior bureaucracy and coercive might, it was more sensitive to the need for effective co-operation with 'political society'. And, being more conscious of the limits to state power, it therefore avoided the humiliations that can often flow from hegemonic ambitions.

Now, Henry III's expansionist thrusts in Ireland faltered partly because of the political unrest in England provoked by royal intrusiveness, and partly because of Irish resistance led by the O'Briens and O'Connors, who knew that the only alternative was their ruin. Yet the Scottish east-coast heartland never disintegrated through resistance to royal power and demands – by comparison with the instability of English national politics in the 1250s and 1260s, even the struggles of Alexander III's minority were remarkably low key. As for relations between Scotland's feudalised core and its outer reaches, any account which fails to give due weight to tension and conflict as well as to peaceful integrative processes would be gravely distorted.[34] But the fact remains that, although tracts of the North and West went to a 'colonial' baronage, these were still areas where individual Norse-Gaelic notables sought and often found accommodation with the new order, and thus possessed in some measure the ability to control and direct the processes of change within their own communities.

In this critical respect, the difference between contemporary Scottish and English approaches to state-making could scarcely have been more stark. The increasingly bureaucratic and standardising modes of English governance in Wales and, more especially, in Ireland made 'the categorization of peoples ... sharper and palpably more discriminating'.[35] But that did not happen in thirteenth-century Scotland. Scotland was like Wales and Ireland in that an

---

[33] Huntington Library, San Marino, California, MS Ellesmere 993.

[34] R. A. McDonald, 'Kings and Princes in Scotland: Aristocratic Interactions in the Anglo-Norman Era' (Guelph University Ph.D. thesis, 1993), focuses on 'Celtic reaction'.

[35] R. R. Davies, *Domination and Conquest: The Experience of Ireland, Scotland and Wales 1100–1300* (Cambridge, 1990), p. 116.

Anglo-Norman nobility had hurried along modernisation and expansion. Yet it was *unlike* Wales and Ireland in that the newcomers to Scotland not only came mainly by invitation but strengthened state power the more effectively because they were never permitted to establish an institutionalised political and cultural primacy. Instead, the deepening of royal control rested above all on the acceptance of difference and 'otherness', and on a productive interaction between feudal and Celtic societies. The Lowlands had already seen a remarkable cultural syncretism, epitomised by the blending of native and incoming elites into a mixed Gaelic-Anglo-Norman aristocracy harnessed to the king's service. In the thirteenth century, this court nobility – notably the Comyns, Fifes, Murrays and Stewarts – carried royal influence much farther afield; yet, at the same time, the Scottish political community was extended to embrace leading northern and west-coast families as part of the governing class. The prominence of accommodation and assimilation, as opposed to exclusion and alienation, is underlined by the Treaty of Perth (1266), which expressly safeguarded the possessions of the western sea-lords and their kin, regardless of past loyalties, and gave them full legal status under Scots law, itself an amalgam of Gaelic and Anglo-Norman practice.[36] Their potency is vividly shown by the career of the former Norwegian client Ewen MacDougall of Argyll, a 'vigorous and handsome knight', a mainstay against King Hakon in 1263, and tied (by his daughter's marriages) to the Strathearns and Abernethies; or that of his son, significantly named Alexander, who attended Parliaments and councils as a baron of Scotland, married a Comyn, and became royal governor in Skye, Lorn and Kintyre.[37] These men and others like them, able to straddle two worlds without deep feelings of disadvantage in either, were vital intermediaries between the Gaelic kin-based society and the kingdom's core. They themselves became leading actors in the process of expansion, and for a full generation after 1266 what is remarkable is how little rather than how much of a 'problem' even the far-flung West presented.

No doubt there will never be an agreed answer to the question: How united was Scotland on the eve of the Wars of Independence? But once we reject the false notion that the only effective form of medieval government was a uniformist and highly demanding one, it is hard not to take a positive view of Scottish state-building, however much its triumphs were later qualified by the strains of protracted international war. It was directed by 'feudal' kings who nevertheless drew heavily on the rituals and traditions of Celtic rulership;[38] and the hybridity of the monarchy was reflected nationally

---

[36] W. D. H. Sellar, 'Celtic law and Scots law: survival and integration', *Scottish Studies*, xxix (1989).

[37] A. A. M. Duncan and A. L. Brown, 'Argyll and the Isles in the earlier Middle Ages', *Proceedings of the Society of Antiquaries of Scotland*, xc (1956–7), pp. 211–17; J. B. Paul, *The Scots Peerage* (Edinburgh, 1904–14), viii, pp. 246–7.

[38] See especially J. Bannerman, 'The king's poet and the inauguration of Alexander III', *Scottish Historical Review*, lxviii (1989).

in hybrid legal, political and social structures, all of which powerfully reinforced a common sense of Scottishness, despite the strength of local, regional and, indeed, cosmopolitan ties. As Geoffrey Barrow has authoritatively put it:

> the kingdom of Scotland, the territory which the king ruled, in which his writs and laws were current, from which he levied his taxes and services ... was ... a unifying concept, not only geographically, bringing together east and west, Lowlands and Highlands ... but also culturally and racially, for the sense of *regnum Scotie* was identical for the native population and the Anglo-Continental incomers alike.[39]

So expansion on the Scottish model stood for a different type of medieval state-making from that of the more 'advanced' English polity in Wales and Ireland. And in Scotland, at least from the standpoint of 1280, it must have seemed that the absorption of the periphery had been more successfully achieved – which reminds us that imperialist policies were not necessarily the most effective means of realising state goals.

This section comes finally to one of Robin Frame's key points earlier in this volume: that a dynastic union between England and Scotland was possible, but that aggressive English colonial strategies had much less prospect of success. The English saw the Wars of Independence not as a collision between two unitary, European-style kingdoms but as a dispute in which contumacious vassals were defying their lawful suzerain.[40] In reality, the scale, intensity and course of the conflict can be understood only by recognising that thirteenth-century Britain contained not one but *two* dominant states or 'superpowers'. England was of course unrivalled in size and wealth; but Alexander III's Scotland, as Rees Davies has recently underscored, exhibited similar degrees of regnal solidity and an equivalent 'match between people and polity'.[41] When the English invaded in 1296, therefore, conquest was attempted on a quite different scale from what had been achieved (over two centuries) in Wales and Ireland. Even then, the tide had already turned against English advances into the Irish heartland; and in north Wales in 1277–83 it had taken a vast mobilisation of state resources to crush the remnants of the native polity. On this argument, it is little wonder that when the Edwards went on to try to conquer Scotland ultimate victory eluded them.

[39] Barrow, *Anglo-Norman Era*, p. 155.
[40] M. Prestwich, 'England and Scotland during the Wars of Independence', in M. Jones and M. Vale (eds.), *England and Her Neighbours, 1066–1453: Essays in Honour of Pierre Chaplais* (London, 1989).
[41] R. R. Davies, 'The peoples of Britain and Ireland 1100–1400: I. Identities', *Transactions of the Royal Historical Society*, 6th ser., iv (1994), p. 19.

Late medieval contributions
Alexander Grant

The fourteenth and fifteenth centuries are an awkward era for the student of 'British history'. In later periods, the successive British Unions provide an essential focus for historical discourse, while in the earlier Middle Ages the seemingly inexorable spread of English power throughout the archipelago is the obvious theme. As Rees Davies and Robin Frame have demonstrated, the experience of Ireland, Scotland and Wales from 1100 to 1300 appears to be one of steadily increasing domination and outright conquest at English hands – though Keith Stringer's analysis (above) shows that with Scotland appearances can be deceptive. In the first half of the fourteenth century, however, the Edwardian juggernaut was halted by the Scots. They resisted English take-over, and by the fifteenth century Anglo-Scottish relations had reverted into being those between two neighbouring, but separate and independent, countries. Thus, if the thirteenth century is the '"British" century *par excellence*',[42] the fourteenth and the fifteenth centuries are the least obviously 'British' of any in the archipelago's history.

Nevertheless, at the beginning of the fourteenth century 'Ireland, Scotland and Wales were taking their due place under what was, ultimately, a single and, increasingly, a uniform pattern of governance ... The day of a truly effective British monarchy ... seemed imminent.'[43] So, if Edward I's conquest of Scotland had succeeded, we would nowadays be contemplating a very different sort of 'British history'. Thus that old question, 'Why did the English fail to conquer Scotland?', is as vital for historians of Britain as a whole as it is for historians of Scotland *per se*; and, although this is not the place to try to answer it in depth, some discussion of it is clearly necessary.

To begin with, Britain's geography militated against a full-scale English military conquest of Scotland. The narrow Anglo-Scottish frontier meant that (in contrast to Wales) individual regions could not be isolated and dealt with piecemeal. Only the South was directly accessible to English armies; Scotland north of the Forth was mostly beyond their reach. Edward I and Edward III outdid their predecessors in leading armies beyond the Forth, but they did not wage lengthy campaigns there. Yet unless the North were conquered, Scottish resistance could not be crushed.

Moreover, military conquest was not simply a matter of invading and winning battles; it also required effective garrisoning. To maintain permanent armies of occupation in Scotland, however, would have been prohibitively expensive. English garrisons in Scottish castles rarely totalled more than 1,000 men overall, and often many fewer; most served in the major castles of southern Scotland, and north of the Forth they were thinly spread. It is not

[42] R. R. Davies (ed.), *The British Isles 1100–1500: Comparisons, Contrasts and Connections* (Edinburgh, 1988), 'Introduction', p. 2.
[43] R. R. Davies, 'In praise of British History', in Davies, *British Isles 1100–1500*, pp. 22–3.

surprising that, whenever Scottish resistance was active, most strongholds other than the main southern castles were usually recaptured fairly quickly.[44]

An alternative was to parcel the conquered territory out to loyal followers – as William I had done in post-Conquest England. Edward I attempted that, but with little success. In 1066 the Anglo-Saxon landowners had been devastated by battles and flight, and the local communities had accepted new Norman landlords. But the early fourteenth-century Scottish landowning class mostly survived the military defeats; and the development of hereditary feudal landholding had probably established close ties between 'rightful lords' and local communities which did not permit easy expropriation. Englishmen given property in Scotland found it unrewarding, while expropriated Scots fought to recover their lands – for example James Douglas, who joined the Bruce cause in 1307 to regain his confiscated inheritance.[45]

Had Scotland been like Wales and Ireland, military conquest might have taken place in another way. Much of the English conquest in Wales and Ireland was not royal but private, achieved by Anglo-Norman *conquistadores* during the twelfth and thirteenth centuries. In Wales their descendants – the Welsh Marchers – were crucial to the final Edwardian conquest; in Ireland their descendants – the 'middle nation' – defended the English colony against Edward Bruce's invasion in 1315–18. Twelfth- and thirteenth-century Scotland had also experienced widespread Anglo-Norman settlement. But Scotland's 'Normans' did not impose English royal authority; their 'invasion' was peaceful, they worked for the Scottish Crown, and they gave it their allegiance. So, when Edward I tried to conquer Scotland, their descendants did not support him, as happened, *mutatis mutandis*, in Wales; instead, many provided essential leadership for the cause of Scottish independence.

That said, Scotland's elites were not consistently patriotic throughout the Wars of Independence. Almost everyone of any importance submitted at least once and often several times, while many collaborated actively. Submissions and collaboration were vital to the kings of England. If Scotland could not be conquered militarily, then they were the only way of bringing Scotland under control – and, at times, that seemed to be happening. The Scottish nobility has therefore been condemned as cowardly and unpatriotic. But resistance and collaboration can be viewed too starkly. After all, wherever the Germans were victorious during the Second World War, submissions and collaboration were rife, despite the strength of modern nationalism; so we should not be surprised that, faced by 'force and violence which cannot be resisted',[46] many

[44] M. Prestwich, *War, Politics and Finance under Edward I* (London, 1972), pp. 111–12; A. A. M. Duncan, 'The War of the Scots, 1306–1323', *Transactions of the Royal Historical Society*, 6th ser., ii (1992), pp. 143–4.

[45] M. Prestwich, 'Colonial Scotland: the English in Scotland under Edward I', in R. A. Mason (ed.), *Scotland and England, 1286–1815* (Edinburgh, 1987), pp. 9–15; Duncan, 'War of the Scots', p. 140; S. Vatjunker, 'A Study in the Career of Sir James Douglas: The Historical Record versus Barbour's Bruce' (Aberdeen University Ph.D. thesis, 1992), ch. 1.

[46] *Acts of the Parliaments of Scotland*, ed. T. Thomson and C. Innes (Edinburgh, 1814–75), i, p. 460.

fourteenth-century Scots surrendered and worked for the English. Yet the main point is that the submissions and collaboration rarely lasted for any length of time. Once immediate English pressure had been removed – which, failing permanent armies of occupation, was bound to happen sooner or later – Scottish revolt invariably broke out again.

At any rate, to see the submissions and revolts in terms of Scottish inconsistency is to look at them the wrong way round. The issue should really be the English kings' failure to gain lasting submissions and reliable loyalty throughout Scotland. And the main reason is surely that persuasion, not 'force and violence', was needed to make the Scottish elite permanently renounce its long-established loyalty to the Scottish Crown. But the English kings, especially Edward I, preferred to bully and threaten rather than to cajole. Even in 1304–6, when Scotland was defeated and Edward was being conciliatory, he merely allowed his erstwhile opponents to buy back their lands; there were no rewards and no bribes for the Scots,[47] because he saw them as rebels. Also, it is unlikely that the Scottish elites would willingly have substituted abrasive English government for the traditional, non-intrusive, Scottish type. In general, they had little vested interest in accepting long-term English rule over Scotland, which explains why that rule was so insecure.

There is an exception, in the Bruce–Comyn civil war in Scotland after 1306. Members of the Comyn/Balliol faction could not accept Bruce as king, and sided with the English; Bruce's *coup d'état* had put them in an agonisingly difficult position. Yet, as Robert I gained the upper hand, many former enemies joined his cause, and only a few irreconcilables left Scotland after Bannockburn. Thus even among those who opposed Bruce so bitterly in 1306, most had long-term Scottish, not English, loyalties. And when, in 1332–3, the irreconcilables' sons – 'the Disinherited' – achieved a temporary Balliol comeback, their final defeat was partly due to their having become totally identified with the English Crown.[48]

We should also remember the significance of the Scottish Church:[49] although religion was a unifying factor in post-Reformation Britain, in the later Middle Ages the Scottish clergy's loyalty to Scotland was bolstered by the desire to remain free of York's ecclesiastical supremacy. Also, the brunt of the Wars of Independence was mostly borne by ordinary Scots. The wealthier peasantry – called 'husbandmen' and 'yeomen' in John Barbour's poem, *The Brus* – together with the lesser landowners and free tenants, provided the bulk of the fighting men. They had their own interests in resisting English conquest, since in 1297 their wool had been requisitioned to help pay for Edward I's French wars and they themselves had feared conscription to serve overseas. And, while on occasions the Scottish leaders may have forced or

[47] Prestwich, 'Colonial Scotland'; Barrow, *Robert Bruce*, pp. 132–6.
[48] Duncan, 'War of the Scots', pp. 125–36; B. Webster, 'Scotland without a king, 1329–1341', in Grant and Stringer, *Medieval Scotland*.
[49] Barrow, *Kingdom of the Scots*, ch. 8.

terrorised them into fighting, in general they were recruited in the customary fashion through the institutionalised obligation on all local communities to provide service for 'the common army of the realm' whenever required.[50]

That brings us back to the status of the kingdom of Scotland, discussed in the previous section. The national institutions of government, including the military machinery, concentrated loyalty on the king and kingdom; so did two centuries of direct male succession combined with a deliberately fostered monarchical ideology. Scottish regnal solidarity was so well established that, in the crises after 1286, it could be maintained without a king: for instance, in the appointment of 'Guardians', in the use of a seal depicting the royal arms and St Andrew to symbolise the kingdom, and in the statement by the defenders of Stirling castle in 1304 that they held it of 'the Lion'.[51] Whatever Edward I might have thought, Scotland was by this period a fully developed kingdom – one of those West European monarchies out of which, as Jean-Philippe Genet stressed at an earlier Anglo-American Conference, the modern state was born during the century 1260–1360.[52]

This highlights the state-building of the twelfth and thirteenth centuries, and reinforces Keith Stringer's view that 'thirteenth-century Britain contained not one but *two* dominant states'. I agree that the main theme of 'British history' to the end of the Scottish Wars of Independence is the roughly parallel expansion of two power blocks: one from Wessex, the other from *Scotia*, eastern Scotland north of the Forth. Both expanded outwards into the Celtic peripheries, and also divided Britain's 'middle kingdom' of Northumbria between them. Such expansion, however, could not continue indefinitely without bringing them into full-scale conflict – as happened from 1296. But neither could conquer the other: English failure in Scotland is paralleled by the Scottish defeat in Ireland and fruitless designs on Wales. In 'British history' terms, the Wars of Independence period produced a stalemate.

English expansionism, however, did not target Scotland alone; in the later Middle Ages France was also invaded, with spectacular if ephemeral success under Edward III and Henry V. After 1337, in fact, the Hundred Years War was the English Crown's main concern. This shift of priorities is often seen as one of the main reasons for the maintenance of Scottish independence.[53] I am not convinced; after all, Edward III had failed to achieve lasting victory north of the Border in 1333–7, just as Edward I had failed between 1296 and 1307 –

[50] G. W. S. Barrow, 'The army of Alexander III's Scotland', in Reid, *Alexander III*; G. W. S. Barrow, 'Lothian in the first War of Independence', *Scottish Historical Review*, lv (1976), pp. 155–7; Barrow, *Robert Bruce*, pp. 80–9; Duncan, 'War of the Scots', pp. 138–46; A. Grant, 'Aspects of national consciousness in medieval Scotland', in Bjørn, Grant and Stringer, *Nations, Nationalism and Patriotism*, pp. 83–8.

[51] E. J. Cowan, 'Myth and identity in early medieval Scotland', *Scottish Historical Review*, lxiii (1984); Barrow, *Robert Bruce*, chs. 1, 6, 7; N. Reid, 'The kingless kingdom: the Scottish guardianships of 1286–1306', *Scottish Historical Review*, lxi (1982).

[52] J.-P. Genet, 'Which state rises?', *Historical Research*, lxv (1992), especially pp. 122, 131–2; cf. J. R. Strayer, *On the Medieval Origins of the Modern State* (Princeton, 1970).

[53] E.g., this is the only reason Hugh Kearney's 'British history' gives for 'the break-up of the Edwardian empire': H. Kearney, *The British Isles: A History of Four Nations* (Cambridge, 1989), p. 90.

yet apart from a few years in the late 1290s, both had concentrated all their war efforts against Scotland. On the other hand, the 'auld alliance' with France (first made in 1295) was certainly important to the Scots; and the Hundred Years War (in which Scotland was also involved) means that the 'British' historian of this period cannot focus exclusively on the British Isles.

But what – apart from the Hundred Years War – was going on in 'British history' after the Wars of Independence petered out? The main themes are no longer those of convergence, domination and conquest; if anything, they are the opposite. In many ways, the rest of the later Middle Ages was a time of disengagement, of divergence instead of convergence. There was a reversal of the 'British' trends of the earlier Middle Ages – and indeed of the general European trends recently described by Robert Bartlett.[54]

Three main areas of disengagement are highlighted here. The first is political. Not only did the Scots check English expansionism, but so too did the French. For most of the Hundred Years War period the English were actually on the defensive, and in the mid-fifteenth century they were driven out of France: the will to maintain conquests abroad had evaporated.[55] In Scotland, meanwhile, after the battle of Neville's Cross in 1346 Edward III took over part of the South, not to annex it but simply to establish a buffer zone against Scottish raiding on northern England. In the later fourteenth century, the Scots regained this buffer zone, but there was no question of further Scottish expansion southwards. English kings did still claim superiority over Scotland, but no longer made serious efforts to achieve it. Instead, Anglo-Scottish conflict mostly consisted of raiding across a Border that was becoming more institutionalised than ever thanks to the refinement during periods of truce of peace-keeping and dispute-settling mechanisms.[56]

There is also political disengagement from the periphery. The emergence of the Pale in Ireland is the clearest case, but in later fifteenth-century Wales, too, actual power came mostly into the hands of native Welsh families.[57] As for Scotland, the last Scottish conquest in the West, the Isle of Man (taken over after 1266) was lost to England after 1333. The institutional integration of the west-coast region, begun in 1293 when King John Balliol created three new sheriffdoms of Skye, Argyll and Kintyre, was mostly abandoned. Only Argyllshire survived in the fourteenth century, to become Campbell private property; the other two were replaced by magnate lordships. Elsewhere, the

---

54 Bartlett, *Making of Europe.*

55 M. Keen, 'The end of the Hundred Years War: Lancastrian France and Lancastrian England', in Jones and Vale, *England and Her Neighbours.*

56 A. Goodman, 'The Anglo-Scottish Marches in the fifteenth century: a frontier society?', in Mason, *Scotland and England*; H. Summerson, 'The early development of the laws of the Anglo-Scottish Marches, 1249–1448', in W. M. Gordon and T. D. Fergus (eds.), *Legal History in the Making* (London, 1991). The buffer zone was regained by 1384, except for Jedburgh, Roxburgh and Berwick, which stayed in English hands until 1409, 1460 and 1461 respectively.

57 A. Cosgrove (ed.), *A New History of Ireland*, vol. II: *Medieval Ireland 1169–1534* (Oxford, 1987), chs. 13, 17–23, by J. A. Watt, A. Cosgrove and D. B. Quinn; G. Williams, *Recovery, Reorientation and Reformation: Wales c.1415–1642* (Oxford, 1987), chs. 7–10.

sheriffdoms of Inverness, Elgin and Forres were incorporated into the new palatine earldom of Moray, and those of Cromarty and Nairn into the earldom of Ross. And the focus of Scottish monarchy moved southwards. The Bruce and Stewart kings granted away their main northern estates, and spent much less time in the North – especially beyond the Tay – than the twelfth- and thirteenth-century kings had done. 'In these times we do not make our residence at Forfar as often as our predecessors', said Robert II in 1372 about one of the traditional royal centres in the North.[58]

Second, there is aristocratic disengagement. Because of the Wars of Independence, land could not be held of the Scottish and English Crowns simultaneously (apart from during the brief peace of 1328–32, and even then 'the Disinherited' were not restored). Thereafter, the rule was applied strictly, except to some monasteries. Admittedly, the 'buffer zone' of 1346–84 was an anomaly: the English Crown granted land within it, and (after 1369) rents were shared between Scottish and English 'owners'. But this ended as the Scots regained the region. When, during Border negotiations in 1398, the earl of Northumberland demanded the lordship of Jedburgh (given him by Edward III), he was rebuffed by Robert III's son, the duke of Rothesay: 'For it wes the Kyngis land, / Off Scotland quha-evyr ware King regnand'.[59] The age of cross-Border landholding by English and Scottish nobles was over.

Aristocratic disengagement has a further dimension. One major feature of thirteenth-century 'British history' is the supranational territorial complexes and connections established throughout all four countries of the British Isles.[60] They can still be found in late medieval England, Wales and Ireland, but they seem less 'British': as the effects of intermarriage, entails, and extinctions of male lines resulted in estates 'becoming concentrated in fewer and fewer hands', they came to be centred mostly in England, while magnate absenteeism became a chronic problem in Wales and English-held Ireland.[61] Again, there are Scottish parallels. The vacuum in northern Scotland left by the destruction of the Comyns was filled by Robert I's creation of the vast earldom of Moray for his nephew, Thomas Randolph. But the Randolph earls of Moray were generally absentees; and after their male line had been

---

[58] A. Macinnes, 'Scotland and the Manx connection', *Proceedings of the Isle of Man Natural History and Antiquarian Society*, viii (1982); Barrow, *Kingdom of the Scots*, p. 383; *Historical Manuscripts Commission, Fourth Report*, pp. 473–85; *Registrum Magni Sigilli Regum Scotorum*, ed. J. M. Thomson *et al.* (Edinburgh, 1882–1912), i, no. 514; appendix I, nos. 8, 31; A. Grant, 'Thanes and thanages, from the eleventh to the thirteenth centuries', in Grant and Stringer, *Medieval Scotland*, pp. 61–70.

[59] Andrew Wyntoun, *The Orygynale Cronykil of Scotland*, ed. D. Laing (Edinburgh, 1872–9), iii, p. 66. See also R. Nicholson, *Scotland: The Later Middle Ages* (Edinburgh, 1974), ch. 6; Goodman, 'Anglo-Scottish Marches', pp. 20–4; and Stringer, 'Identities in thirteenth-century England', pp. 57–8.

[60] See especially R. Frame, 'Aristocracies and the political configuration of the British Isles', in Davies, *British Isles 1100-1500*; also Davies, 'In praise of British History', pp. 15–17.

[61] K. B. McFarlane, *The Nobility of Later Medieval England* (Oxford, 1973), pp. 79–80, and ch. 2; J. F. Lydon, *The Lordship of Ireland in the Middle Ages* (Dublin, 1972), pp. 201–6; R. Frame, *English Lordship in Ireland* (Oxford, 1982), ch. 2; Davies, *Conquest, Coexistence and Change*, pp. 394–8; Williams, *Recovery, Reorientation and Reformation*, pp. 43–6.

extinguished at Neville's Cross, their heirs-general, the Border family of Dunbar, gained only a small part of the earldom – which eventually went to the equally southern Douglases, and then to the Crown when they were overthrown in 1455. Earlier, marriage had brought the Douglases the estates of the other great 'Norman' family of the thirteenth-century Highlands, the Murrays. But the Douglases were rarely active in northern Scotland; and with their forfeiture the pattern of noble withdrawal was accentuated. Meanwhile, male extinction and absenteeism caused a crisis in the early fifteenth-century earldom of Ross, and the earldom of Caithness virtually disintegrated.[62] Thus – though there are exceptions – magnate disengagement from the periphery can be seen as another general 'British' trend of the later Middle Ages.

The third area of disengagement is economic. This is clearest with respect to the currency – which has particular interest, given the arguments over a European currency nowadays. Until the later fourteenth century, there was a 'common British currency': Scotland's and Ireland's coinages had the same weight and quality as England's, and all circulated interchangeably across the British Isles. But in the later fourteenth century the Scots coinage could not be kept in parity, and in 1367 Scotland left the 'sterling area'; Scottish coins were reduced in weight, and the exchange-rate with England steadily worsened: 4:3 from 1373, 2:1 from 1390, 3:1 from 1451. In Ireland, meanwhile, no new coinage was struck in any quantity between the 1330s and 1460; the old coins in circulation were worn and clipped away; in Ulster, Scottish coin circulated at face value, not at the English exchange-rate; and there was widespread counterfeiting ('O'Reilly's money'). In effect, Ireland, too, had left the 'sterling area'; and when after 1460 Irish coins were struck again, they were significantly lighter than English ones. The currency divergence perhaps resulted from the drain of coinage from England in the 1330s and 1340s, which may have had very severe consequences for Scotland and Ireland; worsening trade balances and the general European silver shortage are other likely reasons. Whatever the explanation, one result was that subsequently Scotland's economy followed a different path from England's.[63]

Ireland's currency difficulties were probably also linked to agrarian crises. English-style peasant agriculture was severely hit by native Irish attacks and devastated by the Black Death; while the new availability of land in post-plague England encouraged reverse emigration. In much of Ireland, the rural infrastructure which had sustained English lordship seems to have collapsed. Again, this may be part of a general 'British' trend. In lowland Wales, the Glyn Dŵr revolt did lasting damage to rural society, and the retreat of English settlement is especially noticeable in the towns, where native Welsh

[62] See A. Grant, *Independence and Nationhood* (2nd edn, Edinburgh, 1991), ch. 8; and, for the families, Paul, *Scots Peerage*, ii, pp. 123–31, 318–22; iii, pp. 157–83; vi, pp. 286–310; vii, pp. 239–44.

[63] E. Gemmill and N. Mayhew, *Changing Values in Medieval Scotland* (Cambridge, 1995), chs. 4, 6; M. Dolley, in ch. 29 of *New History of Ireland*, ii, pp. 819–25; M. Prestwich, 'Currency and the economy of early fourteenth-century England', in N. Mayhew (ed.), *Edwardian Monetary Affairs (1279–1344)* (British Archaeological Reports, xxxvi, 1977).

moved in during the fifteenth century.[64] As for Scotland, although we have few details about its late medieval rural society, something similar can be suggested. Evidence for post-plague depopulation can be found in surviving accounts for royal lands from 1358-9, and also in the tax reassessment of 1366, by which the total national valuation was reduced to just over half that of the thirteenth-century 'Old Extent'. But the 1366 figures also show – if not straightforwardly – that the worst falls in value were generally in Highland and western (including south-western) regions: 42% in Ayrshire, 39% in Stirlingshire, 38% in Inverness-shire, and 22% in parts of Argyllshire, for instance, as opposed to 72% in Lothian or 74% in Fife.[65] That suggests a greater loss of rent-paying peasants in those areas. Moreover, the fact that after about 1350 the spread of the English (Scots) language at the expense of Gaelic came to a halt,[66] fixing the English–Gaelic linguistic frontier until the eighteenth century, presumably demonstrates that the earlier medieval expansion of Lowland rural settlement into the Highlands must have ceased.

But disengagement and divergence were not absolute. One 'converging' corollary is the Celtic resurgence – to fill the vacuums. In Wales, where English conquest was followed by Welsh integration, the fifteenth century saw the rise of native *uchelwyr*, or 'squires', who took over administrative tasks on behalf of absentee English lords and high officials. In practice, much of fifteenth-century Wales was run by Welshmen, especially the Herberts, Gruffydd ap Nicholas and his grandson Rhys ap Thomas, and the various Tudors.[67] In Ireland, too, the fifteenth century was dominated (albeit differently) by the native Irish lords – O'Neills, MacMurroughs, MacCarthys, and so on – and by their Anglo-Irish cousins, especially the Desmonds and Kildares. The Irishness of the great Anglo-Irish magnates is disputed. But in the continuous local warfare of late medieval Ireland, they operated in much the same way as Irish chiefs, enforcing authority by means of plundering raids, and maintaining their fighting men through *coinmheadh* or 'coyne', by billeting them on the local peasantry.[68] That is pillage-based lordship, a far cry from what is found in England and most of Scotland; and it is clearly a reverse of the 'feudalising' trend of the twelfth and thirteenth centuries.

The Welsh and Irish experiences have Scottish parallels. Welsh-type integration

[64] K. Down, in ch. 15 of *New History of Ireland*, ii, pp. 449–50, 457, 461–3, 472, 485–7; A. Cosgrove, in ch. 18 of ibid., pp. 552–3; Davies, *Conquest, Coexistence and Change*, pp. 425–9, 456; Williams, *Recovery, Reorientation and Reformation*, pp. 90–5.

[65] Gemmill and Mayhew, *Changing Values*, pp. 18, 364–70; N. Mayhew, 'Alexander III – a silver age? An essay in Scottish medieval economic history', in Reid, *Alexander III*, p. 65; *Act. Parl. Scot.*, i, pp. 499–501 – though for various reasons the figures have to be used with caution.

[66] Barrow, *Kingdom of the Scots*, p. 363; Nicholson, *Later Middle Ages*, pp. 274–5.

[67] R. A. Griffiths, *King and Country: England and Wales in the Fifteenth Century* (London, 1991), chs. 4, 9, 11, 12; R. A. Griffiths, *Sir Rhys ap Thomas and his Family* (Cardiff, 1993); Williams, *Recovery, Reorientation and Reformation*, chs. 7–10.

[68] *New History of Ireland*, ii, chs. 18–23, by Cosgrove and Quinn; R. Frame, 'War and peace in the medieval lordship of Ireland', in J. Lydon (ed.), *The English in Medieval Ireland* (Dublin, 1984); K. Simms, *From Kings to Warlords: The Changing Political Structure of Gaelic Ireland in the Later Middle Ages* (Woodbridge, 1987), especially chs. 7, 8.

is exemplified by the Campbell earls of Argyll, who created a wide hegemony in the central west-coast region by ruthlessly identifying their own interests with the Crown's. And the Irish kind of power structure is found in the even more powerful MacDonald Lordship of the Isles, built up in the aftermath of the Wars of Independence and, at its mid-fifteenth-century height, sprawling over a fifth of Scotland and onto the northern Irish coast. As Stephen Boardman has shown, the MacDonalds, too, imposed their authority through forcible billeting of their fighting men; and their relations with the Crown were more confrontational – at times involving open warfare – than co-operative.[69]

The expansion of the MacDonalds, Campbells, and other kindreds like the MacKenzies, is one aspect of Gaelic resurgence in late medieval Scotland. Another is in the way in which many Highland families, such as the Frasers and Grants, who in previous centuries had been feudalising incomers from the south, increasingly embraced Gaelic culture and attitudes and eventually evolved into clans. The process probably also affected those magnate houses which remained in the Highlands, for instance the earls of Sutherland and the Gordon earls of Huntly; while the best-known instance is the case of Robert II's son, Alexander, Earl of Buchan, the notorious 'Wolf of Badenoch'.[70]

The Gaelic resurgence was not, of course, absolute. Campbell and MacDonald power owed much to such 'feudal' characteristics as primogeniture; Campbell chiefs had major roles in Scottish central government; so, briefly, did a MacDonald chief. And all these Highland families, whether Gaelic or Gaelicised (to use Irish terminology), held their lands by the normal principles of Scots law, and were generally considered fully fledged members of the Scottish political community. Thus they represent a hybrid, 'Scoto-Gaelic' world. That is not new: hybridity had characterised the Scottish landowning class for centuries. But – in contrast with the preceding 'feudal' era – during the later Middle Ages the dynamism came from the Gaelic side.

They can also be regarded as frontier nobles, bridging the Gaelic and 'feudalised' worlds. The same can be said of the 'Gaelicised' Anglo-Irish, and of the new fifteenth-century Welsh lords. This Celtic frontier, however, was not the only one in late medieval Britain; there was also the Anglo-Scottish Border. There, if cross-Border landholding was no longer possible, the fourteenth and fifteenth centuries saw the emergence (partly at the expense of erstwhile cross-Border lords)[71] of a new type of Border lord: obvious examples

[69] S. Boardman, 'Secret armies: the militarisation of the Scottish Highlands in the fourteenth century', in Scotland and War (Association of Scottish Historical Studies, 1995); S. Boardman, 'Campbell lordship in the later Middle Ages', forthcoming; J. Bannerman, 'The Lordship of the Isles', in J. Brown (ed.), Scottish Society in the Fifteenth Century (London, 1977); A. Grant, 'Scotland's "Celtic Fringe" in the later Middle Ages: the Macdonald Lords of the Isles and the kingdom of Scotland', in Davies, British Isles 1100–1500.

[70] Ibid., pp. 121–2, 127–8; A. Grant, 'The Wolf of Badenoch', in W. D. H. Sellar (ed.), Moray: Province and People (Scottish Society for Northern Studies, 1993); I. F. Grant, The Social and Economic Development of Scotland before 1603 (Edinburgh, 1930), pp. 493–502, 513–16. The Sutherlands and Gordons have yet to be the subjects of modern research.

[71] A. Tuck, 'The emergence of a northern nobility, 1250–1400', Northern History, xxii (1986).

are, in England, the Percies and Nevilles, and, in Scotland, the Douglas earls of Douglas and Angus. Their power came not only from land but also from their military functions, notably through March wardenships on either side of the Border. But if we think in terms of 'frontier magnates' with special military roles, we will also find them in Scotland in the Campbells of Argyll and the Gordons of Huntly,[72] in Ireland in the earls of Kildare, Ormond and Desmond, in Wales in the Herberts, the house of Dinefwr and the Tudors, and in England in the Stanleys, whose Cheshire power base was on the Anglo-Welsh frontier. These can be regarded as the new 'British' frontier magnates of the fifteenth century; in most cases their fortunes and misfortunes bulk large in sixteenth-century history as well.

Periphery and frontier, therefore, are as important for 'British history' in the later Middle Ages as in the earlier – albeit in different ways. But there is more to late medieval 'British history' than that. Two broader 'British' themes following from the preceding paragraphs are the forms of lord-man relations to be found across the British Isles, and the practices of feud and dispute-settling. Studies of 'bastard feudalism' usually focus on England, but major work has been done on Scotland and Ireland.[73] Similarly, while dispute-settling is a growth area for late medieval English historians, modern understanding of the topic was initiated by Welsh and Scottish historians.[74] With both topics, the basis now exists for a genuine, highly illuminating, 'British' approach.

This applies to most aspects of late medieval social history. For instance, studies of Scottish local communities, at all levels, are much needed; they will be vital for Scottish history, but will also help to explain the social dynamics of Britain as a whole. In the religious sphere, there is Kathleen Wood-Legh's pioneering study of chantries,[75] which integrates Scottish and English evidence, to be followed up. It has been suggested that lay piety in late fifteenth-century England was conservative in the North and 'modern' in the South; was Scottish piety different, or like that of northern England?[76] Similarly, lay popular culture is an important topic. The Anglo-Scottish Border may have become ever more rigid institutionally, but culturally it was still fluid. Here, the Border ballads are a well-known subject, but the 'Britishness' of late medieval ballads as a whole is worth exploring. Why, for example, were Robin Hood and Little John so popular in Scotland?[77]

[72] See, e.g., the references to their military activities in the Highlands and West in N. Macdougall, *James III* (Edinburgh, 1982), and N. Macdougall, *James IV* (Edinburgh, 1989), *passim*.

[73] E.g., J. Wormald, *Lords and Men in Scotland: Bonds of Manrent, 1442–1603* (Edinburgh, 1985); Frame, *English Lordship in Ireland*, ch. 1; Simms, *From Kings to Warlords*, chs. 5–7.

[74] R. R. Davies, 'The survival of the blood feud in medieval Wales', *History*, liv (1969); J. Wormald, 'Bloodfeud, kindred and government in early modern Scotland', *Past and Present*, lxxxvii (1980).

[75] K. L. Wood-Legh, *Perpetual Chantries in Britain* (Cambridge, 1965).

[76] A. J. Pollard, *North-Eastern England during the Wars of the Roses* (Oxford, 1992), pp. 196–7; cf. M. Lynch, 'Religious life in medieval Scotland', in S. Gilley and W. J. Sheils (eds.), *A History of Religion in Britain* (Oxford, 1994), pp. 116–22.

[77] J. C. Holt, *Robin Hood* (London, 1982), pp. 38, 40–1, 51–2, 160–1; H. Henderson, 'The ballad and popular tradition to 1660', in R. D. S. Jack (ed.), *The History of Scottish Literature*, vol. I: *Origins to 1660* (Aberdeen, 1988).

Study of topics such as these would do much to elucidate the crucial regional, as opposed to 'national', features of 'British history' during the late Middle Ages. Did the Highlands as a whole – or just the West – have more in common with Gaelic Ireland than with Lowland Scotland? How far did the 'Border region' extend – did all of southern Scotland and northern England have more in common with each other than with other parts of their respective countries? For understanding the people of mainland Britain in the later Middle Ages, which are more significant: the Anglo-Scottish Border, or the 'Highland line' and the Mersey-Trent-Humber line?[78]

Work like that would help to balance the fact that, politically, 'the later Middle Ages may seem to shovel less concrete into the "foundations" of the United Kingdom than did the twelfth and thirteenth centuries'[79] (though does the absence of such concrete explain why the edifice seems shaky nowadays?). But for political and institutional history, the late medieval 'British' themes – beyond disengagement and divergence – are perhaps best found in comparisons and contrasts. I have suggested political contrasts elsewhere.[80] Here, I would point to the ways in which both the English *and* the Scottish states developed and were consolidated during the later Middle Ages. Gerald Harriss has drawn our attention to this for England;[81] for Scotland, much the same was going on, albeit differently, and in divergent directions. Thus by the sixteenth century there was even less chance than in 1296 that Scotland could be incorporated into an English state; when it did come to have the same monarch as England, it was as a *partner*, in a dynastic union.

Moreover, if that partnership was or is unhappy, then many of the reasons stem from the later Middle Ages. There is, of course, the mutual hostility which the Anglo-Scottish warfare engendered. More specifically – as several chapters point out below – there is the difference in the way the two kingdoms' institutions operated. Consider, for example, the Parliaments. English parliamentary power owed much to the control over taxation established by the Commons – in particular, between 1298 and 1336, when direct taxation was acceptable, because it went on popular war against Scotland rather than (as previously) on unpopular war against France.[82] In Scotland, conversely, the war against England was fought without recourse to direct taxation (local communities provided men, not money). Therefore, the Scottish Parliament's financial role, and hence its constitutional position, were significantly different – which is crucial to the history of the British Isles between 1603 and 1707.

[78] H. M. Jewell, *The North-South Divide: The Origins of Northern Consciousness in England* (Manchester, 1994).

[79] R. Frame, 'Overlordship and reaction, *c*.1200–*c*.1450', above, p. 83.

[80] A. Grant, 'Crown and nobility in late medieval Britain', in Mason, *Scotland and England*.

[81] G. L. Harriss, 'Political society and the growth of government in late medieval England', *Past and Present*, cxxxviii (1993). For ideas about late medieval government in Scotland, see J. Brown, 'The exercise of power', in Brown, *Scottish Society*; Grant, *Independence and Nationhood*, ch. 6; L. J. Macfarlane, *William Elphinstone and the Kingdom of Scotland* (Aberdeen, 1985), *passim*.

[82] G. L. Harriss, *King, Parliament and Public Finance in Medieval England to 1369* (Oxford, 1975), chs. 4–5, especially p. 79.

This has brought us back to Anglo-Scottish warfare. It is hard to avoid it when discussing 'British history' in the later Middle Ages. And the attitudes it produced are probably the main legacy bequeathed from late medieval Britain. 'Nothing pleases the Scots more than abuse of the English', said Pope Pius II in the mid-fifteenth century;[83] for how many Scots would that be true today?

Yet, in the fourteenth and fifteenth centuries, realistic politicians knew that peace with England was in Scotland's best interests: the devastation caused by war was not. Robert I paid £20,000 to make peace in 1328; subsequently, there was usually a pro-peace lobby of some sort in Scotland. It may have become stronger as the fifteenth century progressed and the issues of the Wars of Independence became less and less relevant in practice. In 1465 a truce, or armistice, was agreed for over fifty years.[84] 'Till [to] honour ennymis is our haile entent',[85] complained the author of the jingoistic poem *The Wallace*; and bellicose Border nobles, including the king's brother, managed to disrupt the peace process and bring about war – in which Berwick was once again lost to England, this time finally. Nevertheless, James III and his government still hoped for peace. Their attitude comes across vividly in the speech which James's Secretary, Mr Archibald Whitelaw, made before Richard III and his council at Nottingham on 11 September 1484: 'Satis enim pugnatum est ...' – 'For there has been enough fighting, enough wrongdoing, enough Christian bloodshed ...'. Whitelaw concluded with a striking piece of 'British' rhetoric:

> It is an unnatural thing that war should be fought between us – we who are bound together within a small island in the western sea, and who are linked by living in the same climate and in neighbouring lands, sharing similarity of physique, language, appearance, colouring and complexion.

Peace, friendship, and close ties with England: that is what James III wanted. The sentiments are similar to those of Alexander III and Edward I in 1284, with which this chapter began. But it was not to be peace at any price. Whitelaw also argued for the return of Berwick; James III, meanwhile, renewed the Franco-Scottish alliance; and a contingent of Scots helped to overthrow Richard III at Bosworth. Scottish policy towards England in the later fifteenth century was thus ambivalent: peace was highly desirable, but the kingdom's integrity had also to be upheld. It was a love-hate – or perhaps rather, given the warfare of the past two centuries, a hate-love – relationship. And that, probably, is the main late medieval Scottish contribution to the future United Kingdom: the ambivalence in attitude towards England, which has done so much to create the enigma of 'British history'.

[83] Nicholson, *Later Middle Ages*, p. 297.
[84] The rest of this paragraph, and the next, are based on A. Grant, 'Richard III and Scotland', in A. J. Pollard (ed.), *The North of England in the Age of Richard III* (Stroud, in press); it also contains D. Shotter's translation of Whitelaw's speech.
[85] *Hary's Wallace*, ed. M. P. McDiarmid (Scottish Text Society, 1968–9), i, Book I, l. 5.

Part III

Building the early modern state

Chapter 7

The High Road from Scotland

Marcus Merriman and *Jenny Wormald*

Stewarts and Tudors in the mid-sixteenth century
Marcus Merriman

If the later Middle Ages was a period of divergence and disengagement in 'British history', in the sixteenth century convergence is firmly back on the agenda. Both Wales and Ireland experienced new assertive English centralising policies. In Wales, these led to the forfeiture and execution of the greatest Welsh lord, Rhys ap Gruffydd of Dinefwr, in 1531, and produced the Acts of Union of 1536 and 1543 which abolished the old principality and marcher lordships. In Ireland, they led to the forfeiture and execution of the greatest Anglo-Irish magnate, Earl Thomas of Kildare, in 1537, and produced the Act of Kingly Title of 1541, which changed Ireland's status from separate lordship to puppet kingdom, to be ruled according to the principles of English kingship.[1] Scotland, meanwhile, stayed independent. But rapprochement is demonstrated by the 1502 Treaty of Perpetual Peace, the first formal Anglo-Scottish peace treaty since the short-lived Treaty of Edinburgh of 1328. And in 1503 the 'marriage of the Thistle and the Rose' between James IV and Margaret Tudor took place, which held out the prospect of Anglo-Scottish dynastic union. In 1521, the Scottish academic John Mair published his clarion call for such a union, *Historia Maioris Brittaniae*.[2] And this duly came to pass in 1603, when Henry VII's granddaughter Queen Elizabeth was succeeded on the English throne by his great-great grandson, King James VI of Scots. The sixteenth century appears to take the British Isles much closer to political unity than at any previous stage in their history.

Such an analysis, however, vastly oversimplifies. While the integration of

---

[1] For 16th-century Wales and Ireland, see initially G. Williams, *Recovery, Reorientation and Reformation: Wales c.1415–1642* (Oxford, 1987), chs. 10–11, 14; and S. G. Ellis, *Tudor Ireland* (London, 1985), chs. 4–9.

[2] *A History of Greater Britain, as well England as Scotland ... by John Major*, ed. and trans. A. Constable (Scottish History Society, 1892). Mair latinised his name to Major, so there is a neat pun in the original title; nowadays 'Major's Britain' has different connotations. For discussion, see, e.g., R. Mason, 'Scotching the Brut: politics, history and national myth in sixteenth-century Britain', in R. Mason (ed.), *Scotland and England 1286–1815* (Edinburgh, 1987); and R. Mason, 'Kingship, nobility and Anglo-Scottish union: John Mair's *History of Greater Britain* (1521)', *Innes Review*, xli (1990).

Wales into the English administrative system was reasonably successful, it encouraged English administrators to try to treat Ireland in roughly the same way – which alienated the Anglo-Irish and the Gaelic Irish alike. Sixteenth-century Ireland continued to be a land of war, despite much greater English efforts than in the past. Not until the end of the Nine Years War (1594–1603) did it seem to have been brought under control – but a generation later the problems exploded again as part of the Wars of the Three Kingdoms.[3]

With Scotland, too, there are severe problems about seeing the sixteenth century as a time of steady movement towards 1603. 'The eventual dynastic merger of 1603 was between kingdoms that differed more widely from each other than would have been the case in 1290':[4] much of this is attributable to late medieval development, but the divergence was especially wide in the sixteenth century. As Jenny Wormald stresses in the following section, the centralising changes in sixteenth-century English government were not mir-rored in Scotland, which was run on much the same basis as in the Middle Ages; when the Union of the Crowns did take place, the differences in the ways that the two kingdoms operated precluded any real 'British' integration.

Moreover, the Union of Crowns itself is all too easily taken for granted. The neatness of the dates almost implies that 1603 followed on automatically from 1503. In 1966, for example, R. B. Wernham intoned:

> ... from the marriage of Margaret Tudor to James IV of Scotland there was born the idea of a united realm of Britain, 'with the sea for its fron-tiers and mutual love for its garrison', that was to haunt statesmen on both sides of the Border until its achievement in 1603.[5]

But that is hardly the case. In Scotland, Mair's arguments for union were out on a limb, and in 1527 his book was eclipsed by Hector Boece's *Scotorum Historiae*, which restated and embellished the nationalist, anti-English account of Scottish history constructed during the Wars of Independence.[6] And those influential Scots who were not anglophobes wanted friendly but separate relations with England (roughly what Secretary Whitelaw had proclaimed to Richard III in 1484).[7] In 1523, when a proposal to invade England on behalf of France was being debated, Lord Forbes warned eloquently of the dangers of English revenge, arguing 'if we would keep amity with the realm of England we were out of all these dangers'.[8]

[3] C. Brady, 'Comparable histories?: Tudor reform in Wales and Ireland', in S. G. Ellis and S. Barber (eds.), *Conquest and Union: Fashioning a British State, 1485–1725* (London, 1995); Ellis, *Tudor Ireland*, chs. 8–9, and 'Conclusion: the Tudor failure'.

[4] R. Frame, 'Overlordship and reaction, *c*.1200–*c*.1450', above, p. 83.

[5] R. B. Wernham, *Before the Armada: English Foreign Policy in the Sixteenth Century* (London, 1966), p. 48.

[6] Hector Boethius, *Scotorum Historiae* (Paris, 1527); conveniently read in *The chronicles of Scotland, compiled by Hector Boece. Translated by John Bellenden, 1531*, ed. R. W. Chambers *et al.* (Scottish Text Society, 1938–41).

[7] See A. Grant, 'Scottish foundations: late medieval contributions', above, p. 108.

[8] Recounted in 1548 by Edward Hall, *The union of the two noble and illustre fameles of York*

In the 1540s, however, we do find Scottish tracts advocating Anglo-Scottish union: for instance, the proposal for uniting the two kingdoms presented to Henry VIII in 1544 by a Highland cleric, John Elder.[9] And three years later an Edinburgh merchant, James Henrison, published *An Exhortacion to the Scottes to conforme themselfes to the honorable, Expedient, & godly Union betweene the two realmes of Englande & Scotland*, in which he declared that

> Herefore dare I boldly say, if these two realms were brought under one Empire and governance, we should see an end of all strife and war, which will never come otherwise to pass: And then should we have this common weal of ours, being now out of all order, and in most miserable state and condition to be most happy and most flourishing.[10]

But Elder and Henrison must not be taken as typical.[11] Both were Protestant exiles from Scotland who had taken refuge in London, and were contributing to English propaganda for a very different kind of dynastic union to that of 1603: the marriage of the young Mary Queen of Scots to Edward VI of England. Thus an English *Proclamation* declared in September 1547:

> We mynd nocht by this conjunctioun of marriage to do ony moir prejudice to this realm of Scotland than to the realme of England, bot with the advice of the noble men and gude men of baith realmes to unite thame togidder in any name by the name of Britounis ...[12]

And in the even more revealing *Prayer* of 1548, God was asked to 'have an eye to this small Isle of Bretaigne' and to complete what he had begun, 'That the Scottish menn and wee might forever and hereafter in love and amitie, knit into one nacion' by the marriage of Edward and Mary. 'Graunt o Lorde that the same might goo forwarde and that our sonnes sonnes and all our posteritie hereafter may fele the benefite and commoditie of thy great gift of unitie graunted in our daies.'[13]

But the *Proclamation* was issued at the time of the duke of Somerset's

---

and Lancaster (London, 1548), fo. 201ᵛ; ed. J. Johnson *et al.* (London, 1809), p. 665. Forbes was not alone: James Hamilton, 1st Earl of Arran, also favoured alliance with England so as to end the miseries of war: *Letters and Papers, Foreign and Domestic, of the Reign of Henry VIII*, ed. J. S. Brewer *et al.* (London, 1862–1910), iv, no. 670.

[9] Printed as 'A Proposal for Uniting Scotland with England, addressed to Henry VIII', in *Bannatyne Miscellany, I* (Edinburgh, 1827).

[10] Reprinted in *The Complaynt of Scotlande*, ed. J. A. H. Murray (Early English Text Society, 1872), pp. 207–36; quote from p. 231.

[11] For Elder and Henrison, see M. Merriman, 'Home thoughts from abroad: national consciousness and Scottish exiles in the mid-sixteenth century', in C. Bjørn, A. Grant and K. J. Stringer (eds.), *Social and Political Identities in Western History* (Copenhagen, 1994), pp. 93–101; and M. Merriman, 'James Henrisoun and 'Great Britain': British union and the Scottish commonweal', in Mason, *Scotland and England*.

[12] Printed in *The Warrender Papers*, ed. A. I. Cameron (Scottish History Society, 1931–2), i, p. 17.

[13] *A prayer for victorie and peace* (London, 1548). The only printed copy of this is in the Pepysian Library, Magdalene College, Cambridge; the manuscript is Public Record Office, SP 10/2 (quote from fo. 11ʳ).

invasion of southern Scotland, in which the Scottish army was defeated at the battle of Pinkie, near Musselburgh, and the *Prayer* was written in its aftermath. The *Prayer* asked God to 'putt away frome us all warre and hostilitie,' but to 'be our sheld and buckle' if conflict continued, and to 'Lay thy sowrd of punyshement uppoun them' that oppose the marriage, or 'converte their hartes to the better waye'. These sentiments were little more than the song of the aggressor over the centuries: 'We only make war to bring peace' – an early modern variant on the twentieth-century motif of 'bombing to the peace table'. A better impression of Anglo-Scottish relations at the time is surely gained from the following contemporary description of the field of Pinkie:

> Dead corpses lying dispersed abroad. Some with their legs cut off; some but ham-strung and left lying half dead; others, with the arms cut off; divers, their necks half asunder; many, their heads cloven; of sundry, the brains smashed out; some others again, their heads quite off; with a thousand other kinds of killing ... And thus, with blood and slaughter of the enemy, this chase was continued.[14]

Pinkie followed Flodden (1513) and Solway Moss (1542) in a sequence of devastating Scottish defeats by the English, in which one king and numerous nobles were killed. The 1502 treaty had brought no more 'perpetual peace' than the treaty of 1328. And if the wars themselves were now the product of contemporary European politics, whenever Anglo-Scottish relations deteriorated, out came the English claims to overlordship: 'I am the very owner of Scotland and he [James IV] holdest of me by homage', said Henry VIII in 1513.[15] The horrors of war did, of course, make the siren calls for peaceful coexistence alluring. The conflicts put severe strains on both countries, especially on their Border communities, and had serious domestic ramifications; little wonder that James VI and I made so much of the 'amity and love' brought by his accession to the English throne. Nevertheless, in the first half of the sixteenth century, Anglo-Scottish relations were essentially in the same state of potential and at times actual warfare that they had been in for much of the later Middle Ages, after the Edwardian attempts at outright conquest had petered out. The Union of 1603 still looks a long way away. To get there, three points must be appreciated. First, despite the military disasters, Scotland was not conquerable by war in the sixteenth century. Second, Anglo-Scottish dynastic union would not simply happen of its own accord; a fortunate combination of circumstances was essential. Third, James VI and indeed Scotland had to be Protestant. Each of these issues will be discussed in turn.

It has been averred that Henry VIII missed an magnificent opportunity

---

[14] *The expedicion into Scotland of ... Edward, duke of Soomerset ... set out ... by William Patten, Londoner* (London, 1548); reprinted in *Tudor Tracts*, ed. A. F. Pollard (London 1903) (quote at p. 102).

[15] J. D. Mackie, 'Henry VIII and Scotland', *Transactions of the Royal Historical Society*, 4th ser., xxix (1947), p. 105. For Elizabethan examples, see *Calendar of State Papers relating to Scotland and Mary, Queen of Scots, 1547–1603*, ed. J. Bain *et al.* (Edinburgh, 1898–), i, nos. 440, 537; and *Calendar of State Papers, Foreign, 1558–59*, ed. J. Stevenson (London, 1863), p. 520.

after Flodden in 1513; had he invaded, he surely must have conquered.[16] This is mistaken: Surrey's army was severely disorganised by its victory, and it was too late in the season for serious invasion. Henry, moreover, had no aims of conquest, either in whole or in part, nor even (despite his rhetoric) of enforcing the claim to overlordship. In reality his policy towards Scotland was purely defensive; he preferred to sport on a far more prestigious field of valour in France. And the same applies to the second and third Anglo-Scottish war of his reign, those of 1522–3 and 1542.[17]

At the end of Henry's reign and the beginning of Edward VI's, however, there were two wars in which the English seriously attempted to bring about Anglo-Scottish union by force of arms; together they constitute what has come to be called 'the Rough Wooing' of Mary Queen of Scots (1544–5, 1547–50). With an infant queen on the Scottish throne (Mary had succeeded in 1542, at the age of one week), and a young prince of Wales waiting to succeed his father in England, the potential for their marriage was immense: in due course, their eldest son (or daughter, failing sons) would inherit both kingdoms. To marry his son and heir to a young queen of Scots was, of course, what Edward I had hoped for in 1290. Then, the death of the 'Maid of Norway' had destroyed the chance of a medieval union of the Crowns, and led instead to the Scottish Wars of Independence. Now, in 1543, Henry VIII tried to turn the clock back – but his proposal for the marriage was eventually rebuffed by the Scottish political elite, who had no serious desire for union with England. Henry, therefore, turned to war in 1544. But he also invaded France, capturing Boulogne in September 1544, and that took priority. Although Edinburgh was assaulted by sea in May 1544, and the Merse and Teviotdale were invaded in September 1545, these attacks seem to have been demonstrations in force, aimed more at forestalling any Scottish invasion of England than at bringing about union.

After Henry's death, however, the Protector, Somerset (who as earl of Hertford had commanded in Scotland in 1544–5) started the Rough Wooing again. The two-and-a-half years from September 1547 to March 1550 witnessed the most intense Anglo-Scottish warfare of the sixteenth century. Somerset had around 15,000 men with him when he won his great victory at Pinkie; he then proceeded to establish garrisons across Lowland Scotland as far north as the Tay. There was another invasion by almost as large an army (about 12,000) in August 1548. A third was planned for 1549; had not

---

[16] J. J. Scarisbrick, *Henry VIII* (London, 1968), pp. 37–8. Scarisbrick also suggests that the period after Solway Moss in 1542 was a golden opportunity lost (ibid., p. 436). For Henry's relations with Scotland, see also R. G. Eaves, *Henry VIII's Scottish Diplomacy: England's Relations with the Regency Government of James V* (New York, 1971); D.M. Head, 'Henry VIII's Scottish policy: a reassessment', *Scottish Historical Review*, lxi (1982); and P. Hotle, 'Tradition, Reform and Diplomacy: Anglo-Scottish Relations, 1528–1542' (Cambridge University Ph.D. thesis, 1992).

[17] Though such ideas occasionally surfaced; e.g., in 1542 the future duke of Northumberland proposed that Henry should add to his dominions 'that parte of Skotland asmoche as ys thisside of the Frithe on theste side, and asmoche as ys athisside Dunebretayne on the west' (*Letters and Papers of Henry VIII*, xvii, no. 1194).

rebellion erupted in England, it probably would have taken place. During this second phase of the Rough Wooing, in fact, Somerset focused as much of England's military might as he possibly could on defeating Scotland. Yet all he achieved was the cementing of the Franco-Scottish alliance. In 1548, Mary Queen of Scots was sent to France, where she was to marry the Dauphin Francis in 1558; while French forces drove Somerset's garrisons out of Scotland between 1548 and 1550.[18]

The lesson of the Rough Wooing, therefore, is that learned by the three Edwards in the fourteenth century: despite crushing victories in the field, Scotland simply could not be made to capitulate through warfare. Anyone who thought otherwise (in particular Somerset) was a fool. The explanation for English failures in Scotland is often found in France, and certainly French help was extremely important to the Scots in 1548–50. That Henry VIII, like Edward III after 1337, was more interested in France is also very significant. But to argue that if Henry had only turned his huge, highly professional army of 1544 on Scotland instead of wasting it on capturing Boulogne, then conquest would inevitably have followed, is to go too far.

Other considerations should be borne in mind. First, there is Scotland's geography, which the English did not comprehend. In March 1544, for instance, Hertford was instructed to do what damage he could to Edinburgh and as many towns about the city as possible, then to pass over to Fife 'and turne upset downe the Cardinalles town of St. Andrews' – all within three weeks – and to be in France for early June![19] It simply could not be done. As in the fourteenth century, the distances involved put most of Scotland beyond the effective reach of the English: an army as large as that of 1544 could not have lived off the land, but would have needed provisioning from England – an impossible operation, even had there been sufficient cartage capacity to supply it for any length of time.

The second critical consideration is money. The 1540s found the Tudor state as wealthy as it ever would be, thanks to the Great Debasement and the Dissolution of the Monasteries. That enabled Henry and Somerset to spend over £3.5 million on more than six years of warfare in France and Scotland. But when this one-off windfall had gone, the Crown was bankrupt, as Northumberland discovered in 1552.[20] Thereafter, the Tudor state never again had the funds to mount major campaigns in the style of Charles V, Francis I of France, or Philip II of Spain. It was all it could do to reconquer Ireland.

In the third place, there were the castles of Edinburgh and Stirling: two of the most formidable defensive strongholds in Europe. In 1544 Somerset (then earl of Hertford) failed utterly to take Edinburgh castle; his attack was

[18] G. Donaldson, *Scotland: James V to James VII* (Edinburgh, 1965), pp. 63–82; W. K. Jordan, *Edward VI: The Young King* (London, 1968), pp. 230–304; M. Bush, *The Government Policy of Protector Somerset* (London, 1975), pp. 7–39.

[19] W. C. Dickinson *et al.* (eds.), *A Source Book of Scottish History* (2nd edn, London, 1958–61), ii, p. 132.

[20] Bush, *Protector Somerset*, pp. 32–4; F. C. Dietz, *English Public Finance* (London, 1920), i, pp. 144–58, 178–87.

repulsed by withering gunfire, and his field engineer found the castle rock impossible to mine. In 1547, after Pinkie, he did not even bother to attack it. Subsequently, the castle was significantly strengthened with extra guns and then by a vast italianate bastion. It simply could not be taken with 1540s technology. And behind Edinburgh stood Stirling, which was undergoing similar modernisation; it implacably guarded Stirling bridge, the key to northern Scotland. One consequence of French entry into Scotland's military establishment in 1547–8 was the erection in the 1550s of yet more modern *trace italienne* fortresses: as Leith, Langholm, Dunbar and Eyemouth were built or re-fortified, so Scotland became even less conquerable.[21]

Finally, nothing indicates that the Scottish political elite – beyond a few malcontents – were seriously prepared to agree to union with England during the 1540s. The Governor, the earl of Arran, did make unionist utterances in 1543, but these were never genuine, being made merely to gain time to consolidate his own political position. Thereafter, he did everything he could to enhance his hold on any future succession to the throne, and the last thing he was prepared to accept was an English marriage for the infant Queen Mary. Instead, when attacked by Somerset, he brought in the French (thus weakening his own chance of power) rather than agree to submit to England.[22]

If the Scots could not be forced into Anglo-Scottish union by acts of war, however, then the only way that that could come about was through dynastic union.[23] But – the second point under consideration – that would not simply happen of its own accord. Nor, as the Rough Wooing demonstrates, would the Scots permit a Scottish queen or princess to be married to an English king, which would produce an English takeover. Thus the 'dynastic initiative', so to speak, had to come from Scotland: for there to be Anglo-Scottish union, it was necessary for a Scottish monarch to inherit the English throne. Throughout their adult lives, Mary Queen of Scots and her son James VI both hoped to do so – and James's hopes eventually came true.

Yet 1603, it must be remembered, was a 'dynastic accident'. To appreciate it, we should consider the two countries' succession systems. Since the late eleventh century, succession to the Scottish Crown had (with the major exception of Robert Bruce's seizure of the throne in the crisis of the early fourteenth century) followed the normal rules of primogeniture, with males being preferred but females not being excluded. Admittedly the Scots did remove certain monarchs – James I in 1437, James III in 1488, and Mary in 1567 – but in each case these were replaced by their sons and heirs. Thus, the concept of Scotland's fabled unbroken hereditary line of native-born rulers

---

[21] M. H. Merriman, 'The forts of Eyemouth: anvils of British union?', *Scottish Historical Review*, lxvii (1988), especially p. 151, note 5.

[22] See J. Wormald, *Mary Queen of Scots: A Study in Failure* (London, 1988), pp. 43–57. A recent study of Arran's politics in 1543 can be found in D. Franklin, *The Scottish Regency of the Earl of Arran: A Study in the Failure of Anglo-Scottish Relations* (Lewiston, New York, 1995).

[23] A union of states negotiated by treaty, as happened in 1707, was not an option open to the English and Scottish statesmen of the Tudor century.

was maintained. In England, on the other hand, while the same rules applied in theory, in practice during the medieval and early modern periods they seem only to have operated when the political elite was prepared to let them do so. In a sense, the English political community 'elected' its rulers: if not formally, as did the Germans, Danes, Poles, Bohemians and Hungarians, in practice the effect was much the same. From 1066 to 1603, fewer than half the instances of English royal succession were simple, with heirs by primogeniture uncomplicatedly succeeding their predecessors. It is not too fanciful to think in terms of the 'elections' of 1066, 1089, 1100, 1135, 1154, 1199, 1216, 1327, 1399, 1461, 1470, 1471, 1483 and of course 1485; and, for a later period, there were those of 1649, 1660, 1688 and 1714.

In the sixteenth century, Henry VIII may have been returned unopposed in 1509, but he did so on the back of his father's successful 'election campaign' at Bosworth – when the then king, Richard III, was deserted by most of the politically conscious classes, or the 'electorate'. Edward VI likewise seems to have had an easy ride in 1547, but his place in the line of succession had to be guaranteed by an Act of Parliament, his father's will had much to do with the form his government took, and there were those two lost days between the death of Henry VIII and the proclamation of his son's succession.[24] As for Mary Tudor, her accession is the clearest example of a decision being made by the country. Northumberland had an alternative regime in being (with Jane Grey as Queen), and 10,000 men to defend it. Mary, however, had more adherents; in effect, she 'won the election'. The point is, it was a contest, and Lady Jane might have won like William III did in 1688, had the wind blown differently in the summer of 1553.[25]

Elizabeth's succession is the most remarkable of all. Her right to succeed depended not on heredity but on a statute of 1544, not to mention *two* Reformations of the English Church. In France, she would have been found a pension, a husband, and a place at court as 'mademoiselle la bâtarde de Bolyn'. In Scotland, something similar would have happened – what did James V's eldest bastard, James Stewart, Earl of Moray, the leader of the faction which removed Queen Mary, really think of Elizabeth? By French and Scottish rules, Elizabeth could not have come to the throne. And it could be argued that what actually happened in 1558 was something akin to a *coup d'état*.[26] Consider, moreover, the extraordinary Bond of Association of 1584. This covenant, drafted by Cecil and Walsingham after the assassination of William

[24] Jordan, *Edward VI: The Young King*, pp. 51–69.

[25] W. K. Jordan, *Edward VI: The Threshold of Power* (London, 1970), pp. 494–535; D. Loades, *Mary Tudor* (London, 1989), pp. 171–83.

[26] The 1536 Act which declared her illegitimate was never specifically repealed; in 1559 Parliament simply declared her 'lawfully descended and come of the blood royal': M. Levine, *The Early Elizabethan Succession Question, 1558–68* (Stamford, 1966). See also M. Levine, *Tudor Dynastic Problems* (London, 1973), pp. 66–74; and W. MacCaffrey, *Elizabeth I* (London, 1993), pp. 12–29. Further, it could be argued that James's accession in 1603 was illegal: see G. Donaldson, *Scotland's History: Approaches and Reflections*, ed. J. Kirk (Edinburgh, 1995), p. 117, where he speaks of it being 'in defiance of statute'.

of Orange, pledged its adherents to defend the queen with all their power. Thousands signed it. But the English ruling elite also pledged that anyone who tried to kill Elizabeth would be summarily slain – *as would the person in whose name the attempt was made*. So, if Elizabeth were assassinated, Mary Queen of Scots was automatically to be murdered, regardless of her complicity. As John Guy has put it, the Association was 'a political vigilante group' determined to execute 'lynch law'.[27] Even James VI could have been despatched because of it. That is not normal hereditary dynasticism in operation.

Moreover, the hindsight with which the Stewart succession of 1603 is so often viewed should be balanced by an exercise in counterfactualism. After all, while historians like to deal with what actually happened, at the time statesmen had constantly to engage in contingency planning. So, when considering 1603, we should never lose sight of a host of 'What ifs'.[28]

What if Francis II of France had lived through adulthood and had sired sons on his wife, Mary Queen of Scots? She would have remained in France. Who would have ruled Scotland: a Catholic French viceroy, or (as actually happened in 1560–1) a Council of Scottish Lords? Would civil war have broken out, much as in the Netherlands – with Moray emerging, like William the Silent, to head a Republic? Or might James Hamilton, Duke of Châtelherault (head of the legitimate Scottish cadet line), have been 'elected' king?

What if Queen Mary had married Don Carlos of Spain after 1560, as was once proposed? She would have lived with Carlos, wherever Philip II sent him. If they had sons, the eldest should eventually have been king of Scotland as well as of the Spanish dominions. Again, a Dutch Republic scenario, or a Hamilton 'election', does not seem far fetched.

What if Elizabeth of England had married, and had borne sons of her own? We surely would not have had Anglo-Scottish union in the early seventeenth century. On the other hand, that might have happened earlier, if Elizabeth had died of her serious illness in 1562. At that time, Mary seems to have been trying not to offend moderate Protestants, and English religious persuasions were mostly Anglican-Catholic (judging by the *Book of Common Prayer*). Or warfare might have erupted: not Thistle against Rose, but an English civil war of religion, which would probably have prevented Anglo-Scottish union.

What if Mary had died childless, in, say, 1557 or 1564? Châtelherault would presumably have succeeded, as King James VI. But the Hamiltons had no family links with the Tudors, so there would have been no dynastic union. Yet, if Mary had died, Henry, Lord Darnley would have been Elizabeth's closest relative. Henry, Lord Darnley, as Henry IX, successor to Elizabeth: the mind reels.[29]

[27] J. Guy, *Tudor England* (London, 1990), pp. 331–3, 344–5, 350. See also J. E. Neale, *Elizabeth and her Parliaments 1584–1601* (London, 1957), pp. 17–18, 33–7, 50–3; and MacCaffrey, *Elizabeth I*, pp. 343–54.

[28] Cf. the illuminating insights produced by Geoffrey Parker's counterfactual essay, 'If the Armada had landed?', *History*, lxi (1976).

[29] Darnley was the son of Matthew Stewart, Earl of Lennox and Margaret Douglas, daughter of

Or, finally and most possibly: what if Darnley had turned out to be an acceptable consort for Mary? Surely, then, Mary would have managed to remove Moray and his anglophile supporters from her Council, as she almost did in 1565. And her son, Charles James, would presumably have been raised a Catholic.[30] What would that have done to his chances of the English throne? By 1603, Protestantism appears to have been established firmly in the English national psyche (especially after the Armada – but would there have been an Armada in these hypothetical circumstances?), and a Catholic succession in England seems, to me at least, impossible. Admittedly, whoever was ruling Scotland towards the end of the century would probably have tailored his or her religious policies to be acceptable to the English ruling elite, or 'electorate'. Nevertheless, the chances of a union of the crowns would have been much slimmer than they were with the real James VI in 1603. And that is the conclusion to be drawn from this counterfactual musing: a very lucky set of dynastic circumstances lay behind the 1603 Union.

To return to actuality: the third point for consideration is that, in 1603, James, and Scotland, had to be Protestant. Two sharply defined moments during the sixteenth century made that possible. One was in 1559–60, when the Scottish Protestant 'Lords of the Congregation' seized power from the French-backed regime of Mary of Guise, regent for her daughter Mary, and brought about the first Scottish Reformation. The other came in 1567, when another aristocratic faction successfully attacked Queen Mary herself and her third husband the earl of Bothwell; a Protestant clique then forced Mary to abdicate, brought about the second Scottish Reformation, and, following Mary's disastrous flight to England and six years of bitter civil war, finally established her son James VI securely on the throne.[31]

One of the many striking features of these two sets of events is that both were accomplished with English assistance. For two-and-a-half centuries, from 1296 to 1548, there had been a long sequence of hostile and often devastating English invasions of Scotland. But in 1560, 1570 and 1573, English armies campaigned north of the Border not as would-be conquerors but as allies of Scotland's Protestant factions, helping crucially first to drive out Mary of Guise's French garrisons, and then to defeat the Marian party in the civil war. This revolution in British political relationships was essentially the achievement of Queen Elizabeth's minister, William Cecil, one of the true 'British' statesmen of the sixteenth century, and to a large extent the architect both of James VI's accession to the Scottish throne and James I's to the English. Throughout his career, Cecil claimed always to be working for Scotland's 'best worldly felicity', namely partnership and, eventually, regnal Union with

the earl of Angus and Margaret Tudor (James IV's widow). His son, of course, did succeed Elizabeth. See J. Dawson, 'Mary Queen of Scots, Lord Darnley, and Anglo-Scottish relations in 1565', *International History Review*, viii (1986).

30 For the prince's name, see M. Lynch, 'Queen Mary's triumph: the baptismal celebrations at Stirling in December 1566', *Scottish Historical Review*, lxix (1990), p. 6.

31 M. Lynch, *Scotland: A New History* (2nd edn, London, 1992), pp. 196–202, 217–22.

England, to uphold the cause of Protestantism – though, of course, England's interests were closest to his heart, which in the 1560s meant ensuring that Scotland was detached from the close relationship with France personified by Mary of Guise and Mary Queen of Scots.[32]

Cecil's first experience of Scotland, however, came as a young man in 1547, when he was employed to record the events of Somerset's invasion for publication to the English governing elite.[33] Whether or not his participation in the second phase of the Rough Wooing shaped his later policy is unclear. But what I, for one, would argue is that the defining events of 1559–60 and 1567–73 would not have come about if it had not been for that really serious English attempt to bring about Anglo-Scottish union by force, made by the duke of Somerset in 1547–9. What that led to, as we have seen, was the French marriage of Mary Queen of Scots – which placed England in considerable peril during the next decade. Had Somerset 'let the Scots be Scots' in 1547, Mary's claim to the English throne would still have been valid and a threat, but she would not have been under French direction. The main purpose of Cecil's intervention in Scotland in 1559–60 was to protect England from French, Catholic scheming; but it would not have been necessary without the crisis created by his former mentor, Somerset.

More to the point, had it not been for the second Rough Wooing, there might not have been a Scottish Reformation at all. Twenty or thirty years ago, such a sweeping assertion would probably have been rejected out of hand: the Reformation was then seen as an inexorable flood engulfing everything that stood in the way, be it aristocratic hesitancy, monarchical resistance, or internal Catholic reform. Nowadays, historical opinion is not so certain.[34] Of course Scotland, in the 1540s and 1550s, produced as powerfully articulate, heroically committed and passionately ardent reformers as did any society in Europe. But that can be said as well of the Huguenots in France. In fact, Reformation 'success' was so often a matter of forces over which ideology, however potent, had no control. It was a domestic (and international) political battle, as well as a war for men's souls, in which faith often lost its engagements through funk, poor tactics and just plain bad luck. We must now recognise that the Scottish Reformation was an extraordinarily close-run thing (as indeed was the English) – in which case the Rough Wooing seems to have been of critical significance.

Reform from within might have saved the Catholic Church in Scotland, had it been given more time. The politics of 1559–60 did not, however, allow that time. The events of those two years – a piece of luck in the truest sense – were absolutely vital to the eventual triumph of the Calvinist faith in

[32] J. Dawson, 'William Cecil and the British dimension of early Elizabethan foreign policy', *History*, lxxiv (1989); J. Dawson, 'Anglo-Scottish Protestant culture and integration in sixteenth-century Britain', in Ellis and Barber, *Conquest and Union*.

[33] See Patten, *Expedicion into Scotland*.

[34] See Lynch, *Scotland: A New History*, ch. 12; and contrast G. Donaldson, *The Scottish Reformation* (Cambridge, 1960), with I. B. Cowan, *The Scottish Reformation* (London, 1982).

Scotland. Without them, there would not have been the *coup d'état* of August 1560. Without them, the Protestant clique could not have taken over the reins of government as they did before Mary Queen of Scots returned from France. In my view, these things could not have happened had it not been for the French presence in Scotland. And without them, too, there would not have been the second *coup d'état* and second Reformation of 1567.

But there are at least two further aspects of the events of 1559–60 which depended on the Rough Wooing of 1547–48.[35] One is that the invasions by the Protestant Somerset included a grievous assault on the Catholic Church in Lowland Scotland: not only were many of its physical workplaces (parish kirks, monasteries, priories) wrecked, burned and plundered by English troops, but physical intimidation by armies and raiding parties forced many clerics to flee their charges, never to return. Numerous clerics were slain, particularly at Pinkie. Also, the financial costs of the war probably bore more heavily upon the Scottish Church than on any other sector of society (except, perhaps, the burgesses). But while mercantile elements could recover, many ecclesiastics were forced to liquidate their capital, leaving the Church further enfeebled. In addition, the Rough Wooing was a cauldron in which Protestant believers could flourish, and a forge on which their faith was strengthened. Had it not been for the war, John Knox probably would not have gone to Geneva.

Secondly, if it had not been for the Rough Wooing, the young Queen Mary herself would presumably have stayed in Scotland. And certainly, without the English aggression in 1547, no French garrisons would have come to Scotland in 1548, to be stationed there still in 1559. In that year, the revolt of the Lords of the Congregation could not have succeeded without its broad-based support – which depended on hatred of the French strangers living in Scotland – and without the assistance of the English troops. Elizabeth, how-ever, would probably not have aided the Scottish rebels had it not been for Mary's French-inspired assumption of the English royal arms. It is simply impossible, for me at least, to conceive of the Scottish Reformation as happen-ing when and as it did without those preconditions. And they, in turn, were the direct result of English actions in the 1540s. In a deeply ironic sense, it can be said that Henry VIII and Somerset did, in what is fatuously described as 'the long term', achieve their broad policy aims of 1543 and 1547: the creation of a pro-English Scotland. Also, perhaps, it is due to them that Scotland became Protestant, and that it was soldered into a Great Britain. But they brought that about despite themselves, and probably did not deserve to do so.

[35] The points in this and the following paragraph derive from M. Merriman, 'The Struggle for the Marriage of Mary Queen of Scots: English and French Intervention in Scotland, 1543–1550' (London University Ph.D. thesis, 1974).

One king, two kingdoms
Jenny Wormald

1603 resolved one thing, and one thing only, for Tudor Englishmen and Stewart Scotsmen. The English acquired a successor to Elizabeth. The Scots lost a full-time king. Beyond that lay nothing but confusion and muddle. Great efforts were, of course, made to play down that muddle, and hide it behind a decent veil of enthusiasm and friendly clarity. The trouble was that the individual voices of 1603 were indeed clear enough; but the things they said were normally contradictory, often incomplete and sometimes violently biased. King James wanted – or was believed to want – a single kingdom of Great Britain. He certainly said so, in the famous proclamation of 1604, which he issued to compensate for the failure of his English Commons to recognise its advantages.[36] And if MPs had expressed strenuous opposition, there were other voices, the voices of those Englishmen who had to state a position outside the House of Commons – men like Cotton or Egerton, as well as poets on the make – who subscribed to the idea. Scottish voices also spoke for closer union. But they all tended to emphasise – over-emphasise, from the English point of view – the ancient kingdom which had given England a king and was now willing to show friendship to the lucky recipient.[37] Protestants on both sides of the Border naturally saw distinctly Protestant advantages in that king. But the English Protestant establishment, as represented by Archbishops Whitgift and Bancroft, had made no secret of their intense dislike of the nature of Scottish Protestantism, while the extremists in the Scottish Church, the Melvillian Presbyterians, had little time for the watered-down version of the English variety. Moreover, as neither Scotland nor England was yet (or ever would be) wholly Protestant, there were also the Catholics, for whom James, son of the sainted Mary, would offer much – or so they told him.[38] Nowhere, however, was there a veil more firmly drawn than over the fundamental problem that the kingdoms of England and Scotland might now share a king, but their political and social traditions remained deeply divided. Historians have tended to follow the lead which King James gave, in looking for similarities. The differences are what matter.

It is, of course, entirely unsurprising that efforts should have been made, in the aftermath of 1603, to identify common ground. But it is equally unfortunate that a real master of prose should be best remembered for that piece of

[36] *Stuart Royal Proclamations*, ed. J. F. Larkin and P. L. Hughes (Oxford, 1973), i, pp. 94–8.

[37] *Acts of the Parliaments of Scotland*, ed. T. Thomson and C. Innes (Edinburgh, 1814–75), iv, pp. 263–4; *Register of the Privy Council of Scotland*, ed. J. H. Burton *et al.* (Edinburgh, 1877–), vii, pp. 535–6. Among the Scottish tracts about the Union in *The Jacobean Union: Six Tracts of 1604*, ed. B. Galloway and B. Levack (Scottish History Society, 1985), see especially John Russell, 'A treatise of the happie and blissed Unioun', pp. 75–142; and see also Russell's unprinted treatise and letter in National Library of Scotland, Edinburgh, MS Advocates 31.4.7, fos. 21r–7v.

[38] See, e.g., the letter from 'The Catholikes of England' to King James, Public Record Office, SP 14/1/56; also SP 14/1/7, 14/1/55 and 14/1/63.

highly dubious propaganda, endlessly quoted in undergraduate essays and elsewhere: 'Here I sit and governe [Scotland] with my Pen, I write and it is done, and by a Clearke of the Councell I governe Scotland now, which others could not do by the sword.' It is one of his most misunderstood statements, far too readily believed. In his 1604 proclamation, the king had stressed those powerful points in common between his kingdoms – their geography, their language, their religion – in arguing for his union. Now, in 1607, he was at pains to tell the English that his Scotsmen were acceptable, civilised and co-operative beings, not the grasping barbarians of fevered English perception. If they had been problematic and difficult in the past, hardly controlled even by the sword, they were now obedient and loyal subjects, whose enthusiasm for union arose not from any particular desire of theirs but directly out of their offer 'allwayes to obey mee ... for the personall reverence and regard they beare unto my Person, and any of my reasonable and iust desires'. It was perhaps somewhat tactless of the king to remind his unenthusiastic English audience that the Scots had shown little interest in union on their own account; he was almost trapped into the admission because of his determi-nation to portray them in a docile and placid light. Thus they were as gentle lambs in the Scottish Parliament. Whereas the English Commons of 1607 showed too clearly their distrust of the Scots, 'no Scottish man ever spake dishonourably of England in Parliament'. None could, such was the power of the Scottish Chancellor to silence dissenting voices. More generally, control of all material to be brought before Parliament, and the king's right of veto, ensured a high level of royal control; again, there is the note of subjects desirous only to please their sovereign, for at the passing of legislation, 'if there bee anything that I dislike, they rase it out before'.[39]

It is all rather sweet in its way. More to the point, it shows the vast gulf between illusion and reality, and, we must presume, the vast ignorance of the English about the Scots on which James was able to play. This heroic attempt to make the Scots appear acceptable could only work with an audience who did not know, or did not care to know, what the Scottish Parliament was really like. We might add that it also shows a somewhat less than sensitive approach to the English Parliament, now asked to admired the subservient and royal-dominated body north of the Border. Indeed, somewhat incon-sistently, that was part of James's point, for incorporated into this section are flashes of criticism of the long-winded grumbling of the English Commons. Moreover, it was hardly flattering to his Scottish Parliament. For this was no subservient body, willing to act as poor relation to its English counterpart in order to please its king. Apart from the fact that it was uni-cameral

[39] *The Political Works of James I*, ed. C. H. McIlwain (reprint, New York, 1965), pp. 301–2. See also *Stuart Proclamations*, i, p. 95: 'the Isle within itself hath almost none ... but one common limit or rather Gard of the Ocean Sea, making the whole a little world within it selfe ... A communitie of Language, the principall meanes of Civil societie, A unitie of Religion, the chiefest band of heartie Union, and the surest knot of lasting Peace.'

in composition – being, on the European model, a meeting of the Three Estates – rather than bi-cameral like the unusual English Parliament, it had a very distinct tradition of considerable political power; one might simply point to the fact that the English Reformation Parliament, acting as junior partner to the Crown, took seven years to achieve less decisive ecclesiastical reform than the Scottish Reformation Parliament, acting in defiance of the Crown, did in just over three weeks. Altogether, therefore, as a piece of rhetoric designed to show the advantages of uniting the kingdoms, the king's analysis can hardly be regarded as a success. What it actually revealed was, in microcosm, the reason why it could not be done.

James himself knew perfectly well that his portrayal of the Scots was untrue; indeed, the very rules which he described as controlling his Scottish Parliament were in fact mostly very recent, introduced in the previous two decades precisely because of problems of control. For present purposes, however, the main point is that they were simpler rules than those that obtained in England. The significance of this can be interpreted in two ways. One is that the later sixteenth century saw Scottish government, its Parliament and council, its lawyers and administrators, very belatedly but determinedly starting to catch up with more developed contemporary kingdoms, notably the kingdom of England. Thus the Scots were beginning to share the English political *mentalité*, even if in practice they still lagged very much behind; rules and conventions would still be simpler, but at least they were now on the right – English – lines and so indeed would produce common ground for the ruler of both kingdoms. There is something to be said for this view. It is true that a lay legal profession was coming into existence, and new rules were being made not only for parliamentary procedure but for admission to the Court of Session; while for the first time the traditional justice of the feud was being seriously challenged, instead of being operated in tandem with the more formal mechanisms of Scotland's Common Law. Attempts were made to introduce JPs into Scotland in 1581 and 1587, and again, more strenuously, in 1609, 1610 and 1617. Laymen were taking over from clerics in administrative offices. It was in James VI's reign that Scotland first experienced long-term regular taxation, to fill the coffers of a spendthrift king. Helped on by the advent of an absentee king, a *noblesse de robe* was coming into existence, and in theory at least this began to shift the balance of political power away from the hereditary aristocracy. As the earl of Dunfermline, a noted beneficiary of the process, boasted to the earl of Salisbury in another attempt to underline the new civility of the Scots, the snub to the mighty northern earl of Huntly when he was refused license in 1605 to go to the king 'will make the courses of all our great ydalgos the more temperate'.[40]

All these things undoubtedly happened, and therefore undoubtedly heightened

---

[40] *Historical Manuscripts Commission, Salisbury MSS*, xvii, p. 149.

perceptions of the similarities between England and Scotland – perceptions which were, because of the Union of the Crowns, a matter of strong political vested interest. King James's whole case, in arguing for a union which went far beyond the personal and royal one, depended utterly upon them. Equally, James's 'new men', whether waiting for the future in the 1590s or living with the new reality in the early years after 1603, had every reason to portray themselves and their political world as comparable to that of the English politicians with whom they would share a common lord. But behind the propaganda lay two very crucial flaws in the case. The first was that the extent to which Scottish political, legal and social *mores* were actually moving closer to those of England was certainly exaggerated. The second was that the king himself was not wholly committed to the changes within his northern kingdom. That being so, our parameters for the debate about the nature of the personal Union of 1603 and its future must change significantly. A move towards an incorporating union of any kind was not just intensely difficult, but utterly impossible. In the previous section, Marcus Merriman discusses the 'defining moments' of the sixteenth century which led to the Union of the Crowns. In 1603 itself, two factors operated. James VI succeeded Elizabeth because he was, despite all the fuss and confusion in which three Tudor monarchs had chosen to bury the principles of succession to the throne, her legitimate heir, challengeable only by conquest. And he was an acceptable successor in the eyes of the English ruling elite because he was adult, male and Protestant. These things made possible a single king of two formerly independent kingdoms. None of them had the slightest relevance to the problem of 'uniting the kingdom'.

The other way of looking at the simpler rules of the Scottish Parliament described in the king's speech of 1607 is that they stand not for a move towards a more developed and 'modern' type of government, but as a reflection of what the Scottish political nation found acceptable; and that could be a very different thing. There was indeed a significant shift away from clerics to laymen in the king's government, created by changing aspirations of the laity and helped on by the reformed Kirk's insistence, by an Act of 1584, on pulling the clergy out of state service. The need to impose greater control on Parliament arose directly out of the political circumstances which dictated the timing of the Reformation, when in 1560 the ascendant Protestant lords were joined in Parliament by a large and clamouring group of lairds, asserting their right to turn up on the grounds of the dead-letter shire election Act of 1428. Thus a new shire election Act came on to the Scottish statute book in 1587 to impose control on this vociferous and volatile group. And the issue of religious debate was the backdrop to the controls imposed by James in the 1580s and 1590s.[41] Likewise, the growing power of the Edinburgh lawyers lay behind the legislation of 1598 and 1600 'anent deidlie

---

[41] *Act. Parl. Scot.*, ii, pp. 525–35; iii, pp. 509–10; also, e.g., iii, p. 354; iv, pp. 56, 69.

feids'.[42] But, to a considerable extent, these apparently 'modernising' and even, in terms of union, anglicising processes were a veneer, beneath which lay much that remained vibrantly resistant to change. Another model is therefore possible.

In a masterly analysis, and with enviable elegance and clarity, Thomas Charles-Edwards has sketched out the relationship between centre and periphery in the early medieval British Isles. Subjects (as James VI and I rather too frequently reminded his exasperated and faithful English Commons) were bound by love to support their monarch. In the seventh century, this meant that they fed him. In the 'centre', this was done by hospitality; those in the area of the normal royal circuit killed the necessary cow, or whatever, and gave him dinner. In the periphery, the same rule operated, but the king was much less often seen. In the outlying areas, which were subjected sub-kingdoms, they trundled the cow out of the byre and sent it off on the hoof, as tribute. Thus those at the centre actually met the king – the great lord, the great patron – and the dinner was the chance to bargain and seek reward. Those in the periphery had less opportunity, but were correspondingly less burdened. And in the outlying parts, grudging acquiescence at best, resentment at worst, were what accompanied the cow sent to the king; only refusal might bring the king in person, and then not as patron, but in force.[43]

No-one writing about early modern England would seek to understand it by invoking its seventh-century past. But the vast problem created by 1603 is strikingly illustrated by the fact that it is still just possible to glimpse Charles-Edwards's three-tier model operating in early modern Scotland. That is the measure of the difference between the two kingdoms. It was at the centre – Edinburgh – where new ideas were coming in, but only at the centre. Thus in 1580 it was observed by an Englishman that 'of lawyers there are but few and those about the Court of Session in Edinburgh, for in the shires all matters are ordered after the great men's pleasures'.[44] The periphery, in other words, remained distinctly traditional; the justice of the feud, the age-old dependence on kin and lords, still flourished. And even the 'centre' was by no means clear-cut about the ways in which it sought to impose control. Thus, in 1587 Parliament and council wrestled with the problem of criminal justice. They came up with three ideas. One looks fairly innovatory. Scotland already had one central court, the Session, for civil justice. Now a central court for criminal justice was proposed by the Privy Council; it would meet in

---

[42] Ibid., iv, pp. 158–9, 233–5. See J. Wormald, 'Bloodfeud, kindred and government in early modern Scotland', *Past and Present*, lxxxvii (1980), pp. 85–7; a rather different interpretation is given by K. M. Brown, *Bloodfeud in Scotland, 1573–1625* (Edinburgh, 1986), pp. 239–46.

[43] T. M. O. Charles-Edwards, 'Early medieval kingships in the British Isles', in S. Bassett (ed.), *The Origins of Anglo-Saxon Kingdoms* (Leicester, 1989), pp. 28–33. In early medieval Scotland, this system operated through the thanages: see G. W. S. Barrow, *The Kingdom of the Scots* (London, 1973), ch. 1 ('Pre-feudal Scotland: shires and thanes'); and A. Grant, 'Thanes and thanages from the eleventh to the fourteenth centuries', in A. Grant and K. J. Stringer (eds.), *Medieval Scotland: Crown, Lordship and Community. Essays presented to G. W. S. Barrow* (Edinburgh, 1993).

[44] *Cal. State Papers Scot.*, v, no. 638.

Edinburgh, and the king would preside in person. But this apparent shift in the relationship between centre and periphery was immediately undermined by the council's own detailed arrangements for a series of local justiciary courts; it would be almost another century before a central court of judiciary was fully in being. The second was anything but novel; it was to revive the justice ayres – the equivalent of the English eyres, last seen in England in 1330 – which had operated in Scotland throughout the later Middle Ages.[45] It was no more successful; but it is the idea of reviving the medieval machinery for supervising local justice which is instructive. In any event, the proposal was dramatically undermined in Parliament by the king himself, who declared that notwithstanding the Act on criminal justice, it was the earl of Huntly's lieutenancy in the north which would determine his approach in that part of his kingdom. He was immediately followed by a senator of the College of Justice, John Graham of Halyards, speaking not as a 'new' lawyer, but as justice-depute to the earl of Argyll, the hereditary Justice-General and thus traditional head of the ayres, who demanded that the Act should not prejudice Argyll's office. If the new approach clashed with the old as far as the periphery was concerned, Huntly and Argyll bring us to the outlying areas, the Highlands and also the Borders. There, as in fourteenth-century England, the government was prepared to resort to local commissions where the ayres failed. But the Scottish variety had none of the politeness of its English counterpart. These were not commissions of the peace; using language as violent as the most violent of its feuding subjects, the government issued commissions of fire and sword. And, less violently, it produced its third idea, one which was utterly traditional and utterly local: the General Band, by which landlords were made responsible for their tenants and dependants.[46] So, in the end, those men of new ideas in Edinburgh could not invoke royal power from the centre, but had to rely on the hope that deep local bonds of kinship and lordship could be made to work in their favour. Small wonder, then, that early Stuart Englishmen were unconvinced by the idea that they could be brought into closer conjunction with a kingdom which was similar to their own.

This was not just because – thanks to the governmental changes of Tudor England, which are of the utmost significance for understanding 'British' as well as 'English' history – the great lords of the English periphery or outlying areas, such as the Percies of Northumberland, were becoming an anachronism,[47] whereas in Scotland their equivalents were still crucial to the control and stability of the kingdom, however much the emerging *noblesse de robe* tried to pretend differently. It was also because the king himself saw control

[45] H. L. MacQueen, *Common Law and Feudal Society in Medieval Scotland* (Edinburgh, 1993), pp. 54–65.

[46] *Reg. Privy Council Scot.*, iv, pp. 217–19; *Act. Parl. Scot.*, iii, pp. 458–67.

[47] Cf. S. G. Ellis, *Tudor Frontiers and Noble Power: The Making of the British State* (Oxford, 1995).

of his kingdom in terms which were profoundly different from those of the Tudor monarchs. He was as keen as they were on a well-governed commonwealth, but he interpreted this in a very different way. Thus he sustained the practice of the aristocracy and lairds of making bonds of maintenance and manrent, as a means of defusing disorder;[48] he believed in his responsibility as arbiter in feuds and disputes. This superb political theorist was also deeply pragmatic. The centralising forces at work in England and in the major European kingdoms might appeal to his Edinburgh lawyers and government officials. But they did not as yet offer a satisfactory answer to the immediate problems of ruling Scotland, so that for the king it was more traditional methods which continued to have an appeal. Nothing is more revealing than the juxtaposition of events which surrounded the death in 1595 of John Maitland of Thirlestane, Chancellor of Scotland and one of the greatest of the men of new ideas, in 1595. Immediately, there were rival candidates for the office and the outbreak of faction-fighting, which was all too familiar to English diplomats who observed the struggle. What was less familiar to them – and is another example of the combination of old and new in James VI's Scotland – was the spectacle of two earls and a duke chasing the office. The king's response was to remove himself to Linlithgow 'where our faccaneres [factioners] will not get such access as they had in Edinburgh'. But he did not go only to Linlithgow. For at this busy time, the earl of Atholl inconveniently died, leaving no male heir, and James therefore set off for Perth, 'to take order with the country of Atholl, which is beginning to break since the earl died'.[49] Local order, maintained by the local earl, was, it seemed, of much more concern than jockeying at court. Indeed, the balance of James's reaction demonstrates very clearly his doubts about an office which had enabled a man to climb to an unacceptable level of political superiority; the chancellorship was kept vacant for three years, which at last does give us an example of similarity, for it was exactly paralleled by his refusal to appoint a Secretary in England for two years after Salisbury's death.

There is, in fact, very little evidence that James sought to temper his Scottish kingship to a model acceptable to his English subjects; indeed he showed considerable reluctance to temper it to the demands of Scottish lawyers and politicians who tried to dent older Scottish political assumption. The fact that they did so with some success was therefore by no means wholly due to a lead from the throne, and inasmuch as there was a lead, it was more the product of the demands of absentee kingship which forced the king, especially after 1603, to admit to the ranks of the aristocracy the politicians and administrators of the 'centre', thus giving them the dignity long held by those whom he described as his 'armes' in the periphery and the outlying areas. The very fact that the man who had a keen eye to the English throne

[48] See, in general, J. Wormald, *Lords and Men in Scotland: Bonds of Manrent, 1442–1603* (Edinburgh, 1985)

[49] These events are described in great detail in *Cal. State Papers Scot.*, xii, especially at pp. 3–69.

did not do more to adjust his style of kingship is a testimony to the fact that he found that his methods of ruling Scotland worked effectively, and were indeed more amenable to him than those which would be imposed on him in the more centralised and bureaucratically and institutionally complex kingdom of England.

When he thought of his English future, therefore, his preoccupations were not primarily with adaptation to English ways of doing things. He never needed to show his mother's obsessive and nagging demands for recognition as Elizabeth's heir, because the Protestant James could be confident, as the Catholic Mary could not, of his acceptability. His anxieties about the English succession lay far more with the Catholic powers of Europe. Thus he sent out confusing signals about his position: hence, for example, the shady diplomacy of 1595–6, when that highly dubious character Pourry Ogilvy went off to persuade Philip II of Spain and Pope Clement VIII of James's desire to restore his kingdom to the true faith, with the somewhat give-away addition in the case of the Pope that some money would greatly help his efforts.[50] James was not wholly unsuccessful in this bluff; rumours of the possibility of his conversion were one factor which influenced the Spanish Infanta when she resisted pressure to try for the English Crown herself, and were still circulating in Rome in 1605, helped on by another Scottish diplomatic rogue, Sir James Lindsay.[51] As Marcus Merriman points out, the Scottish Reformation was an essential pre-condition of the Union of the Crowns, so far as England was concerned. But King James could also see that wool-pulling was a necessary part of the need to distract foreign Catholics, and was skilful enough to walk the English Protestant/European Catholic tightrope. That was much more important than turning himself into an English king. Meanwhile, he turned to something very traditional indeed, in seeking a statement of Scottish support. In 1599, a duke, ten earls and a host of lords and lairds signed a bond which extolled his present government and promised their support in his rightful claim to the English throne.[52] As this gesture hardly made Elizabeth tremble on her throne, or, for that matter, forced the kings of France and Spain or the Pope to back off in the face of Scottish solidarity, we can only assume that it was a response to a bout of irritability about Elizabeth's insistence on survival. But it is a revealing comment on his kingship. James's actions and his attitudes got him his dual Crown. They left him with dual kingdoms.

After 1603, he settled down to exasperate the English. He upset them by demanding a level of unity – a united kingdom – which they found abhorrent,

[50] British Library, MS Cotton Caligula Bviii, fos. 342^r–6^v.

[51] A. J. Loomie, *Guy Fawkes in Spain: The 'Spanish Treason' in Spanish Documents* (*Bulletin of the Institute of Historical Research*, Special Supplement 9, 1971); A. J. Loomie, 'Philip III and the Stuart succession in England', *Revue Belge de Philologie et d'Histoire*, xliii (1965); Public Record Office, SP 14/14/41, fo. 99^r; SP 85, bundle 3, fos. 36^r, 42^r, 46^r, 48^{r-v}, 50^r, 72^r–6^r.

[52] Scottish Record Office, Edinburgh, Dalguise Muniments, GD 38/1/85b; this gives 27 signatures. Another copy gives 41: British Library, MS Sloane 3199, fos. 10^r–11^r.

although his extreme demands were almost certainly made in order to force a moderate and acceptable level of accommodation between his kingdoms which in large measure he achieved.[53] He worried them deeply by his sometimes terrifying theories of kingship. In addition, he infuriated them by his refusal to see the 'centre' as the essential and permanent source of royal power over the periphery. The French ambassador, de la Boderie, simply failed to understand how a king could jeopardise the success of his policies by removing himself from the centre of affairs and going off on his famous hunting trips.[54] But James retained from his Scottish rule a strong sense of the advantages of going out to the periphery, as a means of influencing his subjects and of defusing political tension. The Union of the Crowns fractured the royal 'centre' as it was bound to do. The would-be king of Britain refused to help his cause by acknowledging London as the new and undisputed centre of his kingship.

From the point of view of his new English subjects, the problem began with the king's accession. Uniquely, the new king of England, as they saw him, broke all the normal rules, for now the centre's heart-beat was somewhere in motion on the Great North Road; the 'centre' was literally shifting, down through the English periphery. Cecil, trapped in London, was in an agony of worry about rivals – notably Sir Walter Raleigh – getting to the king. He had grounds for worry. Those who gave the king dinner on his long progress south, those who stood by while he ate it, got their rewards. For a brief moment, the age-old model of kingship – which had never truly died in Scotland – flickered into life in England. Nothing on this scale ever happened again. But it was precisely in such circumstances, when James returned from Scotland in 1617, that the 'Book of Sports' had its birth, when those in Lancashire who hated the rigours of a puritan Sabbath were able to present their grievances directly to the king. More generally, plans to return to Scotland (even if only one visit actually materialised), and threats to move his government to York or to send the heir to the throne, Henry, back to his native kingdom, maintained throughout the reign the gulf between the English who understood successful government in terms of a fixed centre from which it could emanate, and a Scottish king who saw the 'centre' in terms of wherever he happened to be.

There was, then, no 'united kingdom' in the reign of the first British king. There could not be. In time, the inevitable pull of the centre of the more powerful kingdom had its impact on the political style and traditions of its lesser neighbour. Yet, paradoxically, Charles I was to behave in the most traditional of ways when he turned up in force against those members of an

---

[53] This point, stated all too briefly here, is discussed at greater length in my forthcoming article: J. Wormald, 'James VI, James I and the identity of Britain', in B. Bradshaw and J. Morrill (eds.), *The British Problem c.1534–1707: State Formation in the Atlantic Archipelago* (Basingstoke, in press).

[54] *Ambassades de Monsieur de la Boderie en Angleterre, 1606–11* (1750), i, p. 94; ii, pp. 100–2, 165–9.

outlying area of his 'kingdom' when they refused to pay him the tribute he demanded: acceptance of the Scottish prayer-book. And when he did so, he was responding to the greatest example of that most traditional statement of political will, the Scottish bond: the National Covenant of 1638. For all his imperial purpose, reinforced, as he saw it, by divine will, Charles I came to grief by refusing to accept what his father had so well realised.[55] The rhetoric and imagery of union might have made Scotsmen and Englishmen aware that they served one king. But that king had to rule over, and therefore understand, two kingdoms.

[55] For Charles's failure to understand how the Scottish nobles were accustomed to behaving and being treated, see D. Stevenson, 'The English devil of keeping state: élite manners and the downfall of Charles I in Scotland', in R. Mason and N. Macdougall (eds.), *People and Power in Scotland: Essays in Honour of T. C. Smout* (Edinburgh, 1992). For more general discussion, see M. Lee, jr, *The Road to Revolution: Scotland under Charles I, 1625–37* (Illinois, 1985); and A. I. Macinnes, *Charles I and the Making of the Covenanting Movement, 1625–1641* (Edinburgh, 1991).

Chapter 8

Composite monarchies in early modern Europe

The British and Irish example

Conrad Russell

All multiple kingdoms are composite monarchies, but not all composite monarchies are multiple kingdoms. The confusion between the two seems to have been perpetrated by James VI and I, in his speech to the English Parliament in 1607. James compared the relations between the two sovereign kingdoms of England and Scotland (a multiple kingdom) with the fact that England, whatever its myths might say, did not have a single uniform system of law, but had particular laws in, for example, Kent and the County Palatine of Chester (a composite monarchy).[1] England did not have the single uniform system of law characteristic of the single state, and might therefore, with a little effort, be regarded as a composite monarchy: it was not a multiple kingdom.

James's problem was that of ruling over multiple kingdoms: not the problem of rule over a state of many parts, but the problem of rule over several states. I have in the past described the combination of states over which he ruled as 'Britain', and his problem as a 'British problem'. I have been persuaded that this usage is inaccurate. The word 'British' might appear in court masques designed to glorify the king, but in common parlance it was used in Ireland, especially in the province of Ulster, as a shorthand meaning 'English and Scots'. When the word 'British' was used by the Irish, it was used to designate a group different from themselves. Having so often deployed the argument that tampering with the terminology risks imposing the present or the nineteenth century on the past, I cannot resist it in this case, and must therefore speak, more accurately if less simply, of a British and Irish problem.[2]

There is no particular novelty in arguing that the problem of multiple kingdoms was one of the greatest causes of instability in early modern Europe, nor in arguing that it was one of the greatest causes of trouble to the early Stuarts/Stewarts. Both these points were made by J. H. Elliott in the then *Cambridge Historical Journal* in 1955.[3] Since then, they have been

[1] See note 24, below. I am grateful to Professor Paul Monod for clearing my mind on the confusion between these two concepts.

[2] I am grateful to Dr John McCafferty for persuading me of this point.

[3] J. H. Elliott, 'The king and the Catalans 1621–1640', *Cambridge Historical Journal*, ii (1955), p. 253.

developed by innumerable authors, and to repeat these in this essay would be a tediously familiar exercise. What is needed now, and what the body of literature available is now large enough to permit, is the rather more taxing task of distinguishing between genus and species. Which of the difficulties visible in Britain and Ireland are typical of the genus 'multiple kingdom', and which are peculiar to the species found west of Dover? Where difficulties are generic, how often, and how far, do they work out in a way which is specific to the British and Irish example, and for what sorts of reasons?

All the familiar causes of instability we have been taught to look for by students of multiple kingdoms in the Iberian peninsula and elsewhere are present in the British/Irish example. The problems of the prince's residence, of the distribution of offices, of rival constitutional systems for holding the whole together, of division of religion, of foreign affairs and the cost of war, and of outside intervention in disputes between the kingdoms are all visible in Britain and Ireland. If we simply run through our checklist ticking off the items, we will think we have found a typical example of the genus 'multiple kingdom'. This will lead us to write up the problem of multiple kingdoms as if it were a monocausal explanation. By concentrating on the 'problems', it will also lead us to miss the equally interesting successes in running multiple kingdoms.

Parallels are treacherous things. They are like the ball in cricket which looks the same but is not: they encourage playing a stroke which is inappropriate because it does not recognise the difference. To take one example of the point, the genus 'multiple kingdom' suffers from the problem of inducing outlying kingdoms to contribute their share to the cost of war. This problem was as visible to Charles I as it was to Philip IV. The similarity was visible at Charles's court, as is proved by the fact that Secretary Coke, in 1627, proposed copying Olivares's Union of Arms.[4] Yet when we follow the parallel, it comes apart in our hands. The Irish case led to concessions to the major landowners, the Catalan to increased burdens on them. The Irish case created a problem which lasted three years, and, to the dismay of the Old English, faded away again. The Catalan created a problem which lasted the whole of Philip IV's reign. The lack of exact parallel must have something to do with the fact that Catalonia shared a land frontier with Spain's most powerful enemy, while Ireland, however great its strategic importance might be, was a Gallipoli and not a Passchendaele. That fact in turn must have something to do with the fact that Perpignan is now French, while Kinsale is not Spanish. Parallels are treacherous because they are never exact.

Yet some comparative points stand out. Perhaps the most startling is a success. We are not used to thinking of the British and Irish example as a success. For this, I must take some part of the blame. I first approached this subject through that hall of distorting mirrors, the search for the causes of the

---

4 Public Record Office [PRO], State Papers, SP 16/527/44.

English Civil War. This has meant, as Keith Brown and others have justly pointed out, that what I have done has fallen short of true British history. It has also meant that, like S. R. Gardiner, I have done work from which teleology has not been absent. The search for the causes of any upheaval necessarily involves a concentration on the search for things which were wrong. Yet the different and equally valid teleology of the Act of Union of 1707 leads to a search for things which were right. The search for problems should not blot out the successes.

The most remarkable success of the British and Irish union is that so many parts of it are still there. The Union of England and Scotland in 1603 was, in the terminology of the day, an imperfect union: it was a union of sovereign states under a common authority, without a union of laws. In this, it differed from the Union of England and Wales, which was a 'perfect union', involving full integration. The union of England and Ireland was neither of these, and it is as hard to describe accurately as is the doctrine of the Trinity. These three different types of union, under one ruler, encouraged emulation and pressure for uniformity. The imperfect union with Scotland was the one which created most fear of impermanence. One of the union tracts of 1604 said it was like the union of Spain and Portugal, 'wherein there can be no great assurance of continuance'.[5] The parallel illustrates the rationality of the fear, and also the extent to which its failure to come true marks a success for the Union.

Of the other imperfect unions known to the commentators of 1604, some were dissolved long ago, such as the Union of Kalmar, the union of Poland and Lithuania, and the union of Spain with both the northern and the southern Netherlands. Others, such as the union of the Empire and Bohemia and of England and Ireland, lasted into the twentieth century before they were dissolved. Of the imperfect unions which were known to the commentators of 1604, I can only think of four which are still in being: they are the unions of Aragon and Castile, of the Swiss Cantons, of England and Scotland, and, believe it or not, of Great Britain and Northern Ireland. The fact that two of the four imperfect unions still surviving are matters of current controversy seems to illustrate that the commentators of 1604 were right in their view that imperfect unions were likely to be impermanent. Yet it also illustrates that, in the relevant terms of comparison, the unwieldy combination of states ruled by James VI and I must be counted a success.

Yet even here, the parallel is treacherous, and some of the things which made the Union last may also have helped to make it more turbulent. In the checklist of 'things to remember about multiple kingdoms', one of the most important is that difference of religion between the kingdoms caused acute instability. The British and Irish example clearly confirms this thesis. There are three other examples in early modern Europe of multiple kingdoms involving division in religion. They are Spain and the Netherlands, the

[5] *The Jacobean Union: Six Tracts of 1604*, ed. B. Galloway and B. Levack (Scottish History Society, 1985), p. 47.

Empire and Bohemia, and France and Béarn. Two of these caused upheavals even bigger than the British Civil Wars. One led to separation, and the other to a determined attempt at it.

The curiosity is the case of France and Béarn.[6] The chief peculiarity in that case is obviously the extreme disparity in size and power between the kingdoms. Yet it is instructive that the case of England and Scotland (though not so much England and Ireland) is in some ways much more like that of France and Béarn than it is like that of Spain and the Netherlands or of the Empire and Bohemia. Professor Desplat's study of France and Béarn illustrates a tendency among those involved to make cross-border alliances with their co-religionists, rather than national alliances. Louis XIII's Edict of Restitution, restoring to Béarnais Catholics property they had held before 1569, was obviously as likely to worry the French Huguenots as it was to please Béarnais Catholics.

It is that pattern which is reproduced in the exchanges over the Scottish Prayer Book of 1637 and the Scottish National Covenant of 1638. Like the Béarnais Protestants, the Scottish Covenanters were determined to hang on to the support of their co-religionists in the metropolitan kingdom. The Covenanters constantly stressed that this was not a 'national quarrel', but a fight against the Romish superstition which was threatening both kingdoms. The difference between Charles I and Louis XIII was not that they were engaged in different tactical battles, but that Louis had more success in persuading his own religious dissidents not to ally with their co-religionists in the smaller kingdom. In Ireland, where the Irish parliamentary committee of 1641 made a similar attempt to enlist the support of Arundel and Cottington against the political and religious correctitude of Pym, the attempt at a cross-border alliance was less successful.

Throughout the multiple kingdom crisis of the years 1637–51, the three national minorities, English Puritans, Scottish Episcopalians and Irish Protestants, showed the same attachment to union as did the Béarnais Catholics. They all formed their alliances in unionist terms. The 'Scottish imperial' vision of the Covenanters was also a unionist vision to its core. They seem to have calculated that since Scotland was the militarily inferior power, it was only by cross-border alliance based on religion that they could ever hope to build up a winning coalition.

The key difference which separates the crises of the Netherlands and Bohemia from those of Scotland and Béarn appears to lie in the religious complexion of the metropolitan power. Madrid and Vienna were, in effect, one-religion capitals. Those who dealt with them could not make the alliances with co-religionists which were open to those who dealt with Paris and London. The unionist road of dealing with co-religionists in the central kingdom, which was exploited by the Scots and the Béarnais, was not open to

[6] C. Desplat, 'Louis XIII and the union of Béarn to France', in M. Greengrass (ed.), *Conquest and Coalescence: The Shaping of the State in Early Modern Europe* (London, 1991).

those who dealt with Madrid and Vienna. Political forces which were unionist in Scotland and Béarn therefore became separatist in the Netherlands and Bohemia. Neither England nor France was used to thinking of its own internal religious division as a source of strength. In terms of trouble caused in the short term, they were right to identify it as a source of weakness, yet in terms of preserving their unions with outlying kingdoms, that very weakness may have been their biggest source of strength. Insofar as it is possible to make a general rule out of four examples, it appears to be a general rule that religious division broke unions when the central kingdom was united in religion. When the central kingdom was divided in religion, religious troubles in the outlying kingdom might cause much more disruption, but in the end they confirmed the union rather than weakened it. This is because the hopes of religious dissidents in the outlying kingdom were cast in a unionist mould. It is the pattern of which the Scottish Labour Party is the most prominent modern example.

Foreign war, the next of the issues which regularly caused problems in multiple kingdoms, produced remarkably little trouble in Britain and Ireland. Here it is the specific, rather than the general, which is dominant, and the particular specific point which matters is the exceptional absence of war. During the years 1603–42, it was only in 1625–8 that war was a significant political fact. This ratio of peace to war makes Britain and Ireland almost unique in early modern Europe.

Yet this statement, though correct, is misleading. It results from a selection of dates imposed not by British, but by English, domestic history. If the dates chosen were to be 1585–1660, or even more if they were to be 1494–1713, the British and Irish example would look a lot more typical in the European context than it does in the years when England was preoccupied at home trying to mend the leaks in its Exchequer, and France and Spain were trying to recover from financial exhaustion after the Peace of Vervins. During the Elizabethan war with Spain, the Spanish landing at Kinsale and the affair of the Spanish blanks in Scotland show a pattern of continental involvement in British and Irish affairs which is very much in the standard pattern. After the outbreak of the Civil War in England, the doings of the Irish confederates or of Montrose's supporters in Scotland were of very considerable interest to the continental powers.

The one period of serious war during the early seventeenth century, in 1625–8, shows it creating strains between the three kingdoms in a way which would have been entirely recognisable in the Netherlands or Catalonia, or in Naples and Sicily or Sardinia. When Charles I turned to war with Spain, in 1625, it was logical that one of his first fears should be of a Spanish landing in Ireland. It was this fear to which Secretary Coke's Union of Arms was a response. What is specific to the Irish case is that asking the Irish to pay for their own defence might appear as a concession, since it carried with it the trust of allowing Catholics to control armed force, and the security of tenure conferred briefly by the Graces of 1626. It was not the native Irish or the Old English who objected to paying for the costs of their own defence: it was the New English interest, alarmed by the implied concessions to Catholicism. Their fears had much to do with the withdrawal of the Graces on the conclusion of peace. That helps to explain why what might otherwise have been regarded as the imposition of an intolerable burden by a metropolitan authority became instead something the Old English dreamed of getting back, and almost managed to recover in 1641.

This picture provides a very clear contrast with the effect of the war years on Scotland's relations with the Crown. In Scotland, the perception of war pressure was a much more familiar perception of centralising contempt for national privilege and autonomy. In fact, the war years provoked a first crisis of the Union, which has been briefly outlined by Peter Donald.[7] The Act of Revocation, one strand in this crisis, has been much more fully analysed by Allan Macinnes.[8] One of the flash-points was Charles's attempt to raise a regiment of 2,000 men from Scotland. The Scottish Estates 'did altogether refuse it, as a thing unpossible'. The earl of Mar, Lord Treasurer of Scotland, defended the view of the Estates in a stormy interview with the king in London; 'Butt', said his Majesty, 'it is not unpossible, and it shall yett go on.' When Mar tried to continue the debate, Charles revealingly exclaimed: 'ye durst not have done so to my father'.[9]

When the men were eventually raised, they were sent for service against France, Scotland's ancient ally. The earl of Lothian, writing to his father the earl of Ancram in the king's Bedchamber, said, in a letter which can be read several ways, 'there is so general an unwillingness in our country to any war, for I cannot think they except against it because it is against France, for they are only base people that know not how we and France have stood these 8 or 900 years'.[10]

In this crisis of 1625–8, the issues of war finance became entwined with the issue of distribution of offices, for the outbreak of the war coincided with the breakdown of James's Scottish Bedchamber. The key strain on the Bedchamber was the desire of the English *valido*, the duke of Buckingham, to bring it under his own control. In April 1625, when Charles had been two weeks on the throne, the earl of Kellie, James's Scottish Groom of the Stole, told Mar that Charles was resolved not to have any of his father's Bedchamber come into his. He added that Buckingham's power with the king was 'not pleasing to most men neither of one degree nor other'.[11] At the crucial stage of the

---

[7] P. Donald, *An Uncounselled King* (Cambridge, 1990), pp. 14–27.

[8] A. I. Macinnes, *Charles I and the Making of the Covenanting Movement, 1625–1641* (Edinburgh, 1991), pp. 26–102.

[9] *Historical Manuscripts Commission Reports, Mar and Kellie MSS*, i, pp. 134, 145–6.

[10] *Correspondence of Sir Robert Kerr, first Earl of Ancram, and his son William, third Earl of Lothian*, ed. D. Laing (Bannatyne and Roxburghe Clubs, Edinburgh, 1875), i, pp. 44–5. 'They' refers to tenants of Lothian's who had been pressed for the expedition.

[11] *Hist. MSS Comm., Mar and Kellie Supplementary Report*, p. 227. The context does not make clear what meaning Kellie was attaching to the word 'degree'.

crisis over the Revocation and the Scottish regiment, the Bedchamber was in no position to attempt its usual task of mediation. This coincidence between the first crisis of the Union and the collapse of the Bedchamber is a good occasion to ask whether we have misjudged James's handling of the Bedchamber. Seen in a multiple kingdom context, James's handling of the distribution of office may look more successful than it ever did when seen from the Palace of Westminster.

To Neil Cuddy, the historian of James's Bedchamber, it was 'the symbol of failure, and a prime stumbling-block in the relations between king and parliament'.[12] By 'parliament', Cuddy means only the English Parliament. In its own terms, this judgement is correct, yet it is exclusively a municipal judgement in English history. In a discussion of multiple kingdoms and composite monarchies, a wider perspective is needed. For Scotland, the Bedchamber was an essential mechanism for coming to terms with the problem of an absentee king. The stream of requests for favour which filled the papers of the earl of Kellie or the earl of Ancram suggests that, for Scots who knew where to look, the Bedchamber was an excellent means of gaining the attention of an absent king. If Scots were to get a fair share of the patronage of an absent king, some such means were essential. When the earl of Lauderdale, in 1621, wanted a place in the prince's council, his request was sent to the earl of Ancram in the Bedchamber, in order that Ancram should forward it to the king.[13] It is not surprising that there was a crisis of the Union when this system was temporarily superseded by the London-based patronage of the duke of Buckingham. Buckingham did prefer Scots, but they were mostly Anglo-Scots, who tended to have married Buckingham's relations. The system had little to offer Scots whose power base was confined to Scotland.

After 1628, Charles slowly rebuilt his Scottish entourage. The failure of 1637 was not a failure of communication between the Scots and the entourage. Men like Rothes and Cassilis continued, in Jacobean style, to pour out their hearts to Hamilton, Lennox and Morton. Covenanter acceptance of the Jacobean system is implicit in the effort they put into the task of trying to place the earl of Rothes in the Bedchamber.[14] The failure of 1637 was something much more serious. It was a failure in communication between the entourage and the king; and against that personal failure at the top, no system is proof. The Bedchamber system is not to blame.

English protests against that system were the protests of men too little aware of the Union to have much interest in preserving it. They have obscured the fact that, in union terms, the Bedchamber was vital. James's

---

[12] N. Cuddy, 'The revival of the entourage: the Bedchamber of James I, 1603–1625', in D. Starkey et al., The English Court: From the Wars of the Roses to the Civil War (London, 1987), p. 173.

[13] Ancram and Lothian Corresp., i, pp. 26–7.

[14] C. Russell, The Fall of the British Monarchies, 1637–1642 (Oxford, 1991), pp. 49–50, 308. Also Edinburgh, Scottish Record Office, Hamilton MSS, GD406/1/522, 531, 326.1, 646, etc.

proverbial 'stroke of the pen' only worked because the Scottish Privy Council and the Scottish members of the Bedchamber had carefully prepared the piece of paper on which the stroke of the pen was to be placed. It was that relationship which institutionalised the consultation which must be at the heart of any successful system of devolution. In British terms, the Bedchamber was cheap at the price.

To understand the Bedchamber in its multiple kingdom context, we should look at the protests and discontents of the Portuguese at their lack of access to court offices in Madrid. In that context, James's insistence that Scots should have access to court offices in London looks like one of the forces which preserved the Union. That insistence cost James some effort. In April 1603, when James was still on his way to London, the earl of Kinloss arrived in London with James's letters admitting him to the English Privy Council, 'to the disgust of the Lords [of the Council], who pretended that no one but Englishmen should hold honours and office in England'.[15] The Venetian ambassador, who knew where to look for power, reacted by immediately paying a call on Kinloss.

These reflections prompt a comparison of two ways in which multiple kingdoms could handle the outlying kingdoms. One was the system used by James VI in Scotland, which was in essence a system of devolution. The Scottish Privy Council in Edinburgh was in effect a devolved government, in which all the day-to-day work of running Scotland was done by Scots living in Scotland, exercising power in the name of a king with whom they communicated through the Bedchamber. In normal times, royal authority in Scotland was effectively that of the Scottish Privy Council. An ambitious Scot could therefore hope to participate in it, and if he could not participate in it, to influence it through the daily mechanism of social contact in Edinburgh. It was a system which continued a daily political life in Edinburgh, disturbed only by occasional eruptions of royal authority from London.[16]

The alternative system, used in Ireland and Portugal, was that of delegating royal authority to a viceroy or governor general. To a tidy mind, this looks like a better system, because the royal authority is on the spot, and access to it is always possible. In fact, the cases of Ireland and Portugal suggest that the viceregal pattern was a fruitful source of instability. The crux of the problem was that the viceroy was not king, and therefore that anyone discontented

---

[15] J. H. Elliott, 'The Spanish monarchy and the kingdom of Portugal, 1580–1640', in Greengrass, *Conquest and Coalescence*, p. 54; *Calendar of State Papers relating to English Affairs, existing in the Archives ... of Venice* (London, 1864–), x *(1603–7)*, p. 10.

[16] Ironically, the Act of Union of 1707, by destroying the Scottish Privy Council, destroyed any independent Scottish input into the process of patronage. It created a series of patronage-masters who, even though they might be Scots, tended to depend on a power base in London. They therefore became more like governors general than like a Scottish Lord Treasurer under the Union of the Crowns. In this way, the Act of Union brought Scotland to a pattern more like that of Ireland than any which had existed before. W. Ferguson, *Scotland: 1689 to the Present* (Edinburgh, 1968), pp. 54–61, describes Harley's unsuccessful attempt to avoid this consequence.

with his decisions was bound to want to appeal over his head to the king. In that context, the viceregal authority was always either too much or too little. If appeals were allowed, the viceroy lost authority, and if they were not, he lost acceptability. In either case, the viceregal pattern created an interruption in the flow of communication between the country concerned and the metro-politan seat of authority. When, as inevitably happened, people managed to go behind the viceroy's back, the lack of an institutional Bedchamber meant that they went to unaccountable and usually uninformed English Councillors. There was no Irish equivalent of the relationship between the earls of Mar and Kellie, though in a different political constellation the Clanricarde–Essex link might have provided one. Instead, business went to people like the earl of Holland, whose knowledge of Irish matters was not profound. Wentworth became so ruffled by Holland's interventions that on one occasion in 1637 he thanked him for 'the beginning of your respects towards me'.[17] If religion had permitted it, some of the Old English lords could have provided a very effective Irish Bedchamber. It is hard to believe that in those circumstances mix-ups like the Graces and the Plantation of Connacht would have happened as they did. One might ask whether, when James's prolonged hunting trips turned him into an absentee king of England, the earl of Salisbury in London suffered some of the difficulties of a viceroy of England.

Though questions like religion, war and the distribution of offices were always important, in the last resort the break-up or continuation of multiple states depended then, as it does now, on outside intervention. The present boundaries of Catalonia, for example, follow from French willingness to defend Roussillon and Cerdagne when they ceased to defend Catalonia south of the Pyrenees. The independence of the northern Netherlands could not have been sustained without the support, limited though it may have been, of England and France. In Portugal, it was the help and sympathy of the French, the Dutch and the English which enabled Portugal to break away from Spain in 1640, when Catalonia failed.[18] The Portuguese had another asset vital to those who wished to break away from a composite monarchy: a pretender with a hereditary claim. In 1641, when the new Portuguese ambassador arrived in England asking for recognition, Charles asked him by what title his master claimed the crown. The ambassador replied that Cardinal Henry, the last independent heir of Portugal, had died without issue, 'save for some of whom we do not speak', that John of Braganza, the new claimant, was his heir, and therefore that he claimed the crown by succession. Reassured by this information, and by the reports of his own consul in Lisbon that the new king's control of his kingdom was secure, and that the French and the Dutch,

17 Anglesey, Llanfairpwllgwyngyllgogerychwyndrobwulllantysilogogogoch, Plas Newydd MSS, Box XII. I would like to thank the Marquess of Anglesey for permission to examine his family papers.
18 Elliott, 'Spanish monarchy and kingdom of Portugal', p. 65.

'both declared enemies to the Crown of Spain', were likely to support him, Charles took the plunge of recognition.[19]

This list of the hurdles the Portuguese jumped is a good check-list of the hurdles the Irish and the Scots did not jump. Neither had a hereditary successor ready to act as pretender. The Irish would have needed an heir of the old high kings from before the beginning of the English line, and such descents were remote enough to leave plenty of room for rivalry. The Scots had plenty of eligible nobles, but none was ready to take the risk of pretending.

It is more important that Portugal's friends were Spain's enemies, as the friends of the Netherlands had been Spain's enemies. Similarly, anyone who would have supported the breaking away of Ireland or Scotland would have been England's enemy. That would have meant that if England had had a stable alliance with either France or Spain, the other might have been prepared to support independence for Scotland or Ireland. In 1604, when England was making peace with Spain, the French ambassador briefly panicked that this might mean a stable alliance between England and Spain. He said the English were becoming 'eschauffez en l'amitié de l'Espagne', and worried about the rise of Northampton, 'autant declaré ami de l'Espagne qu'enemy ouvert de la France'. As a result, the ambassador said that if things were to change, he could be 'en très beau moyen de séparer ces royaulmes'.[20] It is a good example of how routinely the breaking up of multiple kingdoms was identified as part of the arsenal of great powers.

The French ambassador's fears proved exaggerated. James was not about to enter into a stable friendship with Spain, and the ambassador soon began to realise that. From 1604 down to 1689, England had no stable position in the rivalry of the continental great powers. Because James and Charles had no dependable continental friend, they had no dependable enemy either. There was thus no power which was likely to support a breakaway by Scotland or Ireland. Any power to which England was a certain enemy might have done so, but because James and Charles had no certain friend, they also had no certain enemy. Both France and Spain were always able to hope for the sympathy of England within the next five years. So long as that hope existed, there was no sense in extinguishing it, and turning England into a certain enemy, for the sake of the lesser prize of Scotland or Ireland. In terms of realpolitik, it made no sense for France or Spain to assist a breakaway by Scotland or Ireland. Anyone who thinks this rule ceased to operate during the Interregnum should remember that the Commonwealth's first war was with the Dutch. Moreover, the years of the English Civil War are the last weary

[19] PRO, SP 89/4. fos. 36, 42, 47, 49.
[20] PRO, SP 31/3/37, fos. 13, 34–5. The ambassador's chosen device for separating the kingdoms was to back the duke of Albany (not yet duke of York) as heir to Scotland. He said the Scots were not allowing Albany to leave Scotland, because he would one day be their king.

years before the Peace of Westphalia, when the resources of France and Spain for fishing in troubled waters had run very low.

Just as religious division in London troubled the Union while helping to hold it together, so too did the division in the English Council between the partisans of France and Spain. This is shown very clearly by French tactics during the years 1640–2. From Pym's visit to the French ambassador on 25 October/4 November 1640, if not sooner, every French effort was directed, not towards Scottish independence, but towards using an Anglo-Scottish settlement to strengthen the anti-Spanish party in London. From then down to the ambassador's warning to the Five Members, the French were after the bigger prize.[21] The Scottish Covenanters, who were realists, appreciated very early on that they could not rely on foreign help against England, and this may help to explain why, in David Stevenson's words, independence was 'evidently unthinkable to the Covenanters'.[22] It was only in the context of a new settlement in London that they could regard their own Scottish Revolution as secure. To that end, though not to the end of independence, they could count on consistent French support.

This rule is confirmed by the very different pattern whenever England took on a settled enmity with either France or Spain. Under Elizabeth, settled Anglo-Spanish hostility led to Spanish intervention in Ireland, just as it did to English intervention in the Netherlands. After 1689, settled Anglo-French hostility led to French backing for the Old and Young Pretenders in Scotland. It would be interesting to know whether James VI and I appreciated the fact that his love of peace may have done more to preserve the Union than did any other policy he pursued.

It is possible that the same principle of weaknesses becoming strengths may have applied to the greatest weakness of the English in handling a multiple kingdom. This is their attachment to the notion of a unitary sovereign power, which could do what it would and could not be controlled but by itself. The theory was put forward by Thomas Cromwell as a means of combating papal authority, but it is the long war from 1588 to 1604, against attempts to invade England with papal backing, which really made it take root. This is an idea appropriate only to a unitary state: it simply will not work in a multiple kingdom. It is the curse of politics that ideas come into fashion at precisely the moment when they cease to be useful. The attachment to a unitary theory of sovereignty in 1603, when the onset of a multiple kingdom made it entirely irrelevant, is a case in point.

Lord Burghley, in 1597, had said that an Act of Parliament could make a man a woman. His son the earl of Salisbury repeated that 'I know not what

---

21 Russell, *Fall of the British Monarchies*, pp. 164–6, 449–50.
22 D. Stevenson, *The Scottish Revolution* (Newton Abbot, 1973), p. 132. See also Robert Baillie, *Letters and Journals*, ed. D. Laing (Bannatyne Club, Edinburgh, 1841–2), i, pp. 190–1.

an act of Parliament may not do.' Francis Bacon suggested that an Act of Parliament could abolish Parliament or the monarchy.[23] Yet even if an Act of Parliament could do all these things, it could not regulate relations between England and Scotland, since, unless England were to annex Scotland as it had done Wales, an Act of Parliament would have no authority for the Scots. It shines through all the speeches of Sir Edwin Sandys on the Union that he could not imagine a union which did not have a single Parliament and a single legislative sovereignty. That, as much as sheer obstructionism, may have been why he supported the idea of a perfect union, with a single integrated state and a single sovereign legislature, rather than an imperfect union which might allow different laws and different legislatures in different parts of the state. In France, such a notion would have created no fuss: it was a fact that law was not the same in all of the French provinces, and no Frenchman would have understood an argument which said that France was therefore not a state. The English, on the other hand, came to the task of running a multiple kingdom imprisoned by a theory of authority which turned the very notion of a union of sovereign states, or even the familiar continental composite monarchy, into a contradiction in terms. The English were therefore locked into the nightmare of either believing that England had lost its sovereignty, or believing that no union had taken place. This is an inherited curse from which England has not yet escaped.

King James, on the other hand, wished to unify his countries, not in order to secure a complete uniformity of laws, but in order to ensure that they should be governed by a single law of succession. He simply could not understand why his aim was seen as a fundamental threat to English law and sovereignty. On 31 March 1607 he told the two Houses of Parliament, in terms which no true Cromwellian could accept:

> When I speak of a perfect union, I mean not confusion of all things; you must not take from Scotland those particular privileges that may stand as well with this union, as in England many customs of particular shires (as the customs of Kent, and the royalties of the County Palatine of Chester) do with the common law of the kingdom.

This did not prevent James from hoping the Union would grow closer. When he said it was 'no more unperfect, as now it is projected, than a child which is born without a beard', and added in explanation that it was '*in embrione* perfect', he was invoking an ideal not far different from the 'ever closer union' of the Treaty of Rome.[24]

All this was incomprehensible to members of the English Commons like Thomas Hedley. Hedley identified Scotland, in true Cromwellian style, as a

---

[23] 'Hayward Townshend's journals', ed. A. F. Pollard and M. Blatcher, *Bulletin of the Institute of Historical Research*, xii (1934–5), p. 17; E. R. Foster, *Proceedings in Parliament 1610* (New Haven, 1966), i, p. 66; G. Burgess, *The Politics of the Ancient Constitution* (London, 1992), pp. 22–3.

[24] *House of Commons Journals*, i, pp. 358, 367.

'liberty' and argued: 'if churchmen overthrow law by their privileges, Scotsmen will more'.[25] The anti-papal roots of English hostility to union are very clearly exposed. Laurence Hyde argued in equally Cromwellian terms:

> I am persuaded that the commons and all the Scottish nation except some few great persons that have liberties unfitt for subjects, as power to pardon treasons, felony, murder, manslaughter and other like, would gladly yield to the subjection of our laws: and in this case stood Wales whilst the Earls marchers held their great liberties and powers, and were never united until by H.8 they were discharged of all such regalities, and made even as we, thereby participating all privileges and advantages with us, and are since made as good subjects as any of us.[26]

That was an offer to rescue the Scots from the status of lesser breeds without the law. This Welsh dream constantly recurred in English debates on the Union: it was the only way the English could accept union without abandoning their belief in a single unitary sovereign power. The only union they could understand was annexation.

Any attempt to subject England to any authority above that of its own local King-in-Parliament was seen as a threat to its legal identity. Sir Edward Coke, at the conference of 25 February 1607, said that he was the first who conceived that the change of name, to Britain, could not be with any safety to king and kingdom. Neither Britons, Saxons nor Danes had changed the fundamental law of England; 'the king cannot change the natural law of a nation: this foundation is a firm foundation'.[27] In this invocation of the ancient constitution as a protection against the Union, Coke had drawn attention to a fundamental weakness and lack of authority in the English body politic.

Any serious attempt to regulate the Union would demand changes in the authority of King-in-Parliament inside England. Any attempt to turn England and Scotland into a single state, or even into a multiple state whose parts were governed by some orderly relationship, would demand the imposing of conditions on the authority of the English King-in-Parliament. England's difficulty is that it possessed no source of authority capable of imposing such conditions. Coke had not envisaged the escape route used in 1707 and 1972, of doing it through the device of an international treaty.

In countries like Scotland, which could claim a foundation (albeit mythical), this difficulty did not arise. In a state with a recorded foundation, the authority which set up the institutions of a state could thereafter claim power to regulate them. The heirs of 'Fergus I' in Scotland, or the people in the United Provinces, might claim a power to impose constitutional change

[25] Ibid., i, p. 1017; PRO, SP 14/26/54.
[26] *The Parliamentary Diary of Robert Bowyer*, ed. D. H. Willson (reprinted New York, 1971), p. 211.
[27] PRO, SP 14/26/54.

on a state, though they would need general consent to do it. In England, because no-one created King-in-Parliament or Common Law, no-one had the power to regulate them. The Parliament of England trying to bind its successors is like God finding he cannot drive a golf ball out of his own sight: it is crippled by its omnipotence.

England is unique among the states of Western Europe in that it cannot claim a recorded foundation. We can only say that England became a state sometime between 899 and 956, but the English omitted to make any record of the fact. That this worried Jacobean Englishmen is seen from the attempts to elevate Cnut, Edgar or Egbert of Wessex as a sort of English Fergus I, but the mere fact that the English could not agree on a candidate for founder showed that the attempt was futile. Sir Edwin Sandys, by far the shrewdest of the English opponents of union, spotted that the only way anyone could claim authority to regulate the English King-in-Parliament was by conquest, and the implications of that possibility were frightening.[28] Without the ability to regulate its relations with Scotland, the English Parliament could only pretend that Scotland did not exist. Indeed, it has only accommodated the British Parliament created in 1707 by pretending that it is the same body as the English Parliament which preceded it.

In these circumstances, the English Parliament was forced to pretend that no union had taken place. In 1607, Thomas Wilson reported to Salisbury that the English Parliament had objected to every word in the title and preamble of the bill for abolishing hostile laws, objecting to the words 'continuance and preservation' of the Union because it 'seemed to presuppose an union already made, to which they would not in any wise assent, noe more to any naming of the union at all in the title'. He said 'it seemed they thought the word "union" a spirit, for they shunned the very shadow of the name of it'.[29]

The English Parliament continued to refuse to admit that any union had taken place: if the king chose to be king of Scots in his spare time, that was nothing to do with them. In ecclesiastical matters, where the king could operate on his own, this did not protect Scotland from pressure for uniformity. In matters of secular law, it did. One need only look at the explosion in Anglo-Irish relations when, in 1641, the English Parliament did begin to claim responsibility for Ireland to see what the Scots were spared by the English Parliament's refusal to recognise their existence. So far as the Scots and the English Parliament were concerned, it was a case of the familiar maxim: 'two groups who never meet cannot fight'. It was only the king who met all the groups concerned. The king, therefore, was the only one who could effectively make a mess of the relations between the kingdoms – which King Charles duly did.

---

[28] SP 14/7/63, 65. Sandys even tried to solve the problem of authority by saying it could not be done without 'especiall commission from the country' – possibly a referendum.
[29] SP 14/21/17.

Chapter 9

Irish, Scottish and Welsh responses to centralisation, *c.*1530–*c.*1640
A comparative perspective[1]

Nicholas Canny

In contributing to a volume designed to discuss the 'new British history', I am conscious that my interpretation of events in the three Celtic jurisdictions of the English/British Crown during the sixteenth and seventeenth centuries may appear as ungenerous nationalist carping. To forestall any such criticism I should point out that I have always advocated comparisons between developments in Britain and Ireland, and since my reservations to the new approach are methodological rather than philosophic, I would prefer to be labelled with the modern-sounding tag of 'Brito-Sceptic' rather than with the tired nineteenth-century label of 'Nationalist Historian'.

On those previous occasions when I have sought to dampen the enthusiasm of the zealots of the 'new British history',[2] I have questioned their judgement on three grounds, to which I would now add two more. These are as follows. First, much of what has been praised as exemplary of the genre has been so preoccupied with issues of high politics that the 'new British history' seems to be further widening the rift that already exists in British historiography between political history and social and economic history. Second, the focusing of attention on happenings on the two islands of Britain and Ireland, and the insistence, as John Morrill puts it, 'that the unit of study ought to be the British Isles',[3] imply an integrity for 'These Islands' probably in excess of any that ever existed, and distract our minds from the lively but varied contacts that were maintained by the several different communities on the two islands with the European Continent. Third, much of what appears as

[1] I am grateful to Tom Bartlett, Martin Burke, Pádraig Lenihan and Joe McLaughlin for helpful advice; to Jane Dawson and John Robertson for their comments; and to Ciaran Brady for bibliographic leads.

[2] See my review of C. Russell, *The Fall of the British Monarchies, 1637–1642,* in *Irish Economic and Social History,* xix (1992), pp. 112–15; and N. Canny, 'The attempted anglicization of Ireland in the seventeenth century: an exemplar of "British history"', in R. G. Asch (ed.), *Three Nations – A Common History?* (Bochum, 1993). A slightly emended version of this paper will be reprinted in J. Merritt (ed.), *The Political World of Thomas Wentworth, first Earl of Strafford, 1621–1641* (forthcoming, Cambridge, 1996).

[3] J. Morrill, 'The Britishness of the English Revolution', in ibid., p. 93; it should be noted that John Morrill, out of deference to Irish sensitivities, has dropped the usage 'British Isles', and now favours 'These Islands'.

'new British history' is nothing but 'old English history' in 'Three-Kingdoms' clothing, with the concern still being to explain the origin of events that have always been regarded as pivotal in *England*'s historical development. Fourth, the concern with the holistic approach results in a tendency to emphasise similarity at the expense of difference, and ignores the fundamental diversities that made it so difficult for the several peoples on the two islands to live within a single polity. Fifth, the study of the newly defined subject in all its aspects is beyond the reach of most historians, because it is only those with a good reading knowledge of three Celtic languages as well as English and Latin who can master all the relevant sources.

Because of these various difficulties, I continue to be an advocate of comparative history, where the historian, speaking with the authority that derives from a detailed knowledge of the evidence relating to one society, compares developments there with happenings in the other societies within the same jurisdiction, and compares developments in this larger entity with those in apparently analogous circumstances throughout Europe and in Europe's overseas colonies. It is in this spirit that I have approached my topic, the responses to centralisation in the sixteenth and seventeenth centuries, under the headings of 'Religion', 'Language', and 'Politics'.

Religion

It appears, on a superficial level, that the establishment of Protestantism as the official religion gave the three kingdoms of England, Scotland and Ireland, as well as the principality of Wales, a cause on which to unify during the turbulent years of the first half of the seventeenth century, and saved the fledgling state under the newly united Crowns from the dismemberment that threatened some other composite monarchies in Europe at that time. King James VI and I certainly saw it in that light, as do most of the recent historians who have addressed the problems associated with the Union of the Crowns. Brian Levack, for instance, believes that the Union of Love to which the king aspired was to derive ultimately from loyalty focused on a common religion and a common monarch, and argues that 'the apparently successful precedent' that gave grounds for the optimism of James 'was the union of the Welsh and English people after the constitutional union of 1536 and 1543'. In similar vein, Jane Dawson shows how the relative success of the Reformation in England and Scotland created a common 'Anglo-Scottish Protestant culture' and a common language of *print*.[4] However, while alluding to the sense of unity that did come from a commitment to the same religious cause,

---

[4] B. Levack, *The Formation of the British State: England, Scotland, and the Union, 1603–1707* (Oxford, 1987), p. 179; J. Dawson, 'Anglo-Scottish Protestant culture and the integration of sixteenth-century Britain', in S. G. Ellis and S. Barber (eds.), *Conquest and Union: Forging a Multi-National British State* (London, 1995). I am grateful to Dr Dawson for a preview of this and of others of her papers.

both historians are aware that confessional agreement alone was not sufficient to surmount the various obstacles to unity, and that religious developments in the several dominions of the British Crown contributed as much to division as to unity.

The first problem relates to the different origins and progress of the Reformations in England and Scotland; in the first instance there was a Reformation promoted and firmly guided by the state, and in the second a Reformation advanced and supported by an oligarchy who believed it would consolidate their independence from state authority. The significance of these differences in experience was made manifest only when King Charles I and the Scottish Covenanters each began to contemplate an appropriate scheme of ecclesiastical conformity for the three kingdoms. However, even without the succession of wars that followed upon these later developments, it is clear that the success of the Reformations contributed to divisions both within and between the several jurisdictions of the British/English Crown. Those who have studied the Reformation in Scotland are agreed that its success heightened existing cultural divisions between the Scots- and Gaelic-speaking regions, even to the point where fully evangelised Protestants in the Highlands and Islands were not accepted by ministers in the Lowlands as members of either the same religious or the same cultural community simply because they did not use the language in which the scriptures were printed.[5] England was not troubled by any such acute linguistic divisions, but those areas of the kingdom associated with lingering attachments to the old religion were quickly identified by committed Protestants as 'dark corners of the land'. During the later decades of Elizabeth's reign, when loyalty to Catholicism was taken to imply treasonous intent, the inhabitants of such areas were considered as potential enemies of the community. The acceptance of such ideas at the highest levels of government was to complicate the Crown's dealings with its subjects in both Wales and Ireland, because the Reformation made but slow progress in both jurisdictions down to the middle of the seventeenth century, and the overwhelming number of Protestants in Ireland at that time were officials and settlers from Britain (or their descendants) rather than Irish converts.

Several explanations have been tendered for the slow progress of the Reformation in Wales and Ireland, and Steven Ellis has treated the issue as a common problem for the Tudor state.[6] The causal factors that have been especially isolated are: the low level of interest by the central government in remote areas of their jurisdiction; the limited contact between the peoples of Wales and Ireland and Protestant populations on the Continent; the modest educational attainments of those who would be a reforming clergy, and the

---

[5] J. Dawson, 'Calvinism and the *Gaidhealtachd* in Scotland', in A. Duke *et al.* (eds.), *Calvinism in Europe* (Cambridge, 1994).

[6] S. G. Ellis, 'Economic problems of the Church: why the Reformation failed in Ireland', *Journal of Ecclesiastical History*, xl (1990).

delay in rectifying that situation until the establishment of Jesus College, Oxford, in 1571 and Trinity College, Dublin, in 1592; and the failure of those who were available to work on these two missions to master the linguistic challenges that confronted them. To these shortcomings in the official drive to advance religious reform has been added the rapacity of landowners who gladly seized hold of confiscated monastic land while denying an adequate living to newly appointed Protestant clergy. Such landlord involvement can obviously be interpreted as obstructionist, and it seems to have been true in most cases in both Wales and Ireland that landowners were as concerned to retain their powers of patronage over church appointments as to defraud the Church. However, they seem also to have wished to hinder the arrival in their midst of centrally appointed clergy who would further the political no less than the religious policies of the state.[7]

This first response to the drive for religious uniformity in the outlying Tudor realms might therefore be described as conservative obstruction, and is such as would have occurred in any provincial area of any European state at that time. This alone may have been the principal factor that hindered a more rapid progress of the Reformation in Wales, but it is hardly sufficient to explain developments in Ireland. There the official target during the sixteenth century was the achievement of religious conformity in the anglicised areas of the country and especially the English Pale, and it was generally accepted that the promotion of the Reformation in the Gaelic and Gaelicised regions would have to await the extension of crown authority over the outlying lordships. What makes the Irish situation essentially different from that of Wales is, therefore, that official concern in the sixteenth century was with the leaders of a community who were more given to fawning after royal approval than were any other subjects of the English Crown. These gentry and officials of the Pale were undoubtedly provincials in the sense that their political energies were devoted to advancing local interests, but they were very different from their Welsh counterparts in that they spoke English, were educated after the English manner, and maintained regular contact with the centre of power through correspondence, petition, and delegation. Moreover, those of them who had attended at the Inns of Court aspired to appointment as officials in the Dublin administration (itself a subsidiary branch of crown government), and to this extent were representatives of crown authority in the localities. Why these people ultimately disappointed the government in religious matters therefore calls for a more compelling explanation than that offered for a more purely provincial area such as Wales. But, before advancing such an explanation, we must take account of differences in response, first during the initial phase of reform and then when the Reformation was more advanced.[8]

---

[7] A. Ford, *The Protestant Reformation in Ireland, 1590–1641* (Frankfurt, 1985); G. Williams, *Recovery, Reorientation, and Reformation: Wales c.1415–1642* (Oxford, 1987); T. Herbert and G. E. Jones (eds.), *Tudor Wales* (Cardiff, 1988).

[8] On the nature of society in the English Pale, see N. Canny, *The Formation of the Old English*

When the initial response of the Palesmen is subjected to closer scrutiny it appears that they complied altogether more readily than their Welsh counterparts with the wishes of successive governments in religious matters, at least down to the 1570s. The leaders of the Pale community had no difficulty with outward conformity, and the English-speaking population of Ireland produced even a few people, such as Rowland White, who could perceive of reform in religious terms. However, as with Wales, outward conformity seldom led to sincere attachment to Protestant belief, and many public conformists continued to attend Mass in private while their wives, children and kin remained publicly attached to Catholicism. This recalcitrance was similar to what occurred in Wales, but on a more extensive scale, because public conformity appears to have been more general among the elite of the Pale. To the usual explanations offered by historians for instances where religious compliance did not mature into sincere belief must be added the vulnerability of the Pale community in psychological as well as physical terms. The constant fear of the leaders in the Pale was that their community would be destroyed either by an onslaught from the Gaelic lordships surrounding them or by exactions imposed on the farming and commercial sectors by the lords of Anglo-Norman descent resident within the Pale. Their concerns over such matters formed the subject of their overtures to London, but when it came to discussing questions of religion and morality even professed Protestants like White fell short when it came to admitting deficiencies in themselves and their community. This absence of a capacity for self-criticism, such as was pervasive in the Scottish Lowlands, seems essential to explaining why, in the case of the English Pale, religious compliance did not lead to a commitment to Protestantism.[9]

Another factor which goes towards explaining why conformity did not lead to conviction is that all that the state required of its subjects in Ireland, previous to the mid-years of Elizabeth's reign, was conformity. Thus the leaders of the Pale community continued to enjoy royal favour and to participate in the formulation of policy for Ireland even when the position of governor was held by a metropolitan Englishman, as was invariably the case from the 1530s onwards. The small number of Englishmen who were appointed to civil and ecclesiastical positions during those years were, with few exceptions, as readily absorbed into Pale society as their medieval

Elite (National University of Ireland, O'Donnell Lecture, Dublin, 1975); S. G. Ellis, *The Pale and the Far North* (National University of Ireland, O'Donnell Lecture, Galway, 1986); and a sequence of essays in F. H. A. Aalen and K. Whelan (eds.), *Dublin: City and County from Prehistory to Present* (Dublin, 1992).

[9] See Canny, *Formation of Old English Elite*; 'Rowland White's "Discors Touching Ireland", 1569', ed. N. Canny, *Irish Historical Studies*, xx (1977); 'Rowland White's "The Dyssorders of the Irisshery", 1571', ed. N. Canny, *Studia Hibernica*, xix (1979); and N. Canny, 'Why the Reformation failed in Ireland: une question mal posée', *Journal of Ecclesiastical History*, xxx (1979). A reliable summary of Scottish concern over the corrupt state of the Church is available in J. Wormald, *Court, Kirk, and Community: Scotland, 1470–1625* (London, 1981), pp. 75–108.

predecessors had been; Palesmen were involved with the extension of government authority into the provinces, and even recommended a policy of plantation as a means towards that end.[10] All of this was to change after the 1570s, and one major factor contributing to the change was the appointment to service in Ireland of ardent English Protestants who were highly critical of the church conformism of the Irish-born officials. These incomers recommended that only committed Protestants should hold office in Ireland, and while their opinion did not effect an immediate change in personnel, it did erode the credibility and self-assurance of the Palesmen. Moreover, as the Crown, against the advice of the Palesmen, came to rely more on military means to increase its authority, the presence of Englishmen in positions of authority was dramatically increased, and policy was increasingly decided upon by military officers in consultation with the senior officials in England who were their paymasters.[11]

The social elite in Wales suffered no rejection on the scale of that endured by the Pale community, but both groups responded to the slights that they did suffer in much the same manner: they took to sending their sons to Catholic continental colleges for education. Again, in both instances, many who went to the Continent became priests, but in the case of the Pale some remained laymen and subsequently attended at the Inns of Court for professional training. In both instances, this drift to the Continent involved a rejection of the educational provisions designed for them by the state, but the rejection was more total in the Pale community, which provided hardly any students for the nascent Trinity College, Dublin. Another difference was that, on ordination, many of the Welsh priests were assigned by their spiritual superiors to work in England, whereas the Irish priests returned to their home community where they engaged in missionary work, frequently under the protection and patronage of their kinsmen. The result of these separate developments was that, although the people of Wales generally clung to the old ways, they were left in a weak position to withstand the Protestant missionary onslaught that intensified as the seventeenth century proceeded. The community of the English Pale in Ireland, on the other hand, was rapidly evangelised for the Catholic cause, and became the first coherent Counter-Reformation community under the jurisdiction of the English Crown. Furthermore, this community served as a bridgehead from which to seek to win all the population of Ireland – Gaelic as well as Old English – for the Counter-Reformation.[12]

[10] A good summary of developments in Ireland during these years is available in S. G. Ellis, *Tudor Ireland: Crown, Community, and the Conflict of Cultures, 1470-1603* (London, 1985), pp. 108–227; on the Palesmen and plantation, see 'Edward Walshe's "Conjectures" concerning the state of Ireland, 1552', ed. D. B. Quinn, *Irish Historical Studies*, v (1947).

[11] Ellis, *Tudor Ireland*, pp. 228–75; N. Canny, *The Elizabethan Conquest of Ireland: A Pattern Established, 1565-1576* (Brighton, 1976).

[12] On Wales, see Williams, *Recovery, Reorientation, and Reformation*, pp. 305–31; and P. Jenkins, *A History of Modern Wales, 1536-1990* (London, 1992), pp. 102–23. There is no

The consequence of this religious attachment for the Old English (as this group of Irish Catholics now came to be known) was their exclusion both from government office and from involvement with the plantations that were promoted by the government in provincial Ireland in the aftermath of the Elizabethan Conquest. These favours went instead to convinced Protestants, who before 1603 were usually English, but after that date included Scots who were also permitted a share of the spoils, especially in Ulster. The political response of the Old English to their exclusion from favour was to treat the Protestant Dublin administration as a foreign body that had no care for communal interests, and to negotiate directly with the monarchy. The essential argument of these proto-Unionists when they approached Queen Elizabeth and her two successors was that their record of loyalty to English interests since the Norman conquest of Ireland far outweighed any doubt that might be cast on their reliability because of their religious attachment. At the same time, the Old English as a group compensated for their exclusion from favour by a vigorous expansion of their activities throughout all parts of the country. This was effected in the economic sphere by the rapid acquisition of land, through both purchase and mortgage transactions, from Gaelic and Gaelicised lords who had run into financial difficulties in their efforts to adjust to the new order. Old English merchants also benefited from the quickening of trade that came with more peaceful conditions in the seventeenth century, even when they were forced to share that trade with Protestants and sometimes to concede control of corporations to them. Old English lawyers also found employment with provincial landowners who wished to establish titles to their estates that would be good in Common Law. At the same time, there is considerable evidence of daughters from the Pale being married into landed families in the provinces, while seminary priests from the Pale (sometimes in association with these women) also received hospitality in the houses of Catholic provincial landowners, where they presumably served as tutors while pursuing pastoral work.[13] These social and educational endeavours, which penetrated into the most remote areas, effected such a transformation in the political, religious, and cultural outlook of those provincial lords who chose to endure under a Protestant regime in preference to a military career on the Continent, that one can speak of an Old-Anglicisation and a Catholicisation of Ireland that rivalled the

coherent work on the Counter-Reformation in Ireland, but important aspects are treated in C. Lennon, *The Lords of Dublin in the Age of Reformation* (Dublin, 1989); D. Cregan, 'The social and cultural background of a Counter-Reformation episcopate', in A. Cosgrove and D. McCartney (eds.), *Studies in Irish History Presented to R. Dudley Edwards* (Dublin, 1979); and H. Hammerstein, 'Aspects of the continental education of Irish students in the reign of Elizabeth I', in T. D. Williams (ed.), *Historical Studies VIII* (Dublin, 1971).

[13] The political and religious endeavours of the Old English are well treated by A. Clarke, chs. 7–9 of T. W. Moody, F. X. Martin and F. J. Byrne (eds.), *A New History of Ireland*, vol. III: *Early Modern Ireland, 1534–1691* (Oxford, 1976), and in Lennon, *Lords of Dublin*. The economic rise of the Old English is frequently overlooked but is evident from all local studies; for the most recent, see M. O'Dowd, *Power, Politics and Land: Early Modern Sligo, 1568–1688* (Belfast, 1991).

Anglicisation and Anglic*an*isation[14] intended by the government. The true significance of what occurred becomes apparent when we note the emergence, as negotiators for the Catholic interest from the 1630s onwards, of the bearers of such Galway names as Martin, Donnellan, and Darcy, instead of the Barnewalls, Plunketts, and Dillons of the Pale who had traditionally played that role. These transformations also explain why Old English clergymen like the much quoted David Rothe, Catholic bishop of Ossory, could claim that their missionary efforts complemented rather than conflicted with the concern of the government to 'eliminate barbarous customs, abolish bestial rites, and convert the detestable intercourse of savages into polite manners and a care for maintaining the commonwealth'.[15]

While Rothe and his associates might claim full credit for the advancement of the Counter-Reformation into the remote lordships, their efforts were in fact powerfully supported by missionary priests from Gaelic areas, and full use was made of the Irish language to promote Catholic reform wherever this was appropriate. Some of these Gaelic missionaries were already priests before they ever went to the Continent, and they first went there as part of the exodus from Gaelic Ireland that occurred at the close of the Elizabethan wars. There they had no choice but to enter seminaries if they wished to continue to serve as priests, and they were joined in the seminaries by individuals who had belonged to the privileged learned orders in Gaelic society and who now also found themselves refugees on the Continent. The process by which this cohort of Gaelic seminarians was superimposed on an existing Old English student body sometimes provoked tension in the colleges, but such rivalries were suppressed in the interests of advancing a common missionary endeavour. The training offered, especially at St Anthony's College, Louvain, equipped the priests to work in both Irish and English, and spiritual literature in the Irish language was published from there to meet the needs of the seminarians and also possibly of the literate minority in Gaelic-speaking Ireland. Of equal importance was the encouragement offered to priests who had knowledge of Gaelic metrical forms – particularly those used in popular songs – to compose simple prayers and even catechisms in verse so that they could be more easily memorised by a largely illiterate population.[16]

It is only when account is taken of this Gaelic dimension to the Counter-Reformation in Ireland that we can have a proper understanding of the complexity of the Irish Catholic response to the attempt by the Crown to promote greater unity in its jurisdictions. One generalisation we might posit is that the more English an area was the more Catholic it became, almost as if the population believed that their compliance in civil matters rendered them

[14] This term is favoured by John Morrill; see J. Morrill (ed.), *The Scottish National Covenant in its British Context* (Edinburgh, 1990), 'Introduction', p. 1.

[15] Cited by Clarke in *New History of Ireland*, iii, p. 225.

[16] N. Canny, 'The formation of the Irish mind: religion, politics, and Gaelic Irish literature', *Past and Present*, xcv (1982).

immune from attack because of their allegiance to Catholicism. This would seem to explain the boldness of the Catholic population in the towns, where priests and even bishops worked openly – as is clear from the encounter, described in mocking tone by Thomas Wentworth, between himself and the Catholic clergy of Dublin:

> But I wish you had seen the face of their clergy, such a one in truth as I never saw. The Archbishop in a black suit with a brown cloth cloak and a blue pair of stockings, a fat well-complexioned man, well-fed, I think you would have taken him to have been your country man of Reading if you had seen him stand by a piece of cloth in Leaden Hall. Their doctors in brown cloth suits with all the buttons of their doublets. The rest so suited in colours as John a Knocks with all the Presbytery of Scotland sure were never able to match them.[17]

The Counter-Reformation also met with general, if less visible, success in those rural areas still dominated by Catholic landowners, where priests went discreetly about their pastoral work under the protection of their patrons. Nevertheless, their existence was so well known to the Protestant authorities that in at least two instances these were able to compile diocesan lists of Catholic priests that were as detailed as their visitation reports of their own clergy.[18] Catholic priests had to proceed more cautiously where Protestant landowners were in the ascendant, but even there they could rely on the support of those Catholic landowners who had retained their property, as well as on support from the more prosperous Catholic tenants: thus Catholicism endured even among the natives who resided on the estates of Protestant planters.[19] Indeed, in the case of Ulster, priests under the protection of the Catholic Mac Donnells of Antrim were able to extend their missionary efforts into the Scottish Highlands and Islands in an attempt to stem the Protestantising drive of the Campbells.[20]

There is much in the secondary literature alluding to divisions within the ranks of the Counter-Reformation movement,[21] and there certainly was a fundamental difference in outlook between those clergy who operated in areas under Catholic dominance and those who worked in planted areas. The former tended to be upholders of the status quo, while the latter came to believe that Catholicism could survive into the long term only if there were a

---

[17] Wentworth to Laud, 28 August 1633: Sheffield City Library, Strafford Papers, VIII, fo. 13.

[18] Dublin, National Library of Ireland, MS 8013, IX, 'The names of the Romish Bishop with the surrogate priests and friars within the diocese of Meath and their places of abode', 1622; Strafford Papers, XXb, no. 175, 'The State of the Difference between the Seculars and Regulars'.

[19] See the report of the bishop of Kilmore in County Cavan, 5 November 1633: Strafford Papers, XXb, no. 115.

[20] Dawson, 'Calvinism and the *Gaidhealtachd*'.

[21] The divisions usually cited are those between the regular and secular clergy and those between priests of Old English and Gaelic backgrounds: see, e.g., H. F. Kearney, 'Ecclesiastical politics and the Counter-Reformation in Ireland', *Journal of Ecclesiastical History*, ii (1960).

reversal of the plantations and a return from continental military service of those Irish lords who had been forced into exile at the end of the war.[22] However, the common purpose of religious recovery outweighed these differences, and while some of the Old English clergy, like David Rothe, saw themselves to be fulfilling the cultural agenda laid down by Gerald of Wales in the twelfth century, others, like Geoffrey Keating and John Lynch, sought deliberately to overcome past prejudice and foster a sense of common identity between all Catholics in the country through the fabrication of a new historical past that disregarded the serious animosities that had existed over the centuries between the Gaelic and Anglo-Norman elements of the population.[23]

The Irish Counter-Reformation clearly had no equivalent in any other territory of the British monarchy, but a comparison can be drawn between it and the Reformation in Scotland. Both movements were initially promoted by elite groups against the wishes of a ruling monarch, and both remained beyond the effective control of that monarch's successors. The supporters of Scottish reform also made much of their loyalty to the Crown, even though it was well known from continental experience that the Calvinism they favoured was every bit as antithetical to rulers who would not bend to the wishes of spiritual leaders in religious matters as was Counter-Reformation Catholicism. And perhaps the greatest similarity of all was that both movements were interpreted by their activists as the ultimate fulfilment of the historical role of the descendants of Norman settlers in their respective countries.[24] Again, however, some in Scotland relented from the divisive cultural aspect of the reform, and we learn from Jane Dawson how these Protestant missionaries, under the patronage of the Campbell earls of Argyll, employed the skills of Gaelic bardic poets to promote their message among a largely illiterate population.[25] This is of special interest, not only because it represents one of the few recorded instances where Calvinism overcame the obstacle of illiteracy, but because these Gaelic-speaking Calvinist preachers used the same techniques as priests in Ireland and were competing for souls with those Franciscan missionaries who had gone from Gaelic Ireland into Gaelic Scotland. Such competition indicates that each was also an expansionist religion, and while Irish Catholicism met with but limited success in Scotland, Scottish Calvinism made real progress in Ireland in the wake of Scottish

[22] The question of military exile and its implications for religious developments in Ireland have been skilfully treated in G. Henry, *The Irish Military Community in Spanish Flanders* (Dublin, 1992), and more recently in R. A. Stradling, *The Spanish Monarchy and Irish Mercenaries: The Wild Geese in Spain, 1618–1668* (Dublin, 1994).
[23] J. Gillingham, 'The English invasion of Ireland', in B. Bradshaw *et al.* (eds.), *Representing Ireland: Literature and the Origins of Conflict* (Cambridge, 1993); B. Bradshaw, 'Geoffrey Keating: apologist of Irish Ireland', in ibid.; B. Cunningham, 'Seventeenth-century interpretations of the past: the case of Geoffrey Keating', *Irish Historical Studies*, xxv (1986); J. Lynch, *Cambrensis Eversus, 1662*, trans. M. Kelly (Dublin, 1848–52).
[24] Wormald, *Court, Kirk, and Community*, pp. 95–139.
[25] Dawson, 'Calvinism and the *Gaidhealtachd*'.

settlement there. Moreover, the Scottish ambition to sponsor a Presbyterian Church in England was matched by the desire of many among the Old English to bring England back to the Catholic fold, and they might well have undertaken this mission in the 1640s if the armies of the Confederacy had only been able to provide sustained assistance to King Charles during the Wars of the Three Kingdoms. Another similarity is that both reforms were continentally inspired and were sustained from the Continent. This dimension is clearly evident in the Irish case, but gets little attention in the secondary accounts of the Reformation in Scotland, where authors acknowledge an initial continental influence, but then see the movement as being mediated through England, and sustained through printed Protestant literature from England and through the educational efforts of the Scottish universities. All this is consistent with the evidence, but account must also be taken of the persistent contact that was maintained between Scotland and the most militantly Protestant parts of the Continent through the regular supply of fighting men for the Protestant cause.[26] This might not have resulted, as with the parallel case of Catholic Ireland, in their clergy being educated on the Continent, but it did, as in the case of Ireland, familiarise the most articulate people in their society with the great international issues of the day; and it gave many of them the experience of living in countries where their chosen religion could be seen to enjoy the enthusiastic support of the state. Here perhaps was the factor which, more than any other, made it so difficult for King James VI and I to settle a coherent form of government on his three kingdoms, and which made it calamitous for King Charles when he sought to make good the neglect of his father.

Language

If the English drive to achieve religious conformity or congruity[27] met with either outright rejection or passive acceptance in the Celtic realms, the efforts to promote the English language succeeded to the point where it can be said that, by the middle of the seventeenth century, the ruling elite in all jurisdictions of the British Crown shared a common language. This is not to ignore the several accents and dialects that prevailed even at the highest social level, or the continued existence of Celtic languages as the exclusive vernacular in some areas; but the strides then taken by the English language towards becoming the common property of all subjects of the Crown were never to be reversed. Moreover, this linguistic shift was generally encouraged by the elite, and sometimes their enthusiasm outpaced that of crown and church

---

[26] T. C. Smout, N. C. Landsman and T. M. Devine, 'Scottish emigration in the seventeenth and eighteenth centuries', in N. Canny (ed.), *Europeans on the Move: Studies on European Migration, 1500–1800* (Oxford, 1994).

[27] John Morrill believes that congruity was the extent of the ambition of James VI and I in the religious sphere: Morrill, *Scottish National Covenant*, 'Introduction', p. 8.

officials. In the case of Scotland, the pressure to promote the Anglo-Scots vernacular at the expense of Gaelic came almost entirely from educated reformers and landowners in the Lowlands, and they were supported by the monarchy only when the work was almost accomplished. The effort to establish the linguistic ascendancy of Scots long predated both the Reformation and the Union of the Crowns, and these later developments modified rather than hastened a process that was already well under way.[28] The first modification related to the adoption by Scottish religious reformers of the English-of-England as the language of print,[29] and this, as Dawson points out, resulted (because of the economics of printing) in Scots rapidly losing ground to English as the language of literary composition. This shift had obvious consequences for religious and political discourse, but it is less clear how, other than in matters of vocabulary, it influenced the spoken language of the Lowlands. Far more important here would have been the close associations established with England and English divines by the first generation of Scottish reformers, notably John Knox, and sustained in later generations by Scottish bishops. Such individuals, and also the small but influential group of Scottish noblemen who became courtiers or otherwise became anglicised after the Union of the Crowns, would have at least familiarised Scottish people with how English was spoken south of the Border. However, as Keith Brown has made clear,[30] the cultural influence of these noblemen would have been slight because, once anglicised, they spent most of their time in England; while, at the same time, there were relatively few English administrators in Scotland apart from those associated with the short-lived Cromwellian regime.

On the other hand, two factors that would have worked in favour of the continued use of Scots as a spoken language were the existence in Scotland of its own universities and legal system, and the fact that outward emigration from Scotland was directed towards Ireland and the Continent rather than towards England. And more potent than either of these factors would have been the persistence at home of most Scottish women, who would have transmitted their spoken language to their children, whether male or female. A prime example from Scotland of the different forms of English used by men and women is available in the correspondence between Marion McClellan and her husband Robert Maxwell, when the latter was absent from Scotland and resident on the Irish lands that Marion had inherited from her father. The English used by Maxwell, and also by the secretary who composed most of Marion's letters, is certainly recognisable as Scots but is proximate to the English of England. The one letter written by Marion in her own block print

---

[28] Wormald, *Court, Kirk, and Community*, especially pp. 56–72.

[29] Dawson, 'Anglo-Scottish Protestant culture'.

[30] K. M. Brown, *Kingdom or Province? Scotland and the Regal Union, 1603–1715* (London, 1992), especially pp. 33–59; K. M. Brown, 'Courtiers and Cavaliers: service, anglicisation, and loyalty among the royalist nobility', in Morrill, *Scottish National Covenant*; K. M. Brown, 'The Scottish aristocracy, anglicisation and the court', *Historical Journal*, xxxvi (1993).

and the postscripts she appended to others, however, are barely comprehensible as English and were presumably a phonetic rendering of the language she spoke.[31] Whatever linguistic change occurred in Scotland was therefore part of an evolutionary process rather than the result of any revolution associated with either the Reformation or the Union of the Crowns. Furthermore, as has been noted, the success of the Reformation in some Highland areas did not bring an immediate end to Gaelic as a vernacular, although in the long term the survival of Gaelic was to be closely associated with the survival of a nobility who fostered Catholicism. Even these noblemen would, by the mid-seventeenth century, have known sufficient English to conduct official business with Edinburgh or London, which sustains the point that English had become the language of politics because it was in the interest of the elite to have it so.

It will be evident from what has been said of the Counter-Reformation in Ireland that the experience of language-change there resembled what occurred in Scotland, to the extent that the increased use of English was principally promoted by the elite among the existing English-speaking community in co-operation with landowners in the Gaelic and Gaelicised areas. There the resemblance ends. The first essential difference is that the increase in the use of English in Ireland from the mid-sixteenth century onwards represented the reversal of a decline in the use of English that had been continuous since the fourteenth century.[32] The promoters of the English language in Ireland were therefore working from an altogether less secure foundation than were their Scottish counterparts, and there was a demand for their pedagogic skills only when the provincial lordships were severely disrupted by military intervention by crown forces. Another difference is that the form of English used by the elite of the Pale was (at least in its written form) hardly distinguishable from that used in official circles in England, and those who used it had had the opportunity to reinforce it both through formal education in England and through association with those English-born governors and officials who served in Dublin. The Irish picture is also more complex because the educational activities of the Old English were powerfully supplemented by those thousands of English officials and soldiers who made their careers in Ireland in the sixteenth century, and by those tens of thousands who settled there through the course of the plantations. A few sons of distinguished Gaelic lineage, for example Sir Barnaby Fitzpatrick who was bedfellow and whipping boy to King Edward VI,[33] learned their English in English households, while others such as one of the sons of Shane O'Neill, having

---

[31] F. D. Dow, *Cromwellian Scotland* (Edinburgh, 1979); Edinburgh, Scottish Record Office, Maxwell of Orcharton Papers, RH 15/91/20, nos. 5–9, especially no. 8, February 1641.

[32] Steven Ellis contends that the extent of the decline was exaggerated for political reasons, and his work refers to the absolute maximum extent of enduring English influence in Ireland at the close of the medieval era: see S. G. Ellis, *Reform and Renewal: English Government in Ireland, 1470–1534* (Woodbridge, 1986).

[33] A. Strickland, *Lives of the Bachelor Kings of England* (London, 1861), pp. 212–14.

spent his exile in Scotland, 'spoke English after the Scottish manner'.[34] The influence of Scots was altogether more potent in the seventeenth century, especially in Ulster which accommodated at least 100,000 Scottish settlers before that century was over,[35] and the English then spoken in that province was a variant of Scots. For the remainder of Ireland at that time the language of the elite, whether Protestant or Catholic, was English, and in essence was different only in accent from that spoken at the centre of government.[36] This made it all the easier for stage dramatists to cast such type characters as Captain O'Blunder and Patrick, the servant to the Cromwellian Captain Kil-Tory, for the entertainment of English audiences.[37]

This language shift at the upper reaches of Irish society was without parallel in the three kingdoms, and was adopted by the indigenous lords as a survival strategy within a rapidly changing political order. As change proceeded, the use of English was ever more necessary to these landowners who wanted to live up to their political and social obligations. Consequently, linguistic as well as religious and economic considerations may explain why so many landowners of Gaelic lineage married Old English wives during the first half of the seventeenth century. What is less clear is the extent to which the knowledge and the use of English reached downwards to the lower social levels. The existing peasant dialects persisted in those areas where English had always been spoken, as we learn from Sir William Petty who complained of his inability to comprehend them.[38] My own study of the 1641 depositions indicates that English was known and occasionally used by a wide spread of the native population by that date, and especially where British settlement was intense or where there were historical residues of spoken English.[39] Some contemporary commentators remarked approvingly on this development, and complained that it was being hindered by Irish lords with a view to upholding their traditional control over their followers. This charge was also made in an Irish language source where the anonymous author, if not a landowner himself then certainly a supporter of elite interests, castigated the peasantry for their imitation of English ways and mocked them for their use of broken English.[40] The reality seems to have been that the increased use of English was of mixed benefit for Irish Catholic landowners; it was essential to their own

[34] Lambert to Perrott, 23 October 1584, Public Record Office [PRO], State Papers Ireland, SP 63/112/33.

[35] This is the estimate offered by T. C. Smout in his contribution to Canny, *Europeans on the Move*.

[36] The argument advanced in this section is at variance with that elaborated in A. Bliss, *Spoken English in Ireland, 1600–1740* (Dublin, 1979). For my considered rejection of the method employed by Bliss, see my review of that book in *Studia Hibernica*, xx (1980), pp. 167–172.

[37] I am grateful to Christopher Wheatley for this information, based on his study of Irish drama in the 17th and 18th centuries.

[38] William Petty, *The Political Anatomy of Ireland* (London, 1672), p. 72.

[39] N. Canny, 'The 1641 depositions as a source for the writing of social history: County Cork as a case study', in P. O'Flanagan and C. G. Buttimer (eds.), *Cork: History and Society* (Dublin, 1993).

[40] Huntington Library, San Marino, California, MS Ellesmere 1746, 'A Survey of the Present State of Ireland, anno 1615 ... by E.S.'; *Pairlement Chloinne Tomáis*, ed. N. J. A. Williams (Dublin, 1981).

survival, but it provided their subordinates with access to a wider range of opportunity in the legal, economic, and religious spheres.

If the linguistic history of Ireland during these years is the history of the failure of Catholic landowners to uphold their position as cultural gate-keepers, that of Wales records the pre-eminent success of Welsh landowners in this respect. All historians of Wales are agreed that the principality was 90% Welsh-speaking at the outset of our period, and they believe that this position was little altered by the mid-seventeenth century.[41] Any decline in the use of Welsh that occurred seems to have been in the Welsh-speaking parts of England. For Wales itself, historians point not only to linguistic continuity but to the continued patronage by landowners of Welsh cultural life in all its aspects. It seems that Welsh noblemen who became courtiers and married English wives were able to converse in Welsh even in the eighteenth century,[42] and Welsh had acquired a new status as a language of print when a Welsh edition of the Bible had been published in 1588 following a parliamentary decree.[43] This in itself suggests that the English authorities accepted, even at this early date, that the religious reform of Wales could be effected only in Welsh and with the support of the existing elite. There was every reason for them to believe that this would prove successful, because Welsh squires had previously co-operated in the political reform of their country in a manner that was considered exemplary for Ireland.[44] Moreover, as Glanmor Williams has indicated, Welsh was highly regarded by English antiquarians as the original Britonic language, and Welsh landowners, although considered conservative, were accepted on their record as politically reliable.[45] It was logical, therefore, that the religious reform of Wales should be left to the natural leaders of Wales, for them to proceed with at their own pace and in their own language. The pace, as it transpired, was slow, but Wales did become Protestant without undue disturbance of local rulers or disruption of linguistic continuity. This is not to suggest, however, that Wales remained linguistically frozen in time: we can take it (although this is not mentioned in the literature) that there was a significant increase in bi-lingualism, and that all educated people, and all who were politically and commercially prominent, were capable of conducting their business in English. Thus, although most Welsh people remained monoglot, their society was brought into the world of English speech through the medium of their traditional leaders, whose position was consolidated rather than weakened by the changes that had been effected in the linguistic as well as in the religious sphere.

[41] Jenkins, *History of Modern Wales*, pp. 59–61.

[42] P. Jenkins, *The Making of a Ruling Class: The Glamorgan Gentry, 1640–1790* (Cambridge, 1983), pp. 20–43.

[43] Williams, *Recovery, Reorientation and Reformation*, pp. 323–4.

[44] Canny, *Elizabethan Conquest*, pp. 93–116; the Welsh model for the reform of Ireland is further elaborated upon in C. Brady, 'Comparable histories? Tudor reform in Wales and Ireland', in Ellis and Barber, *Conquest and Union*.

[45] Williams, *Recovery, Reorientation and Reformation*, pp. 429–50.

Politics

Perhaps it was this ability of the landowners in Wales to preserve their local hegemony during a period of rapid change which explains why they proved to be the most compliant subjects within the three Celtic jurisdictions of the Crown. Their counterparts in Scotland and Ireland appear, at first glance, to have been consistently truculent, but it emerges on closer scrutiny that, during the sixteenth century, they engaged in rebellious action only when their local power bases were threatened by outside interference. In the case of Scotland, state interference in the localities usually took the form of the Crown siding with one clan against its rivals, thus forcing the clan that was out of favour to increase the range of its military and diplomatic contacts in an effort to survive. In the case of Ireland, state interference took the form of exploiting animosities within as well as between lordships, and this also resulted in the rapid militarisation of provincial society there. The initial source of military support came from the Highlands and Islands of Scotland, resulting in what Dawson has called a 'Gaelic international',[46] but support was later sought and obtained from England's continental enemies. Such developments were sufficient to steel the will of Queen Elizabeth to seek the total overthrow of her opponents in Ireland, but we should not allow the ultimate polarisation that occurred to blind us to the fact that even her most implacable foes would have come to terms if they had been given assurances that their local authority would remain secure. The earl of Desmond, before he entered into rebellion, had petitioned in vain for some mark of recognition from the Crown that he was a loyal subject, and had been willing to offer almost any security so that he and his son would not be forced to rebel.[47] Similarly, the earl of Tyrone made innumerable attempts to reach agreement with the queen.[48] Tyrone also was contemplating life at the court of King James and a marriage between his son and an Argyll daughter when, in 1607, he suddenly fled to the Continent rather than face charges that would have placed his life in jeopardy.[49] Both Desmond and Tyrone exploited the religious divisions in Europe for political purposes, but neither can be regarded as an exemplary son of the Counter-Reformation, and each was forced, against his better judgement, to oppose the Crown. To have done otherwise would have exposed them to the challenge of rival claimants for power within their lordships when there was no assurance that the Crown would support them against those rivals.

[46] J. Dawson, 'Two kingdoms or three? Ireland in Anglo-Scottish relations in the middle of the sixteenth century', in R. A. Mason (ed.), *Scotland and England, 1286–1815* (Edinburgh, 1987), p. 131; G. A. Hayes-McCoy, *Scots Mercenary Forces in Ireland, 1565–1603* (London, 1937).

[47] Countess of Desmond to Privy Council, 28 June 1580: PRO, SP 63/73/67.

[48] H. Morgan, *Tyrone's Rebellion: The Outbreak of the Nine Years War in Tudor Ireland* (London, 1993); while Morgan details these overtures he does not accept that they were sincerely meant, but I have challenged his assumptions in a review of that book in *Irish Historical Studies*, xxix (1994), pp. 255–7.

[49] N. Canny, 'The flight of the earls, 1607', *Irish Historical Studies*, xvii (1971).

After 1603, the Crown generally desisted from blatant stratagems of divide and rule, but landowners in both Ireland and Scotland still endeavoured to prevent trespass upon their spheres of influence. They were, as we saw, ready to make such minimum concessions to centralisation as would stave off direct intervention in their lordships, but such concessions sometimes presented them with fresh opportunities to mediate between the locality and the centre. These concessions did not, in either Scotland or Ireland, extend to the acceptance of Anglican-style Episcopal Churches, and both groups supported rival Churches which they intended would be reliant upon them for support. When looked at in a three-kingdoms context the result was the effective establishment under a single political authority of three distinct religions, two of which – Calvinism and Counter-Reformation Catholicism – could be seen from continental experience to be incapable of coexisting within a coherent state. Both Kings James and Charles were anxious to rectify this anomaly, but neither seems to have recognised that the religious situation which James allowed to reach maturity was without parallel in any European multiple kingdom, other than in those that had been cantonised. The failure of King James to suppress the Irish Counter-Reformation, when he had the opportunity to do so at the outset of his reign following Elizabeth's comprehensive military victory, was a grave political error, because he then, like the Austrian Habsburgs after the Battle of the White Mountain, might have imposed both political and religious unity upon a disparate inheritance.[50] However, the Scottish landowners who supported a Calvinist Church and the Irish landowners who promoted a Counter-Reformation Church were also politically naive in believing that the spiritual leaders of these Churches would always comply with their wishes simply because they were patronised by them. In the Irish case, the first clear evidence of the pursuit by the Catholic clergy of an independent line was their convening a church synod to coincide with the Parliament of 1613–15, and we can assume that their bold appearances in clerical garb, as described by Wentworth, even at meetings with government officials during the reign of Charles I went against the wishes of their lay patrons.[51] In Scotland, the cultivation of popular fears of popery and the Anti-Christ has been attributed to the initiative of Presbyterian divines, as has the persecution of witches. Jenny Wormald explains such activities by reference to the concern of ministers that their ambition to achieve a perfect society was failing. The principal manifestation of that failure was the evidence of virtual economic collapse symbolised by persistent high migration and intermittent famine. The dire plight of peasants did not prevent the gentry from giving architectural expression to their own continued prosperity during these difficult times, but the lairds were responsive to all grievances that were specifically religious, and seemed to

[50] This comparison with the territories of the Austrian Habsburgs has been inspired by the work of Professor Robert Evans.

[51] See above, at note 17.

realise that if they failed to meet the expectations of the ministers in such matters their authority would be challenged from below.[52] Irish Catholic landowners displayed no such sensitivity to the concerns of the clergy they patronised and, during Charles I's reign, set about negotiating an improved position for Catholicism seemingly without any reference to Catholic church authorities. There is no evidence of an immediate adverse local reaction to this cavalier attitude, but the response of the clergy and the aspirations they expressed when political crisis beset the country at mid-century suggest that they had long since ceased to regard the Catholic gentry as reliable supporters of church interests.

Recent historians, like many from earlier generations, have seen this crisis as but one aspect of a three-kingdoms crisis that was provoked by the single cause of the increased authoritiarianism of the government of Charles I.[53] This seems entirely plausible, but it does not mean that what was considered authoritarian in one kingdom was similarly regarded in another, or that all social groupings in any one society responded similarly to a common authoritarian intrusion. All historians are agreed that the action of the central government that occasioned most offence in Scotland was the attempt by the king to bring the Scottish and English Churches together within a common system of order and discipline – an attempt which culminated in the introduction into Scotland of the English Prayer Book in 1637. What happened then was a confirmation of the forebodings of many Scots over the religious designs of the king ever since his Scottish coronation of 1633 at Holyrood.[54] The first public expression of opposition in 1637 was a popular riot, when, as Keith Brown has made clear, the Scottish elite was surprised by the extent of the animosity towards the innovations that were being proceeded with; they maintained control over events only by becoming leaders, and to an extent prisoners, of the insurgency which was fomented for religious reasons by Presbyterian ministers and 'fuelled by economic grievances'.[55] These events led inexorably to the signing of the National Covenant, but again, as we learn from Brown, the clergy continued to be the driving force behind popular resentment and the squires the seekers of compromise with the king. To say this is not to imply that the Scottish gentry were without political principles or that they were indifferent to interference from England. From the outset, the Scottish Council had feared that the Union of the Crowns would result in Scotland's being reduced (presumably like Ireland) to the status of 'a conquered and slavish province to be governed by a viceroy or deputy', and gentry and merchant interests were always ready to counter any state

[52] Wormald, Court, Kirk and Community, pp. 160–76.
[53] The most recent statements on the subject in relation to Ireland are B. Mac Cuarta (ed.), Ulster 1641: Aspects of the Rising (Belfast, 1993), and M. Perceval-Maxwell, The Outbreak of the 1641 Rebellion in Ireland (Dublin and Montreal, 1994); for a more general statement, see J. Morrill, The Nature of the English Revolution (London, 1993), pp. 6–7.
[54] Morrill, Scottish National Covenant, 'Introduction'.
[55] Brown, Kingdom or Province?, pp. 112–18.

interference in the economic sphere or in the management of their estates.[56] Such concerns gave them good reason to support the Covenant cause, but the primary religious purpose behind the Covenant was defined by the clergy, seemingly without any reference to their social betters, and it was they, too, who mobilised the popular support that made it a national cause.

These events in Scotland and the reactions they provoked in England are now accepted by historians to have exerted a profound influence over subsequent happenings in Ireland. In most standard accounts Thomas Wentworth is identified as the personification in Ireland of the authoritarianism of Caroline government, and the Irish rising of 1641 is taken not only to be the Irish equivalent of the Covenanter challenge of 1637–8, but to have been undertaken in imitation of what had happened in Scotland.[57] There is some substance to all these suggestions, and both English and Irish Protestant observers of the time recognised these very parallels. However, account must also be taken both of the perceptions of Irish Catholics who were involved in these events, and of what actually happened in Ireland during those terrible winter months of 1641–2.

The rule of Thomas Wentworth was unquestionably a disappointment for all Catholics in Ireland, and they would have had even more reason to fear and oppose him if they had been aware of his hidden agenda for Ireland, the details of which were concealed even from the king.[58] The disappointment of the Catholic political leaders stemmed not from Wentworth's authoritarianism but from his failure to deliver the Graces – the promises of the king in relation both to greater religious freedom for Catholics and to granting secure land titles to those Catholic proprietors, particularly in the province of Connacht, who were exposed to the threat of plantation. Such promises had been made against the wishes of the Protestant interest in all three kingdoms, so the Irish Catholic objections were not to authoritarian rule but to the fact that Wentworth refused to use his influence as Governor to have the Irish Parliament (which after 1613–15 had an in-built Protestant majority) give statutory approval to promises made by the king as a sign of royal favour and in return for money.[59] Moreover, as we learn from Aidan Clarke, the most fundamental constitutional objection raised by the Old English to Wentworth's proceedings was that he denied them the right to appeal unpalatable decisions over the head of the government in Dublin to the person of the monarch in England.[60] The essential objection of the Old English was therefore to their being denied access to the benefits of prerogative power. In these respects their fundamental political concerns were the very opposite to

[56] Levack, *The Formation of the British State*, pp. 31–67; the quotation cited on p. 34 implies rather than refers to the Irish parallel.
[57] See the items referred to in note 53, above.
[58] Canny, 'Attempted anglicization of Ireland', especially pp. 64–82.
[59] Clarke, chs. 8, 9 of *New History of Ireland*, iii.
[60] Ibid.; and A. Clarke, 'The history of Poynings' Law, 1615–41', *Irish Historical Studies*, xviii (1972).

those of the Scottish elite, and the fresh fears of Irish Catholics that stemmed from the rapidly changing events of 1640 and 1641 derived not from the authoritarianism of the Crown but from the strident anti-popery that was voiced by both Scottish Covenanters and English Parliamentarians. Consequently, the prime constitutional issue of the day for the Old English became not prerogative power but the pretensions of the English Parliament to legislate for Ireland.[61]

The extent to which knowledge of constitutional issues reached beyond the narrow confines of Irish Parliamentarians remains unclear, but we can be certain that excessive use of the royal prerogative which occasioned such criticism in the other two kingdoms was not regarded adversely, beyond a narrow political circle, in Catholic Ireland. Indeed, those Ulster lords who entered into rebellion in October 1641 claimed that their action enjoyed the prior approval of the king and was with the purpose of upholding his authority against those in Scotland and England who challenged it. That they had struck upon a popular cause is suggested by the fact that hundreds of the Irish captains who followed these early insurgents into rebellion echoed these sentiments, even if many claimed to have risen in support of the Catholic queen or her son rather than of the king. More significantly, among the hundreds of recorded justifications given by these captains for their resort to arms, only two (one of which was from County Wicklow, where Wentworth was notoriously involved in land-jobbery) mention the tyranny of Wentworth's rule as a cause for the action. Instead, whenever Wentworth was referred to it was usually to the effect that his execution was proof that the king had been deprived of his authority, and that the insurgents had acted correctly in taking up arms to defend the royal prerogative.[62]

It seems, therefore, that while the Covenanter movement supplied the Ulster lords with a model and an opportunity to challenge the authority of the government, their action and that of the Covenanters were intended to serve diametrically opposed purposes. The two movements are also different in that the Covenanters challenged the government when they were forced to do so by their ministers and the economically deprived, while the Ulster insurgents seemingly acted without any prompting from below. It also appears that they acted with but vague promises of support from Catholic landowners in the other provinces, and their contemporaries believed that

---

[61] Clarke, in *New History of Ireland*, iii, pp. 285–6; 'Patrick Darcy an Argument', ed. C. E. J. Caldicott, in *Camden Miscellany, XXXI* (London, 1992); this line of argumentation, commenced by the Catholic Darcy, was persisted with by Irish Protestant authors under the very different circumstances of the late 17th century: see J. G. Simms, *William Molyneux of Dublin*, ed. P. H. Kelly (Dublin, 1983).

[62] N. Canny, 'In defense of the constitution? The nature of Irish revolt in the seventeenth century', in L. Bergeron and L. M. Cullen (eds.), *Culture et pratiques politiques en France et en Irlande, XVIe–XVIIIe siècle* (Paris, 1991); an expanded version of this paper is now available under the title 'What really happened in Ireland in 1641?', in J. Ohlmeyer (ed.), *Ireland: From Independence to Occupation 1641–1660* (Cambridge, 1995). More specifically, see Trinity College, Dublin, MS 815, no. 617.

they were a marginal group who threw caution to the wind simply because they were in deep financial trouble. Perhaps their gravest miscalculation was that they acted without taking account of popular sentiment within the Catholic community, and nobody seems to have been more surprised than they when their capture of a few fortified positions in Ulster signalled the outbreak of a Catholic peasant fury that had engulfed most parts of the country within days and weeks of the initial disturbance of 23 October 1641.[63]

This popular aspect of the disturbance in Ireland has not received anything like the attention it deserves, and its occurrence points to yet further differences between the Irish and Scottish responses to centralisation. In my own writing on these disturbances, I have alluded to several dimensions of what was a complex uprising. The first and most universal response was that of popular anger at the extensive settlement of foreigners throughout the country, which took the form of a direct attack upon those settlers and the seizure of their property. Such attacks clearly represented a popular rejection of the government's authority and of the plantations that had been pursued by it, but they also represented a rejection of the influence of landowners within their localities. Those whose authority was rejected included Catholic landowners who not only had acquiesced in these innovations but had aggravated them by inviting foreign Protestants, who would pay higher entry fines and rents than natives could afford, to accept tenancies on their estates. Significantly, the English tenants whom Sir Phelim O'Neill had settled on his estate in County Armagh were among the first victims of the popular disturbance, and O'Neill's inability to defend them is proof that he had lost control of the movement he had initiated. Again, the fact that, in December 1641, Catholic landowners from all parts of Ireland identified openly with the Ulster uprising should be interpreted not as an endorsement by them of what had happened in Ulster during the previous six weeks, but rather as a desperate attempt by these landowners to recover their authority within their own localities.[64]

The role of these landowners as leaders of their communities had, in the first instance, been usurped by dispossessed Catholic tenants and by brothers or younger sons of the landowners themselves who emerged as captains of the insurgency. Priests also became involved in the insurrection from the outset, but usually to direct it towards Godly ends which, as they would have learned in their seminary training, provided the only valid justification for challenging established authority. Individual priests were regularly credited with having saved Protestants from physical harm, but at the price of their conversion to Catholicism as a requirement for their continuing to reside within the community. More generally, priests also insisted upon the recovery of traditional places of worship for Catholic use; they led the insurgents in the

---

[63] Ibid.; and H. Simms, 'Violence in County Armagh', in Mac Cuarta, *Ulster 1641*.
[64] See note 61, above; and Canny, 'The 1641 depositions as a source'.

desecration of Protestant books, buildings and corpses; they reinstated Catholic worship with full pomp and ceremony; and they repeatedly asserted that the only religious guarantee worth having was that which would establish Catholicism as the official religion of Ireland.[65] The advancement of such claims by the Catholic clergy in every part of Ireland from the outset of the insurrection, and the subsequent endorsement of these claims by Rinuccini, the Papal nuncio,[66] indicate that the clergy had long since concluded that Catholic landowners did not have the true interests of religion at heart, and that Catholicism could achieve its rightful position only through direct action by themselves.

The Irish Catholic response to the crisis of the mid-century, like that in Scotland, therefore witnessed the emergence of a clerical group who took it upon themselves to dictate policy for their community independently of their patrons. The positions which they adopted led in both instances to revolution, and we can take it that the sentiments that justified revolutionary action stemmed, also in both instances, from a knowledge of the principles and practice of politics in continental Europe. The Scottish and Irish responses are therefore the very opposite to those in Wales and England where, in the face of severe provocation, subjects still clung to traditional loyalties and entertained revolutionary ideas only in the white heat of war.[67] In both Ireland and Scotland revolutionary sentiments were present from the outset; the history of the Catholic Confederation, like that of the National Covenant, is the history of a landed elite desperately seeking to recover the initiative from a clergy who had forced them into radical positions with which they were never comfortable.

This comparative study of the responses in the Celtic realms to the central-isation measures promoted by the British Crown suggests, therefore, that a conflict between Crown and community in both Scotland and Ireland was always likely from some point in the 1630s, because of the secure existence in both jurisdictions of clerical groups who were fully conversant with justifications for political action to serve religious purposes. The fact that these conflicts, when they came, led to turmoils that eventually embroiled all subjects of the Crown is explained by the facts that the two sets of political objectives were diametrically opposed to each other, and that the fulfilment of one set of ambitions required the utter rejection of the other. It is difficult to see what Charles I, or indeed a monarch more competent than he, could have done to prevent this conflict. In sum, his father had left him a political inheritance that had the potential to become more polarised in religion than

[65] Ibid.
[66] The career of Rinuccini in Ireland is the subject of a thesis by Tadhg Ó h Annracháin, "'Far from *Terra Firma*": The Mission of Gianbattista Rinuccini to Ireland, 1645–9' (presented for the degree of Doctor of the European University Institute, Florence, 1995).
[67] Morrill, *Nature of the English Revolution*, pp. 1–44.

in any other multiple kingdom of that time. When looked at in this light, the ultimate cause of the Wars of the Three Kingdoms must be laid at the door of James VI and I: both because he did too much and because he did too little. He did too much by permitting his officials in Ireland so to alienate the bulk of the population from the government that they were driven into the embrace of the Counter-Reformation; and he did too little by imposing restraints on these same officials who would have crushed the Counter-Reformation in Ireland while it was still in an embryonic stage. Had he followed the advice of his officials in Ireland, when the ways and means were at his disposal to effect a decisive resolution of the religious question, he might well have created a rallying cause that would have brought profit to his Protestant subjects as well as religious cohesion to his multiple kingdoms.[68]

[68] See H. S. Pawlisch, *Sir John Davies and the Conquest of Ireland: A Study in Legal Imperialism* (Cambridge, 1985); those historians who have considered the Union of the Crowns have done so in a two-kingdom context and ignore the fact that the principal benefit that derived from the arrangement for Lowland Scots was the access it gave them to the post-war spoils in Ireland.

Chapter 10

Three kingdoms and one commonwealth?

The enigma of mid-seventeenth-century Britain and Ireland

John Morrill

In December 1653 Oliver Cromwell was installed as the Lord Protector of 'the Commonwealth of England, Scotland and Ireland, and the dominions thereunto belonging'.[1] He ruled the Commonwealth through one Parliament, he presided over a single Council of State which supervised the work of regional commissioners in Scotland and Ireland, and he appointed English judges to preside over the courts of the formerly independent kingdoms of the archipelago. The constitution also established a principle of religious liberty within the Commonwealth for all Protestants who 'professed faith in God by Jesus Christ ... so as they abuse not this liberty to the civil injury of others'. Although the constitution of December 1653 – the Instrument of Government – spoke of the several nations of the Commonwealth, it did not make any distinction between the constituent states or dominions.

From 1653 to 1660 there was thus a single polity in the Atlantic archipelago such as was not dreamed of earlier in the early modern period, nor attempted even in the nineteenth century within the United Kingdom of Great Britain and Ireland. How had this come about?

There has been much recent writing about the 'fashioning of a British state', and 'the development of a British state system if not of a British state'.[2] I have myself contributed at length to that debate, examining the nature of that 'state system'; comparing the experience of the British Isles with that of 'France' and of 'Spain' in the early modern period; examining how far that experience was a natural development from medieval patterns of dynasticism and elite migration; and considering how to make sense of John Pocock's claim that in the early modern period the component peoples of the islands of Britain and Ireland 'interacted so as to modify the conditions of one another's existence'.[3] I have also offered a number of case studies, principally concerned with aspects of Anglo-Scottish relations, suggesting that while the Scots were

[1] S. R. Gardiner, *Constitutional Documents of the Puritan Revolution* (3rd edn, London, 1906), p. 405.
[2] S. G. Ellis and S. Barber (eds.), *Conquest and Union: The Fashioning of the British State 1495–1715* (London, 1995); B. Bradshaw and J. Morrill (eds.), *The British Problem c.1534–1707: State Formation in the Atlantic Archipelago* (Basingstoke, in press), p. 1.
[3] J. Morrill, 'The fashioning of Britain 1534–1660', in Ellis and Barber, *Conquest and Union*; J. Morrill, 'The British problem', in Bradshaw and Morrill, *British Problem*.

victims of a Stuart authoritarianism backed up by the threat of English (and Irish) force, there was no grand design by monarchs, let alone by English elites, to incorporate Scotland into a greater English state.[4]

The events of the 1640s and 1650s have particular appeal as a test-bed for theories about the appropriateness of a British or an archipelagic approach as against separate (if not separatist) histories of England, Ireland, Scotland and Wales. Were the 'Wars of the Three Kingdoms' (or should it be the 'War of the Three Kingdoms'?) one great conflict in different theatres, or were they a series of separate wars that got caught up with one another? Why did the wars end not just with the English putting their king on trial and executing him (remarkable as that event was), but in the eventual abolition of monarchy in all three kingdoms and in the creation of a single Commonwealth? In the past I have attempted one particular line of approach – that for some people it was a single war and for others a number of different wars; that it was both a war of three kingdoms and a series of semi-independent conflicts. To this John Pocock has powerfully retorted that many of the constituent parts of the conflicts making up the War(s) of the Three Kingdoms are unhelpfully described as *civil* wars; he has returned to alternative models of internal war developed by Roman historians to explain what happened in the Roman Empire, and attempts to apply those models to the crisis of the 1640s.[5] I shall return to these models later.

This essay seeks to suggest that a closer examination of the official exchanges between the English and the Scots in the 1640s (and the Irish too, so far as there is space) teaches us a lot about the ambiguous relationships between the polities that were England, Ireland and Scotland. It represents more an attempt to clarify what questions we should be asking than an attempt to state what answers we should be giving; but that seems to me to be as far as we have got.

Much has already been written about how far the collapse of royal authority in each kingdom was the result of the structural instabilities of composite monarchies, and more particularly about how the prior collapse of royal power in Scotland and Ireland caused the English Civil War.[6] As Clarendon put it pretty definitively at the time:

---

[4] J. Morrill (ed.), *The Scottish National Covenant in its British Perspective* (Edinburgh, 1991), 'Introduction'; J. Morrill, 'A British patriarchy? Ecclesiastical imperialism under the early Stuarts', in A. Fletcher and P. Roberts (eds.), *Religion, Culture and Society in Early Modern Britain* (Cambridge, 1994); J. Morrill, 'The English, the Scots and the British', in P. Hodge (ed.), *Scotland and the Union* (Edinburgh, 1994).

[5] J. G. A. Pocock, 'The Atlantic archipelago and the War of the Three Kingdoms', in Bradshaw and Morrill, *British Problem*.

[6] C. Russell, *The Causes of the English Civil War* (Oxford, 1990), chs. 2, 5; C. Russell, *The Fall of the British Monarchies 1637–1642* (Oxford, 1991); C. Russell, *Unrevolutionary England* (London, 1991), chs. 13, 15; J. Morrill, *The Nature of the English Revolution* (London, 1993); K. Brown, 'British history: a sceptical comment', in R. Asch (ed.), *Three Nations – A Common History?* (Bochum, 1992).

though Scotland blew the first trumpet, it was Ireland that drew the first blood; and if they had not at that time rebelled, and in that manner, it is very probable all the miseries which afterwards befell the king *and his dominions* had been prevented.[7]

The first task of this essay is to consider further just how tangled the constitutional relationships between the component parts of the Stuart *imperium* had become, and to look at the consequences for our understanding of those relationships of that near-simultaneous collapse of royal authority in all three kingdoms; the second is to examine just how various parties sought to redefine those relationships; and the final is to ask how we might begin developing a concept of what for the moment I will call the 'War(s) of the Three Kingdoms'.

Dynastic unions and the integration of previously separate dominions were common in early modern Europe (the composite – and multiple – kingdoms of the Valois, Bourbons, and [Spanish and Austrian] Habsburgs, and the Baltic multiple kingdoms). But dis-unions and dis-integrations had also taken place: Ireland could look to the United Provinces, disaggregated from the Habsburg dominions;[8] Scotland could look to Portugal, escaping from regnal union as the 1640s proceeded. But there was a difference. Not the least of the paradoxes of the 1640s is that the English were the least interested in defining the relationship between the three kingdoms, and the people likeliest to disown the dynastic relationship. As Conrad Russell puts it earlier in this volume, speaking of the English Parliaments of James I (and VI): 'if the king chose to be king of Scots in his spare time, that was nothing to do with them'.[9] Thus it was that when the English Parliament abolished monarchy in England in 1649, it abolished it also in Ireland (a dependent kingdom with no existence apart from the Crown of England), but did not then do so in Scotland.[10] The abolition of monarchy in England broke the regnal Union, and left the Scots free to resume their separate historical identity. What caused the war between England and Scotland in 1650–4 was the insistence of many Scots that Charles II of Scotland was also king of England (and therefore of Ireland), their crowning of him as such at Scone, and their swearing to assist him to regain *all* his kingdoms.[11]

This fall of the Stuart monarchies was the culmination of a series of constitutional confusions originating in an unusually untidy and incoherent process of sixteenth-century aggrandisement – on the one hand Tudor/ Stewart dynastic roulette and on the other the inconclusive combination of a

[7] Edward Hyde, Earl of Clarendon, *History of the Great Rebellion*, ed. W. D. Macray (Oxford, 1888), Book VI, pp. 2–3 (my italics).

[8] H. Morgan, 'Hugh O'Neill and the Nine Years War in Ireland', *Historical Journal*, xxxvi (1993); J. Miller, 'The earl of Tyrconnel and James II's Irish policy', *Historical Journal*, xx (1977), pp. 808–10; J. Miller, *James II: A Study in Kingship* (Hove, 1978), pp. 216–18.

[9] C. Russell, 'Composite monarchies in early modern Europe', above, p. 146.

[10] Gardiner, *Constitutional Documents*, pp. 384–6.

[11] Morrill, *Scottish National Covenant*, 'Introduction', pp. 28–30.

half-conceded Irish ancient constitutionalism and half-accomplished modern conquest.

I do not think it coincidental that, in the first month of the Long Parliament, the two most powerful Englishmen after the king during the 1630s both found themselves in the Tower of London on charges initially brought against them (in the case of Strafford) by enemies in Ireland, and (in the case of Laud) by enemies in Scotland. Irish charges and Scottish political pressure later brought both to the scaffold. The confusions of jurisdiction involved demonstrate the constitutional chaos of triple monarchy by 1641. It got worse: in 1649 a High Court established by the Parliament of England voted to execute the king of England, Ireland and Scotland, without consulting, involving or even informing the peoples of Scotland and Ireland; and to add a final twist, three months after the Regicide, the premier nobleman of Scotland, James, first Duke of Hamilton, who had led a Scottish army into England in 1648, was tried in England and beheaded. But he was tried for treason under his title of earl of Cambridge in the English peerage. Herein lies at least one of the enigmas of 'British history': three kingdoms under one king with a confused sense of common identity and destiny.

From the Scots point of view, losing a king to England in 1603 who boasted loudly of seeking a union of kingdoms as well as Crowns, but who had spent the long years of waiting making few solid plans for the various stages towards that greater union, created ever-greater problems. Confronted by his own indolence over making arduous journeys to a much-fantasised destination, by the English neurotic obsession about the sanctity of the Common Law, and by the Scots neurotic obsession with the purity of their Kirk within a perfect union, James settled back on a policy of making the English and Scots more like one another, abandoning a search for constitutional union in favour of a drift towards cultural and intellectual congruity.

James knew those through whom Scotland had to be governed, and he kept in touch by making the Scottish *noblesse de robe* peripatetic (or, at any rate, like so many bungee-jumpers leaping from Edinburgh and almost but not quite getting their feet on the ground in London); but Charles I never got to know Scotland or the Scots. This made the man-management of Scotland impossible. Since policy was *made* where the king was and *enforced* where his Council was, the king lost the ability to recognise that most important of all early modern political skills: identifying the limits of his enforceable will.

Feeling increasingly misunderstood, put upon, and culturally invaded, the Scots came to believe that the king had not only evil counsellors, but alien ones. In 1608 all twelve English judges, sitting in Exchequer Chamber, had had to determine whether a child born to Scottish parents after the Union of the Crowns of England and Scotland – Robert Calvin (*alias* Colville) – could inherit property in England, or whether such an inheritance was to be prevented by the general laws of denization. The case hung on an aspect of the doctrine of the king's two bodies: his natural or physical body and his political body or office. If the former, then feudal law permitted the infant to inherit as a subject of James VI and I; but if the latter, then not, because he was a subject of the political body of James VI but not that of James I. The English judges, having been invited to consider everything from the legal status of the Samaritan leper to the allegiance due to 'Canutus the Danish King', declared that where a king inherited two kingdoms, there was only one 'ligeance', and that anyone born within the king's 'ligeance' was a natural-born subject, and no alien in either of his kingdoms. The natural body had won out over the political body.[12] In a sense the logic of that decision reveals the incoherence of one king and two kingdoms. In much the same way, the *English* advisers of an *English* king could not but give that same *Scottish* king advice that would influence his *Scottish* policy. Advising the natural mind of a king in a composite kingdom meant advising all his political bodies.

The Scots did not have to endure having Englishmen hold office in Scotland; and neither James nor Charles sought to extend the jurisdiction of any English institution over Scotland. They did not, for example, revive the claims of the English Church to a British ecclesiastical patriarchy.[13] But the Scots could not prevent English *influence* over the royal mind; and they would naturally exaggerate its importance when it happened. Such difficulties brought the relations of the kingdoms to crisis point in the 1630s.

The creation of the Kingly Title in Ireland (1541) was intended by its architects not so much to strengthen royal power in Ireland as to strengthen the position of old-settler (medieval-coloniser) interests there. It was supposed to create a separate Irish constitutionalism around a local Council under local elite control, a local Parliament, and secure titles for those who were the loyal subjects of an absentee monarch. For the next hundred and fifty years and more there were those who argued for the effective autonomy of Irish institutions – a sovereign King-in-Parliament, a relationship with the monarch and his representative that shut out English counsellors and the English courts. It was always an unsustainable view. It was not so much the determination of the monarchs themselves and their English advisers that inhibited acceptance of Irish particularism and constitutionalism, as the demands of the military leaders sent over to ensure order and of the new waves of settlers and planters who came in their wake.[14] Many of them wanted Ireland to be a colonial dependency of the English Crown, and the

---

[12] T. B. Howell, *A Complete Collection of State Trials*, ii (London, 1809), cols. 611–58. The best modern discussion is in B. Galloway, *The Union of England and Scotland, 1603–1608* (Edinburgh, 1986), pp. 148–57. I have also drawn on J. R. Tanner, *Constitutional Documents of the Reign of James I, 1603–1625* (Cambridge, 1930), pp. 23–4.

[13] Morrill, 'British patriarchy?', especially pp. 209–10.

[14] B. Bradshaw, *The Irish Constitutional Revolution of the Sixteenth Century* (Cambridge, 1979), chs. 7–9; S. G. Ellis, *Tudor Ireland: Crown, Community and Conflict of Cultures* (London, 1985), chs. 6–9; S. G. Ellis, *Tudor Frontiers and Noble Power: The Making of the British State* (Oxford, 1995), especially chs. 4, 7, and 'Conclusion'.

Catholic population of Ireland (whether Gaelic or Anglo-Norman) to be denied security of title in their lands and – in the case of the Gaelic lords – denied the right even to be seen as civilisable. The pattern of rebellion, subjugation, confiscation, plantation and rebellion that characterised Ireland in the fifty years after 1560 produced levels of violence and hatred beyond anything else seen in the archipelago since the Norman irruptions of the eleventh and twelfth centuries, and resulted in one of the most ethnically, culturally, and religiously polarised regions in Europe.[15]

A great majority of the Gaelic lords sought to protect themselves from state violence by complying with the demands of Dublin and Whitehall to surrender their lands on the promise of regrant of title under the royal seal; and by (in at least one generation) intermarrying either with an English noble family or at least with a New English-in-Ireland one. However, although they surrendered their social and legal culture, they (for the most part) preserved their religion and built a new cultural identity around that.[16] The Old English refined and demanded confirmation of the Irish constitutionalism discussed above, stressing the autonomy and self-reliance of the political institutions of Ireland. They accepted the discipline of Poyning's Law, though they were sometimes unclear what that was.[17] The New English looked to the Crown for support in their search for power within Ireland (such as the creation of new parliamentary seats in areas of recent Plantation), for new opportunities for plunder and plantation, and when the king seemed more interested in holding the ring between rival groups in Ireland, or when the Crown sought to mulct them for the costs of administering and defending Ireland, they looked to the English Parliament to override the Crown. By 1641 there was constitutional deadlock in Ireland, not only over the nature of the political (and religious) rights of the various communities, but also over the extent to which the government of Ireland had been and ought to be assimilated to the government of England. Could the English courts override decisions made in the Irish courts? Could the English Parliament make law for Ireland? Could the English Parliament investigate the activities of English Governors in Ireland? The trial of Strafford before an English Parliament for crimes committed in Ireland was simply the most obvious of these dilemmas.[18]

Once again, the language of the king's two bodies created confusions in a three-kingdom context. The prosecutors of Strafford appeared to need to

[15] For two important recent discussions of these processes, see C. Brady, *The Chief Governors: The Rise and Fall of Reform Government in Tudor Ireland, 1536–1588* (Cambridge, 1995); and H. Morgan, *Tyrone's Rebellion: The Outbreak of the Nine Years War in Tudor Ireland* (Dublin, 1993).

[16] See my forthcoming article, 'Relating to the British: the marriages of Gaelic lords in the seventeenth century'.

[17] M. Perceval-Maxwell, 'Ireland and the monarchy in the early Stuart multiple kingdoms', *Historical Journal*, xxxiv (1991), especially pp. 280–3.

[18] Russell, *Unrevolutionary England*, pp. 263–80; Perceval-Maxwell, 'Ireland and the monarchy'; M. Perceval-Maxwell, *The Outbreak of the Irish Rebellion of 1641* (Dublin and Montreal, 1994) especially chs. 5, 8–9; A. Clarke, 'The genesis of the Ulster rising of 1641', in P. Roebuck (ed.), *Plantation to Partition* (Belfast, 1981).

demonstrate the opposite of the judgement in Calvin's case, for Strafford's clear line of defence, that he was acting for and on behalf of the king, was to be countered by the claim that he was subverting the king's political body and that the permission of the owner of the natural body was not allowable as a defence.[19] But did the king of Ireland have two bodies? If so, was treason against the kingly office in Ireland prosecutable in the *English* courts or only in the Irish courts? If the treason was against the kingly person, could a royal warrant for alleged treasonable acts be pleadable as a defence? Nothing reveals the lack of clarity in English minds about the constitutional relationship between the kingdoms than the oscillation between the two positions as the trial unfolded.[20]

The above serves to reinforce the point made in other recent work that the Long Parliament of 1641 helped to provoke the Rebellion in Ireland by its blatant interference into Irish domestic affairs, and by brushing aside the rights of the Irish Parliament and ignoring Irish constitutionalism. It gave vital and powerful interests in Ireland a profoundly conservative reason for rebellion in the autumn of 1641.[21] All this demonstrates how unstable the relationship of the kingdoms of England and Ireland was in the years before 1641.

The 'Fall of the British Monarchies' began, however, in Scotland. James VI and I followed the model not of the peripatetic Charles V but of the sedentary Philip II – the prototype governor by pen. He was able to do so by having a number of Scots who remained primarily resident in Scotland coming south more or less by rota to bring him up to date and to discuss policy initiatives with him. The Scottish members of the royal household, and the committee of Scottish counsellors in London, were able to co-ordinate policy initiatives which were also debated at the Council Board in Edinburgh. And, in addition, a powerful group of Scottish peers sat on the *English* (though actually *British*) Privy Council, and helped to shape foreign and defence policies there for the whole of Britain.[22]

Gradually the system collapsed. Fewer Scots moved up and down the Great

---

[19] The existing accounts of Strafford's trial are – for the most part – based on inadequate source criticism and anachronistic judgements; for a major exception which looks at an aspect close to the concerns of this paragraph, see C. Russell, 'The theory of treason in the trial of Strafford', in Russell, *Unrevolutionary England*.

[20] I am deeply indebted to Alan Orr, who is completing a Cambridge University Ph.D. thesis on the treason trials of the 1640s, for his helpful discussions of these matters. He holds no responsibility for the way I have framed the argument of this paragraph.

[21] See note 18, above, and the essays in J. Ohlmeyer (ed.), *Ireland: From Independence to Occupation 1641–1660* (Cambridge, 1995).

[22] These themes have been richly explored by Jenny Wormald: J. Wormald, 'The creation of Britain: multiple kingdoms or core and colonies?', *Transactions of the Royal Historical Society*, 6th ser., ii (1992); J. Wormald, 'The union of 1603', in R. A. Mason (ed.), *Scots and Britons: Scottish Political Thought and the Union of 1603* (Cambridge, 1994); and J. Wormald, 'James VI, James I and the identity of Britain', in Bradshaw and Morrill, *British Problem*. See also Morrill, 'British problem'.

North Road between London and Edinburgh; the Scots who dominated the household were permanently based in England; Charles I had as little understanding of geography and social relationships as James had had great understanding. Increasingly, policy for Scotland was made in London by Scottish 'settlers' like the duke of Lennox or the duke of Hamilton, and the Council in Edinburgh became less of a body that made policy and more of a council that enforced policy made in the metropolitan centre (rather like the English regional councils at York or Ludlow). The executive arm of government was atrophying in Caroline Scotland. And so, even more dramatically, was the legislative arm. One reads a lot about the Eleven Years Personal Rule in England. But in the twenty-five years before the calling of the Scottish and English Parliaments of 1639/40 there had been nine English parliamentary sessions lasting over a hundred weeks and two Scottish parliamentary sessions lasting a mere thirteen weeks. Scotland was enduring a lengthy Impersonal Rule.

There was every sign of Scottish constitutional atrophy, therefore, and from a Scottish perspective things were going from bad to worse. The extent of concern, and its neurotic tone, is well caught in the paper presented by the Scottish commissioners to the English Parliament on 14 December 1640 accusing William Laud of being responsible for all the 'novations' that had undermined the purity of the Scottish Church in recent years. It is suggestive that the commissioners called upon the English Parliament to ensure 'that this firebrand may be presently removed from his Majesty's presence; and that he may be put on trial and have his deserved censure, according to the laws of the kingdom'.[23] The English Parliament was to punish him for his interference in the affairs of Scotland. The Scots could not touch him themselves. Wentworth could have been extradited to face trial in Ireland; but Laud could not be extradited to face trial in Scotland. In the event it was not needed. Relentless Scottish pressure was to bring him to an English death.[24]

There were, in other words, constitutional crises in 1641 not only *within* each of the kingdoms, but also *between* them. The challenge of the 1640s is a challenge to comprehend the relationship between the unfolding of interlocking conflicts within and between the kingdoms. They were, in fact, conflicts with a strong centrifugal tendency, and the outcome was at once unanticipatable and yet natural: the destruction of three kingdoms and the creation of a single Commonwealth.

In 1638 enough Scots bonded themselves together in the National Covenant for Charles I and his Scottish counsellors to be rendered powerless to pursue the policies upon which Charles had embarked and in the

---

23 *The Works of ... William Laud*, ed. W. Scott and J. Bliss (Oxford, 1847–60), iii, p. 376.
24 L. Kaplan, *Politics and Religion during the English Civil War* (New York, 1967), ch. 5; W. G. Palmer, 'Invitation to a beheading: factions in Parliament, the Scots and the execution of William Laud', *Historical Magazine of the Protestant Episcopal Church*, 1983.

enforcement of which his counsellors were the often bewildered and reluctant agents. In essence the Scots demanded the reversal of all the innovations in religion since 1592. As they put it:

> we promise and sweare by the Great Name of the Lord our God, to continue in the Profession and obedience of the Foresaid Religion [and] That we shall defend the same and resist all contrary errours and corruptions, according to our vocation. And in like manner and with the same heart, we declare before God and Men, That we have no intention nor desire to attempt any thing that may turne to the dishonour of God, or to the diminution of the Kings greatnesse and authority...[25]

This has often been seen as a self-contradictory statement.[26] How could the Covenanters defy the king and swear to attempt no diminution in his authority in the same breath? The answer, as I have argued elsewhere, is that the Covenanters saw themselves as engaged in an honourable Scottish tradition: bonding together against a king of Scotland to make his will unenforceable. Just as passive non-compliance had caused the abandonment of the Act of Revocation of 1625, so this act of non-compliance with the king's ecclesiastical policies would render them unenforceable. If no-one was willing to punish anyone for not using the new service book, the king's policy would be dead in practice although there had been no overt challenge to his authority. It was a Scottish response to a Scottish problem, and as king of Scots Charles was powerless to effect his policy. But as king of *Britain*, he did have the power to act against his non-complying Scottish subjects. Although the Catholic marquis of Huntly and a few other mainly Highland peers offered to assist the king in enforcing his will by coercion, Charles could not get his way by starting a Scottish civil war; but by calling up the armed might (such as it was) of England, and by invoking the spectre of both an official Protestant and an informal Catholic army from Ireland, he could threaten the Scots with a *British* war in which Scotland's relations to the other kingdoms was to be redefined.[27]

So it was Charles I who began the War(s) of the Three Kingdoms. Thereafter the Scots came gradually to realise that there was no security for themselves or for their liberties outside a redefined federal – or better confederal – union.[28] Initially, in 1638 and 1639, they adopted a double strategy: to force measures through Scottish Parliaments and Scottish General

---

[25] *Acts of the Parliaments of Scotland*, ed. T. Thomson and C. Innes (Edinburgh, 1814–75), v, pp. 272–6.

[26] See the various essays in Morrill, *Scottish National Covenant*, and by David Stevenson and Edward Cowan in R. Mason (ed.), *Scotland and England 1286–1815* (Edinburgh, 1986).

[27] For further definition and discussion of this distinction, see below, pp. 188–90.

[28] J. Morrill, 'The Britishness of the English Revolution', in Asch, *Three Nations*; I am grateful to Allan Macinnes for stressing the advantages of calling the Covenanter proposal confederal rather than federal. He tells me there are sensational revelations on this issue in the Argyll Papers, an electronic version of which he is preparing for publication.

Assemblies that would bring an end to the popery and arbitrary government of recent decades,[29] and to appeal to sympathetic elements in the English political elite to act in such a way as to prevent the king from launching a three-kingdom assault on his Scottish subjects. They did not demand changes in the English (or Irish) constitutions as a condition for laying down their arms; indeed, their self-perception remained essentially defensive.

The events of the middle months of 1640 led to the crystallisation of a new perception, one that was to guide most of the Scottish elite for a decade and more. Faced both by a second royal invasion plan[30] and by the ambiguous attitudes of many English parliamentarians who appeared in the Short Parliament willing to make grants sufficient for large-scale military operations against the Scots in return for the settlement of *English* grievances, the Scots determined that there could be no settlement of one kingdom without a settlement of all three. The Instructions of the Committee of Estates[31] to the Scottish commissioners appointed for the Treaty of London (issued on 4 November 1640) were the germ of all Scottish terms for the next decade.[32]

For the Scots in 1640, settlement required a self-conscious agreement between two peoples: 'you are to decline any of our countrymen to be of the treaty or assist thereat, whether they be in the commission [of king and English Parliament] or not'.[33] The *post-nati* could inherit land in each kingdom, but they remained the subjects of just one of the king's political bodies. Furthermore, their crimes were specific to one kingdom: 'the incendiaries and prime actors are to be tried, the Scotch to be remitted to our own Parliament, and the English to be judged by theirs'.[34]

Yet if the two kingdoms were to remain separate and dis-united, they were to be made to work more closely together. Co-ordination and confederation, not union, were the hallmarks of the Scottish design: clause XIX of the Instructions required that Parliaments should be held (simultaneously) in both nations once every two or three years at most, 'in which wrongs done by either nation to the other are to be tried, and Commissioners appointed to treat about them'. These commissioners of the two independent kingdoms

[29] In this respect the Scots were unlike the English, and dated the beginnings of the misfortunes to the 1590s, when James began his betrayals of the 1581 Confession. See Morrill, *Scottish National Covenant*, 'Introduction'.

[30] The best recent narrative is M. Fissel, *The Bishops' Wars: Charles I's Campaigns against Scotland, 1638–1640* (Cambridge, 1994).

[31] I.e., the Committee of each of the Estates in the Scottish Parliament, granted executive powers by that Parliament for the intermissions between parliamentary sessions. There was such a committee throughout the period 1639–51, but at no other time.

[32] The Instructions are most accessibly to be found in *Calendar of State Papers Domestic, Charles I, 1640–1641* (London, 1881), pp. 244–6, which is a very full summary of Public Record Office, SP 16/471, no. 22, and National Library of Scotland, Edinburgh, Wodrow MSS, Folio Series, vol. 67, fo. 3. The fullest discussion of the negotiations leading to the Treaty of London is in P. Donald, *An Uncounselled King: Charles I and the Scottish Troubles, 1637–1641* (Cambridge, 1990), pp. 273–305.

[33] Instructions of the Committee of Estates, §6.

[34] Ibid., §13.

were also to 'try' differences between the king and his subjects, and also those who had given ill counsel. In addition, between Parliaments, commissioners of both nations (to be entitled *conservatores pacis*) should be chosen, who were to have power jointly to remedy any differences between the two countries. No armies were to be raised in either kingdom without the consent of both; nor was either kingdom to engage in war without the consent of both. The prince of Wales was only to marry with the consent of both kingdoms. Scots 'should have service about the King and Prince, and some in chief places'. Religious reform was less prominently placed in these Instructions than one might have expected, but there was a splash of anti-popery and a bald declaration that 'a common confession of faith should be made for both kingdoms', with mutual obligations to defend it. There was no call for the unity or integration of the Churches, simply a common commitment to an unvarnished and undiluted Protestant creed.[35] This was to be the only area of Anglo-Scottish relations developed in the years that followed, as the demands for a 'conformity of kirks' became more insistent and more detailed. Thus the Solemn League and Covenant (by which the Scots agreed to send 20,000 of their troops to assist their brethren in England) sought to bring the 'Churches of God in the three kingdoms into the nearest conjunction and uniformity in religion, confession of faith, form of church government, directory of worship and catechizing'; but it still spoke of three distinct Churches.[36] The principle remained that of autonomous kingdoms aligned so as to represent no future threat one to another.

The main limitation of the Instructions was, however, that it was a two-kingdom document. It made only passing references to Ireland. It was rooted in a determination to maintain Scotland free from a king who developed policies for Scotland by listening to Englishmen, or who plunged Scotland into wars for England's benefit, or who sought to use English (and Irish) arms to impose his will on Scotland.

I have dwelt on the Instructions of November 1640 because they were indeed the germ of the terms on which all Scottish groups were to insist as the terms for a lasting Anglo-Scottish settlement over the next eleven years. Few in England ever felt any enthusiasm for such terms. As Peter Donald has shown, the English Parliament was happy to initial the first seven clauses of the Treaty of London, which transformed the Scottish Church from a government best described as 'episcopacy-in-presbytery' into a 'pure Presbyterianism', and which redefined the constitutional relationship between the king and the Scottish Parliament and nobility, but it dragged its feet as soon as the

[35] Ibid., §19.
[36] John Rushworth, *Historical Collections* (London, 1659–1701), v, pp. 478–9; reprinted in W. C. Dickinson *et al.* (eds.), *A Source Book of Scottish History* (2nd edn, London, 1958–61), iii, pp. 122–4.

eighth clause, redefining the relationship between the kingdoms, hove into sight.[37] As the 1640s unfolded, the various powerful groups in Scotland – above all those who in the autumn of 1643 entered into a treaty with the English Parliamentarians to send them military assistance against the king, and the separate group who in December 1647 entered into an engagement with the king to send him military help against the out-of-control English Parliament and Army – saw no secure future outside a redefined relationship of the kingdoms of England and Scotland. Only Charles I – *in extremis* – accepted their point of view.

Just as striking, however, is the increasingly confused and menacing language used in Anglo-Scottish official documents about the status and future constitutional integrity of the kingdom of Ireland. The ambiguities of Irish constitutionalism had been abandoned in favour of a frank incorporation of Ireland into a greater English state long before Cromwell set foot on Irish soil on his mission of conquest and retribution.

All these new ambiguities in Anglo-Scottish thinking about the relations of the three kingdoms can be seen in an examination of, in turn, the Solemn League and Covenant of 1643, the Newcastle Propositions, the Heads of the Proposals, the Four Bills, the Engagement of 1648, and the terms on which Charles II was crowned king of Great Britain and Ireland at Scone in January 1651.

At first sight, the Solemn League and Covenant extended the principles of the 1640 Instructions only in one particular: the extension of the co-ordination principle to all three kingdoms. The full title of the document is 'A solemn league and covenant for Reformation and Defence of Religion, the honour and happiness of the King, and the peace and safety of the three kingdoms of England, Scotland and Ireland'. It opens, 'We noblemen, barons, knights, gentlemen, citizens, burgesses, ministers of the Gospel, and commons of all sorts in the kingdoms of England, Scotland and Ireland.' It is striking that the term 'England, Scotland and Ireland' is repeatedly used. The Scots almost always preferred 'Great Britain and Ireland' because the alternative implied a seniority in the realm of England: if 'Britain' was ever disaggregated in Scotland – as at the coronation of Charles I – the order was always 'king of Scotland, England and Ireland'. The usage in the Covenant was a major concession by the Scots, and must have been intended to stress the separateness of the realms.[38] But although the preliminaries and the early clauses use three-kingdom language, the document then slips into dual-monarchy language. Clause IV, for example, speaks of the condign punishment of incendiaries and malignants before 'the supreme judicatories of *both* kingdoms', and clause V speaks of '*both* Parliaments'.

A rather different ambiguity exists in the terms of the Newcastle Propositions put to the king in and after July 1646, 'in the name and on the behalf of the Kingdom [*sic*] of England and Ireland, and the Commissioners of the

[37] Donald, *Uncounselled King*, pp. 273 305.
[38] Rushworth, *Historical Collections*, v, pp. 478–9; *Source Book of Scottish History*, iii, pp. 122–4.

Kingdom of Scotland', which go on to claim that '*both* kingdoms are mutually obliged by the [Solemn League and] Covenant'.[39] The Propositions appear to have incorporated Ireland into an enhanced English state, and to envisage the extinction or at the very least the suspension of the Parliament of Ireland – thus 'a Bill' was to be passed in the English Parliament to abolish archbishops, bishops and so on 'out of the Church of England and dominion of Wales, and out of the Church of Ireland'. Indeed, the Propositions repeatedly speak of the passage of bills for England and Ireland by the English Parliament, 'and the like for the kingdom of Scotland'. Article XVII, for instance, lays down that the English Parliament (and if it is in recess a committee set up by the two Houses) shall make all senior appointments to the Irish executive and judiciary, whereas the Scottish Parliament or its recess committee would nominate the Scottish officers of state.[40]

The Newcastle Propositions were the terms of the Scots and their allies in the English Parliament, especially the so-called 'Presbyterian' grouping headed by the former allies of the earl of Essex in the Lords and by Holles and Stapilton in the Commons. Their strategy for settlement included a widespread disbandment of armies, a significant reduction of the tax burdens on the English people, and the immediate introduction of a diluted form of the agreements of the Westminster Assembly. Such a programme infuriated many members of the Army, who refused to accept the terms of its own dismemberment and articulated a very different set of settlement proposals. In alliance with a powerful bi-cameral grouping headed by the Lords Saye and Northumberland, the Army purged itself and then the two Houses of backsliders, occupied London and simultaneously presented the Heads of the Proposals to the king.

The Heads have normally been seen as a quintessentially English document, preoccupied with constitutional arrangements in post-war England and with a unilateral repudiation of the Covenant. The full title speaks specifically of 'clearing and securing the rights and liberties of *the kingdom*'. Yet clause VIII calls for an Act of Parliament 'for confirmation of the Treaties between the two Kingdoms of England and Scotland, and for appointing conservators of the peace between them'. This was, I think, the only time when an English-generated document conceded the case for a confederal solution to the British problem. On the other hand, the Heads are very unclear about the future constitutional settlement with Ireland: clause III simply sought to create unified military and naval command for 'the peace and security of this kingdom and the service of Ireland', while clause X called for an act voiding the Cessation of 1643 and leaving the prosecution of a war in Ireland to the Lords and Commons. The document is silent about the position of the Scots (settlers, army) in Ireland, and also about the relationship of the Irish Parliament (if it survived) to the English Crown and

[39] Rushworth, *Historical Collections*, vi, pp. 309–17.
[40] Ibid., p. 313.

Parliament, although it is perhaps significant that clause III(4) demanded the establishment of 'a Council of State ... for the peace and safety of this kingdom, *and of Ireland*'. Incorporation seems to have been a real possibility.[41]

In December 1647, after the distractions of the Putney Debates and the flight of the king from Army custody to the Isle of Wight, and as the king plotted his own covenant with the Scots and a renewal of the war in England, a badly rattled Long Parliament approved 'The Four Bills [to be] sent to the King in the Isle of Wight to be passed, together with the Propositions to be sent to him at the same time.' The first Bill empowered the Lords and Commons to have sole control (recruitment, levying, training, deployment, and appointment of commanders) for twenty years of all armed forces by sea and land in 'the kingdoms of England and Ireland and the dominion of Wales', a phrase which implies an incorporation of Ireland along the lines of the incorporation of Wales a century earlier. Certainly it seems that the English Lords and Commons were to have *sole* responsibility for the raising as well as the spending of all moneys for the maintenance of these armies, the implication being the raising of money throughout England, Ireland and Wales; while the fifteenth additional Proposition repeated the call in the Newcastle Propositions for all senior officers in the government of Ireland 'to be nominated by both Houses of the Parliament of England, to continue *quamdiu se bene gesserint*, and in the intervals of Parliament, by [parliamentary commissioners], to be approved or disallowed by both Houses at their next sitting'. The Four Bills ignored the constitutional relationship between England and Scotland, except for a clause in the first Bill prohibiting the forces of either to enter the other 'without consent of the Lords and Commons of England and the Parliament or the Estates of the Parliament of Scotland respectively', a form of words which seemed to rule out the creation of *conservatores pacis*.[42]

Meanwhile the king was formulating his own terms for settlement with the English Parliament and with the Scottish party headed by Hamilton, Lanark and Traquair, but also including many who had taken the National Covenant but who had eschewed the Solemn League and Covenant. In his third response to the Newcastle Propositions, the king went along with the Anglo-Scottish language, referring, for example, to 'the honour of his two kingdoms' and to 'his zeal to the Protestant profession and the union of these two kingdoms'.[43] So when the king turned to the Scots and initialed the Engagement in December 1647, the relationships of the kingdoms were spelled out much more fully than in any other formal document of the time – yet its

---

[41] Ibid., vii, p. 731.

[42] Gardiner, *Constitutional Documents*, pp. 335–8, 346. After 20 years, executive responsibility returned to the king, but the two Houses retained the right to legislate on all matters relating to the militia in England, Ireland and Wales, with the power to override a royal veto.

[43] *Journal of the House of Lords*, ix, p. 193: entry for 12 May 1647.

antecedents can still be found in the Instructions of 1640. There is indeed the pious hope expressed – I think for the only time in Charles's reign – 'that His Majesty, according to the intentions of his father, shall endeavour a complete union of the kingdoms'; but it is accepted that this 'cannot be speedily effected'. Instead, the Engagement and its additional articles lay down that the king and/or the prince of Wales should reside frequently in Scotland as well as in England, should appoint Scotsmen to the English Council and places of trust around the king, queen and prince of Wales, and should appoint Englishmen to the Scottish Council; that all foreign negotiations and treaties should be made by 'Scottish men equally with English'; that there should be free trade between the nations and free access for Scots to English overseas markets; and that English ships should be deployed to protect Scottish trading vessels. No Irish settlement was to be made 'without the advice and consent of the kingdom of Scotland'.[44]

Once more the agreement is silent about quite what any such settlement would contain, although since it would clearly involve the redistribution of parts of Ireland to those who had 'adventured' risk capital in 1642 in the military defence of the Irish Protestant communities, and who were entitled to two million acres of Irish land, and since the Engagement itself anticipated that the huge arrears of the Scots army in Ulster would be met out of confiscated Irish land, a complete conquest and vast series of plantations were clearly built into the calculations. Yet the Engagement has been shown to have been silently a three-kingdom project, with prominent Old English loyalist support for a royal restoration.[45] Thus, a remarkable but unremarked passage of the Engagement states that:

> it is further agreed that *all* such in the kingdoms of England and *Ireland*, as shall join with the Kingdom of Scotland in pursuance of this agreement ... and shall come to the Scotch army and join with them, or else put themselves into other bodies in England and Wales for prosecution of the same ends as the King's Majesty shall judge most convenient, and under such Commanders or Generals of the *English nation* as his Majesty shall think fit ... shall be protected by the Kingdom of Scotland.[46]

This Scottish permission for an Irish invasion of England is certainly the most remarkable feature of the whole document.

By the time of Charles's execution, therefore, the Scots had become ever more convinced that their destiny lay in a separate but closely defined relationship with the kingdom of England, something with which Charles himself had colluded, but something in which the English Parliament had shown at best the most fitful and faint-spirited interest.

The Rump Parliament assumed that the ending of the regnal Union ended

[44] Gardiner, *Constitutional Documents*, pp. 347–53, especially 351, 353.

[45] J. Adamson, 'Strafford's ghost: the British context of Viscount Lisle's lieutenancy of Ireland', in Ohlmeyer, *Ireland: Independence to Occupation*.

[46] Ibid., p. 350.

all formal relations between England and Scotland. The fate of the English monarchy, however, automatically involved the Irish monarchy. Thus, although the Act erecting the High Court of Justice for the trial of the king refers to Charles only as king of England,[47] the charge brought against him and the sentence passed on him – while they itemise only tyrannical acts committed in England since 30 June 1642 – do go on to speak of his commission to

> his son, and other rebels and revolters, both English and foreigners, and to the earl of Ormond, and to the Irish rebels and revolters associated with him, from whom further *invasions*[48] of this land are threatened ...[49]

Once the king was dead, this became more fully articulated. On 13 February 1649 the Rump passed an Act appointing a Council of State. It empowered them to take all steps 'for the reducing of Ireland ... and all other parts and places *belonging to* the Commonwealth of England'.[50] The culmination of this process was the abolition of the monarchy – on the grounds, said the Act of 17 March, 'that it hath been found by experience that the office of a king in this nation and in Ireland ... is unnecessary, burdensome and dangerous to the liberty, safety and public interest of the people'.[51]

Scotland was a free nation, tied to the English only by dynastic accident. It was free to go its own way. Ireland was part of England and had no say in its own destiny – that was the view of the Rumpers. As late as June 1651 the Rump could produce a great seal on one side of which was an image of Parliament in session and the legend 'IN THE THIRD YEAR OF FREEDOME BY GOD'S BLESSING RESTORED 1651', and on the other side an image of England, Wales and Ireland and the legend 'THE GREAT SEALE OF ENGLAND, 1651'.[52]

In a sense, then, the English had dealt with the crisis of constitutional relations within the composite monarchy of Britain and Ireland by incorporating Ireland and rejecting Scotland. As Derek Hirst, David Stevenson, myself and others have argued elsewhere,[53] most Rumpers were desperate *not*

---

[47] Gardiner, *Constitutional Documents*, p. 357.

[48] I have been looking out – thus far in vain – for the use of this word with respect to the Scottish irruptions into England; was it believed that there could be an 'invasion' from one part of the composite monarchy into another? What makes the non-use of this term in relation to the Scots in England the more remarkable is that the word is quite freely used of troops from one region of England entering another.

[49] Gardiner, *Constitutional Documents*, pp. 372–4, 377–80.

[50] C. H. Firth and R. S. Rait, *Acts and Ordinances of the Interregnum* (London, 1911), ii, p. 3. Later clauses reinforce the message – e.g., §5 empowers the Council to act to develop the trade of England and Ireland.

[51] Ibid., pp. 18–20.

[52] For an accessible illustration of this, see J. S. Morrill (ed.), *Revolution and Restoration: England in the 1650s* (London, 1992), p. 41. See the discussion in S. Barber, 'Scotland and Ireland under the Commonwealth', in Ellis and Barber, *Conquest and Union*, pp. 206–8.

[53] D. Hirst, 'The English Republic and the meaning of Britain', in Bradshaw and Morrill, *British Problem*; D. Stevenson, 'Cromwell, Scotland and Ireland', in J. Morrill (ed.), *Oliver Cromwell and the English Revolution* (London, 1990), ch. 6.

to have to conquer and incorporate Scotland. Fairfax refused to serve against the Scots, and Cromwell set forth with a heavy heart. The rhetoric of Cromwell's writings in Ireland and Scotland is striking testimony to the prevailing Puritan priorities. The war against the Irish was driven by divine imperatives – he saw himself delivering 'a righteous judgement of God upon … barbarous wretches who have imb[r]ued their hands in so much innocent blood'. He had come, he told the Irish Catholic clergy, 'to extirpate popery'.[54] In contrast, he had rejoiced that the internal coup by the supporters of the marquis of Argyll which led to the overthrow of the Engagers obviated the need for an English occupation of Scotland in 1648, and he besought the Scottish clergy 'in the bowels of Christ, think it possible you may be mistaken'.[55] But the very men with whom he hoped to do business were adamant that there was no long-term security for Scotland as an independent nation. On 5 February 1649, the day after news of the Regicide reached Edinburgh, the Scottish Parliament declared Charles II 'King of Great Britain, France and Ireland'.[56] Within weeks, they also spurned a formal invitation to enter into a treaty of friendship as two independent nations, demanding that the English disown their own proceedings of the previous months with respect to the execution of the king and the abolition of the monarchy and the House of Lords.[57] Twelve months later a faction of the Covenanters, in the teeth of fierce opposition from 'the Kirk party', agreed to crown Charles as king of Great Britain and Ireland, and on 1 January 1651 they did so. Nothing demonstrates so clearly the consistent and persistent Scottish concern for a confederal union of England and Scotland.[58]

Pressure of space has caused this essay to concentrate on Anglo-Scottish relations. But an equally if not more complex representation of the language of polity and nation, with equally dramatic shifts over time, could be offered with respect to Anglo-Irish or Irish-Scottish relations, and some of the issues have been highlighted in the preceding discussion. One might think that it was in the interests of all Catholic groups in Ireland to play down all the links between the kingdoms except the dynastic ones, and to insist that Ireland was an independent kingdom that shared its king but nothing more with England. Both the Ormondists and the clerical party amongst the Confederates

[54] W. C. Abbott, *The Writings and Speeches of Oliver Cromwell* (Cambridge, Mass., 1934–44), ii, pp. 127, 201–3.

[55] Ibid., ii, pp. 302–5. There was a contrary, 'republican' view held by those who detested the Scots and felt some sympathy for the Irish. Their most voluble representative was Henry Marten; but he spoke for few: see Barber, 'Scotland and Ireland'.

[56] *Act. Parl. Scot.*, vi, part II, p. 157.

[57] Ibid., pp. 435–6; for discussion, see D. Stevenson, *Revolution and Counter-Revolution in Scotland, 1644–1651* (London, 1977), ch. 4.

[58] Even amongst the most hard-line of Scots – those rare beasts, Scottish republicans – we find a similar preoccupation. In an important paper in Cambridge in June 1994, Arthur Williamson drew on the papers of Sir James Hope of Hopetoun to show that there were Scots who looked for a republican confederation made up of the commonwealths of England, Scotland, Ireland and the Netherlands. I look forward to seeing this paper in print in due course.

essentially wanted an Irish Catholic equivalent of what the Scottish Presbyterians secured by the Treaty of London – local self-determination by locally-
selected officials and free parliaments representing local power structures. One
is therefore shocked to find in the Acts of the General Assembly of the Irish
Confederation for October 1642 the following statement:

> XIV. for the avoiding of national distinction between the subjects of his
> Majestie's dominions, which the Assembly doth utterly detest and
> abhor, and which ought not to be endured *in a well-governed
> Commonwealth*; it is ordered and established that ... every Roman
> Catholick, as well English, Welsh or Scotch, who was of that profession
> before the troubles, and who will come and please to reside in this
> kingdom and join the present union shall be preserved and cherished in
> their life, goods and estates ... as fully and freely as any native born
> therein ...

The next clause establishes that

> there shall be no distinction or comparison made betwixt old Irish, and
> old and new English, or betwixt septs and families, or betwixt townsmen
> and countrymen joining in union, upon pain of the highest punishment ...[59]

One way of looking at the conflicts in Ireland in the 1640s, in other words, is
to contrast the *Catholic* perception, which is to play down ethnicity within
Ireland and between Ireland and Britain, while claiming there is no link
between the kingdoms except a dynastic one; and the *Protestant* perception,
which is always to exaggerate the ethnic divides between the 'Irish' (Gaelic
and Old English) and the 'English' and to seek to integrate Ireland into an
expanding British state. One can argue this readily for most, if not all, of the
pro-Parliamentarian groups; and perhaps for the Ormondists too.

For many of those caught up in the wars of the 1640s, the conflicts outside
their own vicinity were remote and unimportant. Even more, for many of
them, the wars outside their own kingdom were barely known and totally
misunderstood. For many others, however, there was one war in several
theatres. I have written elsewhere of some of those for whom that was true.[60]
And the above discussion does not affect that fact. For example, many Irish
Confederates believed that there would be no long-term security for the kind
of Catholic Ireland Charles seemed willing to permit under the Ormond
peace, let alone under the terms offered by the earl of Glamorgan, without a
willingness by the Catholic Irish to send troops to Britain to secure a royal

---

[59] 'Acts of the General Assembly of the Irish Confederation', in J. T. Gilbert (ed.), *A History of
the Irish Confederation* (Dublin, 1882–91), ii, pp. 81–2.
[60] Morrill, 'Britishness of the English Revolution'; Morrill, 'Fashioning of Britain', pp. 28–38.

victory in the British wars.[61] That did not mean that they wanted to see the kind of federated or confederated state that the Covenanters were demanding. It simply meant that they knew that Charles I might, but that his British enemies would not, honour that agreement to create an Ireland assertively independent of the English *state*. That said, it is clear not only that there was a great variety of perceptions about the nature and extent of the war(s) of the 1640s and that those that thought three-dimensionally often made things happen three-dimensionally, not least Charles himself, but also that there are at least three different types of internal war being fought within the archipelago, and that distinguishing these does help us to understand why the 'War of the Three Kingdoms' is more than one war and less than three.

In a recent essay, John Pocock has fruitfully explored the ancient Roman distinction between two kinds of internal war: the *bellum civile* (defined as 'a war between *cives*, citizens of the same polity') and the *bellum sociale* (defined as 'a war between *socii*, polities associated in a system comprising a multiplicity of states'). He goes on to explain that 'the great *bellum sociale* of antiquity turned on the eligibility of Italian *socii* to be treated as *cives Romani*'. He then tentatively suggests that the Scottish and Irish components of the War(s) of the Three Kingdoms are better seen not as part of a pan-archipelagic *bellum civile*, but as *bella socialia*.[62]

This is indeed a fruitful hypothesis. If we paraphrase his distinction as being that between a struggle within a closed political system – such as within the kingdom of England, Scotland or Ireland – for control of existing or transformed political (including religious) institutions, and a struggle by members of one polity within a composite or multiple monarchy to redefine their relations with the other component polities, then we have an analytical tool that sorts out the tangled skeins very neatly.

But I would suggest that we need to add a third component, again well known to Roman historians. This I will call a war of independence or secession. We need to examine whether in Scotland, Ireland and Wales there were those who sought to detach themselves from the Stuart state system, as the Netherlands had done from the Habsburg state system in the later sixteenth century, or as the Portuguese were in the process of doing in the 1640s.

It took me a long time to compose the previous sentence. As I worried away at it, the clouds gathered. I originally wrote '... as the Netherlands had detached themselves from Spain ...'. This was of course a mistake. Charles V was a Burgundian (Netherlander) who inherited (amongst much else) the

---

61 My thinking about the Confederates has been transformed by reading and examining the doctoral thesis of Tadhg Ó h Annracháin, '"Far from *Terra Firma*": The Mission of Gianbattista Rinuccini to Ireland, 1645–9', European University Institute, Florence, 1995, which I hope will speedily be published.
62 Pocock, 'Atlantic archipelago and the War of the Three Kingdoms'.

kingdoms of Spain, and handed most of that inheritance on to his son Philip II. But the ties were dynastic. The fact that Philip sought to govern the Netherlands in ways which owed more to his experience of Southern Europe, and in order to sustain the foreign and military imperatives of an Iberian king, meant that the Netherlands saw him as an unsuitable king. Initially, they believed that the constitutional remedy open to them was to strengthen the elements of self-determination within the seventeen provinces making up the Netherlands. Theirs was to be a *bellum sociale*, a clarification and strengthening of Netherlandish autonomy within a composite Habsburg state system. But the refusal of Philip II to comply with their constitutionalism led to a disowning of his sovereignty.

I therefore changed the above sentence to read 'We need to examine whether in Scotland, Ireland and Wales there were those who sought to detach themselves from the House of Stuart, as the Netherlands had done from the House of Habsburg in the later sixteenth century, or as the Portuguese were in the process of doing in the 1640s.' But this too would be mistaken. One can have a war of independence from a state system without having a war of independence from a ruling house. Indeed this is very clearly demonstrated by what happened in the Atlantic archipelago at the time of the execution of Charles I. In 1649 the *English* abolished monarchy. The option then lay open to the Irish and the Scots to recognise Charles II as king of Ireland or Scotland, and thus to claim independence of a Stuart state system but not of the House of Stuart. A war of independence therefore meant a war to establish a sovereign polity free from any defined (and even more, free from any ill-defined) constitutional relationship with another polity. And so to my final form of words: 'We need to examine whether in Scotland, Ireland and Wales there were those who sought to detach themselves from the Stuart state system ...'. In practice that meant, until 1649, disowning the House of Stuart; and in the 1650s it meant owning the House of Stuart.

England experienced a *bellum civile* in the 1640s. That was a fundamental aspect of its crisis, and for most Englishmen, *the* fundamental experience. But for most of the political elite, for all those living in the northern counties and for many living in the vales of the Severn and the Dee, there was a consciousness – for many of them a distressing and alarming consciousness – that they could become the victims of the *bella socialia* in Ireland and Scotland, as they experienced or anticipated the arrival of troops from Scotland and Ireland who would be determined on intervening in the English Civil War as a means of securing a redefinition of their relationship to England. England also experienced a war of secession, as the metropolitan kingdom sought (perhaps) to prevent the secession of a Catholic kingdom to the west, and (as time went on) to cast off Scotland as an unwanted partner. The refusal of Scotland to be cast off paradoxically resulted in a half-hearted, unconvinced and ill-defended incorporation of Scotland into an integrative union – a sort of unwanted *bellum sociale* from the English perspective.

Scotland experienced first and foremost a *bellum sociale*, a series of military interventions in England whose purpose was to redefine the relationship of two kingdoms, so as to create institutional forms that would preserve the institutions and culture of the smaller, more vulnerable partner. As we have suggested, it may even be that those few Scots who were content to see the dynastic linkage broken by the abolition of monarchy may have wished to see the two commonwealths more closely bound in some republican confederation. There were also, of course, elements of civil war in Scotland, both in the years 1644–6 (the Montrose campaigns) and the years 1649–51 (with the rebellions within the Covenanting movement). But Scottish separatists are hard to find.

Ireland clearly has elements of all three types of internal war, and the dominant form varies from region to region and from year to year. In a sense, the interest in Ireland is in the inextricability of the elements. Thus there was a civil war between the Ormondists and the Confederates, and between Old English Protestants like Inchiquin and (at different times) both the Ormondists and the Confederates. But those same wars can also be seen to represent *bella socialia*, as the Catholics sought to recreate a new Ireland free from the old relationship to England and the English settlers, and as the Protestants sought to create a new closer link to the institutions of the English kingdom. And Inchiquin could fight a *bellum civile* against the Catholics and a fleeting *bellum sociale* against the integrationist Protestant forces of Lord Lisle.[63] Furthermore, as Padraig Lenihan has now shown, there is an embryonic separatism at the heart of Confederate politics in the later 1640s which is not simply the typical whimsy of the embittered *émigré* and the whiskeyed talk of the Wild Geese,[64] but the evolutionary pressure of a movement which had developed so sophisticated and effective a political and administrative structure in the crucible of civil and social war.[65]

What we have, I hope, learned from this essay is that there was an element of Pocock's two forms of internal war in all three kingdoms; and a wraith-like apparition of a third in all of them. Thus the national histories of England, Ireland, Scotland and Wales are necessary but not sufficient in explaining why there were wars in all three kingdoms or what the dynamics of those wars were. If this does not quite identify the enigma of 'British history', it does demonstrate its quintessential ambiguity. The enigma may be that while historians have always known that that was the case, they have yet to realise just what it entails.

---

[63] Adamson, 'Strafford's ghost', pp. 145–58.

[64] T. O'Fiaich, 'Republicanism and separatism in the seventeenth century', *Leachtai Colm Cille*, ii (1971).

[65] P. Lenihan, 'The Irish Confederacy 1642–9: An Irish State at War' (National University of Ireland Ph.D. thesis, 1995), especially pp. 8–15.

Part IV

The age of Union

Chapter 11

Varieties of Britishness
Ireland, Scotland and Wales in the Hanoverian state

S. J. Connolly

In 1745 the army of the Young Pretender overran Scotland and advanced deep into England. Modern historians differ over whether the invaders had any real chance of success.[1] But the incursion was at the very least the most formidable direct challenge offered, at any time in the eighteenth century, to Hanoverian rule over the British Isles. The response to the crisis of the local and metropolitan establishment is correspondingly revealing.

The man in charge of Ireland's affairs during the Young Pretender's sortie was the self-consciously urbane fourth earl of Chesterfield, appointed Lord Lieutenant by a reluctant George II as part of a restructuring of the ministry in January 1745. When a Franco-Jacobite invasion had first been threatened the previous year, Chesterfield's predecessor, the earl of Devonshire, had sanctioned a sudden invocation of the largely dormant laws against Catholic ecclesiastics. Orders had gone out for the arrest of bishops, vicars-general and members of religious orders, and for the suppression of convents and nunneries. Houses were searched for concealed arms and Catholic churches, at least in the towns, were forced to close. Since the 1690s, such measures had been part of the standard response to threats of insurrection or invasion, and though Devonshire had questioned their necessity he had given way to pressure from his Irish advisers. In the much more immediate crisis of 1745, on the other hand, Chesterfield firmly resisted calls for a similar exercise in pre-emptive repression. Instead, he announced his satisfaction with the guarantees of loyal behaviour offered by leading Catholics, and openly mocked the prejudices of what he called 'my good subjects', who 'are in general still at the year 1689, and have not shook off any religious or political prejudice that prevailed at the time'.[2] For Irish historians Chesterfield's viceroyalty is thus generally seen as an episode of relative enlightenment, marking the effective end of serious attempts to interfere with Catholic

---

[1] Compare, e.g.: B. Lenman, *The Jacobite Risings in Britain 1689–1746* (London, 1980), pp. 237–8; W. A. Speck, *The Butcher: The Duke of Cumberland and the Suppression of the '45* (Oxford, 1981), pp. 188–99; and L. Colley, *Britons: Forging the Nation 1707–1837* (2nd edn, London, 1994), pp. 77–85.

[2] S. J. Connolly, *Religion, Law and Power: The Making of Protestant Ireland 1660–1760* (Oxford, 1992), pp. 257–8, 291–2.

religious organisation or practice. In Scottish historical writing, on the other hand, Chesterfield is somewhat differently remembered. One security measure that he did take during the crisis of 1745-6 was to prohibit the export of oats from Ulster to Scotland. His letters to correspondents in England, moreover, recommended that others should do the same, advocating a complete embargo on grain exports into the Highlands as a means of extirpating rebellion there once and for all. This enthusiasm for something close to genocide has led one eminent Scottish historian to resurrect Dr Johnson's verdict on Chesterfield's character: the manners of a dancing master and the morals of a whore.[3]

The contrast between the Irish and the Scottish Chesterfields, between the self-satisfied satirist of Protestant nervousness and the ruthless advocate of mass starvation, is merely one example of what is now a fairly well recognised point: that in the first half of the eighteenth century the main threat to the security of the Hanoverian dominions came not from Ireland, but from Scotland. Local Protestants and British government alike took it for granted that the Catholics who made up three-quarters or more of the population of Ireland were enemies of the state, looking to a restoration of the exiled Stuarts as a means of regaining lost ancestral lands and a Catholic monopoly of power and privilege. But numbers, in a pre-democratic age, were not the crucial consideration they later became. Across the preceding century, the massive appropriation of Irish land that followed the British Civil Wars of 1641-53, the less extensive sequestrations after the Williamite war of 1689-91, and the penal restrictions imposed from 1704 on Catholic landowners, had reduced the Catholic landowning class to an insignificant minority. Confiscation, exile and conformity had together ensured that the social and economic structures, which in Highland Scotland still enabled Jacobite chiefs to summon their human rent onto the battlefield, had in Ireland been shattered beyond repair. The Catholic majority was leaderless and demoralised, cut off from the world of politics both by formal exclusions and by barriers of language and poverty. The Protestant minority, by contrast, was well led, enjoyed sole control of the civil and military administration, and was armed and organised, through the militia, for its own defence.

These practical realities were well understood by contemporary strategists. The Irish army establishment was large, having been fixed in 1697 at 12,000 men. But this was a device to house, and pay for, a general reserve force on a scale that public opinion would not have tolerated in mainland Britain. Thus the response of government to the threat of war, insurrection or rebellion was invariably to move troops out of Ireland to other locations. In 1708, 1714-15, 1719 and 1722, all times of actual or threatened Jacobite invasion, large detachments of soldiers were sent to England and Scotland. At the beginning of the War of the Austrian Succession (1741-8), which formed the

---

[3] Lenman, *Jacobite Risings*, p. 262.

background to the Young Pretender's venture, 700 men from regiments stationed in Ireland were shipped to America, followed by the transfer of 1,400 men to continental Europe in February 1744, and 1,200 more in May 1745. Yet this substantial depletion of the Irish army establishment was accepted with equanimity in Ireland itself. Devonshire, early in 1744, asked that troops should not be withdrawn too quickly, but he did so only to ensure that there was time to 'arm the Protestants, who, if no regular troops invade us, will be able to keep the Papists quiet, and so by degrees if there be occasion we might send over almost all our regular forces'. And, indeed, the response to the Young Pretender's landing in July of the following year was to transfer to Scotland two of the six battalions remaining in Ireland.[4]

Highland Scotland's role as the weak spot in the defences of the British state made it not only the area to which troops were automatically rushed in times of crisis, but also the theatre for methods of repression not seen in any other part of the Hanoverian dominions. Thus it was the Highlands, not Ireland, that were the scene of the great atrocity of King William's reign, the massacre of the Glencoe McDonalds in February 1692. It was the Highlands, not Ireland, that were the scene of the systematic use of military terror to subdue a conquered population in the months after the defeat of the Pretender's forces at Culloden Moor on 16 April 1746. A similar contrast existed in official attitudes to language and culture. Ireland's indigenous language, and the customs and lifestyle of the rural lower classes, were undoubtedly viewed as inferior and barbarous; but the collapse of the political structures of Gaelic Ireland meant that neither was perceived as a political threat. They could be despised but tolerated until they were undermined by the gradual progress of social improvement. In Highland Scotland, on the other hand, the defeat of the Jacobites was followed by a systematic attack on indigenous language and culture. The notorious laws banning the wearing of Highland dress, the use of certain surnames and the playing of the pipes were reinforced by the intensified educational offensive of the Scottish Society for the Propagation of Christian Knowledge, and by the policies of conscious social engineering pursued by the commissioners appointed to administer forfeited Jacobite estates. In each case the aim was to transform the culture of the Highlands, by undermining the traditional clan structure, by disseminating English language and manners, and by instilling in the natives the values of industry, morality and true religion.[5]

These contrasts in the scale and nature of military and cultural repression should by themselves be sufficient to caution against a teleological approach which would see the successful integration of Scotland into the British state,

[4] K. P. Ferguson, 'The Army in Ireland, from the Restoration to the Act of Union' (Trinity College, Dublin, Ph.D. thesis, 1980), p. 99; Devonshire to [Newcastle], 31 January 1744, Public Record Office, MS SP.63/406/32–3.

[5] C. W. J. Withers, *Gaelic Scotland: The Transformation of a Cultural Region* (London, 1988), chs. 2, 3.

and the emergence of Ireland as the United Kingdom's only real nationalist problem, as predetermined outcomes. It could of course be argued that the Scottish Highlands were a special problem. Yet at the beginning of the eighteenth century it would have been difficult to regard the bond between England and any part of Scotland as inherently more stable or permanent than the bond between England and Ireland. There is certainly no parallel in Anglo-Irish relations during this period for the all-out constitutional warfare of the Aliens Act and the Act of Security, or for the literally murderous animosities revealed in an episode like the judicial assassination of three English seamen at Leith in 1705.[6] By 1704 Irish high churchmen were debating how the Presbyterians of Ulster might respond in the event of a war between England and Scotland.[7] Even after the Union, episodes like the Malt Tax riots of 1725 and the Porteous riot of 1736 were at least as alarming, from the point of view of London government, as the rhetorically dramatic but wholly law abiding opposition to Wood's halfpence in Ireland, or even the Dublin anti-union riot of 1759.

Two other reasons can be suggested for avoiding the seductive temptations of determinism in the matter of the success and failure of assimilation into a united multinational state. In the first place, we have to be realistic about the criteria we employ. It is easy enough to itemise various ways in which the eventual separatism of Ireland was prefigured in the differences that, already in the eighteenth century, set it apart from England, Scotland and Wales. But we have to remember that it was not only Ireland that had a separate development in this period. Scotland's integration was made possible, not just by economic prosperity and the willingness of the English elite to admit Scots to a growing share of political and military (especially imperial) patronage, but also by the continued existence of separate Scottish institutions – the law, the Church, the universities – as a focus for national identity and national pride. In Wales the foundations were laid, in the late eighteenth and early nineteenth centuries, for the Nonconformist dominance that was to be a central part of Wales's subsequent separate identity within the United Kingdom. In both cases incorporation into the British state also meant the acceptance of national peculiarities. Any prospectus for the more effective inclusion of Ireland would presumably have meant some similar adaptation.

Second, there is the danger that discussion of eighteenth-century Ireland, warped by an excess of hindsight, will fail to do justice to the strong British element that pervaded its political life. It is of course true that the eighteenth century saw the development of an increasingly assertive Irish patriotism among the Protestant middle and upper classes. But once again it is important not to read history backwards. Irish patriotism was strongly influenced by the English 'real Whig' or 'Country' tradition. Indeed, its political concerns can,

---

6 Lenman, *Jacobite Risings*, pp. 79–82.
7 *Historical Manuscripts Commission Reports, Ormonde MSS*, new series, viii, pp. 78, 86.

to some extent, be seen as no more than the application to Irish conditions of the principles of civic virtue, active citizenship and a commitment to close parliamentary scrutiny of the executive that characterised English 'Country' politics. Irish Protestants continued, well into the eighteenth century, to refer to themselves as Englishmen, using 'Irish' as synonymous with 'Catholic'. When they first began to question what they perceived as the illegitimate intrusion of English government into Irish affairs, the basis of their argument was that they were being denied the constitutional rights of Englishmen. Initially they were prepared to consider a parliamentary union, giving them reasonable representation in the Parliament that would control their lives, as an acceptable alternative to legislative autonomy. In 1703 the Irish Commons actually petitioned for such a union. It was only gradually during the eighteenth century, partly as a response to the growing status of the Irish Parliament and partly through the bitter experience of learning just how little weight appeals to common English kinship carried with London politicians, that Irish patriotism became something that could credibly be presented as the precursor of nineteenth-century nationalism.[8]

Irish patriotism, then, was more British than it looked at first sight. The same holds true, to an even greater extent, for the other distinctive ideology of the first half of the eighteenth century. This was the Jacobitism that constituted, at least up to the 1740s, the primary loyalty of the majority of politically conscious Catholics. Serious investigation of the Irish Jacobite tradition has only recently begun; the subject may well be poised to become, like English Jacobite studies over the past fifteen years or so, a flourishing speciality in its own right.[9] But a proper reassessment of the role of Jacobitism in eighteenth-century Irish society must include a recognition that this loyalty to the exiled Stuart dynasty was not just a potential source of popular disaffection. It was also by its very nature a British political ideology, shared with some Englishmen and many Scots, and concerned with restoring a Scottish dynasty to the combined thrones of England, Scotland and Ireland. The Gaelic poet Eoghan Ruadh O Suilleabhain, stirred to renewed optimism by the American War of Independence, may have written enthusiastically of the coming destruction of 'the wretched troops who speak English' and the 'foreign pirates' sitting in the great houses. But the political framework for these events remained a future in which, with the Stuarts restored, 'all will be

---

[8] Eighteenth-century Irish patriotism has attracted a large literature of varying quality. For an introduction to the complexities of the topic, see, in particular, J. T. Leerssen, 'Anglo-Irish patriotism and its European context: notes towards a reassessment', *Eighteenth-Century Ireland*, iii (1988); D. Hayton, 'Anglo-Irish attitudes: changing perceptions of national identity among the Protestant ascendancy in Ireland *ca* 1690–1750', *Studies in Eighteenth-Century Culture*, xvii (1987); and J. Smyth, '"Like Amphibious Animals": Irish Protestants, Ancient Britons 1691–1707', *Historical Journal*, xxxvi (1993).

[9] B. O Buachalla, 'Irish Jacobite poetry', *Irish Review*, xii (1992); B. O Buachalla, 'Irish Jacobitism in official documents', *Eighteenth-Century Ireland*, viii (1993). See also Connolly, *Religion, Law and Power*, pp. 233–49.

well again in Whitehall, in Ireland and Scotland'.[10] To say this is not to deny that Jacobitism, in Ireland as in Scotland, probably provided a vehicle for the expression of national grievances and of a sense of national distinctiveness. But its central premise was in both cases the continued incorporation of the nation concerned in the British state.

At the other end of the political spectrum, meanwhile, the official political culture of Hanoverian Ireland was constructed on an equally clear assumption that Ireland and Great Britain were a political unit. State festivals in both kingdoms drew on the same shared body of symbols and ceremonial events. Ireland of course had its own political anniversaries, notably the commemoration of the rising of 1641 (23 October) and the victories of Aughrim and the Boyne (1 – later 12 – July).[11] But other festivals – Guy Fawkes' Night, the day of the accession of George I, assorted royal family anniversaries[12] – were common throughout the Hanoverian dominions. There was, likewise, a common iconography of monarchy. In fact Dublin, where statues were erected to George I in 1722 and George II in 1758, appears to have outshone contemporary London in this respect.[13] There was, finally, the same concern for the fortunes of British arms on distant battlefields. In 1740, for example, the neighbourhood of Belfast celebrated news of Admiral Vernon's victory at Porto Bello in spectacular style:

> The inhabitants flocked to the streets, and from thence to the Long Bridge, from whence, to their surprise they saw the neighbouring country all, as it were, on a fire; for those who had not faggots cut, set the hedges of their fields afire, so that (as this town is encircled with a ridge of mountains) one could have counted upwards of one hundred bonfires on the adjacent hills.[14]

The contrast between perceptions of Scotland and Ireland as sources of disaffection, a recognition that political assimilation involved some acceptance of national peculiarities, the strong British element in Irish political culture at every level – all these are reasons for arguing that the successful integration of Scotland into the British state, and the failure similarly to integrate Ireland, should not be approached as a foregone conclusion. But to emphasise that point is to pose rather than to answer questions. For, in the long term,

[10] Eoghan Ruadh O Suilleabhain, 'There are Troubles for George', trans. F. Murphy, *The Bog Irish* (Harmondsworth, 1987), pp. 24–6.

[11] T. C. Barnard, 'The Uses of 23 October 1641 and Irish Protestant celebrations', *English Historical Review*, cvi (1991); J. R. Hill, 'National festivals, the state and "Protestant Ascendancy" in Ireland 1790–1829', *Irish Historical Studies*, xxiv (1984).

[12] Cf. C. A. Whatley, 'Royal day, people's day: the monarch's birthday in Scotland, c.1660–1860', in R. Mason and N. Macdougall (eds.), *People and Power in Scotland* (Edinburgh, 1992).

[13] P. Fagan, *The Second City: Portrait of Dublin 1700–1760* (Dublin, 1986), p. 16. Compare the comments on the paucity of royal statues in London in Colley, *Britons*, p. 203.

[14] *Dublin Daily Post*, 29 March 1740.

Scotland was so integrated and Ireland was not. By the end of the eighteenth century, a combination of Protestant patriotism carried to a logical extreme, French inspired radicalism, and novel forms of popular disaffection together ensured that Ireland had displaced Scotland both as the main trouble spot of the British Isles and as the theatre for methods of repression that were by now considered unacceptable in either of the other two kingdoms. If such an outcome was not predetermined or even, before the late eighteenth century, predictable, then how is it to be explained?

At this point we should perhaps turn to the third and least restive of the Celtic dependencies. Wales is important in this discussion for two main reasons. First, it reveals the limits set, not just by geography and demography, but also by economic and social development. Wales's small size, in both territory and population, and its long-standing administrative assimilation into the English state, are enough to explain why there was no Welsh equivalent to the assertive patriotism of Ireland's Protestant elite. But we also have to explain why Wales failed to develop any parallel to the patriotism of eighteenth-century Scotland, focused on economic and social development rather than on political autonomy. Here the obvious point to stress is Wales's lower level of commercial development, combined possibly with the lack of specifically Welsh institutions of higher education.

Second, the Welsh example confirms the irrelevance, for this period, of those two great staples of nineteenth-century nationalism, history and culture. A recent study sees the acceptance by eighteenth-century Scots of an anglo-centric history as being largely responsible for the subsequent failure to develop a strong and ideologically coherent Scottish nationalism.[15] But this failure to develop a distinctive and confident patriot history is surely a symptom rather than a cause of Scotland's acceptance of assimilation. It is true that the traditional myth of a Scottish monarchy traceable to 330 BC was undermined by new methods of historical scholarship, and that Scotland's past was littered with episodes of violence and, more recently, religious extremism calculated to jar increasingly on polite eighteenth-century sensibilities. But, then, patriotic history has always and everywhere depended on a capacity for selection and omission. The idea that Wales was the home of an ancient British race of Trojan origin had likewise been subjected to sceptical scrutiny as more rigorous historical methods developed in the sixteenth and seventeenth centuries. But it nevertheless survived as a part of patriotic Welsh culture, embellished during the eighteenth century by new accretions of mythology, most notably the obsession with a supposed druidic past.[16] By the same token, if Protestant Irishmen could disregard a centuries-

---

[15] C. Kidd, *Subverting Scotland's Past: Scottish Whig Historians and the Creation of an Anglo-British Identity 1689–c.1830* (Cambridge, 1993). See also R. Mitchison, 'Patriotism and national identity in eighteenth-century Scotland', in T. W. Moody (ed.), *Historical Studies XI: Nationality and the Pursuit of National Independence* (Belfast, 1978), p. 73.

[16] G. H. Jenkins, *The Foundations of Modern Wales, 1642–1780* (Oxford, 1987), pp. 243–52; P. Morgan, 'From a death to a view: the hunt for the Welsh past in the Romantic period',

old legacy of ethnic denigration to develop an exalted image of pre-Norman Ireland as a land of civil liberty, non-Romish Christianity and high cultural achievement, then Scots, if so minded, could surely have worked equivalent interpretative wonders on their national past.[17]

In all three main regions of the Celtic periphery, the late eighteenth century saw a marked growth in interest in history, antiquities, language and folk custom. In each case, however, this cultural revivalism was a force for stability rather than change. In Scotland the new enthusiasm in the late eighteenth and the early nineteenth centuries for a romanticised version of the national past, the idealisation of a vanishing 'traditional' culture, and the elevation of the Highlands from a feared and resented outland to the repository of everything that was best in the Scottish character, can all be seen as part of a depoliticised patriotism, what has been called 'an ideology of noisy inaction'.[18] Alternatively it can be seen as a positively conservative response, mobilising images of vertical solidarity and national tradition in defence of what was perceived as an increasingly threatened social and political order.[19] In Wales, too, the cultural revivalism of the late eighteenth century appealed to, among others, conservative-minded Anglicans concerned to reawaken a partly imagined traditional Wales, uncontaminated by dissent and political insubordination.[20] In Ireland the new interest in Gaelic culture was initially linked to the political patriotism of the Volunteers and the 'constitution of 1782'. After the disasters of the 1790s, however, cultural nationalism largely lost its association with what had in any case been an elitist variety of political self-assertion. Instead, its main political appeal for most of the nineteenth century was to be as a possible instrument of vertical integration, a means by which the Protestant elite might regain the hegemony destroyed by the rise of Catholic mass politics.[21]

From culture and history we turn to the mechanics of the political connection. The management of Scotland and Ireland in the early and mid-eighteenth century was, at first sight, very similar. In each case, government found powerful local agents – in Ireland known as 'undertakers' – to whom the task of political management could be subcontracted. The most

in E. J. Hobsbawm and T. Ranger (eds.), *The Invention of Tradition* (Cambridge, 1983).

[17] N. Vance, 'Celts, Carthaginians and constitutions: Anglo-Irish literary relations 1780–1820', *Irish Historical Studies*, xxii (1981); C. O'Halloran, '"The Island of Saints and Scholars": views of the early Church and sectarian politics in late eighteenth-century Ireland', *Eighteenth-Century Ireland*, v (1990).

[18] The argument of N. T. Phillipson, quoted in R. G. Asch, '"Obscured in Whiskey, Mist and Misery": the role of Scotland and Ireland in British history', in R. G. Asch (ed.), *Three Nations – A Common History?* (Bochum, 1993), p. 43.

[19] B. Lenman, *Integration, Enlightenment and Industrialization: Scotland 1746–1832* (London, 1981), pp. 129–42.

[20] Morgan, 'From a death to a view', p. 94. See also G. Williams, *Religion, Language and Nationality in Wales* (Cardiff, 1979), p. 139.

[21] D. Cairns and S. Richards, *Writing Ireland: Colonialism, Nationalism and Culture* (Manchester, 1988); T. Flanagan, 'Nationalism: the literary tradition', in T. E. Hachey and L. J. McCaffrey (eds.), *Perspectives on Irish Nationalism* (Lexington, 1989).

prominent of these managers – the earl of Islay (later third duke of Argyll) in Scotland, William Conolly and his successor Henry Boyle in Ireland – all occupied the same ambiguous position: ultimately dependent on London's favour, at times vulnerable to shifts in English political life, yet enjoying substantial independent authority.[22] Already in the 1750s, however, we find Boyle, faced with a threat to his power, openly defying government in a way that Islay never attempted.[23] The differences between the two systems became more apparent still following the period of instability that affected British politics generally in the 1760s. In Scotland government found a new manager in the person of Henry Dundas. In Ireland, from the viceroyalty of Townshend (1767–72) onwards, Lords Lieutenant and their increasingly important chief secretaries became directly responsible for political management, dispensing with undertakers in the old sense. This transition to 'direct rule' can in turn been seen as giving patriot politics a new immediacy in the last decades of the eighteenth century.[24]

Why did it prove more difficult to find a satisfactory compromise between central and local power in Ireland than it did in Scotland? The obvious contrast between the two systems is that Ireland retained its own Parliament, while Scottish particularism resided in a set of lesser institutions: the Church, the law, higher education, the royal burghs. There is a tendency to assume that Ireland got the best of the bargain. Dr Johnson, famously, warned that if Ireland accepted a parliamentary union, then England would rob it, as it would have robbed the Scots had they had anything worth stealing.[25] But this perception may well be misleading. Parliamentary autonomy did not prevent large areas of Irish public life – the established Church, the judiciary, the revenue service, the pension list, the peerage – from being used as a reserve of additional patronage for English political purposes. For example, just over half of the occupants of bishoprics in the Church of Ireland during the eighteenth century, and just under half of the judges appointed between 1702 and 1760, had been born on the other side of the Irish Sea.[26] By contrast, the profits of Scotland's domestic public life remained in the hands of Scotsmen. This was not primarily due to the institutional guarantees enshrined in the Union: these, as was demonstrated when heritable jurisdictions were abolished after the 1745 rebellion, were fatally qualified by the doctrine of

[22] J. S. Shaw, *The Management of Scottish Society, 1707–64* (Edinburgh, 1983); D. W. Hayton, 'The beginnings of the "Undertaker System"', in T. Bartlett and D. W. Hayton (eds.), *Penal Era and Golden Age: Essays in Irish History 1690–1800* (Belfast, 1979); D. W. Hayton, 'Walpole and Ireland', in J. Black (ed.), *Britain in the Age of Walpole* (London, 1984).

[23] D. O'Donovan, 'The Money Bill dispute of 1753', in Bartlett and Hayton, *Penal Era and Golden Age*.

[24] D. Lammey, 'The growth of the "Patriot Opposition" in Ireland during the 1770s', *Parliamentary History*, vii (1988).

[25] James Boswell, *Life of Johnson*, ed. R. W. Chapman (Oxford, 1970), p. 1038 (12 October 1779).

[26] J. Falvey, 'The Church of Ireland episcopate in the eighteenth century: an overview', *Eighteenth-Century Ireland*, viii (1993), p. 109; F. G. James, *Ireland in the Empire 1688–1770* (Cambridge, Mass., 1973), p. 131.

absolute parliamentary sovereignty.[27] It was rather the distinctiveness of Scottish institutions – a Presbyterian Church, a legal system founded on different principles – that meant that Scots were not robbed following the Union in a way that many Irishmen felt they were being robbed even without one.

The other problem with the Irish Parliament lay in the development during the eighteenth century of an exalted self-image wholly out of line with its actual status as the representative assembly of a subordinate kingdom. There have been various attempts to fit Ireland into the now fashionable model of the composite monarchy or multiple kingdom. But in many ways such a model is misleading. If the Irish Parliament had in fact been like the Hungarian Diet – a body that over time had evolved certain clearly defined functions as the guardian of provincial liberties – then its role would have been straightforward. British government would no doubt have found it a nuisance, but a working relationship could nevertheless have been established. The reality, however, was that the 1690s began a wholly new phase in the history of the Irish Parliament, as a combination of financial exigency and novel constitutional aspirations transformed it for the first time into a regular part of the kingdom's government. The result was that the members of that Parliament took their self-image and their constitutional aspirations not from some gradually evolving tradition of local representation, but from the model of contemporary England. It was this which made Anglo-Irish politics in the last decades of the century so dangerously unstable. William Pitt's attempt in 1785 to draw up a comprehensive settlement of the economic relationship between the two kingdoms collapsed because the proposals included an acceptance that the Irish Parliament would duplicate English shipping legislation. In 1789 the same Parliament insisted on its independent right to decide when, and on what terms, the Prince of Wales should take power as Regent. In each case the Irish political elite were insisting that their Parliament was not just a guardian of national interests within a composite monarchy, but a sovereign body, not required to defer to its English counterpart even in matters concerning the Crown, diplomacy, peace or war. It was against this background – reminiscent in many ways of the difficulties presented by Scotland in the years before 1707 – that British government policy moved towards the idea of a union.[28]

Compared to Scotland's continued institutional autonomy, then, Ireland's possession of a separate legislature failed to give Irishmen adequate control of their domestic public life, while at the same time it encouraged constitutional aspirations that were in the long term incompatible with continued

[27] Lenman, *Integration, Enlightenment and Industrialization*, p. 1.
[28] For a fuller discussion, see S. J. Connolly, 'Late eighteenth-century Irish politics', *Parliamentary History*, xiii (1994).

incorporation into the Hanoverian state. These two problems, in the eighteenth century at least, seem to do more than culture, geography or earlier history to explain the different political development of the two regions. However, we have still to give proper consideration to the single most obvious difference between Ireland on the one hand and Wales and Scotland on the other: that Ireland, alone among the Hanoverian possessions, had a predominantly Catholic population.

There can be no question but that, in the actual event, religion was a major reason for the failure of the British state to turn political control of Ireland into political integration. Nor is this surprising, particularly in the light of Linda Colley's argument that Protestantism was a crucial ingredient in the new British identity created during the eighteenth century.[29] Yet a review of policy towards Catholic Ireland in the second half of that century must nevertheless raise the question of at what point, if ever, such an outcome became inevitable. From as early as the 1760s, as Thomas Bartlett has shown, government began to re-examine its priorities in relation to Ireland. Such a re-examination was made possible by the disappearance of the Jacobite threat and by the spread of Enlightenment ideas of religious toleration. It was further encouraged by Britain's growing demand for military recruits, which caused British ministers to look with new eyes on Ireland's large reserve of able-bodied but irredeemably popish manpower. After 1789 the threat of French subversion and domestic radicalism provided a powerful additional motive for policies of conciliation. These strategic considerations were reinforced by Britain's growing impatience with the antics of the Protestant patriots, particularly after they had shamelessly taken advantage of the American War to secure commercial and constitutional concessions.[30]

The result of all this was a major change, during the 1780s and 1790s, in the legal position of Irish Catholics. The Relief Acts of 1778 and 1782 removed restrictions on Catholic religious practice, education and economic activity. The Relief Acts of 1792 and 1793 restored the right to vote, to sit on grand juries and municipal corporations, to practise law, to hold military commissions and offices under the Crown. In 1795 the government began to subsidise a seminary at Maynooth for the training of Catholic priests. Catholics were still excluded from Parliament and from top civil and military posts. But a clear strategy of incorporation, what Charles James Fox was later to call 'making the besiegers themselves part of the garrison', was beginning to take shape.[31]

[29] Colley, *Britons*, ch. 1.
[30] T. Bartlett, *The Fall and Rise of the Irish Nation: The Catholic Question 1690–1830* (Dublin, 1992).
[31] Charles James Fox, quoted in T. W. Allen, *The Invention of the White Race*, vol. I: *Racial Oppression and Social Control* (London, 1994), p. 112. Allen's book, despite its rather tendentious overall thesis on the origins of racial prejudice, is a remarkably perceptive account, by an American specialist, of the changing character of British government policy towards Irish Catholics between the 17th and 19th centuries.

In the long run, of course, that strategy was not followed through. By the mid-1790s the government, alarmed by the strength of Protestant reaction to the concessions already granted, set out to reassure Protestant opinion and to damp down Catholic hopes of further gains. Meanwhile popular disaffection was growing rather than abating. From the summer of 1795 the republican United Irishmen reorganised themselves as a clandestine organisation working for an armed insurrection with the backing of Revolutionary France. They also formed an alliance with the Catholic Defenders, a proletarian body inspired by a combination of Catholic sectarianism and crude but potent aspirations to social and political revolution. As arms raids and assassinations multiplied, local and central authorities responded with increasingly ruthless repression: the suspension of normal legal process, the impressment of suspected Defenders into the navy, indiscriminate house burning as a means of subduing whole districts, flogging and pitchcapping to extract information from suspects. The sense of imminent crisis also encouraged an ever more open alliance between the forces of the state and those of militant Protestant-ism, organised since 1795 in the Orange Order. The rebellion which eventually broke out in the summer of 1798 has been described as 'probably the most concentrated episode of violence in Irish history'.[32] An estimated 30,000 persons died in four separate outbreaks, in the counties around Dublin, in the Ulster counties of Antrim, Down and Londonderry, in the south-eastern counties of Wicklow and Wexford, and also, inspired by the belated arrival of a small French force, in parts of the western province of Connacht. In the South-East in particular the insurrection turned into a vicious sectarian war, in which Protestant civilians were plundered and killed. The repression that followed the defeat of the insurgents was likewise brutal and indiscriminate.[33]

The events of 1798 play an understandably large part in Irish historical memory. Indeed, they are often taken as proof of the inherently divided and unstable character of eighteenth-century Irish society. At the same time it is important to bear in mind three points. First, we need to remember the international background of war and revolution against which these events took place. Irish radicalism and popular disaffection alike owed much to the ideas generated or popularised by the American and French Revolutions, to the models of successful political action that both provided, and in the latter case to the prospect of practical support for a revolutionary challenge to the Irish *ancien régime*. Equally important, it was the pressures of war with Revolutionary France that led the British government to adopt an increas-ingly uncompromising and ultimately repressive approach towards middle

---

[32] R. F. Foster, *Modern Ireland, 1600–1972* (London, 1988), p. 280.

[33] The most vivid recent account is Bartlett, *Fall and Rise of the Irish Nation*, chs. 11, 12. See also M. Elliott, *Partners in Revolution: The United Irishmen and France* (Yale, 1982); J. Smyth, *The Men of No Property: Irish Radicals and Popular Politics in the Late Eighteenth Century* (London and Dublin, 1992); and N. J. Curtin, *The United Irishmen: Popular Politics in Ulster and Dublin 1791–1798* (Oxford, 1994).

class radicalism, popular protest and Catholic demands for admission to full political rights. Indeed, any assessment of the long-term history of British rule in Ireland must recognise that the two great crises of that history, in the 1790s and in 1916–22, both developed against a background of large-scale war, with all that this implied for the reduced effectiveness of normal processes of compromise, negotiation and pragmatic adjustment to changing circumstances.

Second, we need to consider the part played in the crisis of the 1790s by accident and miscalculation. How different would the course of events have been if, for example, the earl of Camden, Lord Lieutenant during the crucial period 1795–8, had been less easily dominated by an 'Irish cabinet' composed of hard-line Protestant advocates of repression undiluted by concession? In more concrete terms, it was clearly unfortunate that the Relief Act of 1793, the most dramatic single concession made to Catholics during this period, should have had the inadvertent appearance of being linked with the introduction in the same year of a militia, so that compulsory military service came to be seen as the price the common people paid for the admission of their betters to the franchise.[34] More unfortunate still was the way in which the appointment of the pro-emancipationist Earl Fitzwilliam as Lord Lieutenant in 1795, and Fitzwilliam's own apparent misunderstanding of his role, raised Catholic expectations to unrealistic levels, with the inevitable resulting disillusion when Fitzwilliam was recalled.[35] The polarisation and eventual violence of the 1790s can be seen as the culmination of long-term developments undermining the stability of late eighteenth-century Irish society, and even as a reflection of flaws built into its very structure. But contingency also played at least some part.

Third, and most important, we must not exaggerate the extent to which Catholics, even in 1798, turned their backs on British government. The Defender-United Irish challenge was formidable, but also localised. Even at its high point, in the late 1790s, the organised revolutionary movement was confined largely to the eastern half of the country, and even there its penetration was uneven. When a French invasion fleet appeared in Bantry Bay in December 1796 loyalists were heartened by the willingness of the south-western peasantry to speed troops on their way to repel the invader, and fully aware of how differently things might have gone if the French had appeared instead off the coast of County Antrim. The Catholic church authorities remained implacably hostile to the United Irishmen and Defenders. Most important of all there was Catholic Ireland's military contribution to British security. That one-third of the army that fought Napoleon was Irish is well

---

[34] T. Bartlett, 'An end to Moral Economy: the Irish militia disturbances of 1793', in C. H. E. Philpin (ed.), *Nationalism and Popular Protest in Ireland* (Cambridge, 1987).

[35] Bartlett, *Fall and Rise of the Irish Nation*, pp. 193–201; D. Lindsay, 'The Fitzwilliam episode revisited', in D. Dickson, D. Keogh and K. Whelan (eds.), *The United Irishmen: Republicanism, Radicalism and Rebellion* (Dublin, 1993).

known. But it is equally important to remember that in Ireland itself the largest single group of full-time fighting men available to government was the locally raised and predominantly Catholic militia, and that it was these – along with the mainly but not exclusively Protestant yeomanry – that bore the brunt of the fighting in 1798.[36] Once the rebellion was over, furthermore, the Act of Union was supported by the great majority of propertied Catholics, in the belief that it would quickly be followed by full admission to civil liberties.

What became, after 1800, of the options of conciliation and assimilation? The common assumption is that they ceased to be realistic. Instead, Catholics turned to the demand for repeal of the Act of Union, and for the restoration of parliamentary independence, leaving Protestants to discover that the Union many of them had initially opposed was in fact their best defence against an increasingly well-organised and assertive Catholic majority. But again this is the perspective of hindsight. We have to ask, for example, what would have been the future of the Act of Union if it had been immediately followed, as at one time seemed possible, by full Catholic emancipation and the introduction of state subsidies for the Catholic clergy. We have also to recognise the continued relevance, even after this disappointment, of the assimilationist option within post-Union Catholic politics. George IV's visit to Scotland in 1822 has what is by now a well-established place in the story of the fabrication of a new Scottish cultural identity within the structures of the United Kingdom.[37] The previous year, however, the king had paid a less well-remembered but, in the eyes of contemporaries, equally successful visit to Ireland. As in Scotland, the event was designed to combine displays of British loyalty with the symbolic acknowledgement of national distinctiveness: having established his credentials by disembarking onto Irish soil visibly drunk, the king proclaimed to the welcoming crowds that his heart had always been Irish, and sported a shamrock in his hat as he entered Dublin under a banner proclaiming 'Cead Mile Failte'.[38]

Nor were such gestures left unreciprocated. Daniel O'Connell, already the leader of the Irish Catholics, earned the scorn of English sympathisers like Byron by his extravagant professions of devotion to the visiting monarch, and followed up the visit by the creation of a loyal Georgian dining club. This was of course before the mass agitation for Catholic emancipation of 1823–9. But even after that triumph for the tactics of confrontational brinkmanship,

[36] T. Bartlett, 'Indiscipline and disaffection in the armed forces in Ireland in the 1790s', in P. J. Corish (ed.), *Radicals, Rebels and Establishments* (Belfast, 1985); T. Bartlett, 'Indiscipline and disaffection in the French and Irish armies during the Revolutionary period', in H. Gough and D. Dickson (eds.), *Ireland and the French Revolution* (Dublin, 1990).

[37] H. R. Trevor-Roper, 'The invention of tradition: the Highland tradition of Scotland', in Hobsbawm and Ranger, *Invention of Tradition*, pp. 29–30.

[38] I.e. 'A Hundred Thousand Welcomes': S. J. Connolly, 'Union government, 1812–23', ch. 3 of W. E. Vaughan (ed.), *A New History of Ireland*, vol. V: *Ireland Under the Union, I: 1800–1870* (Oxford, 1989), pp. 67–9.

O'Connell could still return when it suited him to the politics of ostentatious loyalism. Between 1834 and 1840 he abandoned the demand for repeal of the Act of Union in favour of an alliance with the Whig Party, announcing that the people of Ireland were prepared, if treated with justice and equity, 'to become a kind of West Britons'. In 1837 he was to boast that his co-operation had made it possible to release troops from Ireland to suppress both the Chartists in England and the rebellion in Canada. Later he upset Irish-American supporters by his announcement that in exchange for repeal of the Act of Union he would support Britain in its dispute with the United States over the territory of Oregon.[39] Subsequent biographers have tended to dismiss all this as a temporary retreat from O'Connell's real destiny as the champion of Irish self-government. An alternative view would be to see both the royal visit and the Whig alliance as indications that allegiances were, even at this late stage, to some extent negotiable. And in fact Irish Catholic politics were to balance uncertainly, for another half a century, between two alternative lines of development: on the one hand the pursuit of self-determination, on the other assimilation, along with Wales, Scotland, English Nonconformity and a section of the English working class, into the anti-establishment coalition that was British Liberalism.[40] In the century that had elapsed between O'Connell's pragmatic bargaining and the days when Lord Chesterfield had advised on the subjugation of a rebellious Scotland from the tranquillity of Dublin, the odds against a successful integration of Ireland into the British state may well have lengthened. It is more difficult to argue that the outcome was, even now, predetermined.

[39] O. MacDonagh, *The Emancipist: Daniel O'Connell 1830–47* (London, 1989), p. 136; Allen, *Invention of the White Race*, i, p. 112; John Belchem, 'Republican spirit and military science: the "Irish Brigade" and Irish-American nationalism in 1848', *Irish Historical Studies*, xxix (1994), p. 46.

[40] See, in particular, the reassessment of the politics of the 1850s and 1860s offered in R. V. Comerford, *The Fenians in Context: Irish Politics and Society 1848–82* (Dublin, 1985), pp. 142–94; and in R. V. Comerford, chs. 20–3 of *New History of Ireland*, v.

Chapter 12

A nation defined by Empire, 1755–1776

P. J. Marshall

In the last years of the Seven Years War British fleets and armies ranged across the world, dismembering the colonial empires of France and Spain. Yet, as tension rose in the early 1750s and undeclared war gave way to open war, British ministers viewed the prospect of defending the British Isles and Britain's European and world-wide interests with dismay. There seemed to be far too many points of danger. Confident voices about the security of the Scottish Highlands outweighed pessimistic ones, but concern was still being expressed. Many people were alarmed about the west of Ireland. In 1758 the Lord Lieutenant warned that the French could seize Cork or 'land such a body, as may be sufficient in those Popish and disaffected counties to make a place of arms and transfer the seat of war from their own coasts into the south-west of Ireland in the wild parts of Munster and Connaught'.[1] Hessian and Hanoverian troops had to be brought in to defend England. No-one doubted that Hanover itself was vulnerable. Assumptions that Minorca was secure were to be rudely shattered.

On the American continent, the peoples of New England could be presumed to be willing and able to defend themselves. The Virginians might do so after a fashion. Elsewhere, however, there were glaring weaknesses. Nova Scotia was taken to be a particularly acute problem. There the so-called 'neutral' French and their Indian allies would let in the French of New France. Once Halifax had fallen, so alarmist scenarios went, the northern colonies would be rolled up. Pennsylvania was seen as an open incitement to French attack. Its Quaker politicians would do nothing for their own defence and there was a large population of unassimilated Germans whose loyalty seemed questionable. South Carolina and Georgia could not effectively defend themselves against the Cherokees, let alone against a European enemy. In the Caribbean the great wealth of Jamaica was thought to lie open for the picking. The disproportion between slaves and whites was so great that the Jamaica militia was hard pressed to contain slave revolts; it could do nothing to ward off a French or a Spanish attack. The East India Company was

---

[1] Bedford to W. Pitt, 29 August 1758, Public Record Office [PRO], SP 30/8/19, p. 158.

appealing for help against French reinforcements on the coast of Coromandel at the moment when a quite different thunderbolt struck them, as the Nawab of Bengal's troops overwhelmed Calcutta.

This brief summary indicates that mid-eighteenth-century Britain felt itself threatened, not just by the Bourbon enemy from without but by many possible enemies from within: Highland Scots, Irish Catholics, the Indians of the North American continent, non-British settlers in the colonies, the successor states to the Mughal Empire, and African slaves might all turn against Britain. Yet events were soon to show that potential enemies within could be turned into loyal subjects and allies. Highlanders became the flower of the British army. The first very tentative steps were taken towards tapping the resources of Catholic Irish manpower for the forces of the Crown. Pennsylvania Germans were recruited into regiments of Royal Americans. Colonial Americans, if never as many as was hoped, were enlisted into royal regiments, while some 21,000 American Provincial troops were mobilised for the 1758 campaign in North America. By the end of the war the British had engaged on their side most of the Indian peoples in the area of the conflict in America. Within a year of the end of the war, General Amherst was even proposing that a corps of French Americans should be raised for British service.[2] The East India Company enlisted very large numbers of Indian sepoys for the war and formed them into a permanent part of its army, paid for by resources extracted from Indian rulers who were now its docile allies. The Jamaica maroons had been invaluable in suppressing the 1760 slave revolt, and there was a project for raising a regiment of free blacks for the attack on Havana in 1762.[3]

War had thus forced the British greatly to widen the base of their military manpower. Some of those recruited were simply mercenaries, who could be laid off at the end of the war without further consideration. Even the king's own electoral Hanoverian troops were regarded as 'foreign'. The involvement of other troops in British service was, however, part of important processes of change, bringing about the closer integration both of the British Isles and of that complex network of overseas interests which contemporaries were coming to call the British Empire. These two developments were linked. Successful war overseas did much to cement the Union between England and Scotland, as Linda Colley has demonstrated with so much authority.[4] It both provided a focus for a British triumphalism and offered great rewards to the Scots. War overseas also had significant implications for Ireland's relations with Britain. But if war helped to consolidate Britain within the British Isles, it also helped to set limits to any wider Britain. The lesson of war for Britain's

[2] Letter to Halifax, 14 January 1764, enclosing letter from J. Abercrombie, 10 January 1764, PRO, WO 34/74, fos. 250–3.
[3] See correspondence of Egremont and W. Lyttelton, January 1762, 12 May 1762, 11 January [1763]: PRO, CO 137/61, fos. 50, 56, 116, 150.
[4] L. Colley, *Britons: Forging the Nation 1707–1837* (2nd edn, London, 1994).

rulers was that empire required the effective exercise of authority. Whatever the actual scale of their contributions, colonial Americans were judged to have questioned authority. When efforts were made to strengthen the exercise of authority over the colonies after 1763, American questioning escalated into outright resistance. By their resistance, in the eyes of the majority of British people, Americans forfeited their right to be counted as British. So my theme is both the integration of the United Kingdom and the Empire, and the contraction of the nation.

British forces were committed outside Europe, above all in North America, on a scale that was entirely new. The size of this commitment both focused an overwhelming public attention on empire in America and exposed very many British people to service in that Empire. The extent to which the forces deployed in America were British in the widest sense was brought out by a survey ordered by Lord Loudoun of the troops assembled in 1757 at Halifax for the aborted attack on Louisbourg.[5] Returns were required for the nationality of the men from the British Isles, which was defined as English, 'Scotch' or Irish. English – 3,426 – and Irish – 3,138 – were almost equal, with Scots markedly lower at 1,390. Irish officers actually outnumbered the English by 166 to 131, with 71 Scots. There are certain oddities about these figures. In the first place, many of the eleven regiments for which I have found returns had come straight off the Irish establishment. They had therefore been recruiting in Ireland, and the Lord Lieutenant had clearly exercised his patronage rights over the appointment of officers with great tenacity. Since a return for the Highland regiments in America is not included in the Halifax contingent, the Scottish element is certainly too low to represent the Scottish contribution to the army as a whole. A return for Montgomery's Highlanders in South Carolina shows that the regiment was exactly what its name would suggest. All the officers were Scottish and the rank and file were described as 1,001 Highland and 59 Lowland Scots.[6]

Little needs to be added to Colley's account of the importance of the Seven Years War for the integration of the Highlands in particular and Scotland in general into the British Empire. There is much evidence suggesting that Scottish soldiers enlisted very readily for America, and there seems little doubt that they did so as a form of emigration. In 1764 the Provost of Edinburgh deplored the way in which Scotland had contributed quite out of proportion to its population to the war and the fact that of 'the many thousands sent abroad, very few returned'.[7]

Although prohibitions on the recruiting of Irish Catholic soldiers were not officially lifted until 1771, it seems realistic to suppose that there were Catholics among the large number of soldiers classified as Irish. The Lord

---

[5] Lists in Huntington Library, San Marino, California [HL], LO 1345, 1384, 1391, 1683, 1944, 2529, 2533, 3936, 4011–12, 4068.
[6] HL, LO 6695.
[7] Letter to Sandwich, 17 April 1764, PRO, SP 54/45, p. 549.

Lieutenant believed that any regiment recruited in Ireland was likely to contain Papists.[8] That is certainly what Lord Loudoun thought that he had got. He was not prepared to trust the 'prest men' of Otway's regiment fresh from Ireland close enough to the French for others to follow the example of the group that had tried to desert to them.[9] Loudoun tried to hunt Catholics out of his army, but the British government could not for long ignore their potential contribution as manpower. Thomas Bartlett has recently drawn attention to the link between military recruitment and relaxation of the penal laws.[10] Catholic notables clearly saw this as a way to win official recognition. Offers of troops, together with pledges of loyalty to 'their country's cause', were passed on by the Lord Lieutenant in 1762. The Secretary of State received them with caution while welcoming this trend towards 'unanimity among his Majesty's subjects of all denominations'.[11] With the outbreak of the American War caution was abandoned. A full-scale programme of Catholic recruiting was initiated. Lord George Germain commented in 1775 that ministers would not listen to any proposals for raising new corps, 'so long as they flatter themselves with being able to recruit the regiments from Irish Roman Catholics'.[12] Formal relaxation of parts of the penal laws was to follow later in the war.

The needs of war pulled the United Kingdom closer together. The war also brought about very significant changes in relations between Britain and her overseas possessions. These changes gave definition to empire. Some of the changes are well known and I need not treat them at length. Much has been written about the strains put on relations between Britain and the Thirteen Colonies by questions of the raising of provincial regiments and the authority to be exercised over them by British commanders, the quartering of troops, British intervention in Indian affairs, the requisition of labour and transport, and many other issues. Had Lord Loudoun had his way he would have forced a showdown with some of the provinces in 1757. In recalling him Pitt publicly upbraided him for 'exerting too much authority over the people of the country [and] not treating the provincial troops as well so they deserved'.[13] For the rest of the war the colonies were treated with great indulgence as more or less equal partners in war, but the reckoning was only put off. In the eyes of most British commanders, the colonies had not been

---

[8] Bedford to W. Pitt, 3 January 1758, PRO, SP 63/415, fo. 171.
[9] Loudoun to R. Burton, 15 September 1757, HL, LO 1828; *Military Affairs in North America 1748–65*, ed. S. M. Pargellis (New York, 1936), p. 239.
[10] T. Bartlett, *The Fall and Rise of the Irish Nation: The Catholic Question 1690–1830* (Dublin, 1992), pp. 57–9, 85–7.
[11] Halifax to Egremont, February 1762, Egremont to Halifax, 23 February 1762, PRO, SP 63/421, fos. 75–83, 116.
[12] Letter to J. Irwin, 13 September 1775, *Historical Manuscripts Commission Reports, Stopford Sackville MSS*, i, p. 137.
[13] J. Calcraft to Loudoun, 29 December 1757, HL, LO 5140.

partners; they had been not altogether willing subordinates. Much too has been written about how war and its costs transformed the position of the East India Company, leading to ever deeper intervention, first into Indian politics and then into Indian administration, as the Company directly levied taxation to cover the huge costs of its great new standing army.

I would like to pass over these cases and to consider three others that seem to me to illustrate strikingly the way in which the nature of the British Empire was being reassessed: the cases of the Pennsylvania Germans and of the French and the Indians of British North America. They show how metropolitan authority was responding to the 'strangers within the realm', the theme of the excellent collection edited by Bernard Bailyn and Philip Morgan.[14]

'Foreign Protestants' had become an almost universal panacea for any imperial problem. It was assumed that Germany and Switzerland offered a limitless supply of suitable colonists – docile, industrious people with martial qualities. To encourage their settlement in America, the British Parliament had passed acts offering them naturalisation on very easy terms. By the 1750s, however, the concentration of Germans in Pennsylvania – Franklin's estimate of 100,000 out of a provincial population of 190,000 circulated widely – was causing concern. Questions were raised as to how thoroughly they had been assimilated. They gave offence by seeming to vote regularly for Quakers. Doubts were even expressed as to whether they might not 'be led away from the British interest by French emissaries'.[15] To try to turn the Germans into good British subjects, a Society of Nobility and Gentry was formed in London in 1753 with full royal and ministerial support to set up schools to teach English to young Germans in America. The archbishop of Canterbury called this plan 'as great and as necessary to be put into execution as any that was ever laid before the British nation'.[16] Under the pressures of war, however, British ministers looked at the Pennsylvania Germans in a different light. 'An hundred thousand Germans and Swiss, animated by the most amiable principles, zeal for religion, passion for liberty, and a spirit of industry' were described in Parliament as 'a providential resource'.[17] They were to be recruited into special Royal American regiments under foreign officers sent to America from Europe. After the war there was still talk of plans for 'preferring and propagating the English language and preventing the Germans from becoming a separate body and using a separate language, like the Welsh'.[18]

---

[14] B. Bailyn and P. Morgan (eds.), *Strangers within the Realm: Cultural Margins of the first British Empire* (Chapel Hill, North Carolina, 1991).

[15] Pennsylvania Historical Society, Philadelphia [PHS], Minutes of the Trustees for German Schools, W. Smith MSS, reel XR 439.2.

[16] *The Papers of Benjamin Franklin*, ed. L. W. Labaree *et al.* (New Haven, 1959–), v, pp. 217–18.

[17] Horace Walpole on 18 February 1756, *Proceedings and Debates of the British Parliament respecting North America*, ed. R. C. Simmons and P. D. G. Thomas (New York, 1982–6), i, pp. 141–2.

[18] W. Smith to R. Peters, 14 August 1762, PHS, W. Smith MSS, reel XR 439.1.

Further measures for anglicising them were not, however, attempted. Virtually every colony continued to encourage the unrestricted import of foreign Protestants.

At the beginning of the war Catholic French were regarded as enemies rather than subjects. In 1755, 6,000 French were expelled from Acadia. They were to be distributed throughout other British colonies where it was hoped they would be subjected to unremitting anglicisation. Lord Loudoun told them that he would only receive communications from the king's subjects in English; never in French.[19] Lord Halifax wondered why the Governor of South Carolina had not taken away the Acadians' children to be brought up 'in the Protestant religion, by which means they at least, however stubborn their parents might prove, would have become good and useful subjects'.[20] After the capture of Louisbourg in 1758, the destruction of Canadian settlements and the deportation of their inhabitants continued around the estuary of the St Lawrence.

Two years later a marked change in attitudes became apparent. Amherst brought his army into Montreal in 1760, not as the agents of vengeance on what sermon after sermon preached in British America had denounced as that 'mongrel race of French and Indian savages', but as the bringers of a new order of justice and benevolence, a scene commemorated in one of Francis Hayman's great canvasses for Vauxhall. 'I have not hurt the head of a peasant, his wife or his child ... I ... put them quietly in their habitations and they are vastly happy.'[21] He was commended by British ministers and told that Britain did not wish to lose its new French subjects, 'who being now equally his Majesty's subjects are consequently equally entitled to his protection'. They must be allowed to 'enjoy the full benefits of that indulgent and benign government which constitutes the peculiar happiness of all who are subjects of the British Empire'. They should not even be subjected to 'uncharitable reflections on the errors of that mistaken religion, which they unhappily profess'.[22] The line forward to the Quebec Act of 1774 and the official recognition of the Catholic Church in Canada was clear.

The war had forced a serious British reappraisal of the foreign 'strangers within the realm'. Anglicisation had been advocated but tacitly shelved. The British Empire needed manpower, both for war and for settlement. An even greater deployment of British manpower overseas was ruled out. The haemorrhage of Scots and of Irish Protestants to America through the army or peacetime emigration was already causing anxiety. Continental Europeans must be accepted, Protestants for choice, but even Catholics, if need be. Too many conditions could not be imposed on them. But necessity was also being

---

[19] Loudoun to W. Pitt, 25 April 1757, HL, LO 3467.
[20] Letter to W. Lyttelton, 13 August 1756, W. L. Clements Library, Ann Arbor, Michigan [WLCL], Lyttelton MSS.
[21] N. J. O'Conor, *A Servant of the Crown in North America 1736–61* (New York, 1938), p. 143.
[22] Egremont to Amherst, 12 December 1761, WLCL, Amherst MSS, v, no. 114.

embellished by rhetoric, and pride was being taken in a cosmopolitan empire living in prosperity under a benevolent British rule.

The war also forced consideration of non-European strangers. After the acquisition of the Bengal Diwani in 1765, the enormous new responsibilities which this implied became more and more apparent. In 1767 the House of Commons for the first time heard evidence about problems of Indian government and was soon to begin to legislate on them. During and immediately after the war, however, it was American Indian affairs that obsessed the British ministers and a wider public. The success of the French in constructing Indian alliances, together with horrifying stories of massacres along the British American frontier, led to imperial intervention in the appointing of Indian superintendents and to the laying down of rules for the treatment of Indians. Current trends in the historiography of Native Americans stress the limitations on British power, especially after Pontiac's War, and the need to seek accommodation with Indian peoples on the 'middle ground'.[23] But the British and the New England publics took a very different view. Civilising and Christianising the Indians of North America was part of God's providential mission for Britain. From those to whom God had granted great victories much was now expected. Many sermons and addresses were devoted to this topic. In his brief of 1762 for charitable collections for the new colleges in New York and Philadelphia, George III wrote of his satisfaction at the prospect of bringing 'barbarous nations within the pale of religion and civil life'.[24] Much money was raised for the purpose by the Anglican Society for the Propagation of the Gospel, by the Church of Scotland Society for Propagating Christian Knowledge, by the New England Company, and by Presbyterians and Moravians. By 1769 more money was said to be being raised in England and Scotland than could actually be spent on available missionaries and school-masters.[25]

Any kind of systematic theorising about the nature of the 'Empire' which Britain had acquired lagged far behind the fact of acquisition and the need to resolve practical problems in very diverse situations. Nevertheless, certain trends can be detected. In their assumptions about their Empire the British in the eighteenth century, as at later periods, revealed much about their assumptions about themselves. The simplest model for empire was an old but still extremely powerful one. Colonies were dominions of the Crown and the Empire was united by common allegiance to the king. 'The [American] provinces seem to be falling off from their duty to their King in not raising

[23] R. White, *The Middle Ground: Indians, Empires and Republics in the Great Lakes Region 1650–1815* (Cambridge, 1991).

[24] *Acts of the Privy Council of England: Colonial Series*, ed. W. L. Grant and J. Munro (London, 1908–12), iv, p. 545.

[25] [Overseers of Harvard] to J. Mauduit, 30 November 1769, Massachusetts Historical Society, Boston, Miscellaneous Bound MSS.

the number of men his Majesty has been pleased to require of them', Amherst lamented in 1761. He attributed this to 'a want of a due sense of the war being carried on to the general good of his Majesty's subjects'.[26] New peoples could easily be incorporated into the Empire on these principles. They became the king's subjects by right of conquest. This doctrine was immediately applied to the French of North America and Grenada. Indians living in the king's dominions in America were also his subjects, although this was not at first clearly spelled out for the Indians in the vast new territories acquired in 1763; they were said to be peoples 'with whom we are connected and who live under our protection'.[27] Whether Indians who lived in the new provinces of the East India Company were subjects of the Crown was a complex question. In theory they were still subjects of the Mughal emperor, who had delegated his authority to the East India Company. Legal opinion considered, however, that the sovereignty of the Crown extended over conquests made by or grants awarded to British subjects. In 1773 the House of Commons resolved that the Company's possessions belonged to the British state. By then the concept that the British Crown had 'subjects in Asia, as well as those in America'[28] was losing some of its novelty. Burke was to take pleasure in referring to 'our fellow subjects' in India.

For all its apparent simplicity, the doctrine of an empire based on obedience to the Crown had much wider implications by the mid-eighteenth century. When Americans like Franklin took the doctrine literally and proclaimed that their allegiance to Britain was analogous to that of Hanover, that is that it rested solely on obedience owed to a common sovereign, they were reminded that their obedience was, in the words of the Declaratory Act of 1766, to 'the imperial Crown and Parliament of Great Britain', which had full power to make laws binding on them 'in all cases whatsoever'.

Yet even with this most portentous elaboration that obedience to the Crown meant obedience to Parliament, the doctrine of an empire based on a common link of obedience binding together the different subjects of the Crown was an admirably flexible one that could accommodate all sorts of diversity. In return for protection subjects owed obedience, but they did not have to conform in any other way. There was a tradition of diversity under the Crown stretching back to the Middle Ages. 'The Crown of England', Lord Mansfield wrote, 'has always left the conquered their own laws and usage, with a change only as far as sovereignty.'[29]

Throughout the rest of Britain's imperial history many British people have taken pride in the concept of a diverse empire of many 'races', as they usually put it, differing in religion, language, law and custom, but united in obedience to one sovereign. Yet to many others, just as the United Kingdom was more

---

[26] Letter to T. Gage, 16 April 1761, WLCL, Amherst MSS, v, no. 73.
[27] Proclamation, 7 October 1763.
[28] [William Knox], *The Present state of the nation* (London, 1768), p. 85.
[29] *The Grenville Papers*, ed. W. J. Smith (London, 1852–3), iii, pp. 476–7.

than a mere union of separate peoples under a common Crown, the Empire embodied a diffusion of Britishness, which made it a distinctly British empire. Such aspirations were very much alive in the eighteenth century, as attempts to anglicise Acadians or Pennsylvania Germans or to bring Indians within the fold of Christian civilisation clearly indicate. Arthur Young's *Political Essays Concerning the Present State of the British Empire* of 1772 began with a characteristic statement of such aspirations.

> The British dominions consist of Great Britain and Ireland, divers colonies and settlements in all parts of the world and there appears not any just reason for considering these countries in any other light than as a part of a whole ... The clearest method is to consider all as forming one nation, united under one sovereign, speaking the same language and enjoying the same liberty, but living in different parts of the world.[30]

Contemporaries were no doubt as puzzled as historians are by the omission of religion from language and liberty as the elements that constitute a nation, but the implications are clear: Young conceived of empire as more than different peoples 'united under one sovereign'. It was an extension of the British nation overseas. Even Amherst reminded his troops before the attack on Louisbourg of their duty both to their king and to their 'nation'.[31]

In Young's time, as in later periods, such aspirations of course embodied a highly selective view of empire. In postulating a world-wide nation, Young took no account of ethnic and linguistic diversity in America, let alone of the East India Company's dominions. Nevertheless, his belief that the British colonies overseas constituted one nation in terms of language and liberty and, others would have added, of religion would have been very widely shared by people of British origin on both sides of the Atlantic in 1772. Yet within three years the supposed nation began to split apart at Lexington and Concord. It became clear, at least in retrospect, that within the parameters that seemed to unite Britons there were crucial differences. If there was a Britishness that could sustain a union of England, Wales and Scotland and which might, as Sean Connolly suggests, have been extended to Ireland,[32] it could not be extended indefinitely.

About language there was virtually no disagreement throughout the British world. The eighteenth century was the age of the triumphant march of English.[33] It was propagated in the Highlands with official support. The Society for Promoting English Protestant Schools attempted to do the same thing in Ireland. Although the London Society for Schools in Pennsylvania ran out of money, the German communities in the American colonies on

---

[30] Arthur Young, *Political Essays Concerning the Present State of the British Empire* (London, 1772), p. 1.

[31] Address of 3 June 1758, HL, LO 5847.

[32] See S. J. Connolly, 'Varieties of Britishness: Ireland, Scotland and Wales in the Hanoverian state', above, ch. 11.

[33] See the discussion in R. Crawford, *Devolving English Literature* (Oxford, 1992).

their own acquired the English that enabled them to participate in public and commercial life. It has been suggested that even in Germantown the use of German seems to have died out in the second and third generation.[34]

Convention assumed that common ideals of religion and liberty united British of all sorts and conditions. Yet interpretations of what constituted these ideals were beginning to differ.

For the generation of the Seven Years War the British Empire was defined by Protestantism and the war was fought in defence of Protestantism. George Whitefield's *Short Address* warned the British people that '*A French* army and thousands of *Romish* priests threatens us'. They had shown what they intended to

> our fellow subjects in *America*, by the hands of savage *Indians*, instigated thereto by more than savage Popish priests. Speak *Smithfield*, speak ... Speak *Ireland*, speak ... And think you, my dear countrymen, that Rome glutted as it were with Protestant blood, will now rest satisfied, and say 'I have enough'?[35]

In such an emergency Protestants needed to sink their differences. Lord Loudoun, although he thought Quakers unfit for any position of responsibility, tried to rally all shades of Protestant opinion in the colonies. At Boston he attended the Anglican King's Chapel in the morning, went to Dr Sewall's meeting house in the afternoon, and invited a Presbyterian to say Grace at dinner. 'At each of those times and places', one of his entourage commented, 'the parsons preached and prayed so long over and for him that I shall be tempted to think the New England people out of favour with God Almighty if he does not hear them.'[36]

Pitt was a strong upholder of the alliance of all Protestants. He was shocked to hear that the Lord Lieutenant attributed a riot around the Dublin Parliament in 1759 to 'New Light Presbyterians or Twaddlers', who were 'totally Republican and averse to English government, and therefore they are at least equally with the Papists to be guarded against'.[37] Pitt replied that:

> The Presbyterian dissenters in general, must ever deserve to be considered in opposition to the Church of Rome, as a very valuable branch of the Reformation, and that with regard to their civil principles that respectable body have, in all times, shewed themselves, both in England and in Ireland, firm and zealous supporters of the glorious revolution under King William, and the present happy establishment.[38]

---

[34] S. Wolf, *The Urban Village: Population, Community and Family Structure in Germantown, Pennsylvania, 1685–1800* (Princeton, 1976), p. 139.

[35] *A Short Address ... occasioned by the alarm of an intended invasion* (3rd edn, London, 1756), pp. 10, 13.

[36] E. Atkin to W. Lyttelton, 25 January 1757, WLCL, Lyttelton MSS.

[37] Bedford to W. Pitt, 25 December 1759, PRO, SP 63/416, fo. 260.

[38] W. Pitt to Bedford, 5 January 1760, SP 63/417, fo. 152.

The people of New England were said almost to 'idolise' Pitt, and he continued to praise 'the loyal free and Protestant Americans' when it was ceasing to
be fashionable to do so.[39]

Official British policy was generally even-handed in its dealings with all
denominations of colonial Protestants. In 1755 ministers had applied great
pressure on the London Quakers to bring about the voluntary withdrawal of
Quakers from the Pennsylvania Assembly. But this was in fact a compromise
engineered on their behalf by Lord Granville and Lord Halifax to head off
parliamentary action against a people described by Thomas Penn as 'much
respected here'.[40] A Pennsylvania Quaker was present when the British
Friends delivered their address of loyalty on the accession of George III and
received the king's assurance of his 'protection'.[41] Moravians were given
recognition by an Act of Parliament in 1749. The London Society for
German Schools paid subsidies to Calvinist and Lutheran ministers in
Pennsylvania. American Anglicans, especially from the northern Provinces,
were increasingly assertive with the growth of their numbers, but they were
generally disappointed by the attitude of British ministers. They were never
able to win control over the new colleges in the way that the Presbyterians
dominated the College of New Jersey. The colonial bishopric was the issue on
which militant American Anglicans set their hearts. Archbishops of
Canterbury were prepared to take up this cause, but governments were
unresponsive. In 1767 ministers were reported to have warned the archbishop
that they would not support him, because they 'wanted to sustain the
connection between the colonies and strengthen every tye and not break off
any one'.[42]

In 1761 Samuel Davies, the Virginian Presbyterian, delivered a eulogy on
George II. 'In his reign the state had been the guardian of Christians in general
... the defence of the Dissenter as well as of the Conformist: of TOLERATION
as well as of the ESTABLISHMENT.'[43] The British state never formally
abandoned its patronage of Dissent, but the relationship was to fray
somewhat in the years ahead. J. C. D. Clark has recently described the
theological ferment among Dissenters on both sides of the Atlantic in the
reign of George III, which greatly complicated attempts to retain their
support for the government.[44] Outright opposition to government authority
appeared among the Congregationalists of Massachusetts, some of whose
ministers were reported to be abetting riot from the mid-1760s, and among

[39] *Proceedings and Debates*, ed. Simmons and Thomas, ii, p. 161; *Franklin Papers*, ix, p. 403.

[40] J. Fothergill to J. Pemberton, 18 January 1756, PHS, Etting MSS, XXIX, no. 9; H. Brown
to Pemberton, 18 February 1756, PHS, Pemberton MSS, IX, p. 50; T. Penn to R. H. Morris,
13 March 1756, PHS, Thomas Penn MSS, reel XR 186.

[41] *Annual Register*, iii, 1760, p. 248; J. Fothergill to J. Pemberton, 2 November 1761, PHS,
Etting MSS, XXIX, no. 46.

[42] N. Rogers to T. Hutchinson, 2 July 1768, Massachusetts Historical Society, Hutchinson
Transcripts, XXV, p. 267.

[43] *Sermon ... on the death of his late Majesty, King George II* (Boston, 1761), p. 21.

[44] J. C. D. Clark, *The Language of Liberty* (Cambridge, 1993).

the Presbyterians of Ulster in the agrarian disorders of the early 1770s. 'It must appear very extraordinary in England', the Lord Lieutenant mused, 'that the Protestants of Ulster should be so suddenly up in arms.' Among grievances about rents, with which he could sympathise, he also thought he could detect 'a dislike to all government'.[45] From 1775 opposition in England to Lord North's government over America was identified with Dissent, with good reason, as James Bradley has shown: he believes that the majority of pro-Americans were probably Anglicans, but 'Dissenters provided the dominant ideology of opposition and the charismatic leadership for the pro-American agitation.'[46] On their side, British governments seemed to be consorting with High Anglicans but, most reprehensibly from the American point of view, to be extending their indulgence to Catholics, first of all in Grenada, then in Canada, and ultimately in Britain itself.

With the ending of the Seven Years War many Americans began to fear that the association between Britishness and Protestant ecumenism was breaking down. Their fears were exaggerated, but not without some foundation. Anglicanism was gaining a greater degree of official patronage in the Empire, as the establishment of the first colonial bishoprics after the American war was to confirm, while imperial Britain was becoming less and less fastidious as to the faiths, not just Catholicism, but Islam and Hinduism as well, with which it would have dealings.

Arthur Young described the British Empire as a single nation, enjoying 'the same liberty'. By 1772 there were of course sharp disputes as to what constituted British liberty. These disputes have been the subject of a huge literature. It is sufficient to note that the bulk of British opinion did indeed believe that the British Empire was unique among modern European empires in resting on liberty, but that liberty also required obedience to the duly authorised prerogatives of the executive government and to the will of a sovereign parliament. War had reinforced the need for obedience. Americans, on the other hand, had a long record of disobeying their Governors and had recently taken to disregarding Acts of Parliament as well. 'Republican' and 'levelling' principles seemed to be rife among them. For its part, colonial opinion was convinced that Britain was disregarding the common heritage of liberty that had kept the Empire united, and that there was a conspiracy to destroy this on both sides of the Atlantic. Again, of course, they exaggerated greatly, but their fears were, again, not entirely without some foundation. It is irrefutable that the mainstream of British political beliefs was becoming increasingly authoritarian. It was inconceivable that the British Empire should be reconstructed in ways that would deprive its white citizens of representative government, but attempts would be made to strengthen the authority of the executive government and the influence of colonial elites.

[45] Townshend to Rochford, 18 March 1772, PRO, SP 63/435, fos. 145–6.
[46] J. Bradley, *Religion, Revolution and English Radicalism: Non-conformity in Eighteenth-Century Politics and Society* (Cambridge, 1990), p. 158.

There were significant differences across the Atlantic as to what British Protestantism and British liberty implied. How seriously did these differences threaten any sense of a single 'nation'? The evidence from the writings of the colonial elites leaves little doubt that they thought of themselves as part of a British nation until very late in the conflict. The concepts of 'country' and 'nation' constantly recur in their writings. These appear to have had meanings that were clearly distinct. For Washington, for instance, his 'country' was Virginia, but his 'nation' was Britain. 'American' was very widely used as a descriptive term, but it seems only slowly to have been invested with significance as a reference point for identity. One of Franklin's correspondents told him of an encounter in London in 1771, when his describing himself as an 'American' led his British companion to say: 'I hope you don't look on yourself as an American. I told him yes I did and gloried in the name.' But he still felt it necessary to add: 'for that I look'd upon a good Englishman and a good American to be synonymous terms it being impossible to be one without being the other also'.[47] Many of those who called themselves 'Americans' in the 1770s seem to have implied that they were doing so because they had been deprived of their Britishness.

There were innumerable links, such as kinship, religious denomination or business dealings, tying people in Britain to people in the colonies. But whether opinion in Britain itself generally thought of colonial Americans as belonging to a single nation with them is doubtful. It is not difficult to find references in Parliament to Americans as 'our countrymen' as well as 'our fellow subjects'. Yet the rise of the concept of 'American' without distinction as to colony seems to have owed quite a lot to British usage. Historians of Ireland have pointed out that the eighteenth-century English were not good at distinguishing: all Irish people were simply 'Irish' to them and invested with the same qualities. So it was with Americans, who were lumped together and also invested with certain qualities. This implied that they were a distinct people. Lord Halifax made this point explicitly when he commented in 1763 that: 'The people of England seem to consider the inhabitants of these provinces, though H.M.'s subjects, as foreigners.'[48] In the correspondence of Americans in Britain there are many references to the ignorance of British people about the colonies but also to a certain pride of possession over a supposedly subject people. James Fothergill, the London Quaker, warned his American correspondent that, at least until the Stamp Act crisis, 'not one half of this nation knew what country their American brothers sprang from, what language they spoke, whether they were black or white', but 'that American talk of resistance' aroused 'the mastif spirit of John Bull', and 'pride and passion' would 'carry him headlong into battle and to violence'.[49] When

---

[47] *Franklin Papers*, xviii, p. 9.
[48] Letter to Archbishop of Canterbury, 6–7 May 1763, *Calendar of Home Office Papers of the Reign of George III, 1760-3* (London, 1878), p. 279,.
[49] Letter to J. Pemberton, 16 October 1768, PHS, Etting MSS, XXIX, no. 58.

violence broke out very many British people deplored what they saw as a civil war, but there were not enough of them to deter the government from its policies. Burgoyne reported with satisfaction of the army in Boston in 1775 that 'it is firmly attached in principle to the cause of England. The private men, very few rascally drafts and recruits taken out of the Irish jails excepted, have not deserted. On the contrary they appear in general exasperated against the enemy.'[50]

Some colonial Americans came to view the rise of the new cosmopolitan British Empire with dismay. 'They are arming every hand, Protestant and Catholic, English, Irish, Scotch, Hanoverians, Hessians, Indians, Canadians against the devoted colonies', Arthur Lee wrote in anguish in 1775.[51] Yet for most British people the two concepts of empire that I have tried to identify overlapped, rather than competed with, one another. On the one hand, Britain conceived herself as being at the centre of a diversity of peoples tied by obligations of obedience to the British state in return for protection from it. Part of the British elite was beginning to assume the kind of responsibilities in which their successors were to be so deeply involved for generation after generation as Governors of a largely French Quebec, superintendents of Indians, collectors and judges in Bengal. The depth of popular concern for the redemption of the North American Indians, improbable as it may now seem and ineffective as it certainly was, clearly prefigures great popular imperial causes of the future, like anti-slavery or the mobilisation of mass support for missions throughout the Empire. The British were coming to define themselves as a people who ruled over other peoples.

Yet the eighteenth-century Empire and the Empire in all its future incarnations amounted to more than the exercise of rule over other people. Through empire the British aspired to be a world-wide people. The experience of the eighteenth century showed how difficult such aspirations would be to fulfil. It made it clear that Britishness was not a set of immutable principles about religion, language and liberty, but was specific to time and place and had evolved on different historical trajectories in different situations. In crucial respects, the practice of Britishness in America and that in the British Isles had come to deviate from one another, as the Seven Years War and its aftermath were to make clear. The eighteenth-century experience also revealed that 'imagined communities' of Britishness were parochial. English people could perhaps envisage a common community with the Welsh and, often with much difficulty, with the Scots, but they failed to incorporate the Irish or colonial Americans into their idea of nation. Under hard necessity and by what still seems a very extraordinary feat of creative imagination, citizens of individual colonial 'countries' could eventually extend their

[50] Letter to Germain, 20 August 1775, WLCL, Sackville Germain MSS, III.
[51] Letter to [J. Dickinson], 4 September 1775, Houghton Library, Harvard, bMS Am.811.1(62).

loyalties to an idea of America, even while the self-images of many of them probably remained locked in an idealised English nation. This nation rarely included the Scots. The Virginian William Lee thought that to use the phrase 'Britain', rather than 'Great Britain', was to use a 'Scotticism'. 'What chance', he asked, 'can England or America have for a continuance of their liberty or independence when not only the principles, but phraseology of that accursed country is prevalent every where?'[52]

The lesson, for the future of the British Empire, of the war of Britishnesses that broke out in 1775 was that aspirations for the British to be one world-wide people would never be realised. With greater dexterity of imperial management than was shown in the 1760s and 1770s, a loose-jointed Empire and later Commonwealth of more or less British peoples closely allied with one another would certainly endure from the nineteenth century into the twentieth, but 'Greater Britons', merging Canadians, Australians, New Zealanders and white South Africans with Britons, would not come about, however much enthusiasts might desire them. The conventional wisdom that these aspirations were incompatible with colonial nationalism is no doubt true, but they were also incompatible with that deep-rooted plant that was British parochialism.

[52] Letter to F. Lee, 5 September 1774, Houghton Lib., bMS Am.811.1(25).

Chapter 13

Englishness and Britishness
National identities, c.1790–c.1870

Eric Evans

In justly celebrated recent publications, Linda Colley has argued that the experience of waging war during the eighteenth century helped to develop a growing sense of British nationhood. The experience of regular warfare against France – 'the Catholic Other' as she calls it – helped to forge a Protestant British nation from its diverse, and often mutually antagonistic, constituent elements. She discusses the emergence of an expanded social and governing elite which included substantial numbers of Welsh, Scottish and Protestant Anglo-Irish landowners and businessmen. The experience of governing an increasingly complex state in both war and peace brought these elite elements together in pursuit of the common goal of national unity. The image of national identity was particularly prominent in attempts to mobilise support in the long wars against France which lasted, with only two short breaks, from February 1793 to June 1815. One important element in this image-making was the repackaging of George III, who, despite bouts of mental instability, was transmuted in visual representation from bucolic buffer to the symbol of decency, Christian values and proper order in a nation engaged in a desperate struggle against violence, atheism and low-born revolution.[1] As is essential for successful propaganda, the image was substantially more important than the reality.

Yet the development of national identity during the eighteenth century was only partly a function of wartime patriotism: it also reflected growing commercial success, both at home and abroad. James Sharpe's view that, 'By 1760, despite the persistence of localism, a shift had occurred towards a sense of national consciousness',[2] commands widespread assent. Britain in the

---

[1] L. Colley, *Britons: Forging the Nation 1707–1837* (2nd edn, London, 1994), especially pp. 195–319; L. Colley, 'The apotheosis of George III: loyalty, royalty and the British nation, 1760–1820', *Past and Present*, cii (1984); L. Colley, 'Class and national consciousness in Britain, 1750–1870', *Past and Present*, cxiii (1986); L. Colley, 'The reach of the state', in L. Stone (ed.), *An Imperial State at War* (London, 1994).

[2] J. Sharpe, *Early Modern England: A Social History* (London, 1987), p. 120. My own discussion of earlier 18th-century British national identity may be found in E. J. Evans, 'National consciousness: the ambivalences of English identity in the eighteenth century', in C. Bjørn, A. Grant and K. J. Stringer (eds.), *Nations, Nationalism and Patriotism in the European Past* (Copenhagen, 1994).

middle of the eighteenth century was certainly richer and probably more self-confident and self-aware than any other nation in Europe. It was also linguistically and culturally more unified and more knowledgeable both about itself and about its political processes. It was this maturity and self-awareness which seduced Voltaire into thinking that the British political system was more representative and 'advanced' than was actually the case.[3] The authorities had an emerging sense of identity with which to work when the supreme effort to resist French expansionism was required at the end of the century.

It is important to remember, however, that during the eighteenth century patriotism was by no means the preserve of the authorities. Opposition to taxation, for instance, was frequently presented as the struggle by 'freeborn Englishmen' to resist unconstitutional burdens placed on them by a corrupt, unpatriotic government.[4] Important links can be made between those opposition, or 'Country', Tories enraged by Walpole's excise scheme in the 1730s, who invoked the spectre of myriad government agents prying into personal matters, and the early-nineteenth-century rhetoric of William Cobbett, when he told the readers of his *Political Register* in October 1816 that the cause of their 'present miseries' was 'the enormous amount of the taxes which the government compels us to pay for the support of its army, its placemen, its pensioners etc.' Thus the problem confronting 'freeborn Englishmen' was misgovernment, and its remedy was 'a reform in the Commons or People's House of Parliament'.

A growing sense of national identity can, therefore, be a function of patriotic response to external challenge. No challenge to the territorial integrity of England, it may be argued, had been greater since 1066 than that presented by France during the years of war from 1793 to 1815. To resist it, a sense of Protestant British identity was invoked against a French threat variously characterised as Catholic or atheist. The extent to which that identity was sustained by increasing industrial eminence and imperial acquisition during a period of predominant European peace from 1815–1914 may be questioned, but the British Empire was certainly heavily marketed as a source of national pride in the last quarter of the nineteenth century.

This sense of identity may be characterised as 'top-down', and it dominated popular perceptions of patriotism from the 1870s onwards. Before about 1870, however, matters are rendered more complex by the vigorous presence of 'bottom-up' patriotism which stressed the integrity and vitality of what

[3] G. Holmes and D. Szechi, *The Age of Oligarchy: Pre-Industrial Britain, 1722–83* (London, 1993); E. J. Evans, *The Forging of the Modern State: Early Industrial Britain, 1783–1870* (2nd edn, London, 1995), chs. 1–2. The image of a politically corrupt and inert nation, however, is in need of substantial revision; see, e.g., the discussion of political representation in F. O'Gorman, *Voters, Patrons and Parties: The Unreformed Electoral System of Hanoverian England, 1734–1832* (Oxford, 1989).

[4] This theme is more fully developed in Evans, 'English identity in the 18th century', especially pp. 153–8.

many radical writers called the 'productive classes'. Radical patriotism was a particularly potent weapon against the predominantly landed political establishment of Britain in the years 1815–32, when parliamentary reformers characterised their struggle as one between the 'unproductive' landed classes, who drained the wealth of the nation by graft and greed, and the 'productive' who were shut out from political power by a corrupt oligarchy.

Here, therefore, the question of British identities during the period between roughly 1790 and 1870 will be discussed, in three particular ways. First, the use of patriotic language is examined, in order to determine whether nationalism and patriotism were more the preserve of the political left or right. Second, the nature of that national identity is explored, with particular reference to the ambivalence between 'English' and 'British'. Third, the relationship between England and the three smaller nations which comprised 'The United Kingdom of Great Britain and Ireland' is critically considered.

That William Pitt's government used images of nationhood and patriotism as an important weapon to mobilise public opinion against the French is beyond dispute. This involved manipulation on many levels. One was the publication of straightforwardly xenophobic cartoons. A good example of both the visual imagery and the verbal assault with which the British would become extremely familiar during the wars is given by Thomas Rowlandson's *The Contrast* (1793). Two images, of British and French liberty, are offered. The British shows Britannia looking benignly, but protectively, out towards an evidently British vessel. Her left hand carries the scales of justice and her right a scroll inscribed 'Magna Carta'. 'French Liberty' has a harridan holding a trident (upon the middle prong of which is a severed head) and looking aggressively across to Britannia. In case the visual images were considered insufficiently directive, Rowlandson spelled out the contrasts. British Liberty incorporates 'Religion, Morality, Loyalty, Obedience to the Laws, Independance [sic], Personal Security, Justice, Inheritance, Protection, Property, National Prosperity, Happiness'; whereas French Liberty offers 'Atheism, Perjury, Rebelion [sic], Treason, Anarchy, Murder, Equality, Madness, Cruelty, Injustice, Treachery, Ingratitude, Idleness, Famine, National & Private Ruin, Misery'. The redundant caption reads: 'Which is Best?'[5]

The cartoonists also attacked faithless foreign allies. When the first Allied Coalition against France collapsed in 1794, Isaac Cruikshank encapsulated British patriotic frustration with a cartoon entitled *The Faith of Treaties, or John Bull's last effort to oblige his False Friends.* It shows the allies walking away from John Bull, who is represented as a bull charging bravely at French muskets, with the exhortation 'Now my brave Allies, let us all stand firm together and make a bold pushing.' One 'ally' boasts that he has 'fingered the cash from both Sides', while another cares not who wins: 'I'll join the

5 M. Duffy, *The Englishman and the Foreigner* (Cambridge, 1986), p. 286.

Strongest Party.' As this implies, lack of both understanding and trust were to prove substantial obstacles to effective coalitions against the French until the last couple of years of the war.[6]

Loyalist cartoonists also contributed eagerly to the remaking of George III – in the 1760s and 1770s a figure of fervid political controversy – into a symbol of national unity during the French Revolutionary and Napoleonic Wars. He was portrayed as a benign father-figure with simple tastes, around whom folk of very different views could nevertheless unite. And doggerel reinforced the message that patriotic duty to the king involved necessary sacrifice:

> We BRITONS now, to our good king
> Will *grateful* homage pay;
> Nor *murmur*, tho' the war should bring
> Fresh taxes ev'ry day.[7]

Thus, while for roughly ninety-five of the 123 years which the famously unlovely Hanoverian dynasty survived, the term 'popular monarchy' was an oxymoron, during the last thirty years of his reign George III actually achieved unique status as a popular Hanoverian monarch (although, unfortunately, he was only sane enough to enjoy his reputation for fewer than twenty of them). This, of course, was exploited by the government. In January 1795, for instance, during a debate on Grey's Bill to open peace negotiations with France (one of several such opposition motions during the 1790s), Pitt invoked the monarch: 'But with a view to negotiation and to peace, his majesty did not look at it with that view, or for that purpose. He could look for English views and English purposes to see whether it held out the solid grounds for treating.'[8]

The government supported loyalist movements and helped to fund volunteer militias to defend the country. The Reeves Association Movement, for example, received state support once it had been launched in Middlesex in November 1792. A spate of government propaganda against 'Jacobinical and Atheistical' French influences issued forth, of which *Anti-Jacobin* (edited by the young George Canning) was the most famous. A very common theme was simple British virtue contrasted with the meretricious superficialities of new theory. The following typical contribution appeared in Canning's journal in February 1799:

> For to thy Country's foes; 'tis Thine to Claim
> From Britain's genuine sons a British fame –
> Too long French manners our fair isle disgrac'd
> Too long French fashions shamed our native taste

---

[6] Ibid., p. 290; cf. J. M. Sherwig, *Guineas and Gunpowder: British Aid in the Wars with France, 1793–1815* (Harvard, 1969).

[7] Quoted in H. Cunningham, 'The language of patriotism, 1750–1914', *History Workshop Journal*, xii (1981), p. 14.

[8] *The Parliamentary History*, xxxi (1795), column 1213.

> Presumptuous Folly stood in reason's form
> Pleased with power to reason not reform.[9]

The Church of England, as usual, sided with the party of order and contributed a welter of loyalist propaganda. One almost forgotten clergyman, the Suffolk curate William Jones, had enormous success with his *Letters from John Bull* in 1792–3, which warned the lower orders about the dangers of radicalism. John Bull pointed out to his fictional brother Tom the consequences of listening to 'French principles': 'Treason to their King and Ruin to their country! No order! No laws! No Honour! No Justice! King! Religion! or God! – God forbid that *Englishmen* should follow such an example.'[10]

Loyalist patriotism, however, was not merely the synthetic consequence of sharp propaganda in Church and State backed by threats of coercion. It did, in fact, prove genuinely popular, at least as far down the social scale as small shopkeepers. Loyalist literature, including patriotic songs and ballads, had a ready sale. Local organisation was probably more effective than government propaganda in rousing the propertied classes to support the status quo.[11] In most towns, Corresponding Societies advocating universal male suffrage and radical parliamentary reform were outnumbered, and were often driven underground, by loyalist organisations in 1794–5. Fighting the French in the 1790s engendered loyalist and nationalist spirit as never before. This was particularly apparent after the first invasion scare in 1797. One government response was the passage of a Defence of the Realm Act in 1798, which required county-by-county information to be compiled about the number of able-bodied men who would volunteer to defend their country at need. A similar requirement was laid upon harassed parish officials in 1803. The results are striking. Although there are substantial regional variations (independent-minded and Nonconformist East Anglia was notably less loyalist than elsewhere), in total about fifty per cent of men aged between seventeen and fifty-five volunteered to defend their country against invasion.[12] No doubt an unknowable proportion of these 'volunteers' was anything but: parish constables were not short of means of covert coercion. Nevertheless, it is clear that patriotic appeals did not fall on deaf English ears during the French Wars.

The invasion scares of 1803–4 were the occasion for much patriotic iconography. A common theme was Napoleonic pretension. James Gillray

---

[9] *Poetry of the Anti-Jacobin, 1799*, ed. J. H. Frere (Oxford, 1991), pp. 65–9. See also: R. Hole, 'British Counter-Revolutionary popular propaganda in the 1790s', in C. Jones (ed.), *Britain and Revolutionary France: Conflict, Subversion and Propaganda* (Exeter, 1983); A. Booth, 'Popular loyalism and public violence in the north-west of England', *Social History*, viii (1983); H. T. Dickinson, 'Popular Conservatism and militant loyalism, 1789–1815', in H. T. Dickinson (ed.), *Britain and the French Revolution, 1789–1815* (London, 1989).

[10] R. Hole, 'English sermons and tracts as media of debate on the French Revolution, 1789–99', in M. Philip (ed.), *The French Revolution and British Popular Politics* (Cambridge, 1991), pp. 26–7.

[11] Dickinson, 'Popular Conservatism and militant loyalism'; D. Eastwood, 'Patriotism and the English state in the 1790s', in Philip, *French Revolution and British Popular Politics*.

[12] Colley, 'Reach of the state'.

invoked Jonathan Swift in his cartoon *The King of Brobdingnag and Gulliver*, which has George III peering down a telescope at the diminutive figure of Bonaparte; the king's glance suggests amusement tinged with contempt. The image of the 'small' threat was reinforced in a popular print which refers to 'little Boney', afraid to venture out of port to mount the invasion: 'Why don't you come out? Yes, d... you, why don't you come out?' John Bull's composure was also disturbed by news of Bonaparte's plans. His riposte was swift and decisive, if in execrable verse.

> John Bull as he sat in his old easy chair
> An alarmist came to him, and said in his ear,
> 'A Corsican thief has just slipt from his quarters,
> And's coming to ravish your wives and your daughters.'

> 'Let him come and be d...d', thus roar'd out John Bull,
> 'With my crabstick assur'd I will fracture his skull,
> Or I'll squeeze the vile reptile 'twixt my finger and thumb,
> Make him stink like a bug if he dares to presume.'

Britain's island status would help repel the invader. As well as 'a full thousand of flat-bottom'd boats', loyally crewed by patriotic Englishmen, John Bull could also call upon 'my old ally Neptune' to give the French 'a dousing'.

The ironic 'Bonaparte's Answer to John Bull's Card' is one of relatively few songs to invoke the support of all four nations in the new United Kingdom. Boney may rest assured that, in addition to the opposition of 'Johnny Bull', he will also be opposed from the 'mines', 'meadows' and 'fountains' of Wales, the 'stout fleet' of Caledonia, and 'Hibernia's ... snug place'.[13] Another loyalist song, circulated in government-sponsored newspapers, is worth quoting in full. Its first line suggests the king's place as monarch of a greater Britain, and it stresses the unity of purpose of the constituent nations (but strangely omitting Wales) in defiance of Bonaparte:

> At the sign of the George, a national set
> (It fell out on a recent occasion)
> A Briton, a Scot, and Hibernian were met
> To discourse 'bout the threatened invasion.

> The liquor went round, they joked and they laughed,
> Were quite pleasant, facetious and hearty;
> To the health of their king flowing bumpers they quaff'd
> With confusion to great Buonaparte

> Quoth John 'Tis Reported, that snug little strait,
> Which runs betwixt Calais and Dover,
> With a hop, step and jump, that consul elate
> Intends in a trice to skip over.

[13] T. Wright, *A Caricature History of the Georges* (London, 1876), pp. 600–1.

'Let him try every cunning political stroke,
And devise every scheme that he's able;
He'll find us as firm and as hard to be broke,
As the bundle of sticks in the fable.'

The Scot and Hibernian replied – 'You are right –
Let him go the whole length of his tether;
When England, and Scotland and Ireland unite,
They defy the whole world put together.'[14]

Among many patriotic artefacts produced for patriotic purposes in 1803, we should note the plate inscribed 'Oh, de roast beef of Old England', which features the king's head, symbolically stressing the unity of purpose between the Hanoverian monarchy and the British people.[15]

But patriotism was a keenly contested battleground during the 1790s, and the conservatives certainly did not have it all their own way. A vigorous, independent strain of egalitarian, radical patriotism, which depended upon ideas of dispossession by a ruling elite, had existed at least since the English Revolution of 1640–60. The 'Norman Yoke' theory held that English liberties had been lost in 1066; and although kingly despotism was destroyed during the seventeenth century, the great landowners who assumed much greater powers after 'the Glorious Revolution' proved no more mindful of the interests of the people, whom they taxed heavily to subsidise both their own pleasures and an illegitimate system of government. Thus a London artisan in the 1760s might distinguish between his obligation to an employer and his freedom 'as an Englishman ... to chuse my representative'.[16] Thomas Paine, deliberately needling the Whigs, drew on a vigorous tradition when he described the 1689 Bill of Rights as 'a bill of wrongs and of insult'.[17] Radicals in the 1790s argued that the appropriate patriotic response was to agitate for political reform. John Baxter's *New and Impartial History of England*, published in 1796, argued that the English had a right, derived from their Saxon forbears, to challenge the authority of their governors. The conclusion was plain: only a democratic franchise would suffice to give the people the means to end 'Old Corruption'.

Into the second half of the 1790s, opposition Whigs continued to claim leadership of the patriotic reform cause. Charles James Fox's birthday was the occasion for numerous assertions that the leader of the opposition spoke for the people and for Britain. At a dinner held at the Crown and Anchor Tavern in London's West End on 24 January 1798, the duke of Norfolk stated that:

14 Ibid., p. 604.
15 Ibid., p. 602.
16 *Lloyd's Evening Post*, 18–21 July 1760, quoted in S. Yeo, 'Socialism and the state', in R. Colls and P. Dodd (eds.), *Englishness: Politics and Culture, 1880–1920* (Beckenham, 1986), pp. 330–1. For the 'Norman Yoke', see C. Hill, 'The Norman Yoke', in J. Saville (ed.), *Democracy and the Labour Movement* (London, 1954).
17 Thomas Paine, *The Rights of Man* (London, 1791–2), *passim*.

We are met, in a moment of the most serious difficulty, to celebrate the birth of a man dear to the friends of freedom. I shall only recall to your memory, that not twenty years ago, the illustrious George Washington had not more than two thousand men to rally round him when his country was attacked. America is now free. This day full two thousand men are assembled in this place. I leave you to make the application. I propose to you the health of Charles Fox.

Toasts were then offered to 'The Rights of the people', 'Constitutional redress of the wrongs of the people', and 'The genuine principles of the British constitution'. As the evening wore on, and perhaps as drink dulled acuter political sensitivities, the duke even offered 'Our sovereign's health – *the majesty of the people*'. Fox himself gave a toast to the sovereignty of the people of Great Britain, during a meeting of the Whig Club on 1 May 1798.[18]

In his cartoons, Gillray was happy to represent both sides of the patriotism debate. In March 1798, his target was Charles James Fox. After Fox had made one of his now rare interventions in a parliamentary debate to advocate reform, Gillray pictured him as a menacing Frenchman haranguing a suppliant figure: 'Radical Reform or Ruin and Destruction – Debt, Misery, Poverty, Slavery, Oppression, Loss of Liberty'. The cartoon is ironically entitled *John Bull consulting the Oracle*. In *The Tree of Liberty* he depicts Fox as the Devil, tempting John Bull from within a tree labelled 'Rights of Man'. The dialogue has Fox saying 'nice Apple, Johnny, nice Apple'. John Bull, evincing bluff common sense as usual, retorts: 'Very nice Napple indeed ... I hates Medlars, they're so damned rotten that I'se afraid they'll gee me the guts ach for all their vine [fine] looks.' John Bull picks *his* apples from a tree labelled 'Justice', with a crown prominently displayed in its branches; by contrast, the roots of Fox's tree are labelled 'Envy', 'Ambition' and 'Disappointment'.[19] In May 1796, on the other hand, Gillray represented Pitt sitting on a military barracks in front of a furnace, employing the Crown as a bellows to heat a retort which is being used to dissolve the House of Commons, the Bill of Rights and Magna Carta. The occasion of this assault on the prime minister for destroying the British constitution was his proposal to build new barracks without debating the matter in Parliament. The next month, Gillray produced a cartoon called *The Tree of Corruption with John Bull hard at work*. It shows John Bull tugging at a tree and trying to dislodge from its branches Pitt, Henry Dundas and three bags of money, labelled 'Sinecures', 'Pensions' and 'Secret Service Money'. The symbolic attack here is the standard one on government corruption.[20]

This attack was maintained by the opposition after 1815. While the government no longer had such need to evoke patriotic unity, radical

[18] Wright, *Caricature History*, pp. 514–16.
[19] Ibid., pp. 186, 190.
[20] H. T. Dickinson, *Caricatures and the Constitution, 1760–1832* (Cambridge, 1986), pp. 174, 176.

patriotism remained a crucial element in the attack on the old order, not only following the end of the French Wars but also well into the middle of the nineteenth century. The response to the Peterloo Massacre in August 1819, for example, was a rallying cry to all right-thinking Englishmen to cast off the shackles imposed by a corrupt, protectionist government. A reform meeting held on Hunslet Moor in September of that year attracted about 30,000 people, some of them wearing caps of liberty. A flag was displayed showing a man in chains, 'bending under two immense burdens of *National Debt* and *Taxation*. At the top was written *A Free Born Englishman*, and at the bottom, *Britons never shall be slaves.*'[21]

T. J. Wooler took up William Cobbett's theme of government corruption in an issue of *The Black Dwarf*, when he told readers that 'if the plenty of the world were to bring its superfluous corn to the British shores, and offer it at twenty shillings a quarter, the masters of the free-born Englishman would insist upon it that he should not have it at a less price than eighty'. The consequence was that 'the *real* and *only freedom* of an Englishman, is *money* and *money* alone. If rich, what he can *buy* he may have. If great, what he can *take* is his; but your free-born Briton is one of the most miserable of human beings.'[22] A poster displayed in Birmingham in the same month developed the theme of patriotism and liberty:

> BRITONS arise, and yet be free
> Defend your rights and liberty!
> Boroughmongers long have shar'd the spoil
> The working class shares all the toil.[23]

Both the language and the imagery of radical patriotism were prominent during the Reform crisis of 1831–2. John Bull now appeared regularly as a supporter of Reform. In October 1831, after the Lords had thrown out the Reform Bill, a Newcastle-upon-Tyne doctor told a pro-Reform crowd, in which local pitmen were prominent, that national interests must take precedence over sectional concerns: 'Now here we count 80,000 reformers, and if every one was employed to frame a bill of reform no two would be alike; but knowing that unanimity alone can promote our great object, each has, like a true patriot, surrendered his own individual opinion for the purpose of obtaining that unanimity.' When Reform was finally obtained in June 1832, the *Weekly Dispatch* circulated its readers with a free souvenir picture of 'Britannia and the Reform Act'. It shows an armed but smiling Britannia holding a flag upon which are displayed the images of leading

[21] Report of a Meeting on Hunslet Moor in September 1819: housed in the Library of the Thoresby Society, Leeds, and quoted in D. G. Wright, *Democracy and Reform, 1815–85* (London, 1970), pp. 113–14.

[22] *The Black Dwarf*, 8 December 1819.

[23] Quoted in J. Belchem, *Industrialisation and the Working Class: The English Experience, 1750–1900* (Aldershot, 1990), p. 82. For other examples in a similar vein, see Colley, *Britons*, pp. 337–8.

Reformers. The British lion looks out to sea, on which is sailing a ship flying the Union Flag. An anti-Reform vessel is shown sinking nearby.[24]

Radical patriotism was also an element in Chartism, which recent analyses have shown to have been in essence a political movement with a clear democratic agenda. Chartist rhetoric drew heavily upon the older libertarian strains taken from the English Revolution by literate artisans in the eighteenth century, and then adapted to meet new conditions immediately after the French Wars and during the political crisis of 1830–2. The importance of 'noble-minded' and 'liberated patriots' was repeatedly stressed in Chartist publications, and the Chartist Convention of 1839 urged members to cleave to 'the old constitutional right – a right which modern legislators would fain annihilate', and to 'defend the laws and constitutional privileges their ancestors bequeathed to them'.[25]

Until at least the middle of the nineteenth century, therefore, patriotism was manipulated by both the political left and the political right. If anything, before 1850 it put down the deepest roots among radicals and other parliamentary reformers. Admittedly, the manufacture of 'patriots' by a conservative elite had impressive results, especially in the 1790s, when anti-French feeling gripped the propertied classes; while Pitt's government also targeted British Jacobins, accusing them not only of atheism but also of lack of patriotic sentiment. But the radical response to this was cogent and long-lasting; between 1815 and 1832, in particular, radical patriotism held the field. Radicals characterised their struggle as one of loyal, patriotic and down-trodden Britons against a corrupt, profligate and wasteful aristocracy. And not until after 1870, in fact, does it becomes clear that the Conservative interpretation of patriotism – which was basically imperialist, xenophobic and defensive – would hold the field and survive to provide that Party with one of its most permanently bankable electoral assets.

Readers of the previous section will have noticed that both the political left and the political right used the terms 'England' and 'Britain' interchangeably. The quest for a distinctively *English*, as opposed to a *British*, identity in this period is, in fact, one that will prove fruitless. 'British' is the dominant descriptor of patriotic identification; and at any level more local than that of 'Britain', the English were more likely to identify with their own regions and localities than with the whole country of England *per se*.

[24] Ibid., pp. 339–44.
[25] Cunningham, 'Language of patriotism', p. 17. For Chartist rhetoric and language, see: G. S. Jones, 'Rethinking Chartism', in G. S. Jones (ed.), *Languages of Class: Studies in English Working Class History* (Cambridge, 1983); D. K. G. Thompson, *The Early Chartists* (London, 1971); D. K. G. Thompson, *The Chartists: Popular Politics in the Industrial Revolution* (London, 1984); and I. Prothero, *Artisans and Politics in early Nineteenth-Century London* (London, 1979). For a detailed account of the events of 1830–2, see M. Brock, *The Great Reform Act* (London, 1973); a more recent summary is found in E. J. Evans, *The Great Reform Act of 1832* (2nd edn, London, 1994), pp. 45–56.

Since the eighteenth century, when national identity can be identified as an increasingly significant concept in Europe,[26] England has been demographically, economically and politically the dominant partner in 'Great Britain'. The Act of Union in 1800 reduced that demographic dominance somewhat, by adding five million Irish folk to an overall population in the new 'United Kingdom of Great Britain and Ireland' of almost sixteen million; the first official Census, taken the year after the Union, revealed that England comprised almost 54% of the population of the new United Kingdom; Ireland accounted for 33%, while Scotland contributed 10% and Wales only 3%. But thereafter, the impact of the Irish famine and subsequent disproportionate emigration had the effect of increasing England's numerical dominance very substantially: by 1871 England provided 68.7% of the population of the United Kingdom as a whole, as opposed to 14.6% from Scotland and Wales combined and only 16.7% from Ireland.

Yet what these figures also show is that, in contrast to Ireland, Scotland and Wales slightly increased their proportion of the United Kingdom's population between 1801 and 1871. This is because – unlike Ireland – they participated fully with England in the process of industrial growth and substantial urban development. It had not been from any feelings of political closeness, but to participate in early eighteenth-century England's international commercial success, that the Scots had agreed to Union with England in 1707, and from that Union the merchants and industrialists of central Scotland had profited mightily. English students to this day too readily overlook the fact that the textile revolution of west-central Scotland was as rapid and as impressive as that in south Lancashire and north-east Cheshire; the rebuilding of Glasgow as one of nineteenth-century Europe's most substantial, yet elegant, temples to capitalism is testimony to the profitable pay-off of Anglo-Scottish association.[27] Likewise, the valleys of south Wales were transformed during the late eighteenth and early nineteenth centuries, first by iron and then by coal. Cardiff, a tiny place with a population of only 2,000 in 1801, had grown to 40,000 by 1871 and, by 1900, was one of Britain's foremost ports with a population of 164,000; it was created a city in 1905.[28] The Industrial Revolution was undeniably British – and its success underscores the lack of a distinctively English identity.

As Patrick Joyce has recently argued, although industrialism forged common bonds, these were far more likely to be regional than English. Industrial Lancashire, for instance, retained a very clear sense of identity

[26] E. J. Hobsbawm, *Nations and Nationalism since 1780: Programme, Myth, Reality* (2nd edn, Cambridge, 1992). But see also, for an overview from a medievalist's standpoint, K. J. Stringer, 'Social and political communities in European history: some reflections on recent studies', in Bjørn, Grant and Stringer, *Nations, Nationalism and Patriotism*.

[27] M. Lynch, *Scotland: A New History* (2nd edn, London, 1992), ch. 20; R. H. Campbell, *Scotland since 1707: The Rise of an Industrial Society* (2nd edn, London, 1985), *passim*; R. Mitchison, *A History of Scotland* (2nd edn, London, 1982), p. 389.

[28] P. Jenkins, *A History of Modern Wales, 1536–1990* (London, 1992), pp. 239–40.

through its distinctive dialect and dialect poems, which reworked 'the old traditions in new circumstances and for new purposes'. The pamphlet *In Praise of O'Lancashire* identified Lancashire working people as the backbone of the staple industry that made Lancashire and England great: 'Lancashire is the standard bearer of labour and political freedom.'[29] The opening of Manchester's grand Gothic town hall in 1877 was accompanied by massive marches in which all classes participated – an occasion for regional civic pride. Regional identity also infused the creation of a wide variety of public buildings. The Birmingham Council House, for which Joseph Chamberlain laid the foundation stone in 1874, proudly placed sculptured figures around the principal entrance representing literature, art, science, and 'Britannia rewarding Birmingham manufacturers'. The *Leeds Mercury* waxed even more expansive when that city's town hall was opened by Queen Victoria and Prince Albert in 1858: 'For a portion of two days, through the condescension of her Majesty, this old and busy seat of industry becomes in a sense the seat of the Empire.' The opening of buildings such as the lion-guarded Bolton town hall (1873), or Manchester's Royal Corn Exchange, were also accompanied by ceremonial redolent of regionalism and of recognition of participation in a great British enterprise. Distinctively *English* identification was, however, rare.[30]

Historians of the other three nations in the United Kingdom, on the other hand, discover a much clearer sense of identity. Smaller nations gain strength from defensive distinctiveness. D. G. Boyce begins his own study of the Irish, whom he rightly describes as 'marginal Britons', with the recognition that 'it was instinctive for the English to regard the terms English and British as synonymous ... the United Kingdom was ... a coat that fitted snugly and firmly over all the peoples who dwelt in the British Isles'.[31] The Liberal MP James Bryce was pleased to note in 1887 that the Scots and Welsh still treasured 'a distinct national feeling, though happily not incompatible with attachment to the greater nationality of the United Kingdom'. The English-man was different. He 'has but one patriotism, because England and the United Kingdom are to him practically the same thing'.[32]

In political terms, the composition of Parliament amply confirms the dominance of England in the United Kingdom. Between 1707 and 1832, the House of Commons comprised 489 MPs elected from constituencies in England, forty-five from Scotland and twenty-four from Wales. Only the addition of 100 Irish members after the Act of Union in 1800 brought the number of non-English seats up to about twenty-five per cent. The propor-tion of English seats was reduced only marginally, from 74% to 71.5%, by the

[29] P. Joyce, *Visions of the People* (Cambridge, 1991), pp. 279–92.

[30] A. Briggs, *Victorian Cities* (2nd edn, London, 1968), pp. 177, 232; E. J. Evans and J. M. Richards, *A Social History of Britain in Postcards, 1870–1939* (London, 1980), pp. 22–3.

[31] D. G. Boyce, 'The marginal Britons: the Irish', in Colls and Dodd, *Englishness: Politics and Culture*, p. 231.

[32] Ibid., p. 236.

1832 Reform Act, and even more marginally to 70.5% in 1867 (though by then, at last, England's share of parliamentary seats and of the overall population was roughly the same).[33]

Intermarriage of aristocratic families, which increased markedly in the second half of the eighteenth century, ensured that political control was by no means exclusively English. But the structure of politics was such that there was little opportunity for independent-minded Scottish or Welsh voices to be heard in Parliament. Whereas a small, but politically rather significant, minority of English seats before 1832 was elected on a wide franchise and frequently returned MPs critical of government policies, virtually the whole of Scotland operated as a kind of 'rotten borough' in the control either of the Crown or of government ministers. One of the most effective political manipulators, Henry Dundas, was a member of an established Scottish landed family with extensive estates just south of Edinburgh. Dundas was, however, one of William Pitt's most loyal and trusted ministers, holding high office throughout the 1790s, and his presence contributed little to the representation of specifically Scottish interests at Westminster.[34] Indeed he was a particular target of hostility from Scottish radicals and democrats because of his strong support for the Union; they characterised Scotland as 'groaning under the chains of England', and resented Dundas's organisation of petitions pledging undying loyalty to George III. Nevertheless, Dundas did have a sense of Scottishness; for example, like most Scots in public life, he believed the Scottish legal system to be superior in most respects to the English. He told Parliament that no Scot would understand why an Englishman could be sentenced to death for stealing a piece of cheese. In replying to William Adam's proposal in 1794 to introduce greater harmony between the English and Scottish legal codes, he informed the Commons:

> Among the Scots a greater latitude and discretion is indulged their judges. But I affirm that this very circumstance it is that attaches the people to their laws. And I am bold to say, that there will be found fewer crimes to exist among them than in any other country of Europe.[35]

Parliamentary reform after 1832 did breathe fresh life into Scottish politics,[36] but the new political system did not do much to loosen English domination of the United Kingdom's political scene. If nationhood defines itself most readily when it has a cause to fight, or when citizens feel slighted, then the Britain which emerged from the Napoleonic Wars as the strongest

[33] Evans, *Forging of Modern State*, p. 379.

[34] M. Fry, *The Dundas Despotism* (Edinburgh, 1992), pp. 165–206. For a discussion of the political life in the constituencies before 1832, see J. Cannon, *Parliamentary Reform, 1640–1832* (2nd edn, Cambridge, 1980); O'Gorman, *Voters, Patrons and Parties*; and Evans, *Great Reform Act*, pp. 4–14.

[35] *The Parliamentary History*, xxxi (1794), column 63; quoted in Fry, *Dundas Despotism*, p. 165. For links between Scots law and Scottish consciousness after 1707, see H. L. MacQueen, 'Regiam Majestatem, Scots Law, and National Identity', *Scottish Historical Review*, lxxiv (1995), pp. 19–25.

[36] I. C. G. Hutchinson, *A Political History of Scotland, 1832–1924* (Edinburgh, 1986).

nation in the world offered little incentive for the English to assert their separateness from what was now manifestly *Great* Britain.

Finally, the icons representing England *per se* remained resolutely unburnished for much of the nineteenth century. The dominant Union Flag is, by definition, British. England's flag is that of its patron saint, St George, whose claims to Englishness are minimal.[37] It was, and is, unfurled on church towers on the Saint's day, 23 April, but there was in the nineteenth century no concerted attempt to have St George's Day commemorated as a public holiday, a perhaps surprising omission since the same date is also the supposed birthday, and certain date of death, of William Shakespeare. St George's name is, however, attached to numerous nineteenth-century buildings, most notably the famous hall designed for concerts in Liverpool by Charles Cockerell, which was opened in 1854.[38]

If national identity is forged out of external threats, then the substantial influx of predominantly Catholic Irish into Britain during the nineteenth century compels examination. Irish immigration both was very substantial and was widely perceived as threatening. The Census of 1861 recorded 602,000 Irish-born residents in England and Wales (about 3% of the total population), and 204,000 in Scotland (about 7%). In some large towns, of course, the proportion was much higher: Liverpool's proportion of Irish-born in 1851 was 22%, Glasgow's 18%, and Dundee's 19%. The Irish did, however, disperse more widely than is often thought. Bath, Colchester and Newport (Shropshire) all had more than a thousand Irish-born residents by 1861. By 1871, more than two-thirds of the Irish-born lived outside the four major conurbations around Liverpool, Manchester, Glasgow and London.[39] This widespread immigration posed a direct threat to both wage levels and job security in many British towns, especially at times of depression. We might, therefore, expect a combination of economic challenge and distaste for the 'Catholic Other' to produce defensive nationalism at least among the working classes.

Protestant propaganda was certainly active from the late 1830s onwards. The Protestant Association and the Reformation Society placed great emphasis upon awakening nationalist feelings in the indigenous working classes. Branches were established in most English towns, and London had several. One journal specifically aimed at a working-class readership, *Protestant Penny Operative*, achieved considerable success in the 1840s. Its patriotic message was overt, as was its appeal to the skilled worker specifically as a freeborn *Englishman*:

[37] St George, a 4th-century Christian martyr, also doubles as the patron saint of Portugal. It is highly unlikely that he ever came nearer to England than the Middle East; the myth of dragon-slaying appears to have been attributed to him in the 12th century.

[38] D. Watkin, *Life and Work of C. R. Cockerell* (London, 1974).

[39] J. Williamson, 'The impact of the Irish on British labour markets during the Industrial Revolution', in R. Swift and S. Gilley (eds.), *The Irish in Britain* (London, 1989).

Ye Protestant Christians arise!
England summons you now to her aid
Protect and defend me, she cries
Ere freedom and liberty fade.

Firm as a rock be the trust
Of our loyal and Protestant bands
Rome never shall crush to the dust
Our Protestant free artisans.[40]

Protestantism was invoked as the vehicle of progress in wider patriotic appeals. The following flight of rhetoric by a lecturer to the York Protestant Operative Association in 1840 gives the flavour. Britain's love of the English Bible had made it 'the loveliest land on the face of the earth ... While I have a voice ... it shall be Britain for ever! Victoria, our lovely Queen for ever! Protestantism for ever! Three times three for Protestantism.'[41]

Popular newspapers were not slow to categorise the immigrant Irish in crass, stereotypical terms. Journals such as *Family Herald*, *Lloyd's Entertaining Journal* and *Lloyd's Weekly Miscellany* attacked them as stupid, lazy, improvident, feckless, disruptive and, above all, drunken.[42] Influential commentators were not slow to add their weight to the image of the Irish as an ignorant, priest-ridden drag on a vibrant society. Friedrich Engels asserted that:

> Drink is the only thing which makes an Irishman's life worth living; so he revels in drink to the point of the most bestial drunkenness. The southern facile character of the Irishman, his crudity which places him little above the savage, his contempt for all humane enjoyments, in which his very crudeness makes him incapable of sharing, his filth and poverty all favour drunkenness.[43]

Engels also pointed out that 'the English working man' had to struggle 'with a competitor upon the lowest plane possible in any civilised country', who would work for very little wages. The Liverpool Medical Officer of Health, Dr W. H. Duncan, noted in 1859 that mortality rates were highest where the Irish were most numerous. In his view, the Irish were 'not only the most destitute but the most improvident' element in Liverpudlian society.[44] Even the introduction to a Census Report, that for Scotland in 1871, warned against the dangers from the immigrant community:

[40] *Protestant Penny Operative*, 1840; quoted in J. Wolffe, *The Protestant Crusade in Great Britain* (Oxford, 1991), p. 174.

[41] Quoted in ibid., p. 308.

[42] D. G. Paz, *Popular Anti-Catholicism in Mid-Victorian England* (Stamford, California, 1992), pp. 253–9.

[43] Frederick Engels, *The Condition of the Working Class in England in 1844* (London, 1969 edn), pp. 124–5.

[44] C. G. Pooley, 'Segregation or integration? The residential experience of the Irish in mid-Victorian Britain', in Swift and Gilley, *Irish in Britain*, p. 60.

The immigration ... of a body of labourers of the lowest class, with scarcely any education, cannot but have the most prejudicial effects on the population. As yet, the great body of these Irish do not seem to have improved by their residence among us; and it is quite certain that the native Scot who has associated with them has most certainly deteriorated.[45]

Men like Hugh McNeile in the 1840s and William Murphy in the late 1860s and early 1870s also weighed in with anti-popery harangues designed to raise nationalist consciousness.

Yet, while it is easy to find numerous examples of anti-Catholic lessons, it is much harder to determine how receptively the working classes absorbed them. Much of the propaganda was directed at literate artisans, who were encouraged to read reasoned, if prejudiced, articles, to attend meetings and to discuss opinions. Such people, in the main, were not directly challenged by unskilled Irish labourers, though they might well come to a view that the Irish inhibited civilised progress. And in the poorest areas of the cities, where many Irish lived, reaction to them was mixed. Considerable hostility was certainly in evidence from the 1830s to the 1870s, especially in the north-west of England. Street brawls were commonplace in Liverpool in the 1830s and 1840s, particularly after closing time, and there were fights between Orangemen and Irish dockers in 1851. Riots took place in Ashton-under-Lyne, Oldham, Preston, Blackburn and Wigan in 1852–4. Greater violence attended rioting in Failsworth, Ashton and Stalybridge in 1868, when firearms were known to have been used.[46]

The most notorious anti-Irish protests took place in Stockport in June 1852, when three days of street rioting began with the break-up of a peaceful Roman Catholic Sunday-school procession. The timing was doubtless linked to the recent pronouncement by Lord Derby's minority Conservative government that Roman Catholics could no longer display their vestments or religious symbols in public. Popular anti-Catholicism became an important element in the increasing popularity of the Conservative Party in Lancashire from the 1860s onwards. Seats which the Liberals might have been expected to win comfortably on national trend were captured by the Conservatives on an anti-Catholic, anti-Irish vote. Irish-Catholic-rich Lancashire was particularly vulnerable to Tory propaganda. In the otherwise disastrous general election, for the Conservatives, of 1868, Lancashire returned twenty-one Tory MPs to the Liberals' thirteen. Notable prizes included the solid industrial seats of Salford (newly enfranchised in 1867), Bolton, Preston and Blackburn. In south-west Lancashire, famously, Mr Gladstone was driven out.[47] It is worth remembering, however, that the Tories were not exclusively the 'English

---

45   Quoted in J. E. Handley, *The Irish in Modern Scotland* (London, 1947), p. 240.
46   R. Samuel, 'An Irish religion', in R. Samuel (ed.), *Patriotism: The Making and Unmaking of British National Identity* (London, 1989), i, p. 97.
47   Evans, *Forging of Modern State*, pp. 369–70.

party' in Lancashire: Protestant Irish immigrants were an important force in Liverpool, contributed to continuing sectarian violence, and, inevitably, were among the strongest supporters of the Conservatives in the city.[48]

On the other hand, although instances both of anti-Catholic hostility and of Catholics' defence of their Church and its practices are commonplace in the middle years of the century, only occasionally, as in the wake of the Fenian disturbances of 1867–8, did these pose a serious threat to the authorities. More important to the theme of identity, the extent to which they stimulated any developing sense of Englishness is highly debatable. Senses of Protestant and national superiority were indissolubly fused; as in other areas, national identity was as likely to be Protestant British as Protestant English. Some writers also saw in the use of a common language a means of accommodating the rough Irish to British values. The *Working Man's Friend* asserted in 1850: 'When a community begins to speak and read the English language, it is half *Saxonized* even if not a drop of Anglo-Saxon blood runs in the veins.' An issue of *Eliza Cook's Journal*, published three months before the Stockport Riots, even welcomed the fact that

> In England the invidious distinctions of race are rapidly becoming obliterated. We are all so mixed up with Germans, Irish, Norman-French, Jews and people of all countries, that we no longer can pride ourselves on the purity of our 'blood'. Let us hope that the best points of character in all these races will be preserved – the frank generosity and fine personal qualities of the Celt; the diligence and industry of the Saxon ... and we may be proud, as indeed we have reason to already, to bear the name of BRITON.[49]

The extent to which Anglo-Irish hostility contributed to the development of a national consciousness may thus be doubted. Militant Protestant propaganda seems to have had limited impact outside a literate working-class elite, and violence was frequently motivated as much by drink as by defence of either faith or nation. The more fervent defence of the faith, in fact, came from Catholic Irish labourers, for whom priests and icons retained an atavistic power. The evidence of one Protestant evangelical working in the East End of London in the 1880s is indicative: 'Tuesday (St Patrick's Day). The Irish dock labourer is rampant today, and anyone who wishes to be involved in a serious row could not do better than broach the subject of Evangelical religion.'[50] Even the extent to which strictly economic considerations predominated may be questioned. Sensitivity to cultural differences, exacerbated by the defensive tendency of the poorest Irish to congregate in distinct enclaves near the centre of large towns, was at least as important.

[48] Paz, *Popular Anti-Catholicism*, p. 254; N. Kirk, 'Ethnicity and popular Toryism', in K. Lunn (ed.), *Hosts, Immigrants and Minorities* (Folkestone, 1980).
[49] Ibid., p. 77.
[50] Charles Booth, *Life and Labour of the People of London* (London, 1902), iv, p. 197; quoted in Samuel, 'Irish religion', p. 101.

Furthermore, the case of Henry Mayhew shows how English preconceptions about universal Irish fecklessness could be refuted by actual observations. When he visited Irish homes in London in the late 1850s, he noted that costermongers were working 'on the associative principle, by mutual support. In all of the houses that I entered were traces of household care and neatness that I had little expected to have seen.'[51] A series of reports on immigrant life in England published in the Dublin newspaper *The Nation* in 1870–2 – admittedly not an unimpeachable source – provided many other examples of Irish improvement, acceptability and respectability. In 1872, for example, about 5,000 Irish miners were noted as earning good wages around Chesterfield. Their overall condition was described as satisfactory. 'There is sufficient church accommodation ... and ... the Jesuit Fathers ... speak in very favourable terms of the conduct, morals and habits of the Irish people, as contrasted with their English fellow-labourers in the mines and works.'[52] Recent detailed work on the Censuses of 1851, 1861 and 1871 provides some confirmation of this optimistic picture. It reveals that about forty per cent of Irish-born residents in Liverpool, Greenock, Hull and York were in professional or skilled working-class occupations.[53]

The theme of 'backward' Scots and Welsh holding back 'advanced' England in an unprecedentedly prosperous Great Britain was also heard, though less stridently than in the case of the Irish. After all, both Scotland and Wales had impressive industrial achievements to their credit. Scottish and Welsh entrepreneurs chased markets, believed in free trade and grew rich. Prominent politicians from both countries acclimatised readily to Westminster (though some of them then took the lead in berating their fellow countrymen for backwardness). Nevertheless, it was argued that various elements in Scottish and Welsh culture needed amendment, if the smaller nations were to be brought up to scratch.

On most political and administrative criteria, Scotland was more distinctively different from England than was Wales. Scotland retained separate legal and educational systems, which the Welsh did not. The Welsh, however, retained their own language. About two-thirds of Welshmen used Welsh as their first language in 1870; most of these, indeed, were monolingual. In rural north and mid-Wales the proportion was very much higher – between eighty and ninety per cent. Scotland, by contrast, had never been linguistically homogeneous. Since 1707 the Scots language of the Lowlands had been increasingly assimilated to English, especially among the elites, while Gaelic, mostly found in the Highlands, was in steady retreat. In 1870 only

---

[51] Henry Mayhew, *London Labour and the London Poor* (Penguin edn, Harmondsworth, 1985), p. 56.

[52] *The Nation*, 4 September 1872, quoted in A. O'Day (ed.), *A Survey of the Irish in England* (London, 1990), p. 65.

[53] Pooley 'Segregation or integration?', p. 71.

about fifteen per cent of Scots spoke Gaelic, and attempts to preserve the language owed more to pre-echoes of 'heritage' which painlessly extracts the incisors from the jaws of national identity. Minority status was no barrier to the disdain of the Registrar-General at the 1871 Scottish Census: 'The Gaelic language may be what it likes, both as to antiquity and to beauty, but it decidedly stands in the way of the civilisation of the natives [*sic*] making use of it.'[54] Any remaining threats from Highlanders, Jacobites and the clan system having been long dispersed, both sentimental Lowlanders and Queen Victoria's court, which regularly decamped to Balmoral after 1848, could wear the kilt, promote Highland Games, patronise bagpipers and reinvent a safe, sanitised and certainly not separate North Britain.[55]

Wales was rather different. Friedrich Engels may not have been entirely inaccurate when he asserted that 'The English know how to reconcile people of the most diverse races with their rule; the Welsh, who fought tenaciously for their language and culture, have become entirely reconciled with the British Empire.'[56] But he was underestimating the potential of Welsh identity to develop forms which stressed not only 'otherness' but also overt antagonism. The touchstone was usually language. When, in 1847, parliamentary commissioners reported on the state of education in Wales, their message was as clear as it was controversial: Welsh was denounced as 'a peculiar language isolating the mass from the upper portion of society'. The language, in the commissioners' view, was the strongest impediment to civilised advance. The Welsh-speaker 'is left in an underworld of his own, and the march of society goes so completely over his head that he is never heard of, except when the strange and abnormal features of a Revival, or a Rebecca or Chartist outbreak, call attention to a phase of society which could produce so contrary to all we experience elsewhere'.[57] Such disdain was bound to provoke reaction in a society which needed no spur to pronounce the value of its identity. *Eisteddfodau* increased in number throughout the nineteenth century, in industrial south Wales as well as in the more rural north, and the Welsh could celebrate poets and novelists of stature such as William Thomas, Gwilym Hiraethog and Daniel Owen. A Welsh Manuscripts Society was established in 1836, and calls for a separate University of Wales grew in strength. The first University College, at Aberystwyth, opened in 1872.

Meanwhile, the Liberal Party in Wales was emerging as the increasingly potent counterpart to this cultural renaissance. Wales by 1870 was developing as a stronghold of radical Liberalism which, under the direction of Henry Richard, MP for Merthyr Tydfil, was channelling many pro-Welsh sentiments in significant new directions. Richard spoke not for establishment Liberalism but particularly to ordinary Welshmen, many of whom had been enfranchised

[54] K. Robbins, *Nineteenth-Century Britain: Integration and Diversity* (Oxford, 1988), p. 42.
[55] Lynch, *Scotland: A New History*, p. 355.
[56] Jenkins, *History of Modern Wales*, p. 301.
[57] Ibid., p. 310.

in the towns in 1867. The election of 1868 saw a decisive breakthrough for more populist and aggressively Nonconformist Liberalism. The Liberal Party in Wales, after a long period of virtual parity with the Tories, now held roughly two-thirds of the seats and established the long, and still unbroken, tradition of anti-Toryism in the Principality. Many of the defeated Tories were landowners, and evictions of pro-Liberal tenant farmers in 1868–70 served only to emphasise the degree of cultural separation. David Lloyd George – born of course in Manchester but the most 'Welsh' of successful politicians – was only seven years old in 1870; yet the seeds of that radical, anti-aristocratic populism which sustained his early career, and for which he evinced at least romantic fascination much longer, had already been sown.

This study offers three broad conclusions. First, those English who invoked patriotism for much of the nineteenth century were at least as likely to be on the political left as on the right. Radical patriotism drew on old myths, such as the 'Norman Yoke', to establish the model of the 'freeborn Englishman'. This construct was intensely suspicious of state power and egalitarian in temper. It held that, despite the Glorious Revolution, Britain's rulers were unrepresentative and probably corrupt *users* of the nation's wealth rather than its creators. Such a vision inspired Levellers in the 1640s, some independent-minded 'Country-Party' MPs in the first half of the eighteenth century, radical patriots in the 1760s, parliamentary reformers from the 1780s to the early 1830s, and Chartists in the later 1830s and the 1840s. All attacked the system controlled by a landowners' Parliament as 'Old Corruption'. True Englishness, by contrast, was pure and unsullied by graft. Although most adherents to the theory of the 'freeborn Englishman' were radicals, they were joined by many paternalist Tories in their suspicion of a bloated, centralised state. Richard Oastler in 1842 berated both Whigs and Conservatives in the political establishment for introducing centralised administration of the poor law and supporting free trade. He also called for 'the resurrection of that *national* mind, of which our ancestors were so justly proud':

> The people of England are sick of Whiggery in every shape, so thoroughly are they disgusted with the principles of the 'liberal school' that all the talents and power of the Conservatives will not be able to persuade or force Englishmen to submit any longer to a departure from the benign principles of the Constitution.
>
> The New Poor Law and Free Trade, being part and parcel of the same novel, 'enlightened' and unconstitutional scheme, will be warred against successfully by the nation, in spite of every effort which may be made by the Whigs and Conservatives to defeat them.[58]

[58] *The Fleet Papers*, 8 January 1842, p. 10.

It follows from this, in the second place, that neither 'Englishness' nor 'Britishness' is to be understood primarily as an abstract cultural construct devised by an increasingly powerful state as a means of controlling citizens of uncertain loyalty whose allegiance it required. Englishness, patriotism and a sense of national identity each have long but ambiguous histories, which 'the ruled' have helped to formulate. Cultural hegemony as a concept always had greater theoretical attractiveness than practical application; it is of very little use in discussing British national identity.

Third, the combination of a patriotism with intolerant Protestantism is a factor in 'Englishness' as well as in 'Britishness'. Many myths were built around 'Bloody Mary' (1553–8), the wife of the hated Philip II of Spain, who would in 1588 launch the Armada against 'Good Queen Bess'. The myth held that success for the Armada would have imposed slavery and alien, Catholic absolutism upon the freeborn Englishmen. The enduring power of this image, though easily overlooked, is worth remembering. After all, the penal statutes against Roman Catholics were not repealed until 1829. Many Catholic immigrants into Britain had considerable difficulties in assimilating. 'Protestants', in reaction to their presence, presented their national self-awareness in atavistic terms; for them, Catholicism still meant wooden shoes and slavery. Religious rivalry frequently produced violence, especially in the north-west of England. Adherents of Protestant patriotism still survive in the 1990s, though battered, defensive and harbouring dark, and increasingly plausible, thoughts of betrayal. The religious majority in Ulster, its staunchest defenders, cannot understand why few in Britain see compelling reason to sustain the Union of Great Britain and Northern Ireland. Only in the late twentieth century does an overwhelmingly secular Britain seem finally ready to cut Protestant fundamentalism adrift.

It is clear, therefore, that neither 'Englishness' nor 'Britishness' is a separately identifiable phenomenon. Instead, they are the product of complicated cross-cultural developments. The English, certainly, and the wider British, *as British*, are not specially 'patriotic', though plenty of evidence exists, from Palmerston in the 1850s to Thatcher in the 1980s, that they will vote for leaders who successfully identify a national enemy – however puny that enemy might be. In such cases, however, patriotism is not so much a cultural entity as a political weapon. In 1775 Dr Samuel Johnson provided us with his famous aphorism: 'Patriotism is the last refuge of a scoundrel.'[59] The comment had a much more particularist context than is usually assumed. Johnson was referring only to those radical patriots who opposed Britain's going to war with her eastern seaboard American colonies in order to keep them 'English'. This piece of pedantry does, however, suggest one concluding observation: is the 'spirit of England' more an internal political weapon than a symbol of national identity?

[59] The correct quotation is *sic*, not the more usually encountered '... of the scoundrel': *Boswell's Life of Johnson* (Oxford, 1927), i, p. 583.

Chapter 14

An imperial and multinational polity
The 'scene from the centre',1832–1922

Keith Robbins

There is, perhaps, something rather odd in the suggestion that a contribution on the 'formation of the United Kingdom' should begin with that hallowed date in old-style political/electoral history – namely 1832. This is certainly not the place at which to embark on a fundamental reappraisal of the 'Great Reform Act', yet the date selected as the starting-point is not the product of an arbitrary whim. Since this contribution considers the period down to 1922 – that is to say to the partition of Ireland and the end of the United Kingdom of Great Britain and Ireland – it points to the central problem in the nineteenth century of an 'imperial and multinational polity'. I take that problem to be the reconciling of 'democratic' internal pressures on the one hand, and 'imperial' and external aspirations on the other. Our consideration of these matters ends, in time, with the paradox (at least on the surface) of a British government which is apparently forced to 'let go' in Ireland just at the time when 'victory' has been achieved in the Great War and the British Empire has expanded, through the mandates, to an even greater extent.

In short, we are grappling, as other contributors have been in earlier periods, with the definition of the United Kingdom during nearly a century. I need hardly add that the Victorian Age seemed to contemporaries to be one of great dynamism and change, both internally and externally. Thus there was little that was settled and static in the 'destiny' of the United Kingdom, considered either as a 'country' or as a 'power' in the international system. Earlier chapters in this volume have contemplated conquest and resistance, multiple kingdoms, and the varieties of 'Britishness' to be found in the political structures of the 'Eastern Atlantic Archipelago'.[1] Although our colleagues *now* tend to highlight diversity, and rightly stress, at various points, that the constitutional and political relationships within these islands could have evolved in directions which were different from the way in which they in fact did evolve, it remains the case that the predominant *Victorian* assumption was that the United Kingdom of Great Britain and Ireland had finally been 'formed'. All the inhabitants of the islands lying to the north-

---

[1] Cf. R. S. Tompson, *The Atlantic Archipelago: A Political History of the British Isles* (Lewiston, 1986); H. Kearney, *The British Isles: A History of Four Nations* (Cambridge, 1989).

west of France (or to the south-west of Scandinavia), with the exception of the Channel Islands and the Isle of Man, were at length, after 1800, embraced within a single polity with one Parliament and government at Westminster.

It seemed to most Victorian historians and constitutional commentators that this condition was indeed the climax of a process which was 'natural' and desirable. Whether the past that was pressed into service was a past that extended back one, two, three, four or five hundred years – or even a thousand or two thousand years – its telos had been realised. The manifest destiny of a United Kingdom had been achieved. These same writers pinpointed different turning-points along the way, but had little doubt that logic supported what had been accomplished. Coercion and consent, conquest and co-operation had all been present in this long process. There was, no doubt, much to criticise and much to commend in the formation of the United Kingdom but, now that it had happened, there could surely be 'no turning back'.

Such, frequently, was the 'scene from the centre' – hence the title of this paper. 'The centre', in this context, means the world of 'high politics' and the world of historiography. In general, it made little sense in such quarters to dispute the legitimacy, the efficacy and, indeed, the necessity of the United Kingdom. The creation of new states in contemporary Europe – most conspicuously 'Germany' and 'Italy', whether viewed with enthusiasm or apprehension – seemed to be confirmation of the fact that the age of small polities was past. The process of 'unification' exemplified the spirit of the times. The Habsburg or Romanov empires might, in time, disintegrate and allow, for example, the re-emergence of a Polish state, not to mention other conceivable entities; but, dissolution of the remaining empires apart, the prevalent emphasis was upon aggregation and integration, upon the crystall-isation of an identity supposed to be 'national'. The petty states of the Italian peninsula had no place in the 'modern' world. All sorts of arguments could be adduced to explain and endorse what was happening – economic, political, cultural. We know it from innumerable text books as the age of 'nationalism' or of 'the rise of the nation-state'. Of course, it is a picture which over recent decades has been subjected to much detailed criticism, as we have become ever more aware both that the 'nation' is itself a construct and of the extent to which other political calculations lay behind the slogans of nationalism. Many of us have become equally sceptical of the extent to which, in nineteenth-century Europe as a whole, it is possible to place the factors that explain nationalism in a firm hierarchy of significance.[2]

The relevance of debate about nineteenth-century European nationalism to an attempt to define the United Kingdom in 1832 is obvious. Was its formation a shining model and kind upon which, as in other spheres,

[2] M. Fulbrook (ed.), *National Histories and European History* (London, 1993); E. Hobsbawm, *Nations and Nationalism since 1780: Programme, Myth, Reality* (2nd edn, Cambridge, 1992).

mainland Europeans could be expected to gaze with admiration; or, on the contrary, was it a flawed and unstable creation, itself far from immune from the fissiparous tendencies which increasingly afflicted non-national empires on the mainland? If you wanted to form an enduring united kingdom, did you copy the insular variety or take a very different, perhaps contrary, route?[3]

The questions to be addressed, therefore, seem to me to cluster around the meanings we give to 'polity', and the relationship between 'polity' and 'identity', whether 'national' or 'multinational'.[4] I suggest at the outset that we do not necessarily have to decide in a simple and clear-cut fashion whether the United Kingdom was one or the other in the nineteenth century. Indeed, the way in which the United Kingdom was formed seems to me to preclude an unambiguous answer.

One way of evaluating the degree of 'integration' would be to examine the enduring viability of the resulting state-structure. Judged by this test, the Union between Ireland and Great Britain lasted only between 1800 and 1922. Since that latter date, it has only been the Union between Northern Ireland and Great Britain that has subsisted. If we accept that the establishment of the Irish Free State represented, in turn, the triumph of 'Irish nationalism', then it is self-evident that the United Kingdom in the nineteenth century was in reality a multinational state. The rupture, when it came, was the outcome of the inability of two nationalities, 'British' and 'Irish', to work together effectively in one state. On this reading, therefore, the Union of 1800, far from being the final stage in the formation of the United Kingdom, as some Victorians supposed, was merely a temporary arrangement which did not possess even the possibility of enduring viability. It is suggested that, insofar as the word is ever possible, the rupture of 1922 was inevitable. Ireland's 'manifest destiny' left no alternative.

An alternative interpretation, in its way equally extreme, suggests that the elaboration of an Irish national self-consciousness in the nineteenth century in no way made the Union inherently unworkable. It is argued that it was perfectly possible for distinctive national consciousnesses to be developed within 'Great Britain/Ireland', and that such multiple identities posed no threat to the maintenance of the state. In principle, it remained viable, and the path to the break-up of 'Great Britain/Ireland' was not preordained. The disruption of the state might never have occurred, or at least would not have occurred in the manner it did, but for a series of unpredictable events, not the least of which was the Great War.

A central position between these contrasting viewpoints would be to argue

---

[3] D. R. Watson, 'The British parliamentary system and the growth of constitutional government in Western Europe', in C. J. Bartlett (ed.), *Britain Pre-eminent: Studies in British World Influence in the Nineteenth Century* (London, 1969).

[4] W. Bloom, *Personal Identity, National Identity and International Relations* (Cambridge, 1990).

that it was the failure of 'Home Rule' rather than the existence of a sense of Irish identity which made separation highly likely. The United Kingdom, in the form it existed from 1800 onwards, was indeed not a viable creation. However, if Home Rule had been achieved in the last decades of the nineteenth century or before 1914, sufficient 'subsidiarity' would have been established to reconcile most Irishmen to the 'United Kingdom'. On this reading, the United Kingdom was a multinational state – but whether it could remain so depended not on 'nationalism' as such, but on specific constitutional changes, changes which in the event were not forthcoming.

It can also be pointed out that when the rupture between Britain and Ireland came, it was accompanied by the partition of Ireland. A geographically concentrated, religiously distinctive (though not homogeneous) part of the island of Ireland wished by majority to remain within the United Kingdom and to do so on the same basis as other parts. The devolved government in Northern Ireland had not been the original objective of Ulster Unionists, and was initially greeted with some suspicion because it presupposed that there was some kind of 'Ulster' identity. The majority in the North of Ireland took no great exception to the term 'British'. Thus, on the part of the majority in Ireland, the act of asserting the incompatibility of the sense of Irish identity with belonging to 'Britain' led to the partition of 'Ireland'.[5]

It may be argued, however, that Ireland was a 'special case' within the nineteenth-century United Kingdom. Do we not have to distinguish, on the one hand, between the peculiar circumstances of Irish history, over many centuries, which made its incorporation into the United Kingdom always problematic and precarious, and the course of 'British' history 'proper'? If so, the essential question before us concerns the multinational polity of 'Britain' itself. Leaving aside the Irish question as 'special', we need to focus on the question of whether the British polity was 'national' or 'multinational'. What are the relevant criteria to apply? How far back should we go?

Linda Colley, in *Britons* and elsewhere, has powerfully and impressively argued that

> War played a vital part in the invention of a British nation after 1707, but it could never have been so influential without other factors, in particular without the impact of religion. It was their common investment in Protestantism that first allowed the English, the Welsh and the Scots to come together, and to remain so, despite their many cultural divergencies.[6]

Her analysis of the process of 'forging a nation' between 1707 and 1837, as is

---

[5] M. A. G. O Tuathaigh, 'Ireland and Britain under the Union, 1800–1921: an overview', in P. J. Drudy (ed.), *Ireland and Britain since 1922* (Cambridge, 1986).

[6] L. Colley, *Britons: Forging the Nation 1707–1837* (2nd edn, London, 1994), pp. 367–8.

well known, sprang from two linked intentions – to uncover what 'Britons' thought they were being loyal to (against external threats) and to show how a sense of British national identity was forged.

I would not dispute the importance of 'the Other' as a means of sustaining a sense of common identity. Colley instances the fear of militant Catholicism and the existence of one or other hostile continental European power as major elements in the promotion of Britain. After 1707, she writes, the British 'came to define themselves as a single people not because of any political or cultural consensus at home, but rather in reaction to the Other beyond their shores'.[7] The fact that the Other was indeed beyond Britain's *shores* perhaps needs even more emphasis than she gives it. The image of the foreigner continued to be a fundamental means of self-definition throughout the nineteenth century, but while all societies, to a greater or lesser extent, define themselves in this way, it was *insularity* which gave it particular potency in the British case.[8] The perceptions of the French or the Germans were at some distance. The threat they or other peoples might pose at particular moments could be contained so long as command of the sea was maintained. The threat posed by France at the beginning of the nineteenth century could be replaced by the threat posed by Germany without the switch involving any profound cultural transformations. Individuals could be Francophobe, Germanophobe or Russophobe, along lines which had a certain rationality in particular contexts, but a sense of common identity could be sustained at another level by a general suspicion of continental alliances and alignments and a desire to be detached from them.

The issue before us, however, as we move through the nineteenth century, is whether the growing sense of Britishness which Colley has identified in terms of 'us' and 'them' was in the process of gaining any deeper internal grounding. She strongly contests the view that 'Britishness' in her period supplanted and obliterated other loyalties. Great Britain, she writes, did not emerge by way of a 'blending' of the different regional or older national cultures contained within its boundaries, on the one hand, or by the imposition of an English 'core' over a Celtic periphery, on the other. In support of this view she suggests (referring here to the 1990s) that even the briefest acquaintance with Great Britain will confirm that 'the Welsh, the Scottish and the English remain in many ways distinct peoples in cultural terms, just as all three countries continue to be sub-divided into different regions'.[9] That being the case, she believes it follows that a sense of common identity in Britain did not come into being because of an integration and homogenisation of

---

[7] Ibid., p. 6.

[8] C. F. Behrman, *Victorian Myths of the Sea* (Athens, Ohio, 1977); see also my essays, 'Insular outsider? "British History" and European integration', and 'Images of the foreigner in nineteenth- and twentieth-century Britain', both in K. Robbins, *History, Religion and Identity in Modern Britain* (London, 1993).

[9] Colley, *Britons*, p. 6.

disparate cultures but, rather, that it was superimposed over an array of internal differences in response to contact with the Other, particularly in response to *conflict* with the Other.

I have talked elsewhere of the 'Blending of Britain' and know that Colley feels that I am mistaken in the assumption (which I can be thought to share, for different reasons, with Michael Hechter)[10] that Great Britain could come into being only through the creation of some kind of cultural uniformity.[11] I can understand her unease, but do not, in fact, think that my position should be expressed in quite that way. In turn, I have some anxieties about her own view of the myths which could apparently be so effectively superimposed in the eighteenth century over the array of internal differences.

I do not, in fact, subscribe to the view that Great Britain 'could only come into being' through the creation of some kind of cultural uniformity. James VI and I did not style himself King of Great Britain because of a general recognition, north and south of the Border at the time, that cultural convergence had reached the point at which no other solution made sense. The Union of 1707, likewise, was not 'created' as a result of a blending which purveyed every facet of social and cultural life. I would argue, nevertheless, that we cannot be content with examining the question of 'Britishness' as a post-1707 'invention' which was 'superimposed' on internal differences, differences which it seems, in the late twentieth century, have proved as strong as, or stronger than, the superimposed myths. Of course, all historians tend to be prisoners of the particular period on which they focus their attention in a specific monograph. Arguably, however, the 'matter of Britain' has been on the agenda for as long as it is possible to write the history of these islands. Likewise, to infer from the supposed existence today of 'the English', 'the Welsh' and 'the Scottish' as culturally distinct peoples that, during the centuries, there has been no significant blending of their common statehood seems to beg a number of different questions. We need to ask more precisely what we mean by 'culturally distinct peoples', on the one hand, and, on the other, what we mean when we talk of a country 'coming into being'.

In my view, we should beware of imputing a deep underlying core of beliefs, attitudes, values, and genes transmitted in uncontaminated form among the English, the Welsh and the Scottish over centuries, even over a thousand years, upon which 'Britishness' was superimposed at a particular point in time – only for these 'core' cultural features to resume their 'natural' course once internal or external facts appear to diminish its utility. That is not at all to say that there are no cultural differences amongst the peoples of these islands. Colley is clearly right to recognise that even within 'England', 'Wales' and 'Scotland' there have been, and to some extent remain, deep cultural

[10] M. Hechter, *Internal Colonialism: The Celtic Fringe in British National Development, 1536–1966* (London, 1975).
[11] Colley, *Britons*, p. 386.

differences between 'regions' – but we must be wary of endowing such regions with an unchanging identity.[12]

It is, however, notoriously difficult to give precision to 'regions' within the British Isles. The extraordinary difficulty found at present in establishing the British representation on the post-Maastricht European Committee of the Regions is one indication of the problem.[13] The processes by which the English, the Welsh and the Scots became 'peoples', the date by which we may care to believe this to have occurred, and the institutional manifestations (or lack of them) of this distinctiveness cannot be uniformly described. The stereotypes and characterisations which attend these identities have themselves fluctuated over centuries. I am not seeking to deny the importance of some 'continuities', 'heritages' or 'traditions', but wish to make the obvious point that the cultural differences perceived in the present may be very different from the cultural differences perceived at various points in the past.

Great Britain did indeed 'come into existence' as a state at a particular point in time, but, in some sense of the term, 'blending' has been a consistent feature of the history of these islands considered in the *longue durée*. That blending has not been complete and has not occurred to the same extent in all fields of activity, but it is difficult to point to any period in which the communities and regions of 'Britain' as a whole have not established complex patterns of interaction, now in one direction, now in another, on which at different times and for different reasons have been superimposed symbols and myths of 'Englishness', 'Welshness' or 'Scottishness' – superimpositions with which some may feel more comfortable than with 'Britishness', but which, arguably, have no greater historical or eternal validity. Within England, too, mythology and reality mingle when we examine 'North' and 'South'.[14] In addition, in talking of 'regions' we must not overlook the enormous growth of London, capital of England, Great Britain, the United Kingdom and the British Empire. It was in London that communities gathered and dissolved from all over Britain/Ireland. In other words, at different times, for different levels of society, for different communities, for different individuals, it has been prudent or accurate to emphasise the one facet of identity rather than the other.

I do not believe, therefore, that the British state was 'created' by cultural homogeneity; but I do believe that its endurance during the period 1832–1922

[12] Ibid., p. 6.
[13] M. Kolinsky (ed.), *Divided Loyalties: British Regional Assertion and European Integration* (Manchester, 1978); C. Harvie, *The Rise of Regional Europe* (London, 1994).
[14] C. Kidd, *Subverting Scotland's Past: Scottish Whig Historians and the Creation of an Anglo-British Identity, 1689–c.1830* (Cambridge, 1993); N. Evans, 'Gogs, Cardis and Hwntws: regions, nation and state in Wales, 1840–1940', in N. Evans (ed.), *National Identity in the British Isles* (Harlech, 1989); P. Payton, *The Making of Modern Cornwall* (Redruth, 1992); and, for a long perspective, see H. M. Jewell, *The North–South Divide: The Origins of Northern Consciousness in England* (Manchester, 1994).

has to be explained not only by self-identification in relation to the Other and to that 'Protestantism' which Linda Colley stresses in the eighteenth century, but also by the fact that the process of 'blending' continued, even accelerated, in many spheres of life. It was assisted by travel, railways, education, migration, sport, commerce and literature, which did produce a certain blending that 'integrated' Britain. I have discussed some of these matters at greater length elsewhere and would not wish to repeat my comments here.[15] However, I do not wish to claim that this complex pattern of interaction and contact resulted in a culturally homogeneous country which totally obliterated distinct and separate pasts, whether conceived to be national or regional. It is not sufficient, in Scotland or Wales, to talk about a century which witnessed 'anglicisation', even supposing we know precisely what that term means. In short, there was a process of integration, but diversity was not eliminated and few sought to eliminate it. It was a process of integration, part contrived, part beyond the reach of contrivance, which makes it not inappropriate to speak of the making of a British nation whose sense of common identity and purpose outweighed in importance the still abiding consciousness of difference.

I would argue that, on balance, the successive extensions of the franchise and the broadening of political participation increased that sense of being part of a single political society. The mid-Victorian political elite had to seek to embrace the entire kingdom and undertake arduous and not altogether welcome travel to demonstrate their interest. In the person of William Gladstone, for example, one remarkable man served as an individual unifier of the kingdom by virtue of his own ancestry and connections. His role was even more important than that of the queen. He blended Britain as no-one else could.[16] Can we describe him, however, as a Scot? If so, he was a Scot who talked about 'England' in Scotland when referring to the British state.

Both major parties, however, succeeded in maintaining themselves – admittedly differentially in terms of support – throughout Britain during the nineteenth century. That is not to say that the tone and character of politics in Scotland was precisely the same as in England, or to claim that there were no substantial issues which were peculiar, at least in their intensity and resonance, in different parts of the country. In the decades immediately before 1914, 'Home Rule' became a significant issue within the Liberal politics of Scotland and Wales. It failed to make substantial progress as much because of regional differences within Scotland and Wales as for any other reason. The prominence of non-English politicians in the higher reaches of British

[15] K. Robbins, *Nineteenth-Century Britain: Integration and Diversity* (Oxford, 1988); paperback edition entitled *Nineteenth-Century Britain: England, Scotland and Wales: The Making of a Nation* (Oxford, 1989; new edn, 1995).

[16] Besides his Scottish links, Gladstone also had strong Welsh connections: see my 'Palmerston, Bright and Gladstone in north Wales', in K. Robbins, *Politicians, Diplomacy and War in Modern British History* (London, 1994).

governments was not confined to periods of Liberal government. There could not be a more convincing demonstration of the fact that Britain was *both* a multinational *and* a national country. No doubt partly in pursuit of a solution to the Irish question, prominent Liberal politicians, from the Foreign Secretary downwards, were explicit in their recognition both that there were three 'nations' within Britain and that they were inseparably linked to their mutual benefit.[17] Not the least of those benefits was the fact that the help of Scotland and Wales was normally required in order to make Liberal government possible. If Scotland had followed the path of Norway and seceded from a united kingdom, life would have become more difficult for English Liberals. Notwithstanding the fact that Scotsmen, by one definition or another, dominated the emerging Labour movement and talked sometimes of Home Rule, there was no doubt that Labour was firmly 'British'. The problems of the twentieth century would be solved by a united British working class. It is worth stressing, too, that these political tendencies went hand in hand with a burgeoning civil service whose perspective was largely unitary and metropolitan.

Ironically, however, it is in the sphere of religion that the differences between the nations of Britain remained explicit and contentious in the nineteenth century.[18] If we refer again to Linda Colley, she makes great play with the fact that as 'an invented nation' Britain was heavily dependent internally upon a broadly Protestant culture as an aspect of its *raison d'être*. Much depends upon how broad 'broadly Protestant' is conceived to be. It hardly needs to be said that 'Britain' had no Protestant Church. Study of the ecclesiastical/political relations between England and Scotland in the sixteenth and seventeenth centuries hardly suggests that 'Protestantism' in itself could provide a basis for agreement.[19] In the nineteenth century, the Churches of the three nations conspicuously did not blend. The splits and divisions in the Church of Scotland were scarcely comprehensible south of the Border. The issue of Disestablishment gave ecclesiastical politics a distinct flavour in Wales. Thus, while it may be conceded that Protestantism remained a kind of badge of common identity over against Catholic states, it is only at a very general level that this can apply. As much as providing a necessary support to 'Britishness', therefore, the ecclesiastical divisions within 'Protestantism' showed, as nothing else did to the same degree, that 'Britain' was a country of very considerable diversity and indeed disunity.[20] Even English Protestant

---

[17] 'There is an Irish national feeling and there is a national feeling in other parts of the United Kingdom. You cannot help it. The thing is there.' Cited in K. Robbins, *Sir Edward Grey: A Biography of Lord Grey of Fallodon* (London, 1971), p. 281.

[18] K. Robbins, 'Religion and community in Scotland and Wales since 1800', in S. Gilley and W. J. Sheils (eds.), *A History of Religion in Britain* (Oxford, 1994).

[19] See my 'Religion and identity in modern British history', in Robbins, *History, Religion and Identity*.

[20] See the review of Colley, *Britons*, by H. Wellenreuther, *Bulletin of the German Historical Institute, London*, xvi (2) (1994), pp. 11–17.

Dissenters could share with Roman Catholics a common sense of exclusion from the established order despite the theological differences between them.

The 'scene from the centre', as we have approached it, therefore presents a Britain which was unified but not uniform. It is difficult, however, to think of any episode, even including land struggles in Wales and Scotland, which seriously endangered the fabric of the state. By public gesture and legislation, the distinctiveness of the nations of Britain received recognition, though whether it was sufficient and whether it was patronising were matters on which there was and remains argument. It is difficult to be dogmatic as to whether this state of affairs represents 'integration', since the concept itself is puzzling. I have suggested that the 'national unity' of the Great War seemed to confirm the cohesion of Britain even as it rendered suspect the integrity of Britain/Ireland. The perception of the Other scarcely wavered. The contrast is made sharp if we compare the internal condition of Austria-Hungary as a 'multinational state' with Great Britain as a 'multinational state'. Judged by this yardstick, Britain could properly be considered a 'nation-state'.

No doubt, the integrity of 'Britain' was reinforced and strengthened further by the expansion of empire beyond even anything imagined in the eighteenth century. Whatever might have been the nature of the unity of the country within these islands, it was overseas that, through settlement, 'Greater Britain' became a reality. Whether in Canada, Australia or New Zealand, to take only three examples, 'England', 'Scotland' and 'Wales' could not be transplanted neat into a distant environment. Settlers were inescapably 'British' – though there were, of course, particular concentrations which gave individual communities a 'Scottish' ethos, for example – at least initially. Likewise, in India, Africa or elsewhere in the dependent Empire, 'the British' governed, traded, evangelised or fought, though within all these spheres little national niches could be found. Whatever Britain had been in the past, whatever it was in the process of becoming in the present, its global external projection – even if sometimes described as *The Expansion of England* – was a common focus of enterprise, pride and achievement. That such a small collection of islands should come to such a commanding position in the world could be explained, or at least justified, by a notion of providential mission or manifest destiny. The collection of virtues, capacities and qualities which had evolved in Britain were those required by an imperial race. Britain was itself now the centre of an imperial scene.

Yet alongside self-confidence went self-doubt, to be found even at the apogee of empire – as it retrospectively appeared. Could the Empire remain 'British'? Was not some imposing and effective mechanism of imperial federation required to sustain 'Britain overseas' and stave off the ambitions of nascent colonial nationalism? The 'Empire at War' between 1914 and 1918 gave grounds for both optimism and despondency about the 'endless adventure' that was the British mission in the world. The doomed character of these hopes and expectations needs little emphasis.[21]

The 'Formation of the United Kingdom' now excites interest not so much because it is seen as an inexorable process but because the nature of the United Kingdom now appears more problematic than ever it did in the long nineteenth century. Looked at over a long period of time, it may seem that the period between 1832 and 1922 was a 'sport' rather than a 'norm'. Whether the 'break-up of Britain', should it at length occur, is something which will benefit all the peoples of Britain is not something which the historian, *qua* historian, can determine. Perhaps that is just as well. We cannot fail to note, however, that historians of the United Kingdom seem, to outside observers, either outrageously explicit or curiously coy in the articulation of their own personal preferences and attitudes. 'Frameworks', it should be apparent, do not present themselves. They have to be constructed or deconstructed by historians – with political consequences of an unpredictable character.[22] A reading of the past suggests that even those whose detachment is most icy can only go so far in distancing themselves from the aspirations and assumptions of their own time as they seek to penetrate the totality of relationships within these islands. It does no harm to remind ourselves of this fact.

[21] For example, see E. M. Andrews, *The Anzac Illusion: Anglo-Australian Relations during World War I* (Cambridge, 1993).

[22] See my 'History, historians and twentieth-century British public life', in Robbins, *History, Religion and Identity*; and K. Robbins, *The Eclipse of a Great Power: Modern Britain, 1870–1992* (London, 1994).

Chapter 15

Letting go

The Conservative Party and the end of the Union with Ireland

John Turner

> To the Irish people said Mr Gladstone,
> 'The land which thou formerly hadst, own.'
> He never chopped down the thinnest tree
> Without thinking how it would affect his Ministry.[1]

This verse, written by an English schoolboy in the 1890s, happily captures two of the three themes of this essay. The first theme is that, from an English perspective, the role of Ireland in the United Kingdom was distinctive and ambiguous, and raises important questions about the nature of the Union at the end of the nineteenth century. The second theme is that the great developments in the history of the Union in the late nineteenth and early twentieth centuries, which culminated in the establishment of the Irish Free State but did not change the relationships between Scotland and Wales and the rest of the Union, were entangled in the struggles of Westminster politics. The third theme of the essay is that the First World War cast a strong, if unnatural, light on British attitudes to the nature of the Union, from which there is much to be learned about Britain as a national or multi-national state. Each of these themes is illustrated by an examination of the position taken by the Conservative and Unionist Party, whose very name and existence were predicated on maintaining the Union with Ireland, towards the separation of Southern Ireland as it developed from nightmare to reality between 1917 and 1921.

The dissolution of the Union with Ireland, which was brought about by the Irish Treaty of 1921, reminds the historian of two things. The first is that we cannot afford to be Whiggish about the unity of the United Kingdom. It was quite possible for the processes which formed the Union to be challenged by contrary processes which tended to dissolve it. The second is that although the nature of the United Kingdom must be understood socially, culturally and economically well as politically, politics can sometimes dominate the long-term outcome by contingent events in the short term. Between 1917 and 1921

---

[1] Unattributed verse, originally composed between 1891 and 1893, from E. C. Bentley *et al.*, *The First Clerihews* (Oxford, 1982), p. 44.

there was an attempt to stabilise the Union which ended with a fairly convincing bid to give most of Ireland away in order to preserve the rest. Like any political process it was conducted in a fog of uncertainty; its outcome owed as much to the unintended consequences of action as to the wisdom of a plan; and it was all done in a language which has concealed as much from historians as it ever conveyed to contemporaries. In a volume devoted to the problematic nature of the United Kingdom, it seems only appropriate to contribute a little more to the ambiguity of explanation by exploring this challenging episode in some depth. The Conservative and Unionist Party dominated British government for the whole period during which the separation was first fought over, and then negotiated. Yet it was able to contemplate the establishment of the Free State and the effective 'loss' of the area which is now the Irish Republic. To explain this conundrum we have to look more closely at the forces which shaped British politics in the early twentieth century. This closer look suggests that the fate of the Union depended more and more on the vagaries of Westminster politics, and that the hegemony of 'Britain' as a definition of the United Kingdom was strongly influenced by the political needs of England.

Recent work on patriotism has revealed the essentially problematic nature of British national identity.[2] Patriotism was by no means the preserve of the governing classes, political or military, and once it escaped the confines of a national governing class it was hard to pin down and especially hard to associate with an unambiguous notion of the United Kingdom as a unitary nation-state. Much recent discussion has focused on the patriotism and national feeling of the working classes and (something different) of the left,[3] but this has very often been taken from the point of view of the English working classes, especially those of the metropolitan areas. This is not entirely unreasonable: the overwhelming majority of the inhabitants of Great Britain were English, and the overwhelming majority lived in towns, with a bias towards the conurbations of London, Lancashire and the West Riding (but also towards those of the banks of the Clyde). Being English, however, did not exclude the possibility of feeling different from English people from other areas and defining them as 'the Other'. The perceived differences between Yorkshire and Lancashire were more than a music-hall joke: Norman Tebbit's recently defined 'cricket test' for national identity would clearly have shown the two counties to be hostile nations. It is significant that one of the most powerful working-class organisations at the turn of the century, the Miners' Federation of Great Britain, had to adopt a loose federal structure to accommodate the regional differences in its members' interests. Moreover the

---

[2] R. Samuel, *Patriotism: The Making and Unmaking of British National Identity*, vol. I: *History and Politics* (London, 1989).

[3] P. Ward, 'Englishness, patriotism and the British left, 1881–1924' (London University Ph.D. thesis, 1994). See also E. Evans, 'Englishness and Britishness: national identities, *c*.1790–*c*.1870', above, ch. 13.

sentiments of Glaswegians, and of the inhabitants of south Wales, were inextricably bound up with not being English. Even more obviously, the inhabitants of north Wales, and those from the south who still spoke Welsh, were manifestly not English at all, a point which could be made in respect of language, of both high and popular culture, and of politics. The self-conscious revival of Celtic languages at the turn of the century, coupled with a marked revival of nonconformist Protestant religion which rejected the Anglican Church, can leave us in little doubt that, whatever pressures there were for a political and cultural convergence within Great Britain, centrifugal forces were also at work. It is therefore not unreasonable to regard the Union at the turn of the twentieth century as being genuinely divided into distinct, and self-conscious, nations, which were often further divided into localities which were themselves the objects of loyalty and were the means of self-definition for individuals. It was common to distinguish between Highland and Lowland Scots, between those from south Wales and those from the central and northern regions, between Londoners and Liverpudlians or between Yorkshiremen and 'Geordies'.

This generalisation, of course, requires immediate qualification. Whereas a Scottish or Welsh sense of nationhood could be discussed, as Gladstone once discussed it, in the same context as the emergent nationalisms of Eastern, Central and Southern Europe (he put Irish nationalism low on the list, far below that of the Czechs), it would be difficult to discuss English nationalism in the same sense, because English politics and culture were as hegemonic as the politics and culture of Vienna. However, the smaller partners in the Union were fertile ground for the self-assertion which had long been part of the Romantic political tradition in Europe. Scottish and Welsh national identities were partly manufactured by middle-class antiquarians, professional explorers in the past who brought back trophies rather than systematic understanding. Yet that was no less true of the English traditions and cultural identities being manufactured with all sorts of ulterior motives by writers from Dickens to William Morris and from Robert Blatchford to Rudyard Kipling. One consequence was that identity became consolidated at a convenient level which could readily be understood and transmitted in fiction or popular journalism, and the Scottish and Welsh 'nations' were just such convenient levels. There was no necessary incompatibility between being Welsh and being British, but there was a real incompatibility between being Welsh and being English which could take many forms. The appearance of Welsh chapels in south London at the turn of the century to serve the Welsh community in its metropolitan exile was entirely benign towards the Union, as were the revived Eisteddfod meetings. The anti-English rhetoric in David Lloyd George's early anti-landlord campaigns in north Wales in the 1880s was more strident. Without the benefit of a living second language, but helped by a larger population and a longer tradition of high culture backed by an ancient university system and independent legal and ecclesiastical structures, Scotland also maintained a sense of separateness. Scotland, even more than Wales, had its parallel elites and its own Established Church.

All this is perhaps only to make the point that late nineteenth-century society in Great Britain allowed many cultural and social representations of nationhood, some of which were complementary to a supranational United Kingdom and some of which were somewhat at odds with it. In political terms this diversity was matched by a diversity of political preference. Notoriously, the Liberal Party was strongest in what contemporaries liked to call the 'Celtic fringe' and in some rural areas, while the Conservative Party, especially after the electoral reforms of 1883–5, saw most of its parliamentary strength in England and especially in the suburban seats. Political parties were themselves national, in the minimum sense that the same party labels were used throughout England, Wales and Scotland, and that MPs once elected also tended to conform to a common party discipline. There were nonetheless marked differences between the countries of Great Britain in the extent to which political allegiance was focused on Westminster or on local groupings. In Scotland, which throughout the period between the 1883–5 reforms and the First World War was consistently more favourable to the Liberals than to the Conservatives, parliamentary politics could seem an entirely Westminster affair. In 1912 H. H. Asquith, then Prime Minister of a glitteringly talented Liberal government and himself a K.C. and the MP for East Fife, contentedly observed a Scottish landscape and remarked that 'as far as the eye can see, these rolling hills are represented at Westminster by London barristers'. It was not so in Wales, where an even stronger Liberal group of MPs was largely home-grown, was capable of and inclined towards caucusing together for Welsh (Liberal) interests, and allowed itself a bitter feud when Lloyd George and D. A. Thomas battled for the leadership before the Boer War.

The differences between the three countries of Great Britain on the one hand and Ireland, the fourth member of the Union, on the other therefore need to be handled rather cautiously. Politically, administratively, legally, economically and culturally each part of the Union had a different relationship with England and London. Wales had a common legal system and a close economic integration with English industry, but a distinctive political style and a resurgent national language and culture. It shared an Established Church with England, but the majority of church-goers were Nonconformist. It had a territorial aristocracy which was closely associated with England but was regarded as Welsh by the English. Scotland had a distinct legal and administrative system but close economic integration, and a self-confident indigenous culture expressed in Scots English rather than in Gaelic, but a political system which had converged with the English party system. It had its own Established Church, and a plurality of denominational allegiances. Its aristocracy was more obviously Scottish than the Welsh was obviously Welsh.

Ireland, unlike either Wales or Scotland, was unlike England as well.

Divisions within Irish society were more marked, and more widely recognised outside Ireland, than were divisions in Welsh or Scottish society. Divisions in the agricultural south between a Catholic peasantry and an Anglican (and often absent) landowning class were bitter and notorious; in the north an urban manufacturing sector dominated by a Protestant nonconformist population was by the end of the nineteenth century lightly admixed with an immigrant Catholic community in Belfast. Since the Act of Union in 1800 the internal politics of Ireland had been dominated by the shortage of land in the South and by sectarian conflict in the North-East, in both urban and rural areas; indeed the jerky progress towards the political enfranchisement of southern Irish Catholics had been accompanied during the nineteenth century by an equally jerky development of Orangeism which had its roots in rural Protestant Ulster but which had become a political movement of urban areas whose effect, and perhaps also whose purpose, was to inhibit the emergence of a self-conscious working class in the industrial North-East.

Moreover, the massive emigration of the Irish to Great Britain, whether as a destination or as a resting place on the way to North America, made Irish problems known, if not understood, in England and Scotland in the late nineteenth century. Glasgow, Liverpool and Manchester had significant populations of immigrants and first-generation descendants of immigrants. David Fitzpatrick has shown that these immigrants were dispersed beyond the main conurbations, and has further shown that the Protestant population of north-east Ireland was responsible for significant emigration to Scotland,[4] which was consistent with the close economic integration between the predominantly Protestant counties of Ulster and the industrial areas of the west of Scotland and the north-west of England.

Ireland thus appeared to Britain in a number of guises. Since the Act of Union, it was legally part of the same nation-state with the same Established Church and the same Parliament. Social problems within Ireland were perceived as the special consequence of a peculiarly unhappy combination of economic misfortune (in the shape of the Famine) and an unhelpful land-tenure system. Westminster politicians could thus argue over the rights and wrongs of maintaining the established social structure of southern Ireland, and although the point was contested there was a widespread support for the Disraelian view which saw the inevitability of some change in a system which inherently had no future. But British political responses to Ireland were also influenced by the predicament of the Irish in Britain, who constituted a depressed and underprivileged minority, readily identifiable and associated with all sorts of social and economic problems characteristic of the poorer parts of cities. In the west of Scotland and in Liverpool the full range of Irish social antagonisms was simply transplanted to British soil, with violent

---

[4] D. Fitzpatrick, 'A curious middle place: the Irish in Britain, 1871–1921', in R. Swift and S. Gilley (eds.), *The Irish In Britain 1815–1939* (London, 1989).

sectarian conflict a normal part of the political process.[5] Welsh and Scottish immigrants to English cities did not bring their politics with them, were not associated in popular discourse[6] with poverty and crime, and did not have a socio-political problem back home with which the host community could engage. In fact the relative indifference of the Irish in Britain to the political problems of the Ireland which they had left has been well documented by historians, but these were subtleties of which neither the British public nor, apparently, the British political classes were fully aware.[7] Ireland, in short, was different, and this difference goes some way to explain why its part in the Union was differently perceived by those whose political instincts were to defend the Union.

Furthermore, Ireland was in many ways treated as a colony, with a separate system for enforcing public order based on Resident Magistrates, and an administrative system which emphasised subordination as well as difference by locating power in a Lord Lieutenant or viceroy with an administration in Dublin castle which was under the political tutelage of a single minister, the Chief Secretary, who was not always even in the Cabinet.[8] Westminster-inspired 'solutions' of the Irish 'problem' were delivered by an imperial metropolis to a colonial dependency, whether they were straightforwardly oppressive after the fashion of successive Liberal and Conservative 'Coercion Acts' which withdrew various civil liberties from Irish subjects of the Crown, or socially palliative like the Land Acts, or devised to deliver political concessions like the ill-fated Home Rule Bills of 1886 and 1894. At the same time the Catholic Irish, whether they lived in Ireland or in England, whether they were peasants, migrant labourers, professionals or politicians, were treated by the English political elite as an inferior race.[9]

The end of the Union with Ireland, a process with its immediate antecedents in the Liberal government's decision in 1912 to make a third attempt to grant

[5] See, e.g., P. Waller, *Democracy and Sectarianism: A Political and Social History of Liverpool, 1868–1939* (Liverpool, 1981); S. Gilley, 'English attitudes to the Irish in England, 1780–1900', in C. Holmes (ed.), *Immigrants and Minorities in British Society* (London, 1978); cf. Evans, 'Englishness and Britishness', above, pp. 236–40.

[6] Or indeed in expert discourse: Mayhew, Booth, Rowntree and all their imitators were preoccupied with the identifiable relationship between Irish populations and social stress.

[7] I. O'Day, 'The political organisation of the Irish in Britain, 1867–90', in Swift and Gilley, *Irish in Britain*.

[8] See C. Townshend, *Political Violence in Ireland: Government and Resistance since 1848* (Oxford, 1983); C. Townshend, *Making the Peace: Public Order and Public Security in Modern Britain* (Oxford, 1993), pp. 23–4. Townshend refers to the 'demi-colonial' status of Ireland.

[9] I am obliged to Professor the Earl Russell for the following Irish 'joke' which family legend attributed to his great-grandfather, Lord John Russell: 'An Irish Member was addressing the House of Commons with great emotion on an agricultural subject. From the public gallery a coconut was hurled down into the chamber, splitting in two upon the Irishman's skull. "Mr Speaker," said the affronted Member, "I must protest. A man has spat upon my head."' A similar cast of mind is evident in the depiction of the Irish, simian in features and in intellect, in contemporary *Punch* cartoons.

Home Rule to the country, has not lacked historians. The outline of events is therefore fairly clear. Seen as a problem in British and imperial politics, the Irish Union was fairly secure until the end of the first decade of the twentieth century. Of the competing Liberal and Conservative solutions to the problem of discontent in Ireland, the Conservative solution had won through with Wyndham's 1903 Land Act, which not only set up a legal framework for changing tenancies into freeholds and thus permitting the consolidation of holdings into larger and more economic units, but also made finance available to carry the policy through. The Act thus gave to Ireland what Gladstone's Land Acts had quite failed to give, despite their good intentions: a firm basis for capitalist agriculture. A slowly growing prosperity began to marginalise the discontent which had powered the Nationalist political movement.

By 1912 Irish Nationalist members, more numerous than the population of Ireland would justify, were more or less reliable but subordinate partners in the Liberal–Labour–Irish parliamentary group which supported the Liberal government after the 1910 elections. At local level the Nationalist Party, originally built up by Charles Stuart Parnell, was secure, relying on the support of the Catholic Church and on local elites, even though the agrarian distress on which its early successes had been based during the 1870s and 1880s had diminished in significance. The party was also recovering from the effects of the split between Parnellites and anti-Parnellites occasioned by Parnell's unconventional private life; and despite the solid if unimaginative leadership of John Redmond it still faced competition in Cork from the All for Ireland League under William O'Brien and Tim Healy. While the Nationalist Party itself was too weak to rock the Westminster boat with its, by now routine, demand for a limited form of devolution to an Irish assembly, the more extreme forms of nationalist sentiment had only the limited expression of cultural organisations such as the Gaelic League and movements such as *Sinn Fein* which sought, rather as movements were doing all over Europe, to recreate a nation in the image of a partially forgotten culture. It was difficult to imagine any form of Irish nationalism as a serious threat to the status quo.

The conventional wisdom about what happened next is interestingly anti-Whiggish. In this conventional view a number of contingencies first turned this stable situation into an unstable one, and then the resultant mess caused the post-War government to lose commitment to the efforts involved in restoring a stable Union. The Free State ensued, which already had an independent spirit and soon acquired an independent status. The contingencies in themselves make a fairly impressive narrative catalogue. In 1912, to appease their Irish parliamentary supporters, Asquith's Liberal government blew the dust off the 1894 Home Rule Bill and presented it to Parliament;[10]

---

[10] See P. Jalland, *The Liberals and Ireland: The Ulster Question in British Politics to 1914* (Brighton, 1980), which indicates the narrow limits within which Liberal politicians conceived the problem they faced when setting up new constitutional arrangements for Ireland, and rightly emphasises the Liberals' concentration on Westminster problems while a civil war developed in north-east Ireland.

Ulster and Ulster's Conservative allies brewed up a fierce resistance, and the conflagration was only damped down by the outbreak of war, which Asquith appropriately and candidly described as an amazing stroke of luck.[11]

With the Home Rule Act sitting on the statute book in a 'suspended' state which no-one could define, the government ignored Ireland's problems until the Easter of 1916, when a handful of patriots launched a futile and unpopular *coup de théâtre* in Dublin. By chance, an unusually incompetent British officer was in command in Ireland, and the subsequent brutal and ineffective repression turned decent apathetic Irish citizens into active nationalists whose political safety-valve was not the Nationalist Party but the *Sinn Fein* movement, which soon turned itself into a political organisation. Meanwhile the Liberal Prime Minister, operating in the uncomfortable context of a coalition whose Conservative members he despised, tried to solve a number of political problems at once by handing the poisoned chalice of the Irish problem to his great Liberal rival, David Lloyd George. Lloyd George stitched up an agreement with Redmond, the Nationalist leader, and Sir Edward Carson, the Ulster Unionist leader, which predictably annoyed the Conservative Party and the Irish Unionists outside Ulster, and was therefore rejected. Although this expedient did not help the Irish problem at all, it succeeded in distracting Lloyd George for a while, which was entirely to its credit from Asquith's point of view. In Ireland *Sinn Fein* went from strength to strength in by-elections and public demonstrations, while in London the Irish problem was soon redefined as the problem of keeping Ireland loyal not to the Empire but to the Nationalist Party, which was at least a safer pair of hands than those of the separatists.

The contingent argument goes on in a suitably contingent vein. Because the leaders in London, whose strategy this was, were rather preoccupied with other great events such as the battle of the Somme, the near-collapse of sterling in the autumn of 1916, and the replacement of Asquith by Lloyd George as the leader of a new and more Conservative coalition in December, they omitted to make any progress towards an Irish settlement. By March 1917 the issue had been put off long enough for it to be submitted to the collective wisdom of the Dominion Prime Ministers, who had been summoned to London for an 'Imperial War Cabinet'. Meanwhile the mutual impatience of Ulster Unionists and Irish Nationalists had led to angry confrontations in the House of Commons. The deadlock was apparently broken by the invention of the Irish Convention, a strange cross between a constituent assembly and a Buddhist retreat, in which Nationalist and Unionist politicians, all Irish, agreed to talk about the future shape of an Irish political settlement. This allowed Redmond, Carson and their close colleagues to assure unhappy supporters that some progress was being made or (in Carson's case) that no progress was really being made at all. The Convention

---

[11] C. Hazlehurst, *Politicians at War, 1914–1915* (London, 1970).

opened at Trinity College, Dublin, in July 1917, and most Westminster politicians, especially those in government, hoped that they need not think further about Ireland for a very long time.

Historians differ in their emphasis on the reasons for the failure of the Irish Convention, which broke up acrimoniously in May 1918. One school of thought, citing the repeated attempts by the Convention's chairman Horace Plunkett to bring the British government back into play, holds that it fell apart under the weight of its own internal contradictions. *Sinn Fein* was absent, the Ulster Unionists were under the close supervision of a monitoring committee whose job was to ensure that the delegates did not agree to anything, and the majority of the Irish Nationalist delegates were drawn from the most fossilised parts of the machine. Only the more flexible Nationalists and the Southern Unionists were prepared to have a meeting of minds which could encourage the Unionists into a governing structure which Nationalists would accept. The other school of thought points to the negligence of the Westminster government, which made little effort to help the Convention around difficult corners, and finally destroyed all hope of progress by insisting in May 1918 that military conscription should be applied immediately to Ireland, which had hitherto been exempt.[12]

Both explanations clearly have something to contribute, and both play a part in a sequence of contingent explanations which accounts for why the population of southern Ireland was, by the end of the year, so disenchanted with the Nationalists and with the British government that it returned a slate of *Sinn Fein* members in the general election of 1918. With the Nationalist Party, ironically, reduced to a handful of seats in Ulster, and the Ulster Unionists as defiant as ever, the prospect of negotiating a way out of Ireland's problems retreated. The year 1919 saw the outbreak of guerrilla warfare which soon escalated into the first campaign of the long retreat from empire.[13] The government, led in this regard by a Conservative, Walter Long, prepared the 1920 Government of Ireland Act on federal lines, which would have devolved limited power both to Ulster and to Southern Ireland.[14] Even this was overtaken by events, and by 1921 it was all over: both sides had fought to exhaustion and the best way forward seemed to be an agreement for a *de facto* divorce. British public opinion and the British government had lost the stomach for a fight.[15] Partition, which had often been discussed but never embraced wholeheartedly by political leaders, was adopted by default. The

[12] For internal contradictions, see the *locus classicus* R. B. McDowell, *The Irish Convention, 1917–1918* (London, 1970); for conscription and neglect, see A. J. Ward, 'Lloyd George and the 1918 Conscription Crisis', *Historical Journal*, xvii (1974); and, more fully, J. Turner, *British Politics and the Great War* (New Haven and London, 1992), pp. 242–8, 278–93.

[13] C. Townshend, *The British Campaign in Ireland, 1919–21* (Oxford, 1975).

[14] Although the importance of federalism in Britain's Irish policy has been carefully treated in J. E. Kendle, *Ireland and the Federal Solution: The Debate over the United Kingdom Constitution, 1870–1921* (Kingston, Ontario, 1989), the mechanics of policy-making over the Bill in 1919–20 await a full analysis.

[15] D. G. Boyce, *Englishmen and Irish Troubles* (London, 1972).

Union was renamed 'The United Kingdom of Great Britain and Northern Ireland', and the traditional hatreds of Irish politics slumbered uneasily for nearly fifty years until 1969.

After such a catalogue of woeful accidents and misjudgements, it is easy enough to conclude that but for the circumstances of the 1912 Bill, or the War, or the decision to impose conscription, or the distraction of opinion in Great Britain in the early 1920s, there would have been no such breakdown in a relationship which had, if anything, become more stable if not actually affectionate in the century since the Act of Union. But as an historical judgement, this account depends rather heavily on the presumption that the policy of late nineteenth-century governments towards Ireland had indeed had the effect of 'pacifying' the country, and that the antagonisms latent in Irish society were indeed cooling by 1911. As such, it is no more satisfactory than the alternative, and highly Whiggish, view that the emergent nationalism of nineteenth-century Ireland, once blessed by the great figure of W. E. Gladstone, was bound to triumph over Unionism in the end, just as the working classes were more or less at the same time bound to achieve a political apotheosis in Labour's defeat of Liberalism.

An alternative reading which deserves exploration depends much more on an analysis of the nature of Unionist preoccupations during the half-century before the Irish Treaty. To get at an idea of what the Union was, let us try to explore what Unionism thought it was about. It might be appropriate to start at the end, with a remark made by an experienced Unionist politician, William Bridgeman, during the House of Commons debates over the Irish Treaty Bill in December 1921. He wrote to his wife:

> I don't feel that the position is a difficult one to defend – but there will always be people who learn nothing & can't get out of the old ruts. It is said to be a surrender to murder. It may have been a surrender to enter into conference with murderers – but we were asked to do that by the Southern Unionists (Midleton etc.) – & if you were to negotiate at all there was no one else to negotiate with. But in the settlement we have surrendered nothing which in my opinion we could not have agreed at any time since 1914, when we were beaten over the Union ... The Unionist Party got Ulster out of the Home Rule Bill and kept her out.
>
> The real issue was this. Were we to fight it out till we had exterminated the Sinn Feinians (in America, Australia etc. as well as Ireland) which would have entailed the devastation of southern and western Ireland, or to make a last effort for a settlement by negotiation.
>
> If the settlement is a failure as the bigots predict, & results in more murders & the invasion of Ulster we shall be in no worse a position than we were in before. On the contrary we shall be in a better position, for we shall then fight them with the whole civilised world assured that we

have gone to the furthest possible limit of conciliation – & universal opinion will be with us & not against us.[16]

This passage, admittedly the private thought of a single individual, but certainly representing the dominant political position of the Conservative leadership in late 1921, has much to yield. First, the rejection of the Diehards is characteristic of the mind of Conservative leaders in the early twentieth century. Bitter experience over the Parliament Act of 1911 had convinced most of them that a party divided would always lose, and could be more gravely injured by standing in the path of a juggernaut, wherever that juggernaut happened to be going. Second, the analysis of what had happened in 1914 is particularly cogent: the Unionists had already lost the Union, and the remaining task was the protection of Ulster, which had been achieved by the 1921 Treaty. Third, the withdrawal from southern and western Ireland is a manoeuvre to be executed in the light of international publicity. The 'civilised world' – which in this case seems to mean public opinion in the Dominions and the United States – was expecting a decent settlement. A distant but telling analogy could be drawn with the Conservative Party's internal discussions in the 1950s and early 1960s about withdrawal from the African empire. Then the government drew up a balance sheet of the costs and benefits of holding on to the African colonies, concluded that the costs were greater than the benefits, and negotiated its way out of Africa over a ten-year period, trying with very limited success to protect the interests of white settlers (whose political role among Westminster Tories was not unlike that of Ulster politicians in the first and second decades of the twentieth century). In short, the retreat from the Irish Union was seen, *even at the time*, as a process of decolonisation rather than as a dismemberment of the integrity of the United Kingdom.

How might this have come about? Once more, one element of the explanation must be sought in the evolution of Unionist language during the latter part of the nineteenth century; another element is the entanglement of Unionism with a system of party politics whose focus and *raison d'être* were by now English rather than British. Let us take these points in order.

On the one hand, the nature of the 'Irish problem' as understood by Westminster politicians underwent a significant change after the 1870s. Early perceptions of its nature in Britain were so closely focused on the agrarian problem that solutions were sought in land reform (the carrot) and coercive measures against agrarian unrest (the stick). This was the essence of Gladstone's policy in his first government. It could not survive the change in political tactics by Irish politicians who united the idea of agrarian reform with the idea of self-government. As John Vincent showed years ago, the

---

[16] Bridgeman to C. Bridgeman, 19 December 1921, from the Bridgeman Papers, reprinted in *The Modernisation of Conservative Politics: The Diaries and Letters of William Bridgeman, 1904–1935*, ed. P. Williamson (London, 1988), p. 154.

adoption of a Home Rule position by Gladstone in 1885 is best understood as part of a game of double-bluff in the long-running contest for the leadership of the Liberal Party.[17] The Conservative Party had traditionally taken a line about Irish social change which was more robust (and more hostile to the Catholic Church) than Gladstone's early Liberal policy, but the differences of principle were not great. In the 1880s Randolph Churchill took matters further by marrying his own vision of educational and social reform in Ireland to the idea of an alliance between energetic Tories and Redmond's new-minted Nationalist movement. He had earlier observed, in 1877, that 'England had years of wrong, years of crime, years of tyranny, years of oppression, years of general misgovernment to make amends for in Ireland';[18] and this was a line pursued with the closest Churchill could get to consistency in the next few years. It goes without saying that Randolph Churchill was not a typical Conservative, but on Ireland his position was at this time consistent with, and largely derived from, opinions which were held in moderate Unionist circles in Dublin. It was not inconsistent with an aggressive hostility to Home Rule when that was first proposed by the Liberals. Nor was it inconsistent with the political tactic of exciting Ulster opinion against the Catholic south.

The majority of Conservative leaders in the 1880s, when they thought about Ireland at all, regarded it as a country with a unique and unfortunate past which, although it was populated by a native race with distinctly mutinous tendencies, was steadily being integrated into the Union. Conservative legislation towards Ireland followed this pattern of thought, in its legislation on county councils (1888), its educational legislation, and even its land legislation culminating in Wyndham's Act (1903). However, the rhetoric of union within the United Kingdom was steadily being overhauled by an alternative rhetoric of imperial unity, which gained considerable impetus from the launch of the Tariff Reform movement in 1903 and also emerged in the active discussions of closer imperial union associated with Lord Milner after his return from South Africa in 1905.

The rhetoric of imperial unity was, as some of its critics were keenly aware, highly subversive of the status quo in the United Kingdom. It sought to legitimise British imperial domination of the Empire by re-inventing the Westminster Parliament as an 'Imperial Parliament', a phrase and a concept which crop up with increasing frequency in political debate during the Edwardian decade. This was not wholly welcome to the self-governing white dominions, and the leading proponents of imperial unity had some trouble in persuading Australian and Canadian politicians that the idea was not a recolonisation of their societies. The price of doing so was a protracted discussion of the formal devolution of power to subordinate assemblies, of

[17] J. R. Vincent, 'Gladstone and Ireland', *Proceedings of the British Academy*, lxiii (1977).
[18] A speech in 1877 at the Woodstock Agricultural Show, cited by R. F. Foster, *Randolph Churchill* (Oxford, 1981), p. 43.

which the best known examples are in the work of Lionel Curtis and the Round Table movement.[19] Curtis was not widely admired in British politics, but Milner's influence was greater, and the willingness of politicians such as the earl of Selborne (Milner's successor in South Africa) to discuss the idea made it an important one. Simultaneously the pressure of business at Westminster, coupled with the strictly partisan feeling that Liberals were neglecting important matters such as the Empire in order to pass their wicked socialist measures, led Conservatives such as Walter Long to contemplate the establishment of subordinate legislative assemblies in the United Kingdom.[20]

In many ways the idea of United Kingdom devolution was a dangerous temptation for Conservative defenders of the Union with Ireland. Under the guise of 'Home Rule All Round' it was a convenient wrecking phrase when the idea of Irish Home Rule was revived in 1911–12.[21] Yet it seemed to encourage some Conservative politicians either to accept, albeit covertly, the general thrust of the Liberal government's proposals, or to deflect them into directions which were not what the Liberals had first intended but still compromised a pure Unionist position. Take as an example the sentiments of J. L. Garvin of the *Observer*, writing to Balfour in October 1910:

> Thinking the present Dublin Castle system now untenable – some form of devolution inevitable – I cannot think it now impossible to frame a safe constructive compromise between the Gladstonian Home Rule which has perished – what greater justification of the struggle against it? – and the old Unionist position which has now lost so much of its old basis. Since then a generation has passed away ...
>
> Would not an Ireland under Federal Home Rule on the Quebec model or so, send a solid *majority* of Conservatives to help defend in the Imperial Parliament nearly all we care for?[22]

This was just slightly less of a fantasy than might have been imagined; Conservative and Unionist candidates could regularly turn out 60,000 votes in Ireland, just under a tenth of the electorate, but Garvin's reasoning was that most of the Nationalist votes would evaporate once some version of devolution had been granted.

Garvin's suggestion was immediately repudiated by Austen Chamberlain, but not in terms which would indicate a difference of principle: he objected to Garvin's shouting the idea from the house-tops in his newspaper, and feared the consequences if either Liberal or Irish politicians took it as the first step on the road to independence, rather than as a final settlement. But at the same

---

[19] J. E. Kendle, *The Round Table Movement and Imperial Union* (Toronto, 1975).

[20] This is discussed fully in R. P. Murphy, 'Walter Long and the Conservative Party, 1905–1921' (Bristol University Ph.D. thesis, 1984), and R. P. Murphy, 'Faction in the Conservative Party and the Home Rule Crisis, 1912–14', *Historical Journal*, lxxi (1986).

[21] J. E. Kendle, 'The Round Table Movement and "Home Rule All Round"', *Historical Journal*, xi (1968).

[22] Quoted in Austen Chamberlain, *Politics from Inside: An Epistolary Chronicle* (London, 1936), p. 280.

time the Tory leadership was receiving, and considering very seriously, coalition proposals from Lloyd George which would have encompassed, besides a settlement of a large number of other outstanding disagreements, including the 1909 Budget and the question of naval armaments, a devolution of some powers to Provincial Councils, including an Irish Council.[23] The internal Conservative debate on the Irish proposals was very fierce, revealing a flexibility among some leaders – notably Chamberlain – and a desperate clinging to the Union by others. Lord Salisbury was even prepared to concede the introduction of elected or nominated members of the House of Lords rather than to submit to Liberal proposals for Home Rule because 'We are fighting not for our hereditary privileges, but for the Union, and we are prepared to make even the greatest sacrifices.'[24]

The coalition proposals were part of a political manoeuvre which failed to come off for many reasons, only one of which was the intransigence of the extreme Unionists in the Conservative Party.[25] Instead, the constitutional deadlock of 1910 over the powers of the House of Lords was resolved by a general election which the Liberals just managed to win, and the Liberals continued to govern with support from the Irish Nationalist Party and the Labour Party. The contingencies mentioned at the beginning of this essay took over, Unionist hostility to Home Rule *as it was presented to them* became intense, and the result was that Conservative objection to the government's policy was carried to the length of appearing to support armed insurrection in Ulster.

It is at this point, though, that it seems proper to introduce another aspect of the alternative reading of Conservative attitudes. This is that between 1886 and 1912 the Conservatives, while formalising their links with the Liberal Unionists and thus with the name and form of Unionism as a political objective, had in fact become increasingly an *English* party with a strategic objective focused on Westminster. Even Randolph Churchill, whose understanding of Irish problems was rather greater than that of most of his contemporaries, was mostly concerned to beat the Liberals, and it was a delicate question whether to do so in alliance with the Irish Nationalists or in violent antagonism to them and in support of the fiercest Orange Ulstermen. By 1912 the political questions in England had changed, but the primacy of English politics was even more obvious. The Conservatives since 1903 had tried to establish themselves as a popular party in urban England by adopting Tariff Reform and defending the economic interests of the middle classes. Despite their best efforts, this had lost them three general elections. Two possible ways forward were, on the one hand, to change the venue by

[23] J. D. Fair, *British Inter-Party Conferences: A Study of the Procedure of Conciliation in British Politics, 1867–1921* (Oxford, 1980), pp. 77–102.

[24] Salisbury to Lansdowne, 6 September 1910, British Library, Balfour Papers, MS Additional 49730.

[25] The most extreme interpretation of its significance is in R. J. Scally, *The Origins of the Lloyd George Coalition* (Princeton, 1976), pp. 172–210, in which the discussions are seen as a dry run for the coalition which in due course did concede Partition and a form of Home Rule.

contemplating a political system in which England (where they were in a strong majority) was protected from the political opinions of Scotland, Wales and Ireland; or, on the other, to change the argument by attacking the Liberals on a subject which (Conservatives hoped) the Liberals would not find vast popular sympathy.

Implicitly, the breakdown of the Constitutional Conference in 1910 postponed the first expedient, and the Ulster crisis brought the second to the forefront. However, it is clear that only a minority of Conservative leaders were sympathetic to the Ulster position in its pure form. Walter Long and Lord Lansdowne, later to play a full part in negotiations over the future of Ireland, cared most for the position of the Unionists in southern Ireland: they were appalled at the implications of any partition arrangement in which Ulster would in effect cut loose from the South, leaving Southern Unionists in a helpless minority. Others such as F. E. Smith and, to some extent, the leader Andrew Bonar Law would do anything to discredit the Liberals, but showed little passionate enthusiasm for Ulster's cause in its own right. One of the most poignant documents of the Ulster crisis is the diary of Sir Henry Wilson, one of the officers most involved in the so-called Curragh Mutiny, who spent hours explaining to Bonar Law why he should support those officers who wished to refuse to serve in military enforcement of the law in Ulster. While full of explanations of what Wilson said to Bonar Law, there is scarcely a word of what Bonar Law said back to Wilson.[26] Unless the Conservatives had actually been able to stop the Liberal legislative juggernaut in its tracks, their only hope was in civil war: and that is no position for a Conservative Party to occupy.

It therefore seems quite right that Bridgeman should have identified the passage of the Home Rule Act in 1914 as a turning point – wreckage from which the survival of Ulster was the one thing to be preserved. Tactically, Conservatives were unable during the War to achieve any other outcome. Carson, the Ulster leader, had a strong following on the Conservative back bench because of his outspoken views on matters unrelated to Ireland, such as the importance of military conscription, the desirability of an economic war after the War against Germany, and the necessity of removing Asquith from the premiership. Until March 1917 this discouraged any political leader from doing anything in Ireland which Carson did not want, but it did not help those whose primary interests were in the preservation of the Union with the whole of Ireland. In 1916, when Lloyd George persuaded Carson and Redmond to agree on a policy which would very probably lead to partition,

[26] The Curragh 'mutiny' of 20–21 March 1914 arose because army officers, when confronted with the hypothetical possibility of being ordered into action against rebellious Ulster Volunteers, sought ways to avoid obeying such orders. The Secretary of State for War, J. E. B. Seely, and the Chief of the Imperial General Staff, Sir John French (himself an Ulster Protestant), conceded their position, but the Cabinet repudiated them, so Seely and French resigned. Throughout the incident the disgruntled officers and their friends were in close touch with Conservative leaders. See *The Army and the Curragh Incident, 1914*, ed. I. F. W. Beckett (Army Records Society, 1986).

with the six Protestant counties of Ulster remaining with the Westminster Parliament and the rest of Ireland falling under a Dublin Parliament, the objections from Long and Lansdowne were even more passionate. Long aroused the back bench in the House of Commons and the result was almost a victory for those who wished to topple Bonar Law from the Conservative leadership. But in the discussions within the party, which eventually saw the resignation of one senior minister, so much was already implicitly conceded that it is hard to see the back-bench passion as other than a means to Bonar Law's discomfiture. Even the resigning minister, Lord Selborne, admitted that

> I understood, and I believe that my Unionist colleagues understood, that an effort was to be made to get the Ulster Unionists and the Nationalists of Ireland to agree to the exclusion of Ulster or of a part of Ulster from the operation of the Government of Ireland Act, and in addition to see whether there were any safeguards which would induce the Unionists of the south, centre and west of Ireland to accept a government and parliament in Dublin for the rest of Ireland. If an agreement on these points could be reached an Act amending the Government of Ireland Act would be passed during the war, but it never entered our heads that anyone contemplated bringing in the Government of Ireland Act, amended or unamended, modified or unmodified, into operation during the war.[27]

The effect was that even those who went so far as to resign, and most did not, were resigning not over the fact of the proposal to renegotiate the settlement which had been passed rather hastily in 1914, but merely over the proposal to introduce changes before the War was over.

With Ulster protected and the South exposed, it was difficult to elaborate and stick to a Conservative policy other than one of measured retreat. From 1918 onwards, with the Irish Convention in its terminal illness, the principal *Conservative* proposal to deal with Ireland was federal devolution, now proposed by Austen Chamberlain as a condition of his return to the ministry, and taken up with enormous enthusiasm by Walter Long, who became an 'Overlord' of Irish policy after the conscription crisis. Where devolution had once been the worst acceptable outcome, it had become the best: an attempt to give Southern Ireland some of the same protection which had been 'negotiated' for the North by the intransigence of Ulster.

But Bridgeman was also right to point to the irrelevance of Diehard resistance. The Union was no longer the stuff of Conservative politics after the First World War. It had been replaced by a fear and loathing of socialism, which would have become a serious basis for political reconstruction had not the party feared and loathed Lloyd George even more. Instead, those Conservatives who retained a concern for the future of Ireland were reduced to a restatement of the nature of the Union which quite repudiated the notion

---

[27] 'Memorandum on the Crisis in Irish Affairs which caused my resignation from the Cabinet June 1916', by the earl of Selborne, 30 June 1916: Oxford, Bodleian Library, Selborne Papers 80/226.

of a closer integration. Take Lord Selborne's letter to his brother-in-law and old friend the marquess of Salisbury in June 1918.

> I entirely agree that under present circumstances self-government in Ireland is absolutely out of the question, unless it be for the six counties of Ulster. I am quite prepared to rule the rest of Ireland as a Crown Colony for the present whether under the present constitution or under a revised constitution ...
>
> I am pushing forward federation as by far the most conservative thing that can now be done, far the greatest stabilising force possible to our constitution as it now exists. I know of no other means of making secure what I most love and prize in the institutions and customs of my country.

He went on to repeat a point which we have already heard from J. L. Garvin, that 'it is worthy of note that in all [countries with a federal system] the Conservative Party seems to draw its strength from the subordinate legislatures'.[28]

This was the position which Walter Long took in his development of the 1920 Government of Ireland Act. It was a flexible strategy, and its outcome was the fruit of unintended consequences. In effect, an important element in the Conservative Party had abandoned the Union with Ireland by 1920. A partitioned Ireland, with an entrenched and intransigent Protestant majority in the North, was not the object of their policy, but it was the most likely outcome when that policy was confronted with the real world. By making the Union with Ireland part of a larger concept of empire they had abandoned the ambition of closer integration of the Kingdom, and then the contingencies of English politics took over.

In conclusion, it is useful to compare the Irish experience very briefly with the experience of the two other smaller partners in the Union during the period of the First World War. Scotland's relationship to the Union and to England posed little problem to English politicians in the early twentieth century. Asquith's contented contemplation of the banks of the Firth of Forth has already been mentioned; but Conservatives also felt comfortable north of the Border. Two successive Conservative leaders, Balfour and Bonar Law, had strong Scottish connections themselves, and although the party was less successful in Scotland than its Liberal competitors were, the Liberal Unionist wing still retained a presence. To look at it another way, there was no political or cultural movement in Scotland which challenged either the Union or the Conservative Party, let alone one which challenged both, as the

---

[28] Selborne to Salisbury, 17 June 1918, Selborne Papers 7/33; reprinted in *The Crisis of British Unionism: The Domestic Political Papers of the Second Earl of Selborne, 1885–1922*, ed. D. G. Boyce (London, 1987), pp. 218–19.

Irish Nationalist movement undoubtedly did. Moreover the Scottish and English elites were thoroughly mingled within the social milieu of Conservatism. The result was an almost unctuous exploitation of the congruence between a Scottish identity and a British identity. Consider this observation from the brother of F. S. Oliver, one of the principal ideologues of imperial unity and later of federalism for Ireland, but also a wealthy businessman. William Oliver, who had inquired, at the age of forty-seven, about the possibility of enlisting as a private in a Highland regiment, lived in Canada. In May 1915 he had a conversation with the captain of HMS *Kent*, which had been prominent in Admiral Sturdee's action off the Falklands.

> He has a lot of Scotch fishermen who, he says, are the pick of the crew, for strength anyhow. The gun crews were so completely Scotchmen that they were actually split up into clans. One crew was called McLeod – another clan McPherson. The captain told me he would back up one against the other as, e.g., to the McPhersons, 'You wouldn't let clan McLeod beat you.'[29]

A similar attitude to the congruence between national or local patriotism and British or imperial patriotism was manifest in a strange incident during the autumn of 1917, when miners in the south Wales coalfield were resisting the 'comb-out' of industrial labour for the trenches and striking for higher pay. General J. C. Smuts, who had arrived from South Africa for the Dominion Prime Ministers' meeting in March and stayed on as a member of Lloyd George's War Cabinet, went to south Wales and addressed a meeting at Tonypandy.

> In front of me there was a vast crowd numbering thousands and thousands of angry miners, and when I got up I could feel the electricity in the air.
>
> I started by saying: 'Gentlemen, I come from far away as you know. I do not belong to this country. I have come a long way to do my bit in this war, and I am going to talk to you to-night about this trouble. But I have heard in my country that the Welsh are among the greatest singers in the world, and before I start, I want you first of all to sing me some of the songs of your people.'
>
> Like a flash, somebody in that huge mass struck up 'Land of My Fathers'. Every soul present sang in Welsh and with the deepest fervour. When they had finished, they just stood, and I could see that the thing was over. I said: 'Well, Gentlemen! It is not necessary for me to say much here to-night. You know what has happened on the Western Front. You know your comrades ... are risking their lives ... You know it as well as I do, and I am sure that you are going to defend the Land of

[29] W. Oliver to F. S. Oliver, 27 May 1915, in *The Anvil of War: Letters between F. S. Oliver and his Brother, 1914–1918*, ed. S. Gwynn (London, 1936), p. 104.

your Fathers of which you have sung here to-night, and that you will defend it to the uttermost – and that no trouble you may have with the Government about pay or anything else will ever stand in the way of your defence of the Land of your Fathers.'[30]

This is a fine story, though its provenance and details encourage circumspection. Although Lloyd George's memoirs, where it is quoted, are full and firmly based on primary sources, nothing is there without an ulterior purpose, and it was Lloyd George's way to romanticise about Welshness. It is very unlikely, in Tonypandy, that all the audience could have sung in Welsh, since many of them were English-speaking monoglots who had come, with their fathers, from the west of England or from Ireland within a generation. Smuts, out of either ignorance or cunning, was appealing to a manufactured local cultural patriotism in order to place it in the context of an imperial patriotism in which he, who did not 'belong to this country', could participate.

An alternative view of Welshness and imperial patriotism had been illustrated by Lord Kitchener as Secretary of State for War at the beginning of the conflict, who while accepting the recruitment of Welshmen into Welsh regiments, had first resisted the appointment of Nonconformist ministers as chaplains at the front, and had then refused to allow the use of Welsh either on parade or in barracks. Both positions got him into trouble with Lloyd George.[31] In due course he gave in, but even this concession presented a contrast to his treatment of Irish aspirations, North and South. On the one hand the 36th (Ulster) Division, made up largely (but not exclusively) of former members of the paramilitary Ulster Volunteers organised under their own officers, was allowed to fly the Ulster flag (the Red Hand) almost from the beginning;[32] on the other hand the aspirations of the southern Irish divisions were scorned even by Liberals. Asquith remarked in December 1914:

> Poor Birrell[33] ... is clamouring (at Redmond's instigation) for a 'Badge' for the new Irish division, on the plea that the Welsh & Ulster Divisions already have one. They had gone so far as to invent a shield surmounted by a gold crown, & with the Arms of the 3 provinces (I suppose excluding Ulster). K[itchener], it appears, won't hear of it, and thinks that a 'shamrock on a shoulder strap' meets the needs of the situation ... Redmond is in a fine frenzy...[34]

---

[30] Cited in David Lloyd George, *War Memoirs* (London, 1938), i, pp. 814–15.

[31] J. Grigg, *Lloyd George: From Peace to War, 1912–1916* (London, 1985), pp. 173–8.

[32] See T. Bowman, 'Composing divisions: the recruitment of Ulster and National Volunteers into the British Army in 1914', *Causeway*, ii (1995), pp. 24–9.

[33] Augustine Birrell, the Chief Secretary for Ireland.

[34] Asquith to Venetia Stanley, 29 December 1914, in *H. H. Asquith: Letters to Venetia Stanley*, ed. M. and E. Brock (Oxford, 1982), p. 343.

Welshness, like Irishness, was acceptable as a way of getting people to fight for Britain, just as the many 'Pals' battalions were recruited from English localities, but it was not to be used to assert itself. Such national identities were always slightly suspect to the Conservative political elite, and more than one Conservative minister readily observed that during the industrial unrest of 1916 and 1917 it was the Scottish and the Welsh who were discontented. F. S. Oliver, admittedly a loudmouth, explained to his brother that the executions of Irish participants in the Easter Rising was a good policy 'because if we had not, we should have had the uprising which was planned over the whole of Ireland, we should have had another on the Clyde, another in South Wales, and probably industrial trouble in all sorts of quarters'.[35] This remark goes even farther than others in its suggestion that there was a potential Celtic dissidence which was something other than industrial in its origin. In fact the evidence for British patriotism provided by the rate of voluntary enlistment before the first conscription legislation in December 1915 suggests that the patriotism of Scotland and Wales was at the same level as that of England, with minor variations almost certainly caused by minor differences in age structure and employment conditions.[36] The willingness of the southern Irish population to enlist was limited at the beginning of the War and went rapidly downhill as the Irish divisions were spurned by the War Office: the case of William Redmond, MP, John Redmond's brother, who was killed in action on the Western Front, serves if anything to highlight the gap between the Nationalist elite who were still prepared to work on the surviving link between Ireland and Britain and the rest of the population which was rapidly losing interest.

These examples suggest that from the English Conservative point of view the national identity of non-English parts of the Union was always to be regarded instrumentally. By the time of the First World War the combination of anglocentrism and the growth of the Empire had produced a sense of British identity which was fundamentally intolerant of the Celtic alternative. The incorporation of any particular non-English element in the Union had come to be seen as a matter of convenience rather than of principle. In that light, the readiness with which Conservatism abandoned the Union with Ireland in 1921 is hardly surprising. What had been an object of intense passion, because of the exigencies of English politics, in 1912–14, became a matter of indifference after 1919 when the costs seemed to outweigh the benefits. The Union with the South was let go, and a more robust and defensible political system, posing little threat to Conservative political hegemony in England, took its place.

[35] Gwynn, *Anvil of War*, p. 145.
[36] I. Beckett, 'The British Army, 1914–1918', in J. Turner (ed.), *Britain and the First World War* (London, 1988), p. 105. 26.9% of Scotland's male population enlisted, compared with 24.2% of the male population of England and Wales (which were consolidated in the records).

Part V

Epilogue

Chapter 16

How united is the modern United Kingdom?

David Marquand

I take it as axiomatic that large and complex modern societies are never united over goals or ends; and that, if their rulers pretend otherwise, they are deceiving themselves or their listeners. Modern liberal democracies are, in Michael Oakeshott's language, nomocratic, not teleocratic: they are held together by common rules, not by shared purposes. Even totalitarian regimes, which aspire to govern teleocratically, do not do so in fact. Indeed, totalitarian practice itself confounds totalitarian claims: there are always more dissidents, more internal *émigrés*, more enemies of the people to be rooted out. So to say that modern Britain is not, and never has been, held together by a common purpose or purposes is to say nothing very startling. It would be astonishing if it were.

That said, it is clear that states may be more or less legitimate: that they may rest on a more or less secure basis of popular support. It is also clear that the identities which states claim to embody can be more or less in contention and more or less problematic. Finally, it is clear that political economies can be more or less prone to generate social cohesion. These three notions – legitimacy, identity and social cohesion – provide the governing themes of this essay. I shall argue that, compared with the situation thirty or forty years ago, the British state today is much less legitimate, the identity or identities it claims to embody are more contentious and more problematic, and the political economy is less prone to generate social cohesion. And having argued these three propositions, I shall then try to speculate about the reasons and about some of the implications.

I shall look at these issues through the prism of two sets of ideas from social science. The first is the now famous triad analysed by the American economist, Albert Hirschman – the triad of 'exit', 'voice' and 'loyalty'.[1] For Hirschman, 'exit' and 'voice' were two alternative mechanisms through which consumers could control producers. 'Exit' was the paradigmatic mechanism of the market place. If you do not like the product you go to a different producer. If enough customers go to a different producer, the producer who

---

[1] A. O. Hirschman, *Exit, Voice and Loyalty: Responses to Decline in Firms, Organisations and States* (Cambridge, Mass., 1970).

has failed to satisfy them goes out of business. The threat of consumer 'exit' keeps producers on their toes; through 'exit' and the threat of 'exit', consumers exert control. The alternative mechanism, the mechanism of 'voice', is quintessentially the mechanism of politics. Control is achieved, or attempted to be achieved, by argument, by nagging, by protest, by complaint. If consumers are not satisfied by the producer, they raise hell. And they try to control what the producer produces through this process of hell-raising.

'Loyalty', the third term in the triad, is often forgotten. Yet it seems to me to be crucial to Hirschman's whole argument. 'Loyalty', as Hirschman sees it, is a precondition of effective 'voice'; more intriguingly still, there is also a sense in which 'voice' is a source of 'loyalty'. I will listen to you only if, in some sense or other, you are loyal to me: if you are not loyal, why should I pay you any attention? Old and valued customers can hell-raise effectively. Birds of passage cannot. Moreover, and in some ways even more importantly, the opportunity to exercise 'voice' and the experience of exercising it success-fully – the opportunity to nag, complain, argue and debate and the experience of being listened to when one does so – themselves help to generate 'loyalty'.

The implications go further than is sometimes realised. If 'loyalty' declines for any reason, 'voice' will decline as well; the more 'voice' declines, the more 'loyalty' will decline. The decline of 'voice', in other words, can become self-reinforcing, until only 'exit' is left. By the same token, if increasing reliance is placed on 'exit', 'loyalty' is likely to be eroded; and, insofar as 'loyalty' is eroded, it will become more difficult to return to 'voice' at some stage in the future. 'Exit', too, is self-reinforcing.

The second social-science notion on which I want to draw is that put forward by the American political theorist, Michael Waltzer, in his *Spheres of Justice*.[2] In part of this extremely rich and suggestive study, Waltzer argues that every society contains a number of different social 'spheres', each with its own principles for the allocation of social goods. In the sphere of the market, goods are properly allocated by the market principles of supply and demand, and by the market mechanisms of price and competition. But it is considered wrong to allocate the goods of the political sphere by market principles. Political offices are not to be bought and sold. In the political sphere, goods are allocated according to a different set of principles – according to the principles of one person one vote, of a secret ballot, and so forth. In another sphere, the sphere of sexual favour, most present-day Western societies consider it wrong to allocate goods either by political or by market principles. There we believe that some kind of emotional principle should apply.

Now, Waltzer goes on, because of the special peculiarities of money, the quintessential medium of the market sphere – because, in his marvellous phrase, money is the 'universal pandar' which can be used not only in the market sphere where it is appropriate, but also in other spheres where it is not – the

---

[2] M. Waltzer, *Spheres of Justice: A Defence of Pluralism and Equality* (New York, 1983).

market domain is peculiarly expansionist. The boundaries that separate different social spheres from each other are therefore under constant threat from what Waltzer calls 'market imperialism', or at least from the possibility of market imperialism. Money can leak illegitimately from its proper sphere to other spheres. Goods like political office or love or respect – goods which belong to non-market spheres and ought not to be treated as commodities to be bought and sold – can be wrongly commodified. And through the operation of the universal pandar of money, goods which have been de-commodified, placed in a non-market sphere, can be re-commodified. That is market imperialism.

Against that background, I now want to look at the first of my three propositions – the proposition that the British state has become less legitimate, that it enjoys less popular support, than was the case thirty or forty years ago. I shall argue that the legitimacy, the authority and the efficacy of the British state were on a rising curve from around 1920 to around 1950; and that from around 1960 to the present day they have been on a declining curve, so that now they are at lower levels than in the years after the First World War.

It is true that, for thirty years or so before the First World War, the forms and structures of the British state were bitterly disputed. Irish Home Rule, the powers of the House of Lords, women's suffrage and even the popular referendum all loomed large in political debate. After 1918, however, these battles died down; and the next half century was marked by a broad constitutional consensus extending over most (though not quite all) of the political spectrum. Consensus, moreover, went hand in hand with success. In the two World Wars of this century, the British state raised great armies, spent huge sums, mobilised its people and resources with extraordinary skill, and triumphed conclusively over its enemies. Partly because of all this – because of the constitutional consensus on the one hand, and because of the British state's success in meeting the primordial test of war on the other – the British version of the Keynesian welfare state, which the second-best compromises of the post-war period spawned all over Western Europe, took shape unusually quickly and seemed, at the time, to be unusually well founded. It was universally assumed that Beveridge and Keynes had, between them, discovered the solutions to the poverty and unemployment which had disfigured Britain before World War Two. It was also universally assumed that the government machine would be willing and able to put these discoveries into practice; and that, in doing so, it would light a beacon for mankind.

That mood lasted for fifteen years or so. But by the early 1960s, fissures had begun to appear in the granite certainties of the war and early post-war years. The heroic age of Beveridge and Keynes – the age, if you prefer, of Bevin and Cripps – had given way to doubts, self-questioning and self-mockery: to the age of the satirical television programme, *That Was The Week*

That Was. Few now saw the British version of the Keynesian welfare state as a model for lesser breeds; instead, the British elite was beginning to ask itself what foreign models had most to teach it. Under Harold Macmillan in the early 1960s, and with gathering speed under Harold Wilson and Edward Heath, institutional complacency gave way to a strange kind of institutional St Vitus's Dance. The 1960s and 1970s saw a host of new bodies – the National Economic Development Council, the National Board for Prices and Incomes, the Industrial Reorganisation Corporation, the Pay Board, the Prices Commission, the Central Policy Review Staff – and of commissions of enquiry. There was a Royal Commission on the Civil Service, a Royal Commission on Local Government, even a Royal Commission on the Constitution. Old departments of state were amalgamated into new ones; new ones were set up, only to be incontinently closed down. Ancient counties were swept away, and ancient cities demoted into district councils. Huge quantities of legislative time were devoted to unsuccessful attempts to 'reform' the House of Lords and to set up elected assemblies in Wales and Scotland.

The most obvious features of these attempts to re-arrange the furniture on the deck of the *Titanic* were their intellectual incoherence and mutual incompatibility. The Royal Commission on the Civil Service was debarred from enquiring into the relationship between civil servants and ministers – the spinal cord of the whole administrative system. The structure of local government was examined in isolation from its financing; its financing, in isolation from its structure. The legislation designed to establish elected assemblies in Wales and Scotland paid no heed to the project's inevitable repercussions on the governance of England. Less obvious, but in some ways even more significant, was a remarkable combination of apparent radicalism and fundamental conservatism. For example, in 1964 the Department of Economic Affairs was set up to act as a counterweight to the Treasury. But the division of responsibilities between the DEA and the Treasury – the DEA focusing on planning for the medium term, the Treasury on the balance of payments and the exchange rate in the short term – ensured that, in any conflict between the two, the latter would have by far the louder voice. And thus, the new tripartite bodies set up to plan the economy and police the resultant wage controls logically implied a form of corporatist power-sharing on the model of Scandinavia and Central Europe; but the governments which established them stuck rigidly to the doctrines and practices of Westminster parliamentarianism, with which corporatist power-sharing is incompatible.

The one great exception – belated entry into the then European Community – proved the rule. This change, perhaps the most far-reaching change in the governance of Britain since the foundation of the United Kingdom of Great Britain in 1707, was accomplished with ruthless skill and complete success. But, as a long line of Euro-sceptics has pointed out, the governments concerned sedulously pretended – to themselves even more fatally than to others – that the institutions and understandings of the British state would be unaffected. This was gross self-deception. The incoming tide of European legislation was bound to sweep, slowly, gently but inexorably, through the British system. More important still, participation in a supranational project that depends on power-sharing and coalition-building was bound to confront a political class accustomed to the *mores* of Westminster and Whitehall with a steep and painful learning curve. Yet these well-known features of the Community system were hidden or glossed over.

The much more dramatic – and enormously more complex – changes of the 1980s must be seen against that background. As is well known, there is an irony about these changes. The withdrawal of the state from civil society, which the early New Right theorists saw as the centre-piece of their whole project, has been conspicuous by its absence. The percentage of Gross Domestic Product going to public expenditure has fallen only trivially, if at all; the burden of taxation is no lighter than it was. Though financial markets have been de-regulated, the labour market has been re-regulated: employers are less tightly constrained than they used to be, but the trade unions are more so. Large swathes of the public sector have been privatised, but it can at least be argued that the regulators who now control their pricing policies allow them less freedom of action than they enjoyed before. The real achievement of the Thatcher and Major governments has been to reconstruct the state, not to curtail its scope and still less to diminish its power.

In the first place, the balance of power between the central state and the local authorities has been tilted dramatically in favour of the central state. Local authorities still exist, local councils are still elected, local councillors still take a range of decisions. But a huge range of functions formally exercised by local authorities have been taken away from them; and their ability to raise and spend resources as they wish has been drastically curtailed. Secondly, and in some ways more significantly still, a range of intermediate institutions, which stand or stood between the individual and the central state, have had their wings clipped. Universities, the trade unions, the BBC and the professions have all felt the lash of a radical centralism, more Jacobin than Tory and with no real precedent in British history. Thirdly, the core executive at the apex of the government machine has engaged in a systematic process of what the political scientist, Rod Rhodes, has called the 'hollowing out of the state'.[3] A huge range of public functions (carrying with them formidable spending consequences) have been transferred to appointed bodies – development corporations, hospital trusts, Training and Enterprise Councils and the like – while responsibility for delivering most of the services which still remain within the public sector has been farmed out to the so-called 'next steps agencies' at arm's length from government. As an impish recent complaint by Gerald Kaufman underlines, the implications for ministerial responsibility are profound:

[3] R. A. W. Rhodes, 'The hollowing out of the state: the changing nature of the public service in Britain', *Political Quarterly*, April–June 1994.

Bichard [Chief Executive, Benefits Agency] keeps writing to me, and I want him to stop. Whenever I have a constituency case involving a social security problem, I write about that case to the government minister responsible: these days, Peter Lilley, Secretary of State for Social Security.

Lilley passes my letter to Bichard. Bichard then writes to tell me he is looking into the case.[4]

Partly as cause, and partly as consequence, constitutional issues now have a higher place on the political agenda than at any time since 1914. Charter 88, the cross-party pressure group committed to a new constitutional settlement, has almost 50,000 signatories. Not long ago a Mori poll conducted for the Rowntree Reform Trust showed that 63% of those polled thought that the system needed either 'a great deal' or 'quite a lot' of improvement, whereas only 4% thought that the system worked 'extremely well'.[5] The Scottish Claim of Right, the constitutional convention, the opinion polls and the stands taken by all the political parties save the Unionists make it clear that a majority of the Scottish people now wish to re-negotiate the terms on which the Scottish nation-state voluntarily joined with the English nation-state to create a new multinational British state in 1707. The Labour Party is now committed to a Bill of Rights, to Home Rule for Scotland and Wales, to some form of regional government in England, and to an elected second chamber. For their part, the Liberal Democrats are for this reform agenda virtually in its entirety. Because of all this, it seems fairly clear that the next general election will be fought, at least in part, on the constitutional question, in a sense which has not been true of any previous general election since the First World War. The Conservative Party will be fighting on the proposition that no changes should be made in the unwritten British constitution – the embodiment of the traditions and history of the British people – and the opposition parties will be fighting on the proposition that the constitution is in desperate need of fundamental reform.

All this, it is important to note, has been accompanied by growing tension between the politicians and the officials at the heart of the British state and the institutions of the increasingly proto-federal European Union. It is true that the public at large seems indifferent to this tension. Yet the 'European question' clearly divides the political class more acutely than any constitutional question has done since the battles over Irish Home Rule. It also seems fairly clear that the issue has at least the potential to split the Conservative Party in the 1990s, much as the Irish question split the Liberal Party in the 1880s.

The question is, 'Why?' Why is the British constitution – for so long a byword for stability and consensus – in such contention? Why has the British

[4] Ibid., p. 148.
[5] T. Smith, 'Citizenship and the Constitution', *Parliamentary Affairs*, xliv (1991).

state undergone such a radical reconstruction at the hands of its ostensible defenders? Above all, how are we to explain the loss of legitimacy – or at least of acceptability – which that state has experienced in the last thirty years or so?

This is where the social-science notions I discussed a moment ago come back into the argument. I believe that all of the developments I described above – the institutional disarray of the 1960s and 1970s; the hollowing out and restructuring of the 1980s and 1990s; the renewal of constitutional debate of the sort we knew around the turn of the century; the continuing tension between Westminster and Whitehall on the one hand and Brussels, Luxembourg and Strasbourg on the other – are symptoms of a deepening crisis of the British state which can best be described as a crisis of the last *ancien régime* in Europe. Second, I believe that this crisis has come about because the structures, the operational codes and the constitutive understandings of the British *ancien régime* do not provide, and never have provided, opportunities for 'voice' adequate to the needs of a pluralist, multinational society in a pluralist, supranational European Union. Finally I believe that, because opportunities for 'voice' are inadequate, there is a profound sense in which the British state is an 'exit state' in Hirschman's sense of the term, not a 'voice state'. And because it is an 'exit state', 'loyalty' is lacking.

More particularly, I believe that the current crisis of the state reflects a deep incompatibility between the doctrine which lies at the very heart of British statehood – the doctrine of the absolute and inalienable sovereignty of the Crown in Parliament – and any form of power-sharing. The doctrine of absolute parliamentary sovereignty makes it extraordinarily difficult for the British state to share power with its partners in the European Union and also with the institutions of the Union itself. Power-sharing between the central state in London and lower tiers of government inside the United Kingdom is equally difficult. So is power-sharing between the state and the organised interests that are characteristic of all complex, modern industrial societies. In one of the most suggestive phrases in his majestic *Machiavellian Moment*, John Pocock writes that democracy came to Britain 'through the medieval technique of expanding the King-in-Parliament to include new categories of counsellors and representatives'.[6] Unfortunately, the absolute sovereignty of the King-in-Parliament, which that technique presupposes, has set narrow limits on the expansion, certainly in our own day.

Pre-eminent among the consequences of this basic incompatibility are the uncertainties, confusions, misunderstandings and policy failures which have marked Britain's membership of the European Union. There is an instructive parallel between these policy failures and the policy failures which marked the approach of successive British governments to the Irish question in the thirty years before the First World War. In the end, as everyone knows, the Irish question turned out to be unanswerable within the terms set by the past

[6] J. G. A. Pocock, *The Machiavellian Moment. Florentine Political Thought and the Atlantic Republican Tradition* (Princeton, 1975), p. 547.

history of the British state and by the political culture which that history had helped to create. That is why the twenty-six counties of southern Ireland now form a separate, sovereign nation-state of their own, instead of enjoying provincial autonomy within a federal, or at least partially federal, United Kingdom. But there was nothing in the nature of the Irish people or the Irish identity to make Home Rule impossible and secession inevitable. The barriers of feeling and assumption that stood in the way of Home Rule and ensured that Irish aspirations could be satisfied only in a separate state were to be found in mainland Britain, not in Ireland. The problem, in essence, was that most (though not, of course, all) of the British political class simply could not understand the notion of federalist power-sharing; and that because that federalism was incomprehensible to most British politicians, it was also intolerable to them. By an extraordinary paradox, it was easier for the British state to answer the Irish question through the 'exit' mechanism of complete secession than to create a federalist structure based on 'voice'.

Exactly the same is true of contemporary British attitudes to the European Union and its institutions. The British political class cannot comprehend how it is possible for a state, with all the attributes and the appurtenances of sovereignty as that notion has traditionally been understood, to share power with the institutions of the European Union and with the other Member States. Irrespective of party, the managers of the British state have seen power in zero-sum terms, as a hard, impervious cricket ball, which is either held or not held, and which cannot, by its very nature, be shared. But, of course, power-sharing is of the essence of the European Union, as it is of all federal or even confederal systems.

Another result of the situation I have been trying to describe is that the British version of the Keynesian welfare state, which had seemed unusually well founded when it came into existence at the beginning of the post-1945 period, turned out to be, on the contrary, extraordinarily fragile. Here, Waltzer's notion of market imperialism comes back into the argument. In essence, the rationale of the Keynesian welfare state was to curb market imperialism. Its purpose was to construct clear boundaries around the domain of the market place, to replace 'exit' relationships with 'voice' relationships, at least in certain spheres. But because the British state was not truly a 'voice state', because it did not give adequate opportunities for 'voice', the British version of the Keynesian welfare state did not do this in practice. Instead of replacing the 'exit' relationships of the market place with the 'voice' relationships of the forum, it replaced them with hierarchical relationships centred upon a benevolent, essentially technocratic mandarinate.

An emblematic episode in the history of the post-war Keynesian welfare state was Aneurin Bevan's decision to nationalise the hospital service when he started to frame his proposals for the future National Health Service in 1945.

There was a bitter battle in the cabinet over this question. The prestigious, but bankrupt, voluntary hospitals had to be brought within a publicly funded system if they were to survive at all. The question was whether to put them under municipal control, like the existing local authority hospitals, or to put them under national control. The consultants bitterly opposed the first answer, in essence because it threatened their professional power. Bevan solved the problem by placing all the hospitals – both voluntary and local authority – under national control; and defended his decision on grounds of efficiency and uniformity. Herbert Morrison, old leader of the London County Council and perhaps the greatest municipal socialist in British history, opposed him on grounds of local democracy. Though Morrison was then at the height of his power, as Attlee's deputy and grand panjandrum of Home policy, while Bevan was a comparative political stripling with only a few months of cabinet office behind him, victory went to the latter. It is hard to quarrel with Rudolph Klein's summary of the issues at stake.

> In its final form ... the NHS represented the victory of the values of rationality, efficiency and equity: it was designed to be the instrument of national policies for delivering health care in a rational, efficient and fair way across the country. But as the debates between 1939 and 1948 showed, there are other values. The case for local government control was based not just on the defence of a particular interest – the existing local authorities – but on a view of the world anchored in the values of localism: a view which stressed responsiveness rather than efficiency, differentiation rather than uniformity, self-government rather than national equity.[7]

The implications go deeper than is sometimes realised. Social citizenship took a giant step forward when the National Health Service came into being, but there is an important sense in which political citizenship took a step back, in which 'voice' had less scope after 1945 than it had had before. Whatever its other merits, the new nationalised hospital service was more impervious to democratic control than the municipal hospital service had been in pre-war days. As Morrison pointed out in cabinet, the same was true of Gas and Electricity. There, too, large local authority sectors – hitherto controlled by elected local councils – were taken out of local hands, in the name of efficiency and rationality.

In the golden years of the post-war boom, the mandarin collectivism which Bevan had championed in his battle with Morrison, and which suffused the mental universe in which the Keynesian welfare state took shape, reigned virtually unchallenged. But when the economic climate turned cold, and hard decisions had to be made, its blithe indifference to 'voice' turned out to be a fatal handicap. Because they were not rooted in 'voice' relationships, because the institutions of social citizenship had grown up in a subject, rather than in

[7] R. Klein, *The Politics of the National Health Service* (London, 1983), p. 28.

a civic, political culture, the barriers which the post-war government erected against the threat of market imperialism turned out to be far more fragile than they looked. Social goods which had been de-commodified after the War were re-commodified in the 1980s with an ease which would have astonished the post-war generation; the universal pandar of money returned to sphere after sphere from which it had been banished. All this was, of course, the product of a hegemonic political project, pursued with crusading zeal by one of the most resolute governments in British history. But, almost by definition, hegemony is a two-way street. Hegemonic projects succeed only if the culture is already hospitable to them. And one of the reasons why British culture was hospitable to the New Right project of the 1970s and 1980s is that the supposed beneficiaries of the social-citizenship state of the post-war period did not feel that they owned the institutions that composed it.

This leads on to a more general point. By the 1970s, Britain's political economy was plainly in crisis. A balance of payments crisis interacted with a fiscal crisis to produce a crisis of governability, manifested in the failure of successive governments to mobilise consent for the wages policies without which the post-war commitment to full employment could not be squared with tolerable levels of inflation. Somehow or other, the crisis had to be resolved, by default if not by design. As everyone knows, the resolution was accomplished by the New Right. But the New Right's way out of the crisis was not the only possible one. In principle, there were at least two other possibilities. There was a left-socialist option, involving more vigorous state intervention in the supply-side of the economy, import controls to protect the balance of payments, and secession from the European Community. And, though it was never articulated as such, there was also a social- (or perhaps christian-) democratic option, involving more explicit forms of corporatist power-sharing and closer identification with the European Community. But the second and third options would have entailed a sharp break with the institutions, understandings, assumptions and operational codes of the British *ancien régime*. No-one in the political class was prepared for such a break; and the New Right option won by default. Having won, it fed – as Hirschman's theory would have predicted – on itself.

That is only the beginning of the story. As I tried to show earlier, implicit in Hirschman's whole argument is the notion that 'voice' depends on 'loyalty'. I suggest that 'loyalty', in turn, depends on identity. To feel loyal to a political community is to feel bound by the compact between the dead, the living and the unborn, which is of its essence. And to feel bound by such a compact is to identify with the community in question.

Against that background, the rise of the New Right and the increasing reliance on 'exit' which is its concomitant take on a new colour. For most of its history, the identity embodied by the British state was quintessentially global, oceanic, imperial and, by virtue of this, non- or at least extra-European. Like many other identities, it was a factitious construct, not an emanation of irresistible sentiment. It emerged after the Act of Union, during the eighteenth-century race for empire with Bourbon France. Its purpose was to enable both Scots and English to transcend old national animosities in a blaze of glory; and that purpose was largely achieved.[8] The new British state – a much more fragile creature, it should be remembered, than it looks in retrospect – acquired a new and special legitimacy: the legitimacy of imperial success. Its justification was that it was a better predator than other states; that the pickings of its Empire were richer; that the blaze of glory that surrounded it was brighter. Later, when success had bred more success, when the global pre-eminence of the British state seemed beyond challenge, a more relaxed tone came to predominate. Now its justification was the *pax Britannica*: its role as the guarantor and linchpin of the global market which the guns of the Royal Navy had brought into being. In its relaxed later stages as much as in its tense early ones, however, the grandeurs and servitudes of empire were of its very essence; and the same grandeurs and servitudes inevitably shaped the identity it claimed to embody.

The result was a vision of the British state and people which I have elsewhere called 'whig imperialist'.[9] It had a multitude of monuments: poems ranging from the haunting to the banal; war memorials in remote Highland villages; regimental battle honours hanging in obscure cathedral corners; the spine-tingling ritual of a Remembrance Day parade. At its heart lay the twin themes of globalism and constitutionalism. The British state was, by definition, a global state; and the British people, by definition, was a global people. As Winston Churchill put it in the House of Commons in May 1945, the British sovereign embodied 'a multiple kingship unique in the world of today'. Of that kingship, 'we in these islands are but a single member'. To it, however, all the other governments of the Empire felt 'an equal allegiance and an equal right'.[10] But the Whig dimension of the vision was as important as the imperial dimension. Not only were the British a uniquely global people; they were also a uniquely freedom-loving one: the inventors of constitutional government and the rule of law. As Sir Ivor Jennings put it: 'Written constitutions are based on theories or principles of government, but theories are suggested by experience and the nations who dare to call themselves free have built largely on British experience.'[11] That experience was Britain's gift to the world, and the matrix in which the British state and nation had been formed.

The Whig imperialist vision of the British state helped to shape the mentality of the entire political class, left as well as right. The post-war

[8] For this process, see L. Colley, *Britons: Forging the Nation 1707–1837* (2nd edn, London, 1994).

[9] D. Marquand, 'The twilight of the British state? Henry Dubb versus sceptred awe', *Political Quarterly*, April–June 1993.

[10] *House of Commons Debates*, 5th ser., vol. 410, 15 May 1945, cols. 2305–7.

[11] W. I. Jennings, *The Law and the Constitution* (3rd edn, London, 1943), p. 8.

Labour government's foreign and imperial policies cannot be understood without taking it into account; nor can its reverential attitude to the state and to the famous unwritten constitution it had inherited from its predecessors. Indeed, the same vision still lurked in the collective sub-conscious of the Labour leadership in the 1960s and 1970s. For, on the central questions of identity and nationhood – fundamental to any state – it enjoyed a kind of hegemony. The left had little distinctive to say about identity. The solidarities it evoked were those of class, not those of nation. As a result, Whig-imperialist Britain was not one among several possible Britains, in the way that Republican France is – or, at least, used to be – one among several possible Frances. Whig-imperialist Britain *was* Britain. The British state was the child as well as the parent of empire. Its iconography, its operational codes, the instinctive reflexes of its rulers and managers were stamped through and through with the presuppositions of empire. By the same token, the identity it claimed to embody and helped to create was, of necessity, imperial: it could not be anything else. Empire was not an optional extra for the British, in the way that republicanism was an optional extra for the French. It was their vocation, their reason for being British as opposed to being English or Scots or Welsh. Shorn of empire, 'Britain' had no meaning.

Hence there was a crucial, if elusive, contrast between Britain and France in the post-war period. The loss of the French Empire was plainly a very painful matter for the French. But, with astonishing skill and *chutzpah*, Charles de Gaulle contrived to reconstitute French identity around a post-imperial vision of grandeur, of civilisation, of France's vocation as the linchpin of a *Europe des patries*, a bastion against the pretensions and vulgarities of the so-called 'Anglo-Saxons'. In the early post-war period, no British leader even attempted to do anything comparable. Rather, British governments in the early post-war period sought to minimise the pain involved in the loss of empire by pretending that it was not happening – that Britain's vocation as a quintes-sentially imperial and global power could be realised as well through the headship of the British Commonwealth as it had been through ruling the Empire. But from the early 1960s, this manoeuvre ceased to carry conviction. The British state was now a would-be (later, an actual) member of the European Community. The British Commonwealth was no longer the chief focus for Britain's role in the world, and it was absurd to pretend otherwise. But no-one managed to invent a new British identity, centred upon a new European destiny. Edward Heath tried, but failed. No-one else even tried.

It is sometimes suggested that Mrs Thatcher was a British de Gaulle, and there is an obvious sense in which she merits the description. She undoubt-edly sought to reassert British greatness in the way that de Gaulle had reasserted the greatness of France. Where de Gaulle tried to re-invent the France of the seventeenth century, she tried to re-invent the Britain of the nineteenth – the nineteenth century being Britain's *grand siècle*. But because it is by definition impossible for Britain as such to be post-imperial, Thatcher could not be a truly British de Gaulle; she could only be an English one. What she really did was to assert a particular vision of belligerent English nationhood; and because England's identity is not quintessentially and inescapably imperial in the way that Britain's is, such a vision could resonate even in a post-imperial world.

Here, too, the implications go wider than may appear at first sight. The British loyalties and language on which the post-war Labour government could draw gradually ceased to be available to subsequent governments. When the Keynseian welfare state of the post-war period encountered the cold climate that followed the long boom, attempts to appeal to those loyalties and speak that language fell flat, as the unfortunate Harold Wilson discovered when he tried to evoke the Dunkirk spirit. At the same time, Scottish, Welsh and English identities and loyalties began to revive. This revival of an English identity, accompanied by a corresponding revival of Scottish and Welsh identities, had profound consequences, both for the party system and for the state. It helped Mrs Thatcher to create a new social coalition which so far has given the Conservative Party over a decade and a half of power. It made life correspondingly more difficult for the Labour and Liberal Parties, both of which are doomed to be British in a sense which is not true of the Conservatives. The Labour and Liberal Parties depend not just on the English periphery – the old industrial regions in the case of the Labour Party, and the south-west in the case of the Liberal Party – but on the non-English nations of the United Kingdom. And, in recent times at least, this has been spectacularly untrue of the Conservatives.

There is, however, a paradox in all this. The Conservative Party has been, for most of its history, the party of the British state and of the institutions and symbols of the state: the party of the monarchy, of the Established Church, of the complex web of traditions encapsulated in the doctrines of Westminster absolutism. Now, the British state is, and always has been, multinational, not national. Scotland and Wales are indispensable to it; if they were not part of it, it would not be British at all. But the more the governing party becomes an exclusively English party, the more it is thought to be indifferent or hostile to the interests and aspirations of the non-English nations of Britain, the more unstable that state is bound to become. The legitimacy and authority of the London government may perhaps have been strengthened in the parts of England where the New Right social coalition rides high, but they have been weakened in the non-English parts of the United Kingdom and perhaps in the English periphery as well. The historic party of the Union has become, in practice, a force for disunity.

By the same token, and for essentially the same reason, the party that took Britain into the European Community has become, in practice, the anti-European party. The Scots and Welsh both have, or can at least easily construct, pluralist European identities. It is quite easy for a Scot to retrieve ancient memories of the 'auld alliance' with France, of the eighteenth-century

Scottish Enlightenment, of Scotland as a historic European nation, and of Edinburgh as a great European capital. By virtue of these memories, Scots can say, 'I am Scottish, I am European and I am also British', much as Catalans can say, 'I am Catalan, I am European and I am also Spanish.' The same is true in a different kind of way of Wales. But, for reasons which are not altogether clear, it does not seem to be true of England. No-one has succeeded – and I suggest that no-one has tried – to construct a similarly plural and similarly European English identity. The myths, the iconography, the symbols of English nationhood are as non-, or even anti-, European as are the myths, symbols and iconography of British nationhood. The myth of English nationhood is the myth of the White Cliffs of Dover, of Drake's Drum, of England as a bastion of liberty resisting an encroaching continental despotism. As a result, it is very difficult to re-invent an older English identity, in which England would be a great European nation, as closely involved with the rest of the Continent as are France or Germany or Italy.

Against that background, let me turn to the third of my opening propositions – the proposition that, in the period under discussion, Britain's political economy has become less prone to generate social cohesion. I begin with the now familiar distinction between 'Rhenish' and 'neo-American' capitalism, offered by the French economist, Michel Albert.[12] His schema is, no doubt, over-simplified. His description of the 'neo-American' model does not do full justice to the extraordinary diversity and complexity of American practice, and his picture of 'Rhenish' capitalism is somewhat stylised as well.

As a device to clarify issues and stimulate debate, however, his distinction is helpful. And it is clear that the neo-American model of capitalism (to use his terminology) is 'exit'-based, whereas the Rhenish model depends much more heavily on 'voice'. It is also clear, presumably because of this, that the neo-American model is less socially cohesive. Finally, it is clear that British capitalism was always closer to the neo-American model than was the rest of Western Europe; and that, during the course of the 1980s and 1990s, it moved still further along the neo-American road.

Once more, the question is, 'Why?' The answer, I believe, is less comfortable than proponents of 'Rhenish' capitalism generally believe. Given the structure of comparative advantages which the Thatcher government inherited from the past, and given Britain's place in a global political economy in the throes of an extremely disorientating transition, it is hard to see how any British government in the 1980s could have followed an economic strategy significantly different from the one actually followed by the Thatcherites after they took office in 1979. It is worth noting that, in Australia and New Zealand, both of whose political and economic cultures were similar to Britain's, Labour governments followed policies remarkably

---

12 M. Albert, *Capitalisme contre Capitalisme* (Paris, 1991).

similar to the policies followed by the Thatcher government in the United Kingdom. Of course, we cannot know what would have happened if a Labour government had been in power in Britain in the early 1980s (and if James Callaghan had called a general election in October 1978, as he was expected to do, a Labour government might well have been in power in Britain in the early 1980s). Perhaps it would have broken out of its inherited constraints, in quite new ways. But, to put it at its lowest, that seems unlikely. It is much more likely that, if Labour had been in power in the early 1980s, operating within the structure of comparative advantage that then existed and facing the turbulent global political economy of the time, it would have followed a course much closer to the course the Thatcherites actually followed than to that of the 1950s or 1960s. It was, after all, Denis Healey, not Geoffrey Howe, who first broke with the Keynesian orthodoxies of the post-war settlement; and the logic that forced him to do so would still have been in operation.

It follows that the real question is not why the governments of the 1980s followed the macro-economic policies they followed; given the nature of British capitalism in 1979, they had no real alternative. The question is whether that nature was inevitable. There is a powerful recent historiography, the most effective popular champion of which is the economic historian W. D. Rubinstein,[13] which suggests that the answer is 'yes'. British capitalism, according to this school of thought, has always been finance-led, not industry-led. Britain's comparative advantage has always lain in financial services, not in industry – even during the early nineteenth century. And, this school of thought continues, the course of British economic history has been largely determined by an alliance between the state and finance capital, going back to the early eighteenth century. To put it in Hirschman's language, an 'exit state' has reinforced, and been reinforced by, an 'exit' political economy.

I suspect that there have also been elements of Michel Albert's 'Rhenish' capitalism in the industrial provinces. Alfred Marshall's well-known description of the mixture of co-operation and competition in the Sheffield cutlery trade in the 1880s certainly suggests that there were.[14] The fact remains that these 'Rhenish' elements were swamped by elements closer to Albert's 'neo-American' model; and that, by the 1980s, the resultant structural constraints left the managers of the British state no room for manoeuvre. All sorts of questions arise. Was there ever a chance of a 'productivist' alliance between industrial capital, or at least parts of industrial capital, and organised labour? Could the thrust of state policy have been shifted in favour of industry, at the expense of finance? Which social forces would have had to be mobilised for such a shift to take place, and why did no-one mobilise them? But these are subjects for a different essay.

---

[13] W. D. Rubinstein, *Capitalism, Culture and Decline in Britain, 1750–1990* (London, 1993).
[14] A. Marshall, *Principles of Economics* (London, 1910 edn), p. 296.

Chapter 17

Conclusion
Contingency, identity, sovereignty

J. G. A. Pocock

It would be easy, if fatal, for me to present these concluding reflections in the character of old Simeon in the Temple.[1] About twenty years ago, I began calling for the development of a new sub-field or subject, to be named 'British history' and designed as a history of the interlocking peoples and cultures inhabiting what I proposed calling 'the Atlantic Archipelago'.[2] Although Richard Tompson of Utah published a book called *The Atlantic Archipelago* in 1986,[3] and Hugh Kearney, then of Pittsburgh, published *The British Isles: A History of Four Nations* in 1989,[4] it was long the fashion to commiserate with me on the poverty of response to my suggestion; indeed, David Cannadine took no account of it at all in his memorable *Past and Present* essay on 'British History: past, present – and future?'[5] Yet the tide has abruptly turned, as the essays in this volume and the conference from which they derive make strikingly evident; and though this has had little to do with my rather uncertain trumpet before the dawn, and far more to do with the works of Conrad Russell, John Morrill, Linda Colley, Rees Davies and Robin Frame,[6] we can now claim 'British history' as a field of study well enough established to have both its paradigms and its critics – that the latter are mainly Irish is a reminder of how necessary they are. It would therefore be possible, easy and perhaps not unfitting for me to cry 'Nunc dimittis, Domine' – 'Lord, now lettest thou thy servant depart in peace' – and vanish into my own prophetic past.

---

[1] See *Luke*, 2: 25–35.

[2] J. G. A. Pocock, 'British History: a plea for a new subject', *New Zealand Historical Journal*, viii (1974), reprinted in *Journal of Modern History*, xlvii (1975); subsequently, J. G. A. Pocock, 'The limits and divisions of British History: in search of the unknown subject', *American Historical Review*, lxxxvii (1982).

[3] R. S. Tompson, *The Atlantic Archipelago: A Political History of the British Isles* (Lewiston, 1986). There is now allusion in some writings to an 'Eastern Atlantic Archipelago', distinct from the Scandinavian-American archipelago westwards from Iceland.

[4] H. Kearney, *The British Isles: A History of Four Nations* (Cambridge, 1989).

[5] D. Cannadine, 'British History: past, present – and future?', *Past and Present*, cxvi (1987).

[6] E.g., C. Russell, *The Fall of the British Monarchies, 1637–1642* (Oxford, 1991); J. S. Morrill, *The Nature of the English Revolution* (London and New York, 1993); L. Colley, *Britons: Forging the Nation 1707–1837* (2nd edn, London, 1994); R. R. Davies (ed.), *The British Isles 1100–1500: Comparisons, Contrasts and Connections* (Edinburgh, 1989); R. Frame, *The Political Development of the British Isles 1100–1400* (Oxford, 1990).

I have no intention of doing so; the field is too full, not only of folk, but of problems which remain crucial to my work as a historian and to my consciousness as a historical being – so that even the prophetic role I slipped into may not yet be exhausted. There is more work to be done and already in hand, and I should like to introduce this conclusion by describing one of the projects composing it. At the Folger Institute Center for the History of British Political Thought, situated at the Folger Shakespeare Library in Washington, we are engaged (it could be said) in mapping history as revealed, as constructed, and even as distorted, in the various political languages which have from time to time been employed in debating history as it happened to the discussants during the course of the early modern period. We recently published a volume entitled *The Varieties of British Political Thought, 1500–1800*,[7] a collection of essays surveying the field as it has come to appear to us; and it was necessary to confess that this was an anglocentric volume, for the reasons that the enormous output of the London print industry, and the intensity with which the English of the sixteenth, seventeenth and eighteenth centuries debated their affairs and their theological and philosophical implications, gave their political thought a hegemony in the historiography, which reflected that which they had exercised in the history, of the Three Kingdoms. Only in the chapters of this volume which deal with the eighteenth century does it manage to look beyond England, into the rest of Britain and even beyond.[8]

We were not prepared to remain satisfied with this achievement, and proceeded to organise further seminars at the Center, designed in the first place to establish something like a tentative canon for Scottish political thought as a distinct body of discourse, and in the second to use it in opening up the topic of 'Britain', a concept which was in some measure a Scottish invention.[9] These seminars have given rise to two further volumes: one with Roger Mason as its editor and the Union of the Crowns as its subject;[10] and another in which John Robertson and others examine the Union of the Parliaments and the creation of the United Kingdom of Great Britain.[11] I want to give emphasis to two ways in which the latter of these volumes points to future work and indicates unfinished business. In the first place, it claims an association between the Anglo-Scottish Union and the American Revolution. To understand why the former of these had to be an

---

[7] J. G. A. Pocock (ed.), *The Varieties of British Political Thought, 1500–1800* (Cambridge, 1993).

[8] Namely, N. Phillipson, 'Politics and politeness in the reigns of Anne and the early Hanoverians' (ch. 7); and J. G. A. Pocock, 'Political thought in the English-speaking Atlantic: (i) The imperial crisis', and '(ii) Empire, revolution and an end of early modernity' (chs. 8–9).

[9] A. H. Williamson, *Scottish National Consciousness in the Age of James VI* (Edinburgh, 1979); B. P. Levack, *The Formation of the British State: England, Scotland and the Union, 1603–1707* (Oxford, 1987).

[10] R. A. Mason (ed.), *Scots and Britons: Scottish Political Thought and the Union of 1603* (Cambridge, 1994).

[11] J. Robertson (ed.), *A Union for Empire: Political Thought and the British Union of 1707* (Cambridge, 1995).

'incorporating' and not a 'federating' union is to understand an important set of reasons why the American colonies could not be joined in a confederation with Great Britain and could not be incorporated within it either; just as it is to understand some of the problems of the contemporary United Kingdom. In work appearing elsewhere,[12] I have argued that the inability of the English Parliament to enter into confederal relations arose from the absolute sovereignty, the absolute incorporation of Crown and Parliament, Church and kingdom, established at the Henrician Reformation and bitterly contested in civil wars from 1637 to 1745. It was not just bloody-minded ethnic chauvinism which moved the English in their dealings with associated peoples; it was also the intensity of their own problems and the need to settle them among themselves. Has that altogether changed?

A further implication, however, is that 'British history' in the eighteenth century is not confined to that of the United Kingdom but extends to that of an Atlantic empire linking the archipelago with another continent, and is not the history of four nations alone but of at least five; it has an American dimension. There is the paradox that 'British history' extends to, and offers to explain, the point at which the American colonists declare themselves thirteen states independent of the Crown and one people no longer linked with another – as they declare 'the British' to be – and depart from British history altogether.[13] The history of British political thought, we have found, can be made to include the language of the Declaration of Independence; but it cannot include that of the Philadelphia Convention, the *Federalist Papers* and the Constitution of the United States, for the reason that the language of confederation and federation was profoundly alien to British discourse, and has remained so. But if United States history begins at this point, so too does that of multinational Canada, in the sense that the desire of American Loyalists to continue as subjects of the Crown imposes an association with the newly conquered French of Quebec and Acadia, as well as with the indigenous 'first nations' in several regions. British history at this point has enduringly escaped from the confines, broad as they are, of the Atlantic archipelago considered as off-shore islands of the European peninsulas.

United States history both is and is not British; and 'British history' includes the reasons why it ceased to be British. This formula, or set of paradoxes, is highly relevant both to the directions being taken by the plans of the Folger Center and to the perceptions demonstrated in the present

---

[12] Pocock, 'Political thought in the English-speaking Atlantic', in Pocock, *Varieties of British Political Thought*; J. G. A. Pocock, 'Empire, state and confederation: the War of American Independence as a crisis in multiple monarchy', in Robertson, *A Union for Empire*. See also J. G. A. Pocock, *Sovranita Britannica e Federalismo Americana: la ricostruzione di un impero* (Macerata: Laboratorio di Storia Costituzionale Antoine Barnave, forthcoming).

[13] This process is placed in the context here indicated by J. P. Greene, *Peripheries and Center: Constitutional Development in the Extended Politics of the British Empire and the United State, 1607–1788* (New York, 1990). Cf. P. J. Marshall, 'A Nation defined by Empire, 1755–1776', above, ch. 12.

volume. All together look towards the second great secession which has marked the course of British history. Participants in the work of the Folger Center have realised that if the Anglo-Scottish Union of 1707 can be linked to the American Revolution of 1776 and the Constitution of the United States in 1789, the history of the imperial crisis of 1763–83 is incomplete without close attention to the crisis in Irish history between 1780 and 1801, and to that third and fatal Union, which created the United Kingdom of Great Britain and Ireland, brought to an end (so it is argued) the English *ancien régime* between 1829 and 1832,[14] and inaugurated a period in British and Irish history which did not altogether finish in 1922. Just as we realised that we could not adequately study the two Anglo-Scottish Unions without a history of political discourse distinctively Scottish, so we are now contemplating a series of seminars on the even more diverse discourses to be found in Ireland, since the time when Tudor policies inaugurated the period in British history known by the name of the Three Kingdoms.

This is to consider Irish history within the construct of 'British history', and to this Irish historians predictably and understandably raise objections. They point out that the term 'British' has at various times meant 'Romano-Celtic', then 'Anglo-Welsh',[15] then 'Anglo-Scottish'; and that Ireland is inhabited by peoples of whom a majority were never included within any of these imposed groupings and have strenuously resisted attempts to include them. The point is wholly valid, but is most powerfully so when directed against a contention which I do not think anybody is currently putting forward: namely, that 'British history' is the name of a paradigm which offers to include every aspect of the history of every people formed within the territory of the second United Kingdom (1801–1922) – or the full extent of the Atlantic archipelago from Sark to the Shetlands – and reduce it to a common history, the history of a single formed identity. This would obviously be an imperialist contention, but it is not being advanced and there is no more than a precautionary need to reject it; yet its presence indicates a category confusion which is at the back of our minds and does need to be cleared up.

'Irish history' is not part of 'British history', for the very good reason that it is largely the history of a largely successful resistance to being included in it; yet it is part of 'British history', for exactly the same reason. In saying this, we move from the illusion, or verbal confusion, that 'British history' is the history of a shared identity with a shared past, to the more focused realisation that it is the history of the attempt, with its successes and failures, to create such an identity. The term remains a paradigm, but it is a paradigm

[14] J. C. D. Clark, *English Society, 1688–1832: Ideology, Social Structure and Political Practice during the Ancien Régime* (Cambridge, 1985).

[15] This may be the point at which to interject that the reconstruction of 'British' political discourse does not yet include a history of discourse which is distinctively Welsh. Such a discourse no doubt exists and ought to be studied. If it has not yet been brought to light, this is because – like other Celtic-language discourses – it was not deposited at the centres of an institutionally autonomous political system. That is not a reason why it should not be studied.

incessantly contested and even self-contested. It includes its own exclusions: the history of how American colonists established an 'English' (rather than a 'British') identity and then transformed it in the process of seceding from 'British history' to construct a history of their own; the history of how some of the Irish peoples (there is one signal exception) successfully maintained the claim that they had never been part of 'British history', yet have not established a history from which the 'British' presence can be altogether excluded. From the standpoint from which a historian of discourse views this history, the term 'British political discourse' denotes not a shared discourse in which the various nations subject to the Crown conducted the affairs of a shared polity, but rather a discourse as to whether such a discourse, and the political structures presupposed by it, could or should be established; if so how, and if not what should replace it? It is primarily a discourse about the invention of Britain; secondarily, contestably and with contestable degrees of success, a discourse arising from the *fait accompli* of such an invention. If 'Irish history' is not part of 'British history', it has by that fact – or by the 'if-ness' of such a fact – done much to make 'British history' what it is, just as 'British history' has done much to make 'Irish history' what it is: two propositions that appear to border on the self-evident, in past, present and future. We shall therefore be considering the Irish contributions to the being and the non-being of 'British political thought', though it may be wise to reserve the title *The Varieties of Irish Political Thought* for denoting the programme as a whole.

The present collection of essays very clearly resembles the programme I have described in treating 'British history' as a history which contests, which questions – though, it is important to add, which does not automatically negate – its own identity. It has examined the history of the United Kingdom with an eye to asking how it happened, whether it is going to last, whether it might – even whether it should not – have happened otherwise. Given the view of the Parliamentary Union and the American Revolution which I outlined earlier, I have been interested to note the emphasis that has been placed on the imposition of full imperial sovereignty, on the absolute and irrevocable incorporation of Crown and Parliament, on the United Kingdom if not on its Atlantic Empire; and interested also to note a recurrent nostalgia for an alternative history in which something more like confederation and less like incorporation might have marked the road which in fact was not taken. In other places than this,[16] I have argued that it was not merely a chauvinist or an imperialist impulse – strongly present though these impulses visibly were – that drove the English to impose the unity of their own kingdom on the larger imperial monarchy into which it was never absorbed, but the bitter experience of civil war which had taught them how hard that unity had become to maintain and what shattering breakdowns must follow from the failure to maintain it. We must not let the hugely enlightening concept of a

---

[16] See the references in notes 12, above, and 18, below.

War or Wars of the Three Kingdoms tempt us into talking as if the English
Civil War did not really happen. The English did not want such a war, but
found that they had to fight it with each other; and they hated it so much that
they imposed it on Scotland and Ireland in the attempt to resolve it. The
imperial sovereignty they imposed on other nations was an effect of the
imperial sovereignty they had imposed on themselves; this is one reason,
among others, why 'British history' has been so often written as the history
of England with excrescences.

That history, English and British, constitutes a past which is continuously
and insistently present. We feel the nostalgia of which I spoke – the half wish,
half belief, that it might have been otherwise and may be represented almost
as if it had been – because it is the history of an undivided and imperial
parliamentary sovereignty which has never consented, or condescended, to
enter into confederations, and therefore presents serious problems to a United
Kingdom desirous of entering into new patterns of relationships with the
Irish Republic and, more ambitiously, with the European Union. There is a
past which will not go away, and which renders *you* – the Anglo-British
audience to which this book is chiefly addressed – uncertain whether you
really want it to; in that sense the politicians who talk about 'a thousand years
of history' are not quite as Whiggishly stupid as David Cannadine so understandably makes them appear. If politicians have problems in deciding what
they are saying, so have you.

I have now turned from '*we*' to '*you*', the better to present a further set of
reasons why it is not my intention to cry 'Nunc dimittis' and withdraw from
the field. My original paper, 'British History: the need for a new subject', was
first delivered as the J. C. Beaglehole Memorial Lecture to the New Zealand
Historical Association, meeting at the University of Canterbury in 1973. That
is, it was composed and delivered after the great divorce which occurred when
you told us that you were now Europeans, which we, as New Zealanders,
were not; so that after all those generations in which you had allowed the
notion of empire to shape your identity (or so you now tell us, by way of
justifying what you do now, since you no longer have the Empire), we were
to learn that you cared as little for our past as for our future. What you did,
of course, was irrevocably and unilaterally to disrupt a concept of Britishness
which we had supposed we shared with you; it was not free from causing us
problems (as the Canadian historian Ged Martin points out), but we had
supposed you knew that. In effect, you threw your identity, as well as ours,
into a condition of contingency, in which you have to decide whether it is
possible to be both British and European (given that you do not particularly
believe in either), while we have to decide in what sense if any we continue to
be British or have a British history. You did not pause to consider what you
were doing to us – but you did it to yourselves at the same time.

This condition calls for intensive historical rethinking by all of a now
disrupted '*us*'. You have to rethink yourselves and therefore your history;

as this volume has been rethinking the history of the United Kingdom, so you need – if you any longer have the nerve – to rethink the history of Europe and your place in it, ceasing to use 'Europe' as a means of denaturing British and English history and focusing instead on the ways in which the latter history – yours, whoever you may be – has helped to make the history of Europe what it is (or what it may be thought of as being).[17] We are at the same time – whoever 'we' were and now are – having to rethink our history, which, for more reasons than one, entails rethinking your history and that of other cultures and peoples. Whether I was already formulating the need for all this when calling for a 'British history' in 1973, I cannot of course say now; but that is how the matter must appear in retrospect. The word of the Lord – old Simeon might say – came to him at Ilam House in Christchurch twenty-two years ago; and after the usual interval, this volume and its parent conference are evidence that both Israel and Judah are attentive to it now.

But why have we heard the word, and what is the word we have heard? The lesson seems to be that the history of every nation – or rather, every political community claiming a past of its own making – must be read as both contingent and relative. By contingent I mean that it has been shaped by circumstances exterior to itself, rather than by the logic of its own history. The present *locus classicus* of this contention has been Conrad Russell's 'British' explanation of the English Civil War. Carried to an extreme beyond anything which its author asserted, this would mean that there were no 'English' causes for civil war and consequently no 'English Civil War' at all; the English merely found themselves caught up in a general collapse of governing authority and a general resort to armed violence, common to all the British kingdoms and arising from causes scattered indifferently throughout the three of them. To this it would have to be replied – what to a historian of political discourse is declared inescapably by the evidence – that however the English got into domestic conflict, and however bitterly they perceived it as unnatural and unnecessary, they discovered once they were in it that there were deep-seated problems in their polity, both ecclesiastical and civil, over which they were fighting one another and which they would have to settle if they were ever to stop fighting one another. As we have seen, they imposed their search for a settlement of these problems on the Scots and the Irish, whom they saw as impeding it. In this sense there was an English civil war; and I have asked in another place whether the Scots fought one another over the nature of the Scottish polity which certainly existed, and whether the wars in Ireland can be described as wars in which 'Irishmen' fought one another over

[17] For explorations of this theme, see J. G. A. Pocock, 'Deconstructing Europe', *London Review of Books*, 19 December 1991, reprinted in *History of European Ideas*, xviii (1994); J. G. A. Pocock, 'Vous autres Européens – or inventing Europe', *Filozofski Vestnik* (Liubljana: Slovenska Akademija Znanoski in Umatnasti), xiv (1993).

the nature of a shared 'Irish' polity.[18] I do not want the question to determine the answer; yet it is important that such questions can be asked.

They go further than the problem which they immediately raise: that of the relation between *Aussenpolitik* and *Innerpolitik*. We are asking ourselves how far – indeed we are being pushed towards asking ourselves whether – any sovereign political society establishes the logic of its own history. Our present inclination is hostile not merely to the hegemony, but actually to the existence of the assumption that it can do this; to assert that the English fought a civil war within the structure of royal government in Church and State is liable to be condemned and derided as 'Whiggish', and we neglect to ask whether, or how far, the 'Whig' structures of Protestant constitutionalism succeeded in furnishing the parameters within which 'English history' was obliged to operate. It is possible to say that there could not have been an English civil war had there not been a rebellion in Scotland, a rebellion in Ireland, a Welsh (and Cornish) decision to furnish the king with regiments without which he could not have fought a war at all; to insist that the War(s) of the Three Kingdoms happened in three or more national histories, whether or not a set of 'British' circumstances can be found common to all of them; and yet to conclude that there was an English civil war whose outcome determined, or was imposed upon, much of what happened in all the kingdoms and principalities. It is necessary only to recognise that this may be part of what happened, and to tell this story in interaction with other stories that need to be told; it can then be told contingently, which is not the same as denying that it is there to be told at all.

All this has an ideological dimension; it is history with a present tense. We live in times when the autonomous political community (whether or not it be 'national') finds it difficult to maintain its sovereignty and identity in face of a global money-market which it cannot control and which threatens in many ways – economic, political, technological, cultural – to displace and perhaps replace it.[19] In these circumstances there is great value in a historiography which asks how, how far, and whether the sovereign or national state has ever been the author of its own history; which suggests that we have long been exaggerating the extent to which it has, and points out that there are other ways of telling the story of what happened in the past. Because it treats sovereignty as precarious and contestable – the great lesson, incidentally, which the English learned from their civil wars – such a historiography is a critical, scientific and even moral device for dealing with a world in which sovereignty is more precarious and contestable than ever, and we may (or may not) have to begin living without it. But such a historiography (like every

---

[18] J. G. A. Pocock, 'The Atlantic Archipelago and the War of the Three Kingdoms', in B. Bradshaw and J. Morrill (eds.), *The British Problem, c.1534–1707: State Formation in the Atlantic Archipelago* (Basingstoke, in press).

[19] I explore some of these problems in the essays cited in note 17, above, and in J. G. A. Pocock, 'Notes of an occidental tourist', *Common Knowledge*, ii, 2 (1992), pp. 1–5, 8–18.

other) ceases to be criticism and becomes cant the instant it begins to use closed assumptions and to operate on the unspoken premise that national sovereignty and history never existed, never should have existed, or are at the point of disappearing forever (and a good thing too). The contributors to this volume have not fallen into cant of this kind; we have avoided studying the history of the United Kingdom on the assumption that it is an illusion, a mistake, a crime, or an episode closed off by its ending; and yet we have operated in a climate of discourse such that we knew we could have said or implied these things though we did not. We are living in a crisis of confidence, without which we would not have chosen this subject or joined in this programme; but we can claim to have shown how to live in such a crisis, without submitting to its dictatorship.

The same considerations apply when we turn from history as 'contingent' to history as 'relative'. By the latter term I mean that 'British history', as it has shaped itself over the last two decades, has emerged as a 'multicultural' history in the proper sense: a history of a number of cultural and historical identities, forming themselves and each other, and possibly, at some points, in some cases, and in some particulars, merging in a common identity which may have a history, a past, and a future. That language represents it as a history which is highly contingent, but at this point we come to see it as relative, in the sense that we encounter the politics of identity formation. We are reminded that traditions are invented and communities imagined, and that selves invent and imagine others in the act of inventing and imagining themselves; the English, it is argued, could not have invented themselves without imagining the Welsh, the Scots and the Irish (and the French) in the process, while the Irish, a conquered and colonised set of peoples, had to begin imagining themselves as a people largely in response to the ways in which the English imagined them. The 'new historicism' (an unfortunate term) applying itself to the study of Elizabethan literature[20] has valuably reminded us that identities are imagined and invented in a process of interaction, highly and even paranoically complex and very often both brutal and tragic.

What is perhaps harder to face – since guilt comes easy to most of us – is that we live at the outcomes of many such processes, and have to decide what to do with the many legacies they have left us. Here too there is a cant – a cant of 'political correctness' – which this volume has had to avoid, and has been successful in avoiding. It is disturbingly easy for the critical intellectual (in this case including the historian) to point out how every identity has been constructed, with the implication that it is for the critic to say how and when it is to be deconstructed; to contend that the construction of every identity entails the construction of an Other, and that the Self is false in exact proportion to the falsity of the image of the Other. To point out that this is

[20] In particular, among the many works of many authors, R. F. Helgerson, *Forms of Nationhood: The Elizabethan Writing of England* (Chicago, 1992).

all too often the case is good history and good morality; to assume that it is invariably and necessarily the case, and that all identities are targeted for a kind of righteous demolition, is to elevate the critical intellectual to the office of grand inquisitor. There is too much of this kind of cant, and those who engage in it may be doing the work of the global market, which likes to demolish and reconstruct human communities as the needs of salesmanship dictate. Not so the contributors to this volume, who as historians stand on ground constantly shifting but never fragile.

Sovereignty and identity have been our themes, as they have played so large a part in making the historical discipline what it has been. We have been enquiring into the history of the United Kingdom because we want to know what sovereignty and identity it has displayed in the past, and whether it will continue to display sovereignty and identity in the future. Those of us who are Irish are as interested in the outcome as those who are British, and as a New Zealander excluded from Europe I am interested in it in my own way; I have my own history to attend to, and this is part of it. In this respect I believe that should Hugh Kearney ever rewrite his 'history of four nations' by the inclusion of a fifth, this is less likely to be made up of the Caribbean, African and Asian settlers in this island[21] – deeply interesting as their future is – than of the last of the historic nations formed in the past of this archipelago: the Protestant people of Northern Ireland, now asserting that they are 'British' whether or not the other 'British' peoples want them to be, and justly suspicious of a conspiracy to classify them as 'Irish' without their consent. I do not endorse the brutality of their extremists' methods when I say that I know what they are about.

I want to finish by remarking that to treat sovereignty and identity as contingent and relative, imagined, invented and negotiable – and that is what is being done throughout this volume – does not lead to their disappearance as a foreordained conclusion; that is the cant to which we have not succumbed. The owl of Minerva, we are told, takes flight in the gathering dusk, but it sounds a call to which others may respond, and it lays eggs which may hatch out in unexpected life-forms. In the original spoken version of David Cannadine's paper,[22] he followed a sustained attack on the uncritical and unoriginal invention of an Anglo-British[23] past by politicians, by talking nevertheless of 'how we look at our national past and how we are changing the ways we look at that national past', and of the responsible public function of historians as 'the keepers of our nation's collective memory'. Who are this 'we', I wonder, and is he not 'a villain, and a bastard, and a knave, and a

---

[21] As Professor Kearney suggested during the Conference discussions.
[22] D. Cannadine, 'British history as a "new subject": politics, perspectives, and prospects', above, ch. 2 (but in revising and abbreviating his spoken text, Cannadine has cut the passages quoted here).
[23] This useful adjective is recommended by Colin Kidd in his *Subverting Scotland's Past: Scottish Whig Historians and the Creation of an Anglo-British Identity 1689–c.1830* (Cambridge, 1993).

rascal'[24] who speaks of our nation? Evidently not; Cannadine avoids post-modernist cant like the rest of us, and some deep-seated reconstruction, not a deconstruction, of 'us', 'our past', and 'our nation' may be going on behind his words. (I only wish I knew who will be included in it.) And when we render sovereignty contestable, do we not open up questions to which only sovereignty can give answers? It may be that our enquiry takes place in one of those creative loops of which we read in cybernetics. For this reason I am, if not sanguine about our future as citizens, at least unashamed about what we have been doing in our present as historians.[25] A nation, or a multiple nation, which has always been debatable continues its history by continuing the debate. 'Non nunc dimittis, Domine', therefore; suffer us yet a little and we will show thee that we have somewhat yet to speak on several peoples' behalf.

[24] Captain Macmorris, in William Shakespeare, *King Henry V*, Act III, Sc. 2.
[25] Cf. J. G. A. Pocock, 'History and sovereignty: the historiographic response to Europeanisation in two British cultures', *Journal of British Studies*, xxxi (1992).

Index